FIRST GRANDCHILD

初孫

FIRSTLING!

A NEVER BEFORE SEEN

久保帯人

Chapters 150 and 151 in this volume were featured on the cover of *Weekly Shonen Jump* and printed in color for two straight weeks. According to the editor in chief, it was a first for the magazine. I'm thankful. Firsts are always nice. I love them.
-Tite Kubo

BLEACH is author Tite Kubo's second title. Kubo made his debut with *ZOMBIEPOWDER.*, a four-volume series for *WEEKLY SHONEN JUMP*. To date, *BLEACH* has been translated into numerous languages and has also inspired an animated TV series that began airing in the U.S. in 2006. Beginning its serialization in 2001, *BLEACH* is still a mainstay in the pages of *WEEKLY SHONEN JUMP*. In 2005, *BLEACH* was awarded the prestigious Shogakukan Manga Award in the *shonen* (boys) category.

BLEACH
Vol. 18: THE DEATHBERRY RETURNS
The SHONEN JUMP Manga Edition

STORY AND ART BY
TITE KUBO

English Adaptation/Lance Caselman
Translation/Joe Yamazaki
Touch-Up Art & Lettering/Andy Ristaino
Design/Sean Lee
Editor/Yuki Takagaki

Managing Editor/Frances E. Wall
Editorial Director/Elizabeth Kawasaki
VP & Editor in Chief/Yumi Hoashi
Sr. Director of Acquisitions/Rika Inouye
Sr. VP of Marketing/Liza Coppola
Exec. VP of Sales & Marketing/John Easum
Publisher/Hyoe Narita

Printed in the U.S.A.

Published by VIZ Media, LLC
P.O. Box 77010
San Francisco, CA 94107

SHONEN JUMP Manga Edition
10 9 8 7 6 5 4 3 2 1
First printing, April 2007

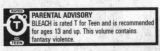

PARENTAL ADVISORY
BLEACH is rated T for Teen and is recommended
for ages 13 and up. This volume contains
fantasy violence.

www.viz.com

THE WORLD'S
MOST POPULAR MANGA

www.shonenjump.com

Your shadow, quietly
Like a vagrant poison needle,
Stitches my footsteps.

Your radiance, lithely
Like lightning striking a water tower,
Cuts down the source of my life.

BLEACH18 THE DEATHBERRY RETURNS

STARS AND

浮竹十四郎

Jûshirô Ukitake

Ichigo Kurosaki

黒崎一護

Shunsui Kyôraku

京楽春水

plot

As Rukia's date with death looms ever nearer, Ichigo struggles desperately to achieve Bankai. Meanwhile, Orihime and the others, lacking a leader, enlist the aid of the fearsome Kenpachi Zaraki. And Renji, fearing that Ichigo will be too late to save Rukia, goes to save her himself, only to be intercepted by the deadly Byakuya Kuchiki!

BLEACH ALL

砕蜂

Soi Fon

山本元柳斎重國

**Shigekuni Genryûsai
Yamamoto**

Yoruichi Shihôin

四楓院夜一

STORIES

BLEACH18

THE DEATHBERRY RETURNS

Contents

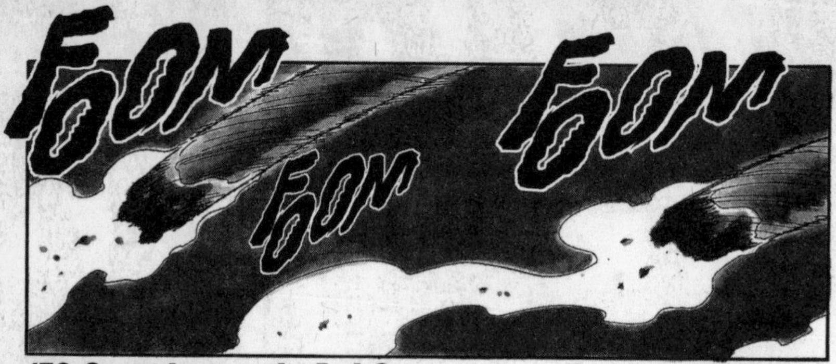
BOOM
BOOM
BOOM

150. Countdown to the End: 0

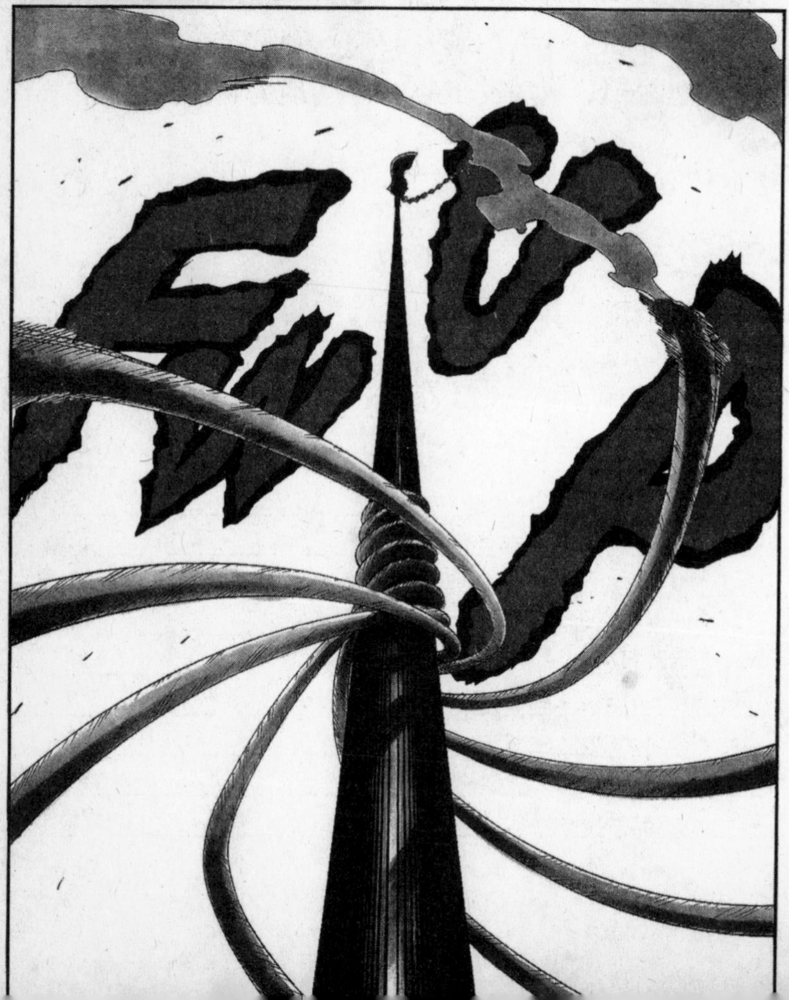

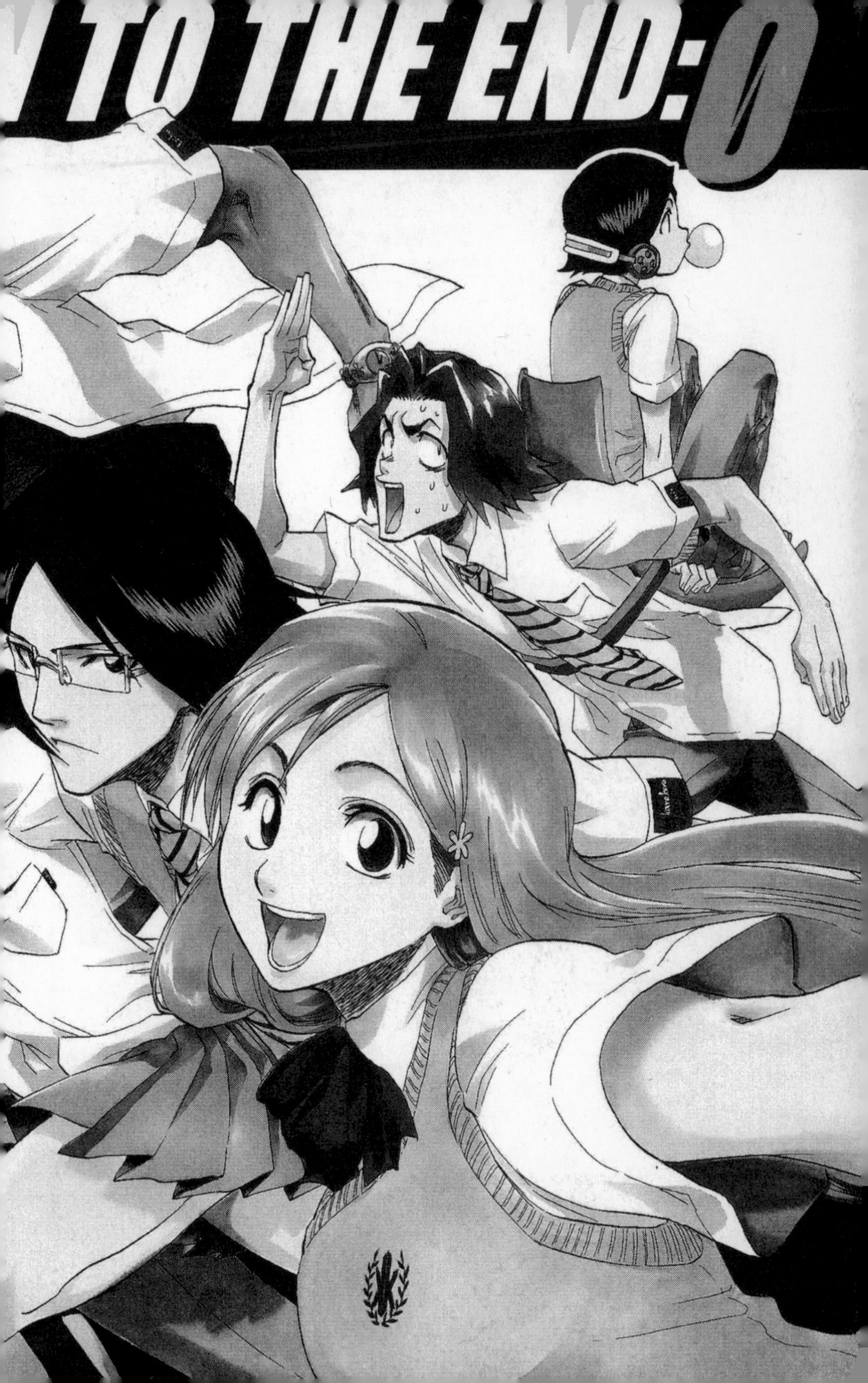
TO THE END: 0

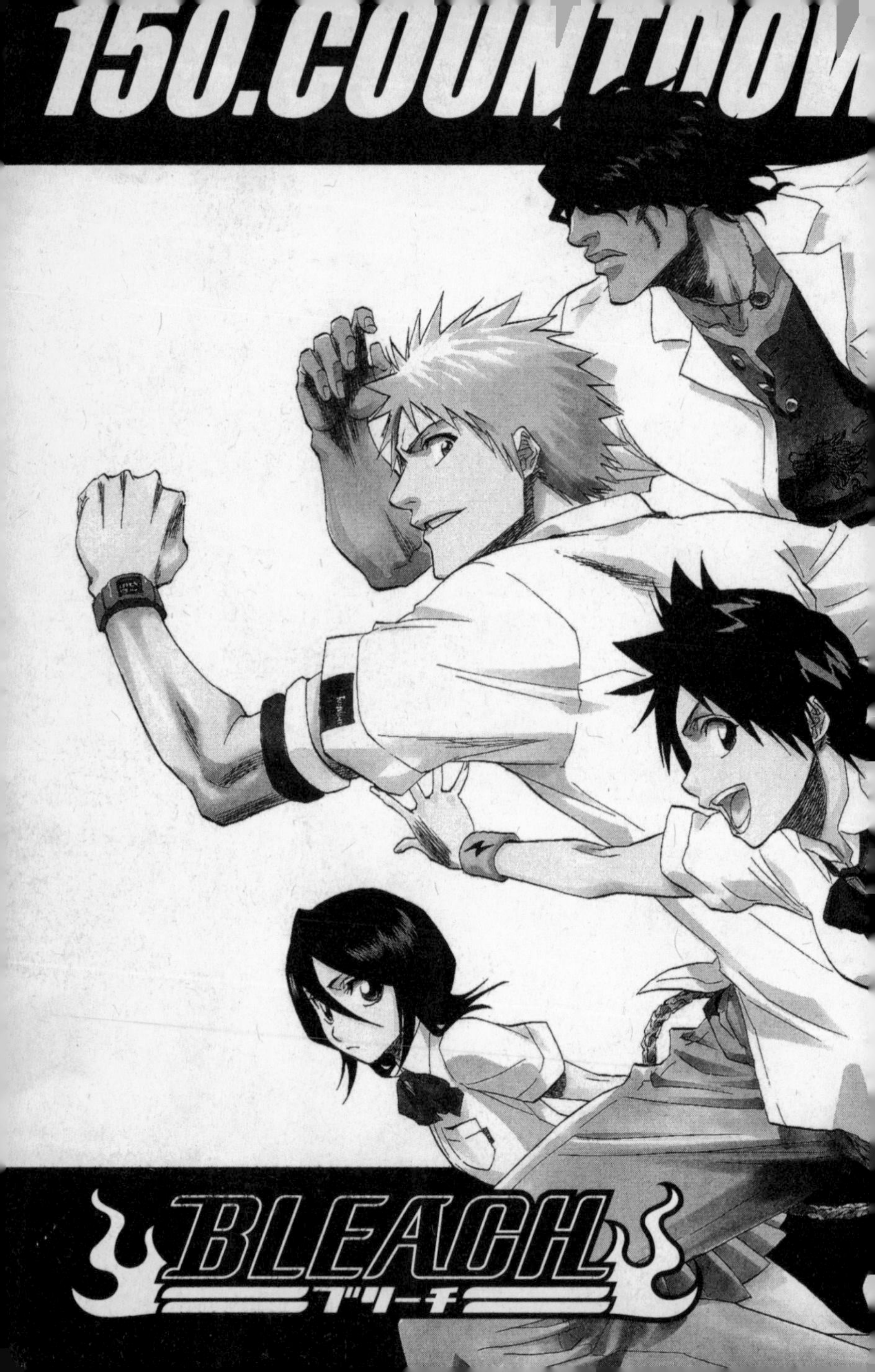
150.COUNTDOW
BLEACH
ブリーチ

BLEACH
ブリーチ

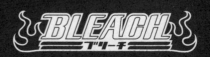

THE SÔKYOKU...

LOOK!

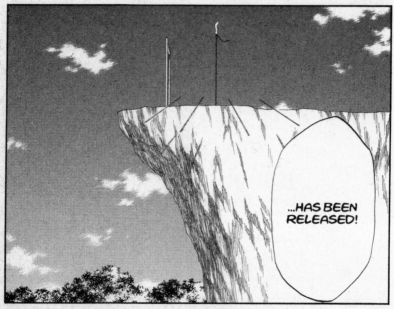

...HAS BEEN RELEASED!

CHUNK

CHUNK CHUNK

CHUNK

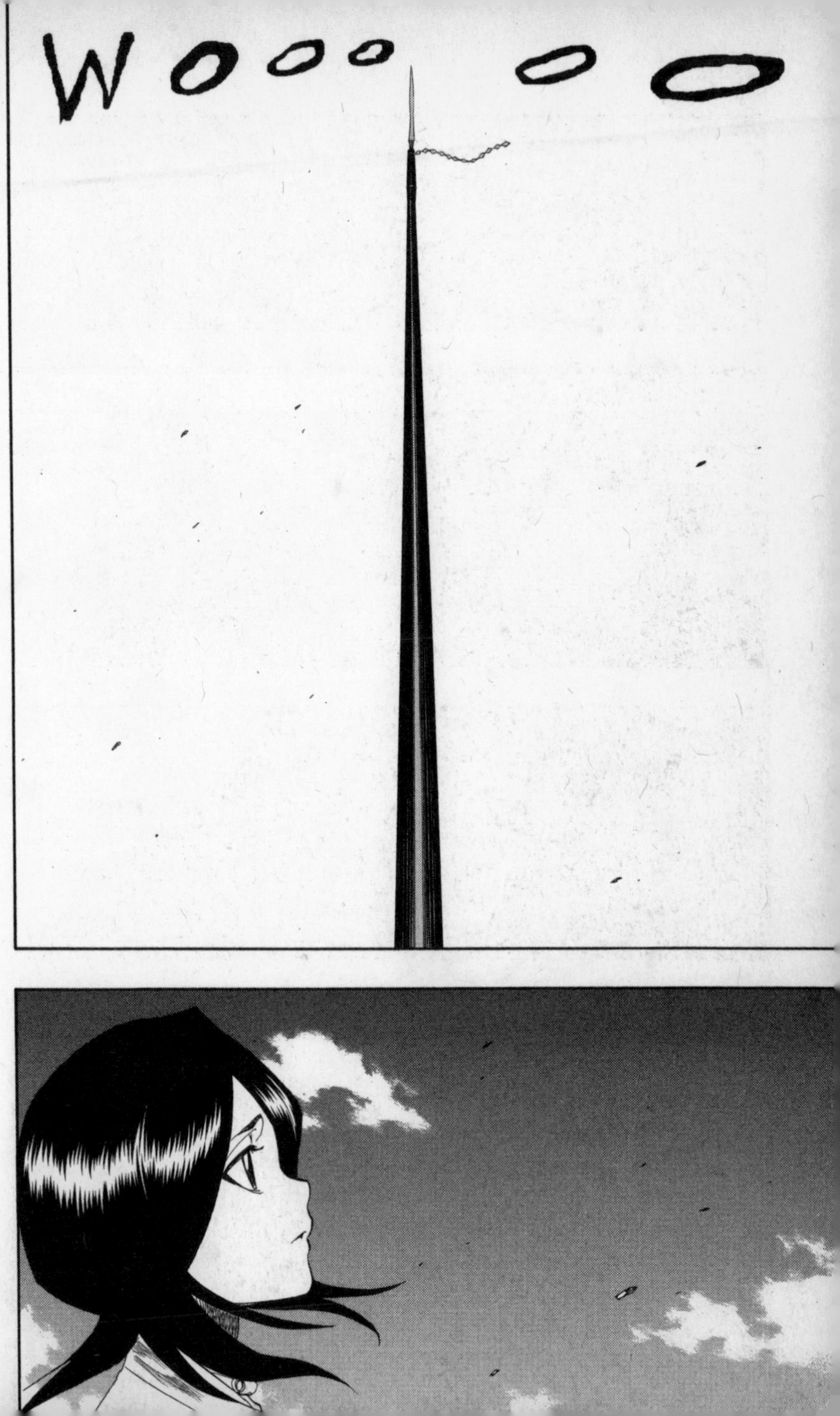
WOOOOO

READ THIS WAY

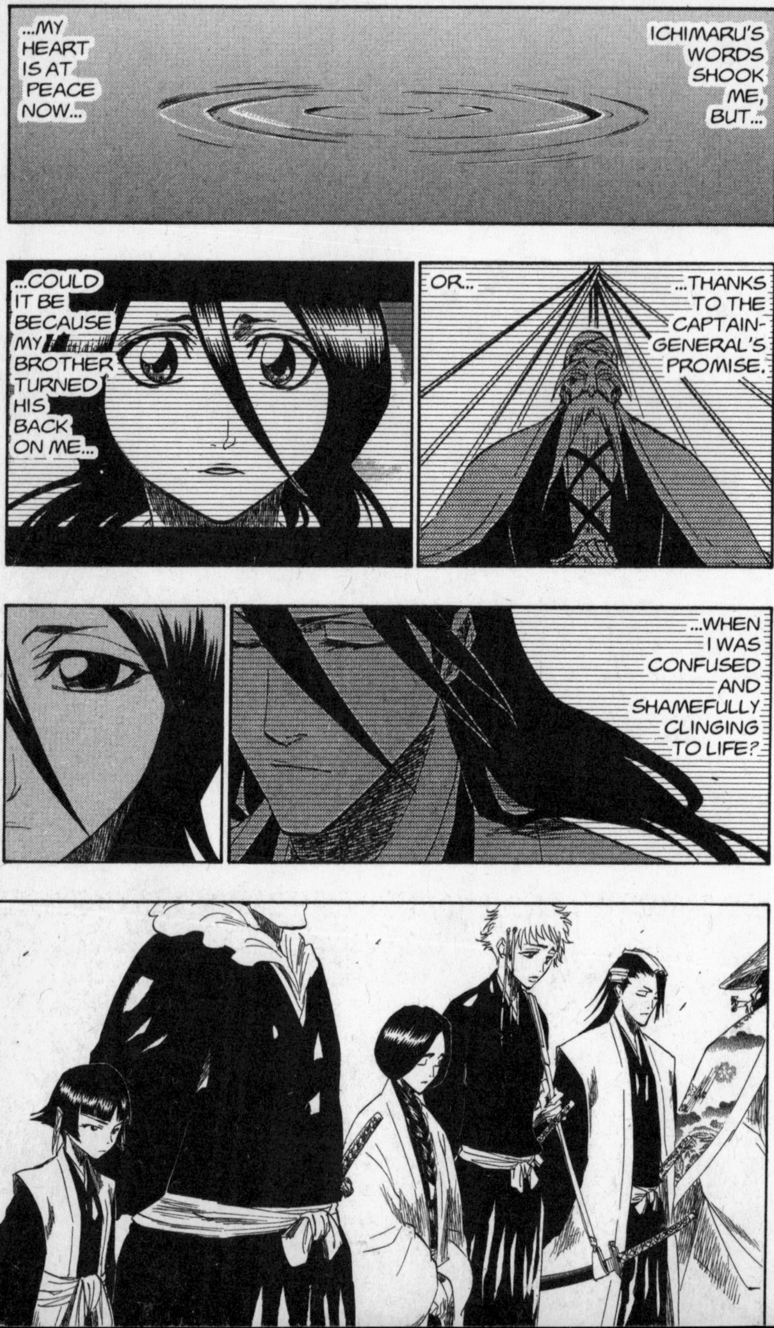

ICHIMARU'S WORDS SHOOK ME, BUT...
...MY HEART IS AT PEACE NOW...
OR...
...THANKS TO THE CAPTAIN-GENERAL'S PROMISE.
...COULD IT BE BECAUSE MY BROTHER TURNED HIS BACK ON ME...
...WHEN I WAS CONFUSED AND SHAMEFULLY CLINGING TO LIFE?

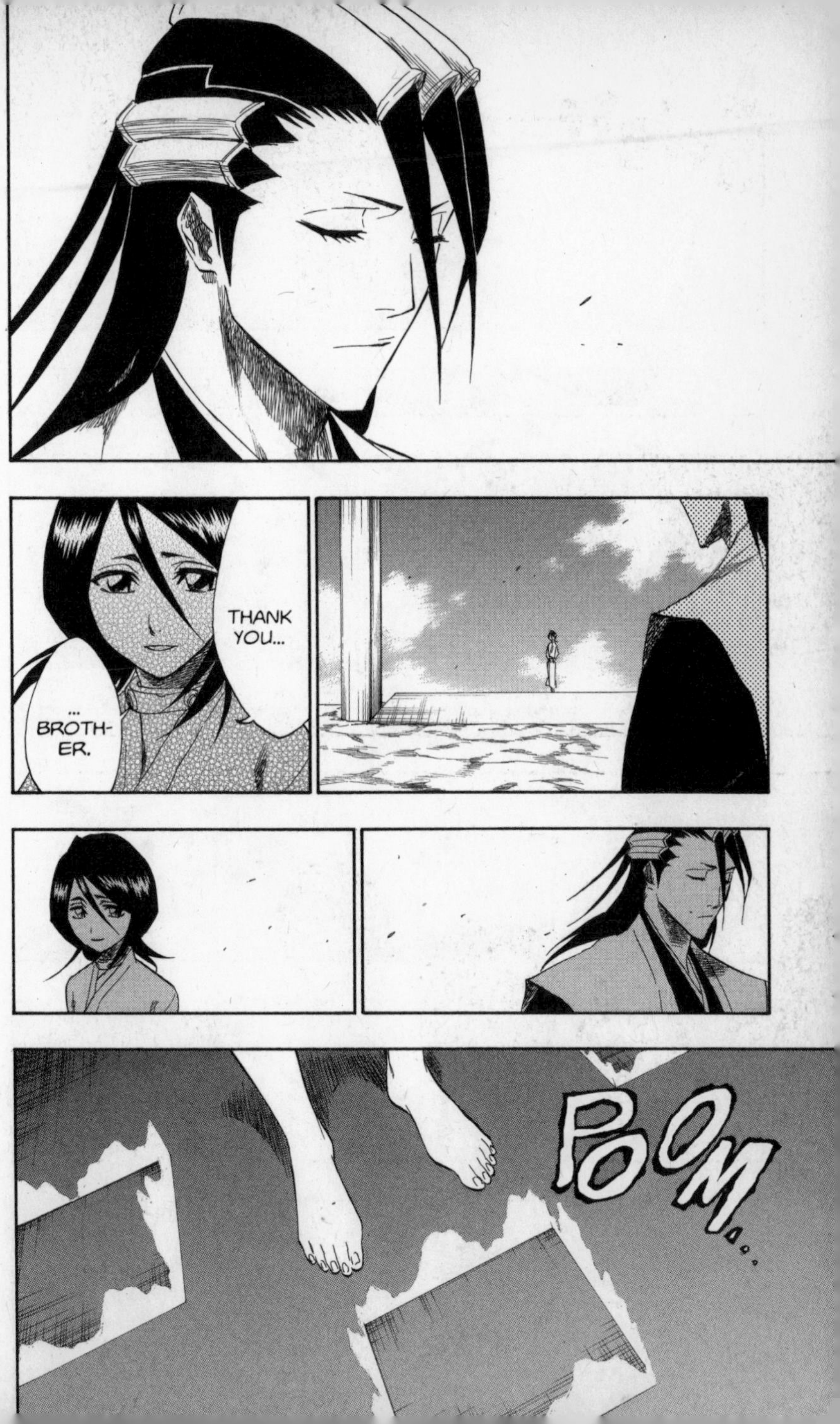
THANK YOU...
... BROTH-ER.
POOM..

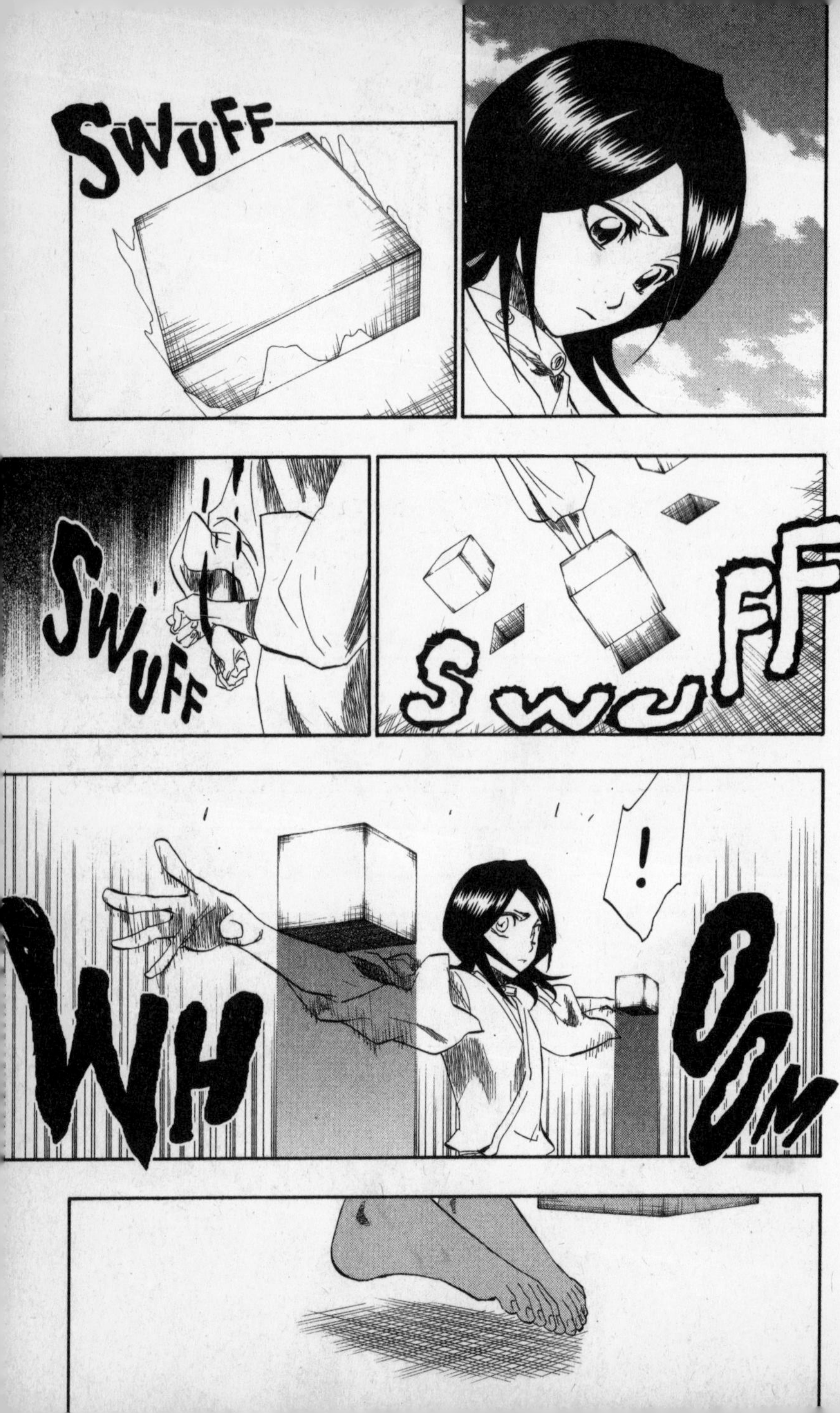
SWUFF
SWUFF
SWUFF
!
WHOOM

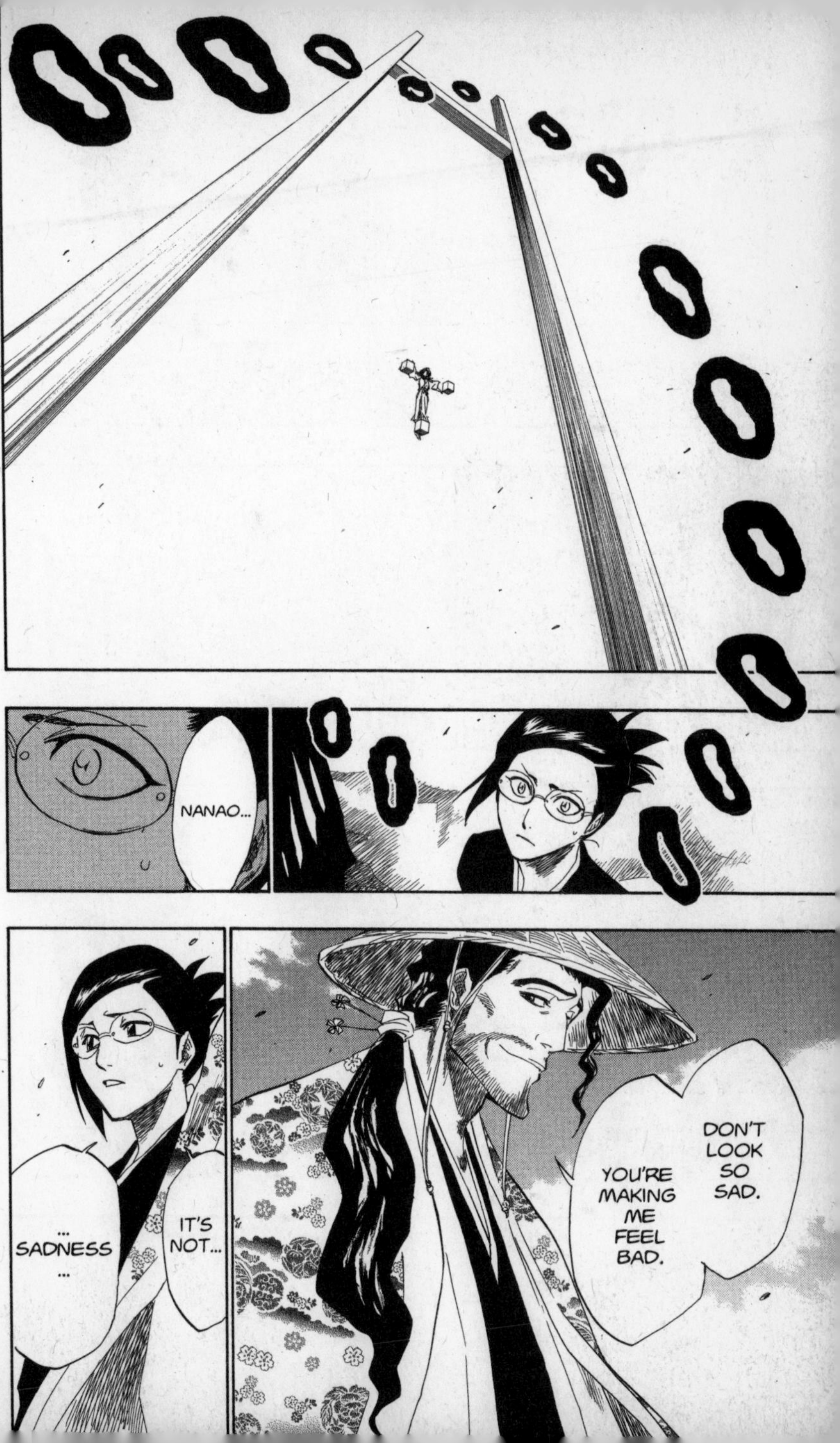
NANAO...
DON'T LOOK SO SAD.
YOU'RE MAKING ME FEEL BAD.
IT'S NOT...
...SADNESS...

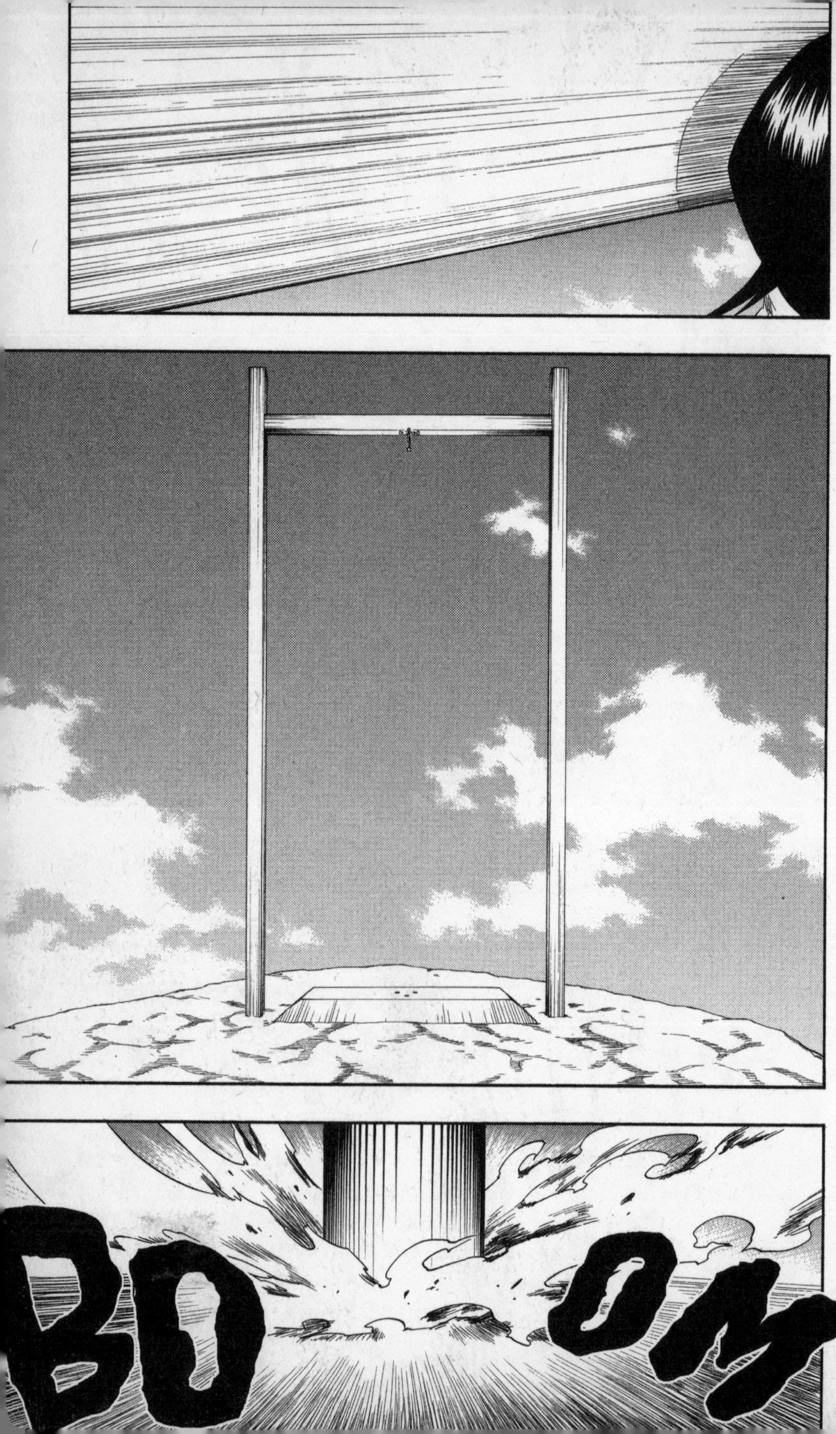
BOOM

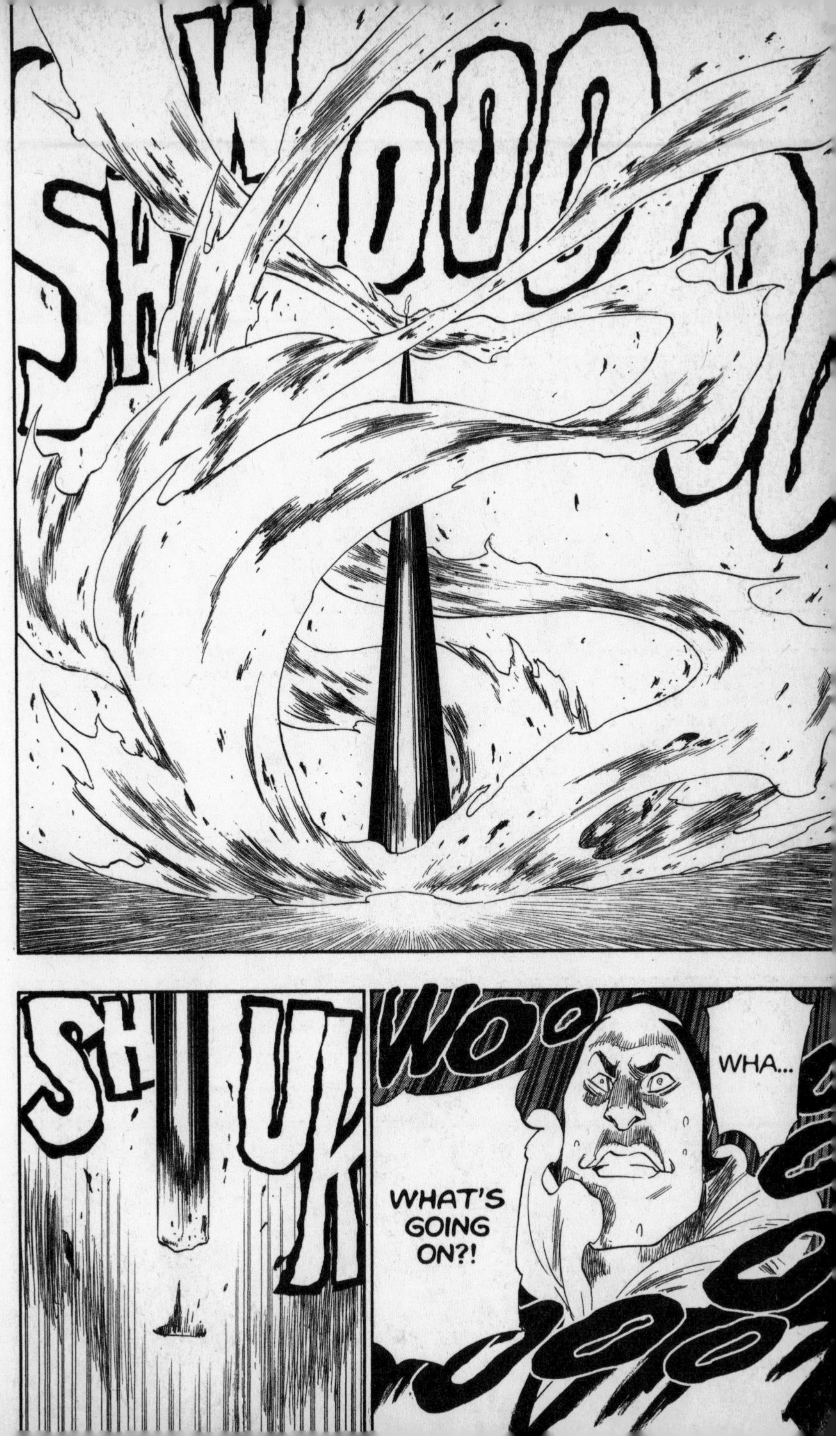
SHWOOOO
WOOOOOO
WHA...
WHAT'S GOING ON?!
SHUK

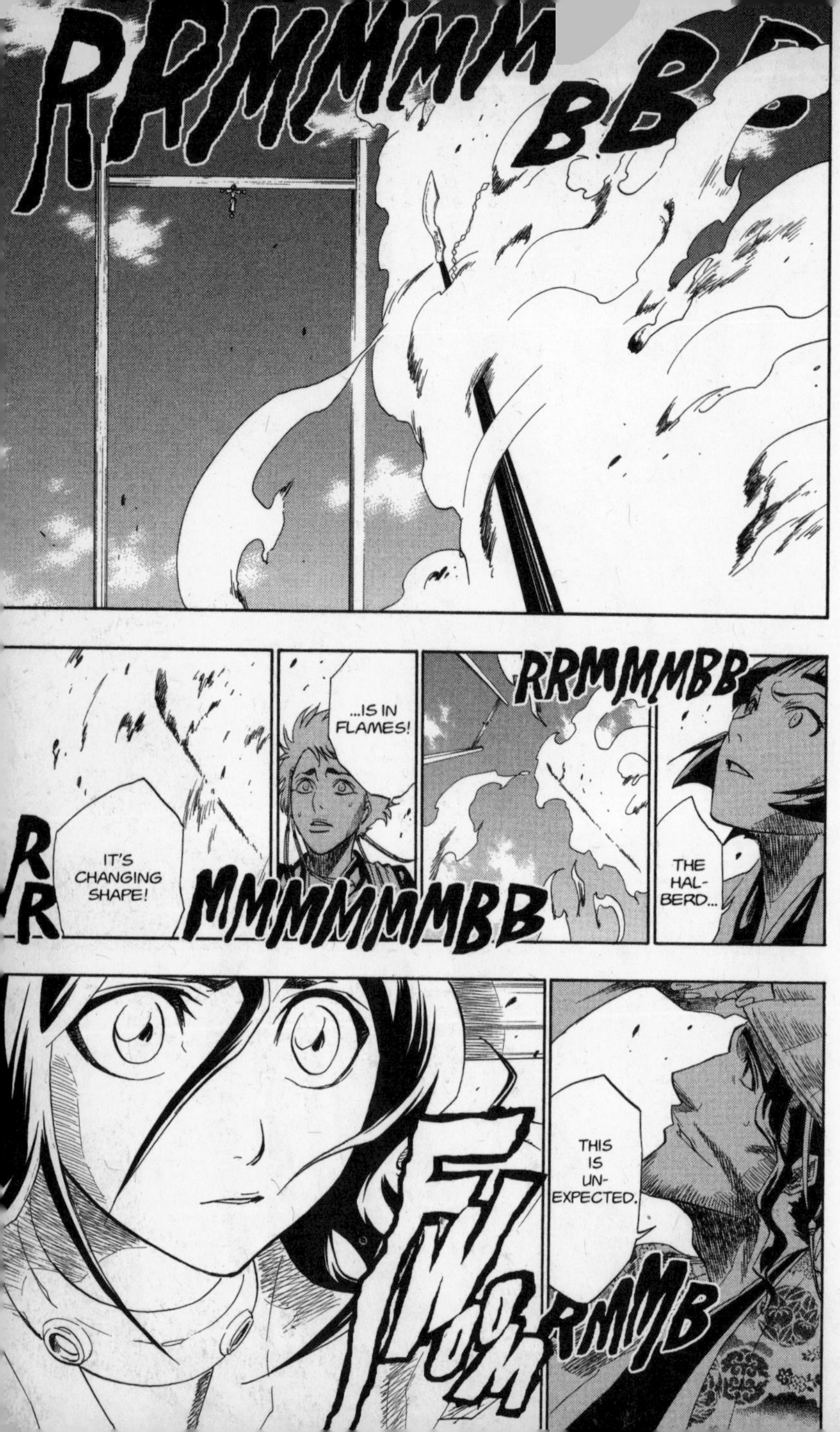
RRMMMMMBB
THE HAL-BERD...
RRMMMBB
...IS IN FLAMES!
IT'S CHANGING SHAPE!
RRMMMMMMMBB
THIS IS UN-EXPECTED.
RMMB
FWOOM

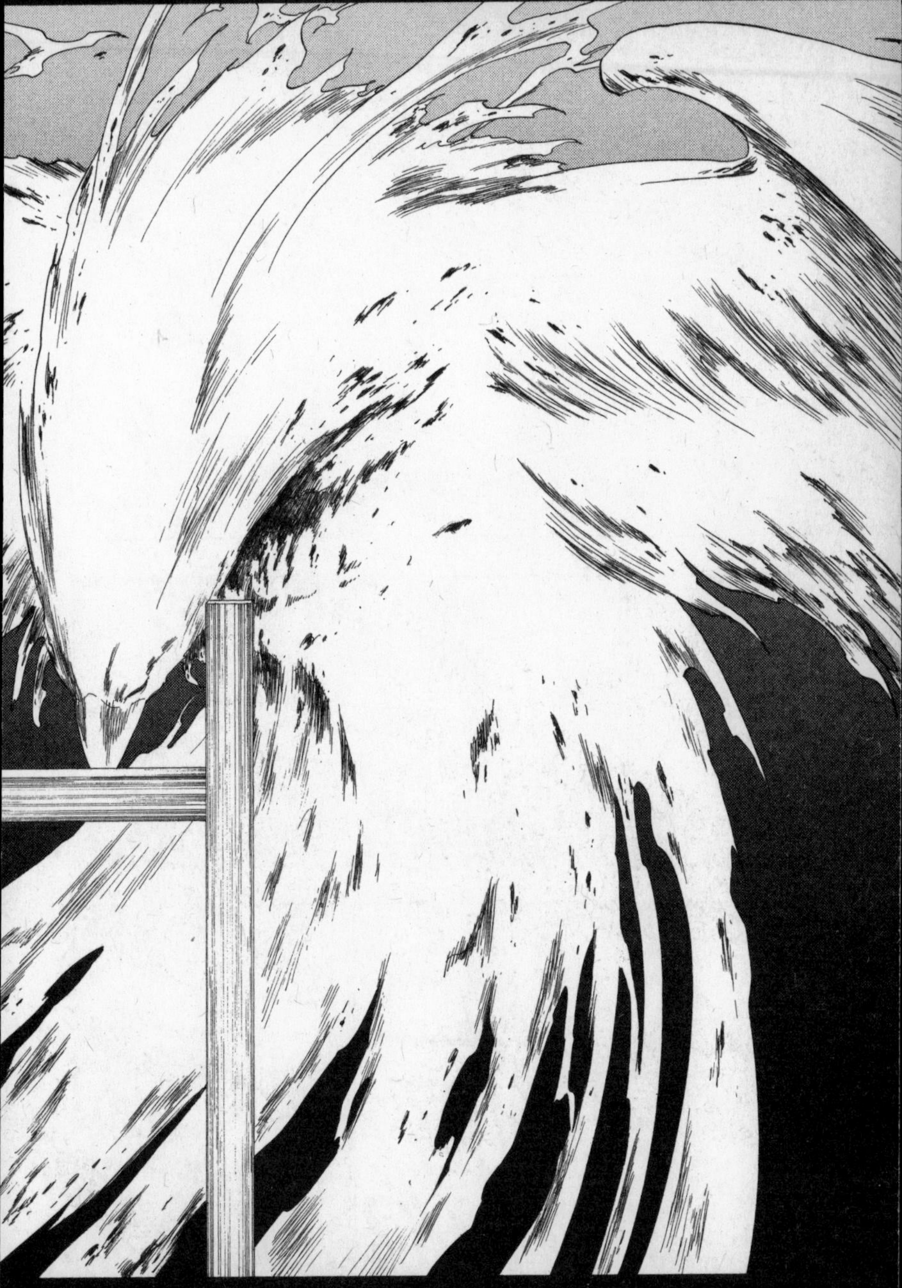

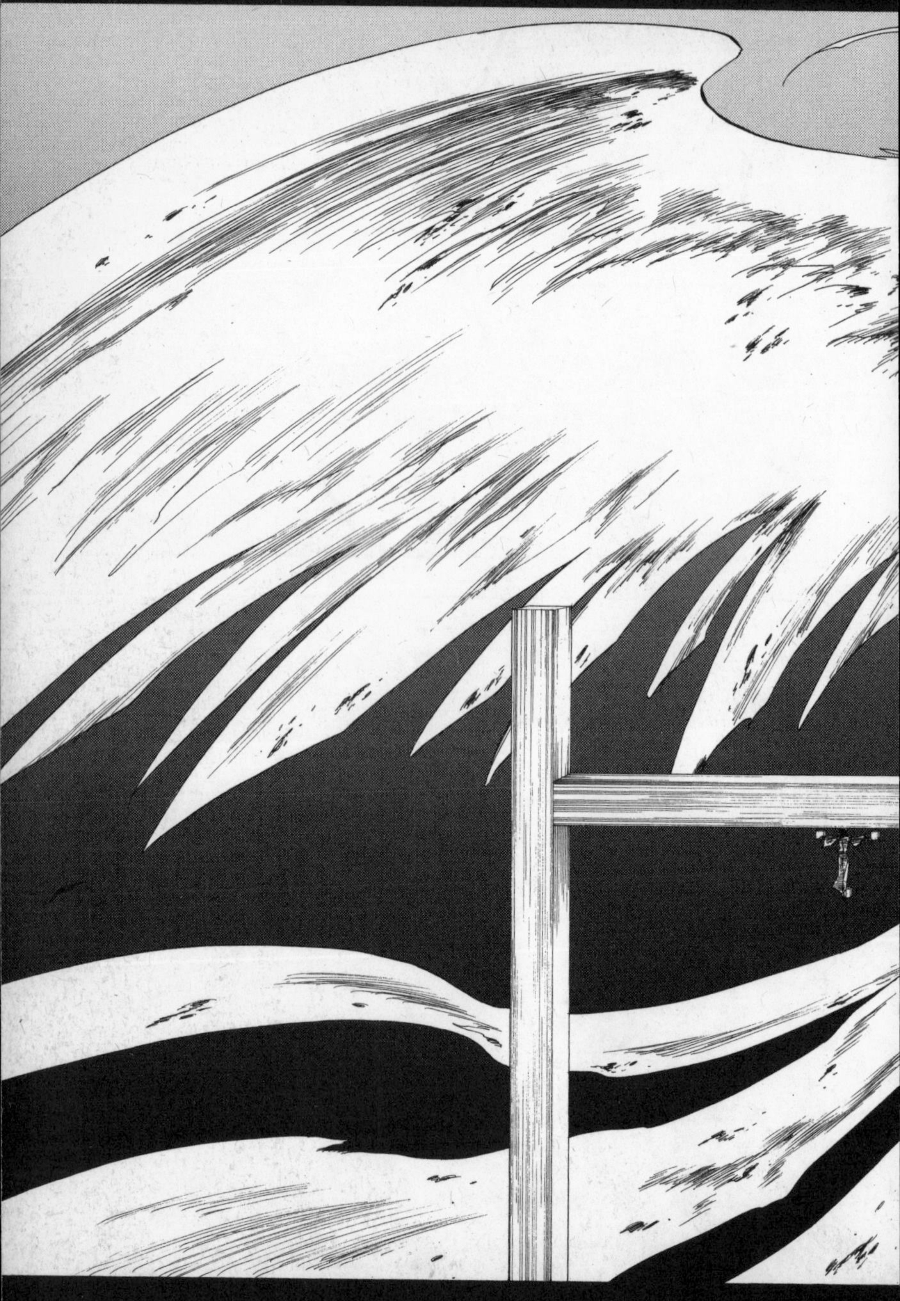

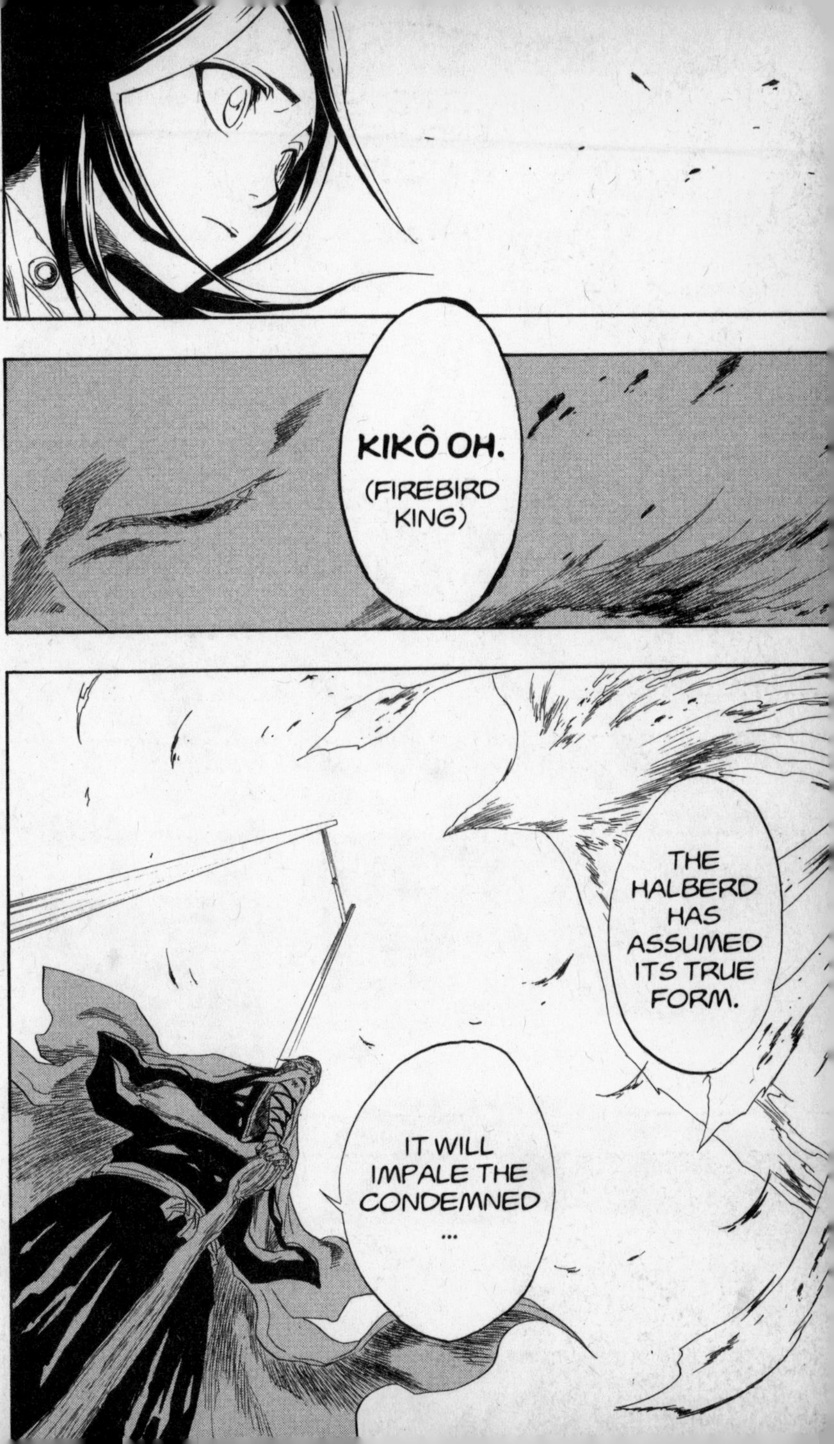
KIKÔ OH.
(FIREBIRD KING)
THE HALBERD HAS ASSUMED ITS TRUE FORM.
IT WILL IMPALE THE CONDEMNED ...

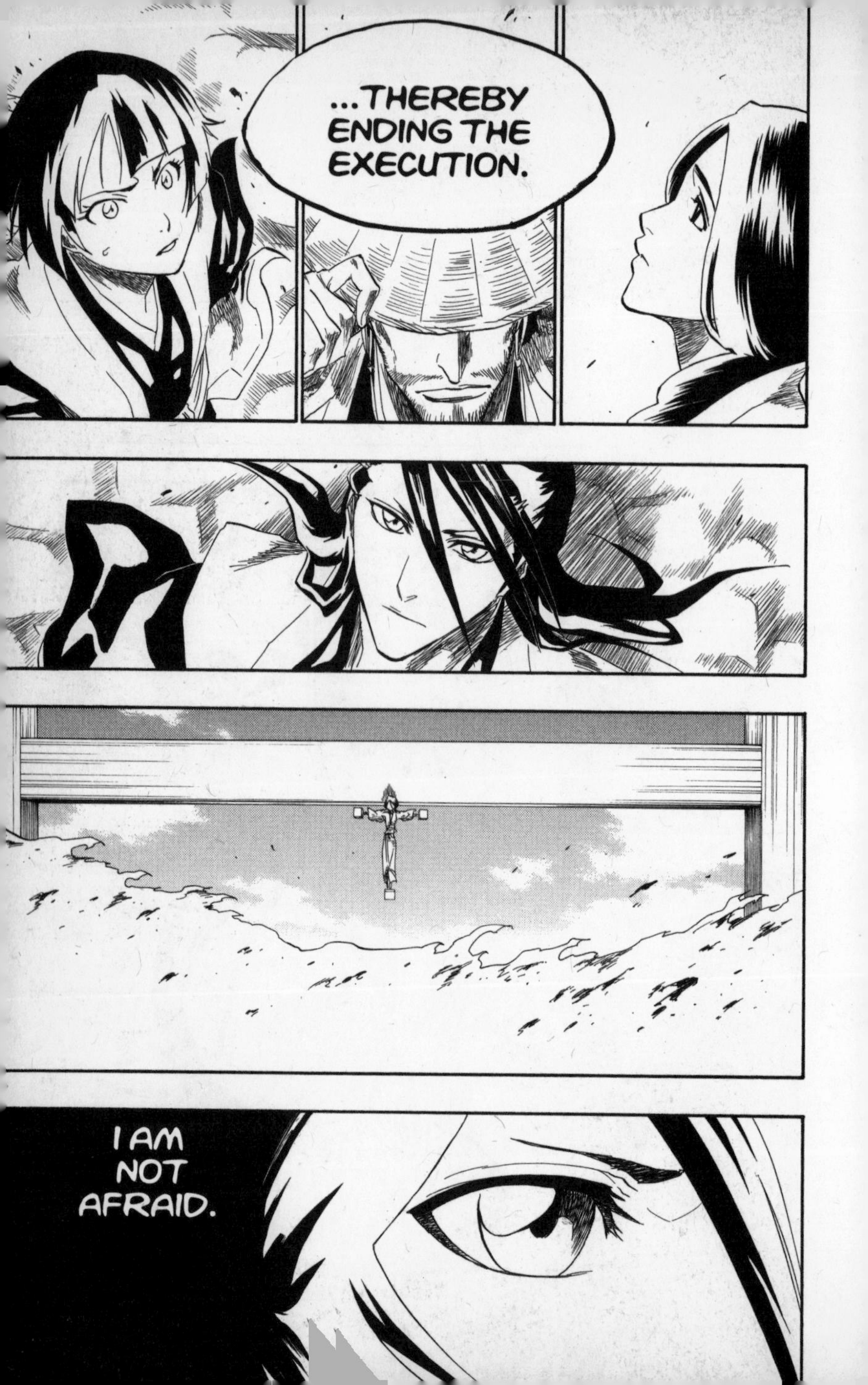
...THEREBY ENDING THE EXECUTION.
I AM NOT AFRAID.

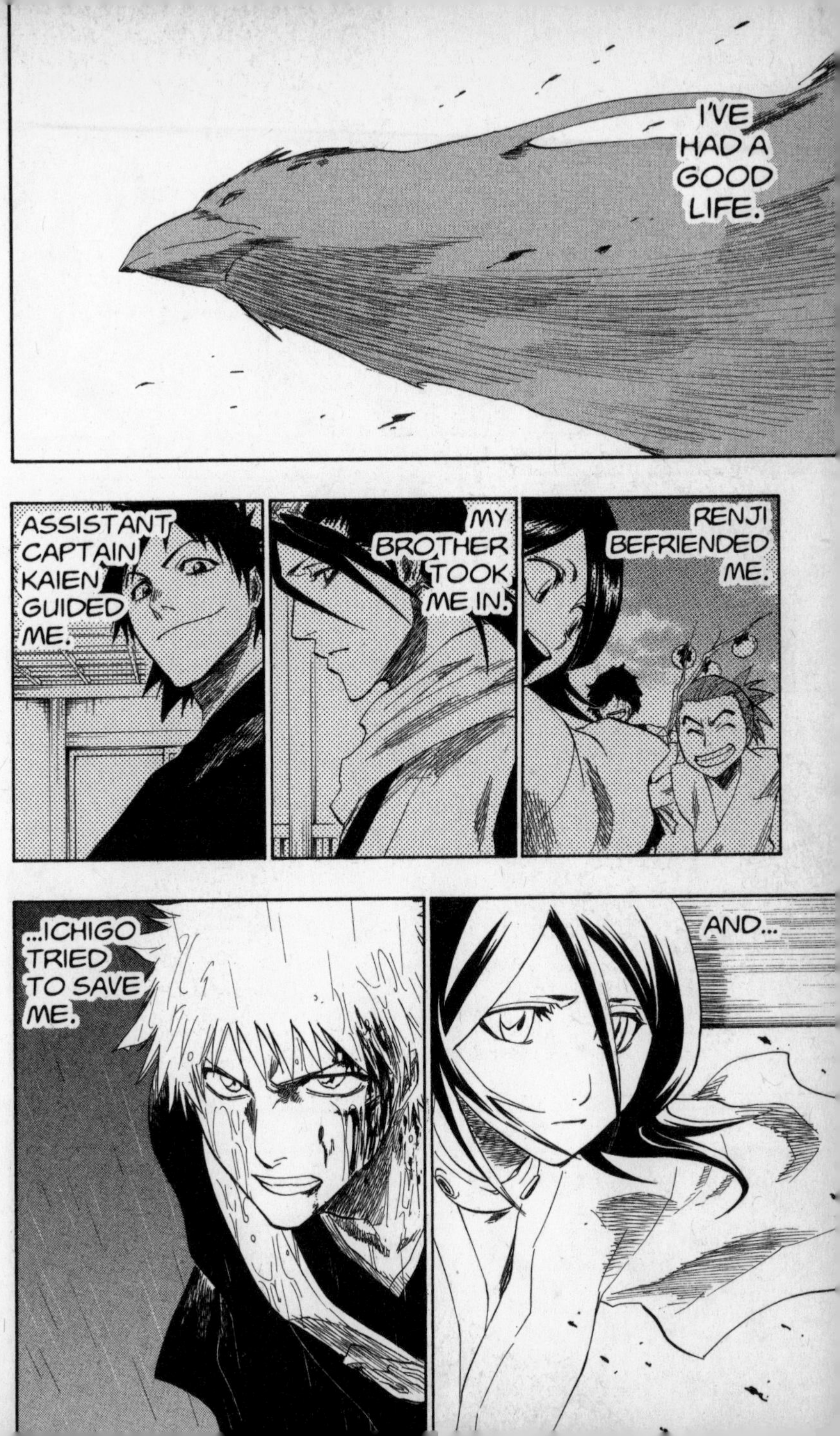
I'VE HAD A GOOD LIFE.
RENJI BEFRIENDED ME.
MY BROTHER TOOK ME IN.
ASSISTANT CAPTAIN KAIEN GUIDED ME.
AND...
...ICHIGO TRIED TO SAVE ME.

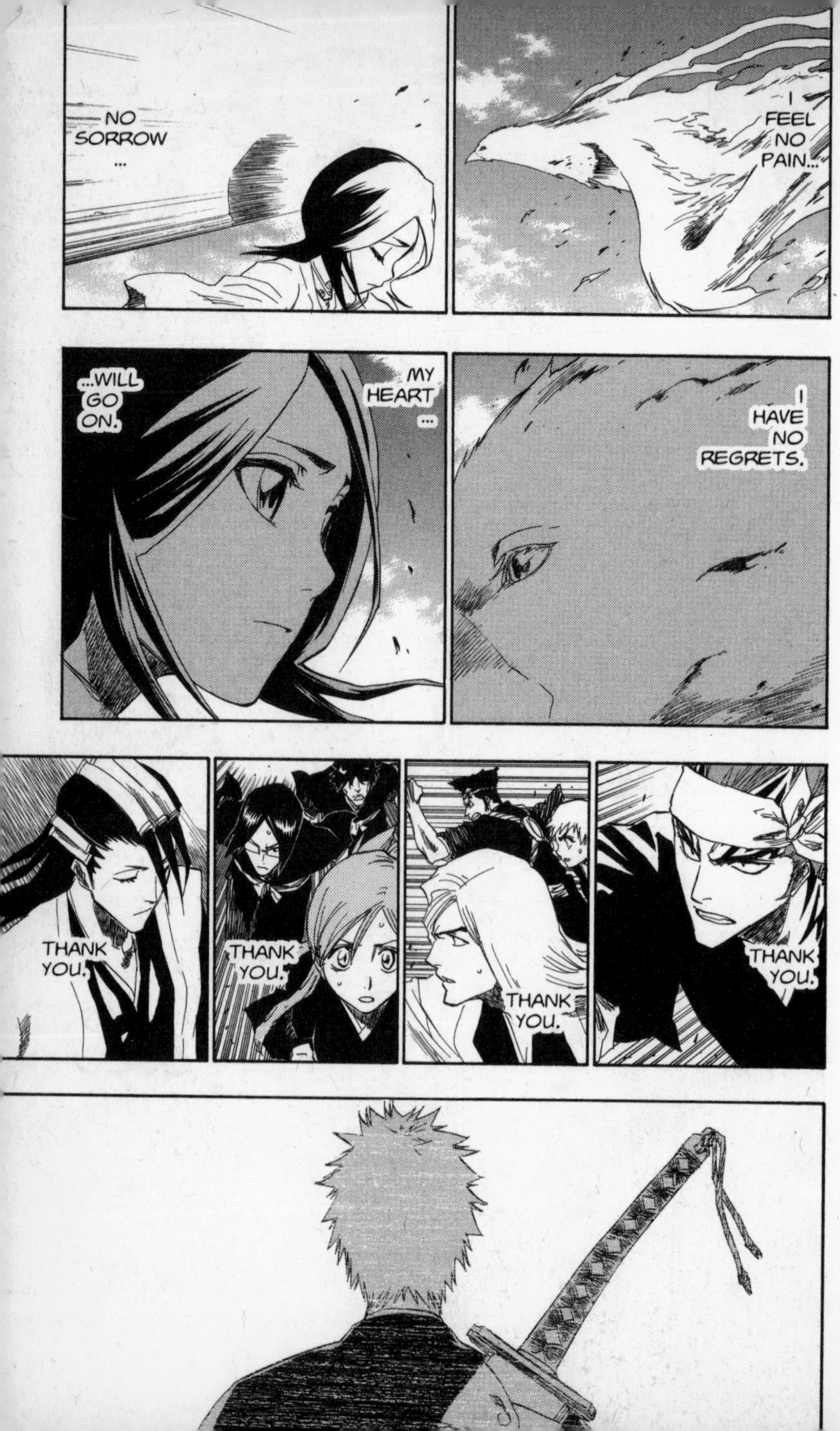
I FEEL NO PAIN...
NO SORROW ...
I HAVE NO REGRETS.
MY HEART ...
...WILL GO ON.
THANK YOU.
THANK YOU.
THANK YOU.
THANK YOU.

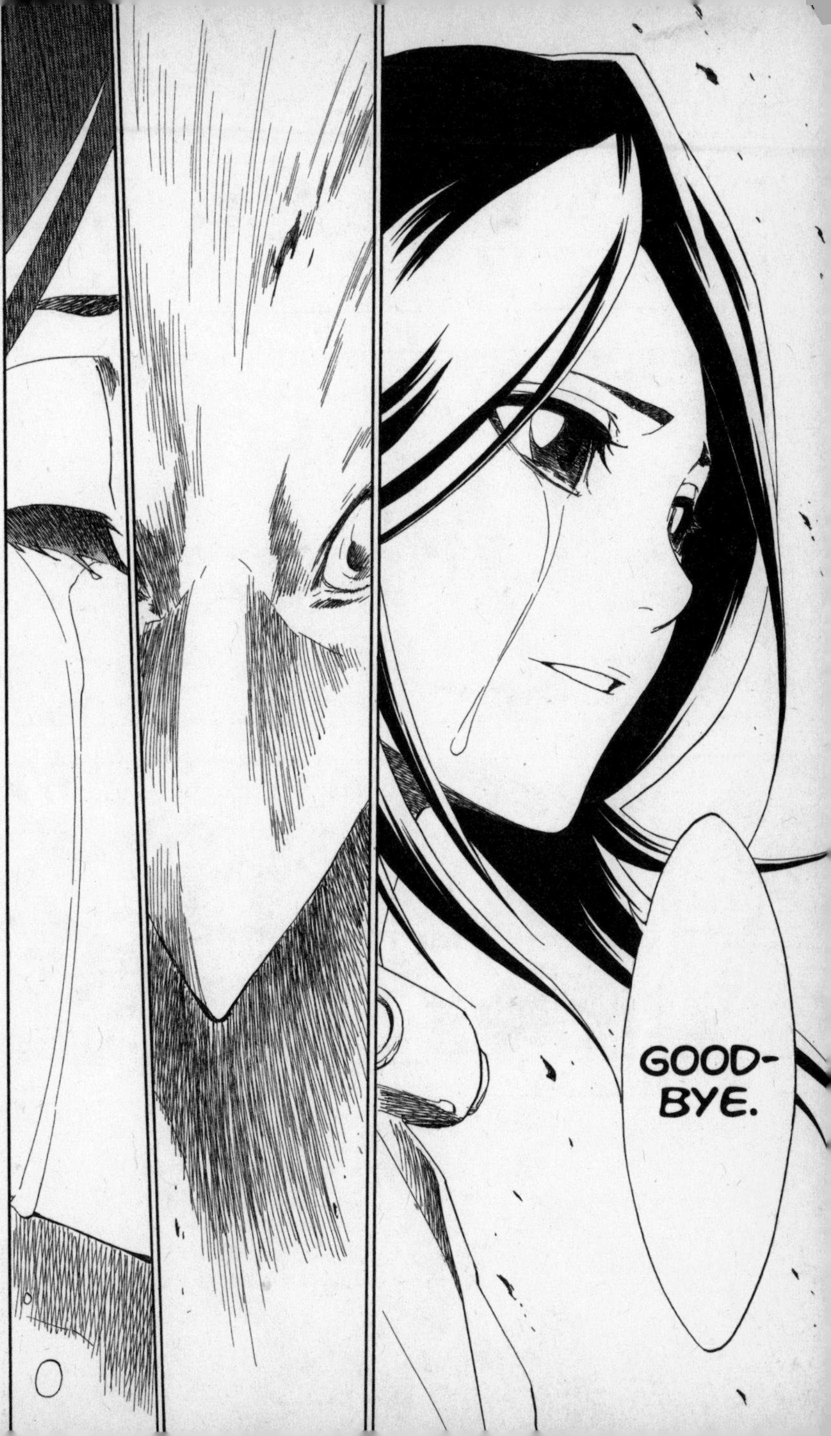
GOOD-BYE.

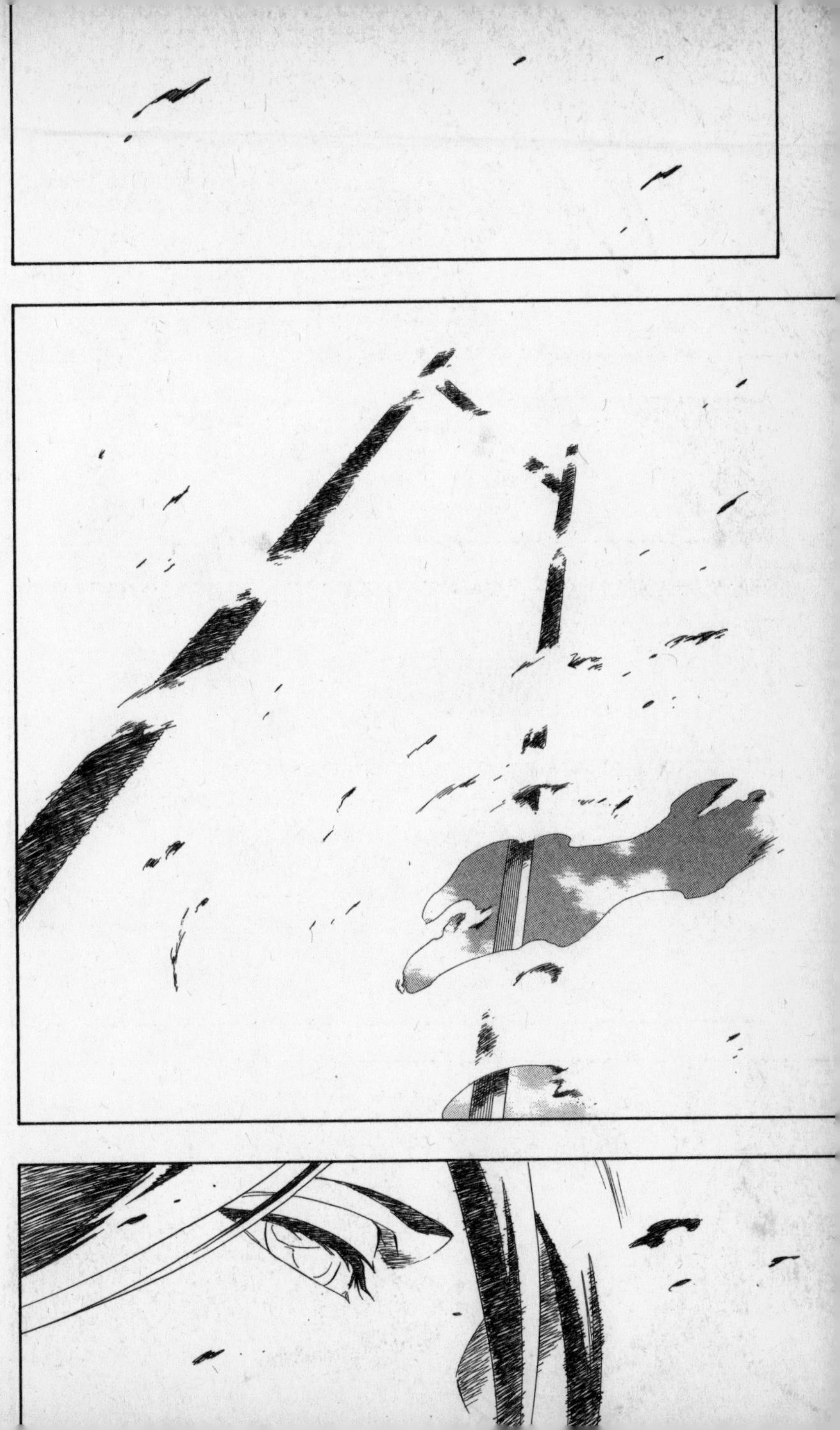

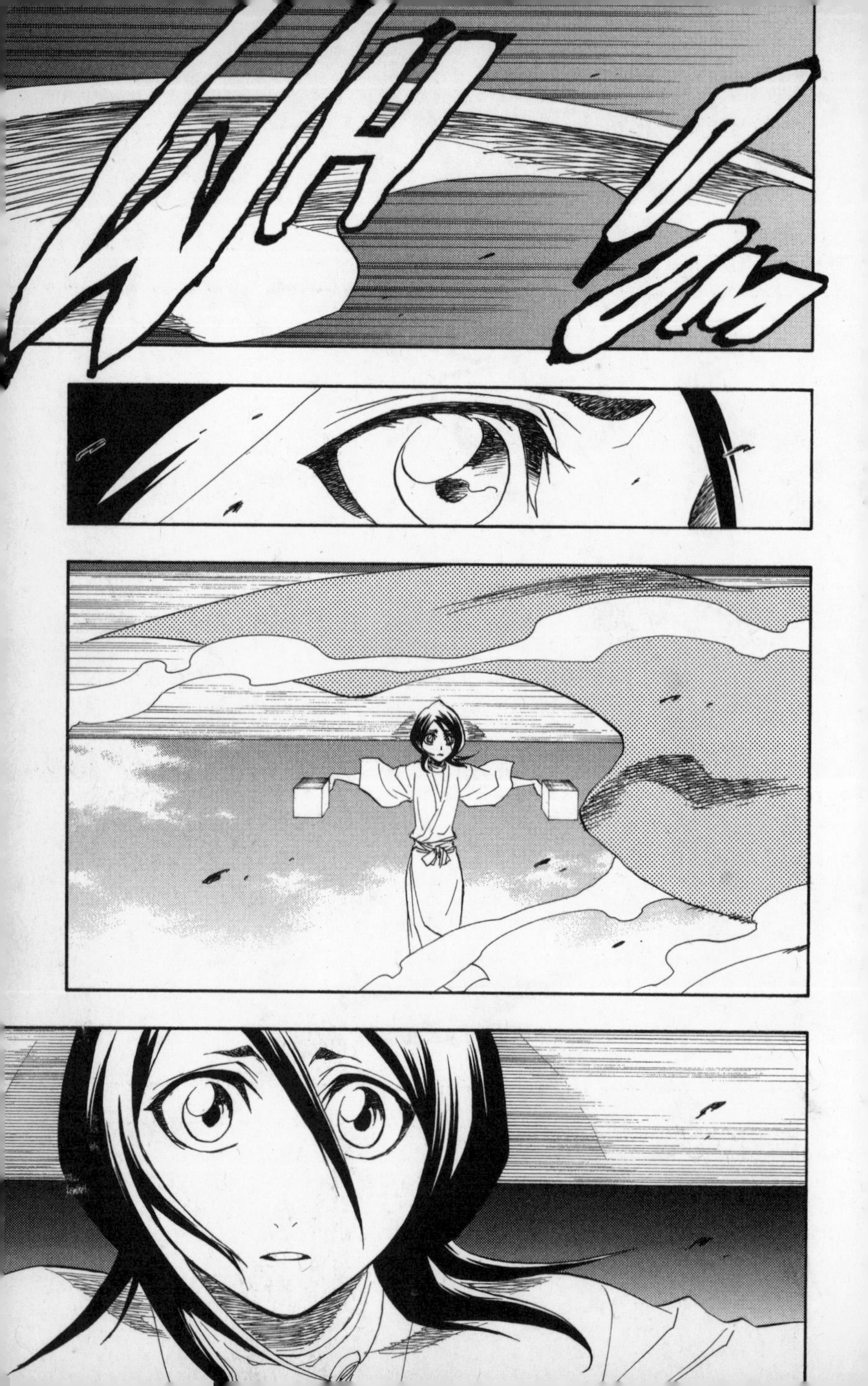
WHOM

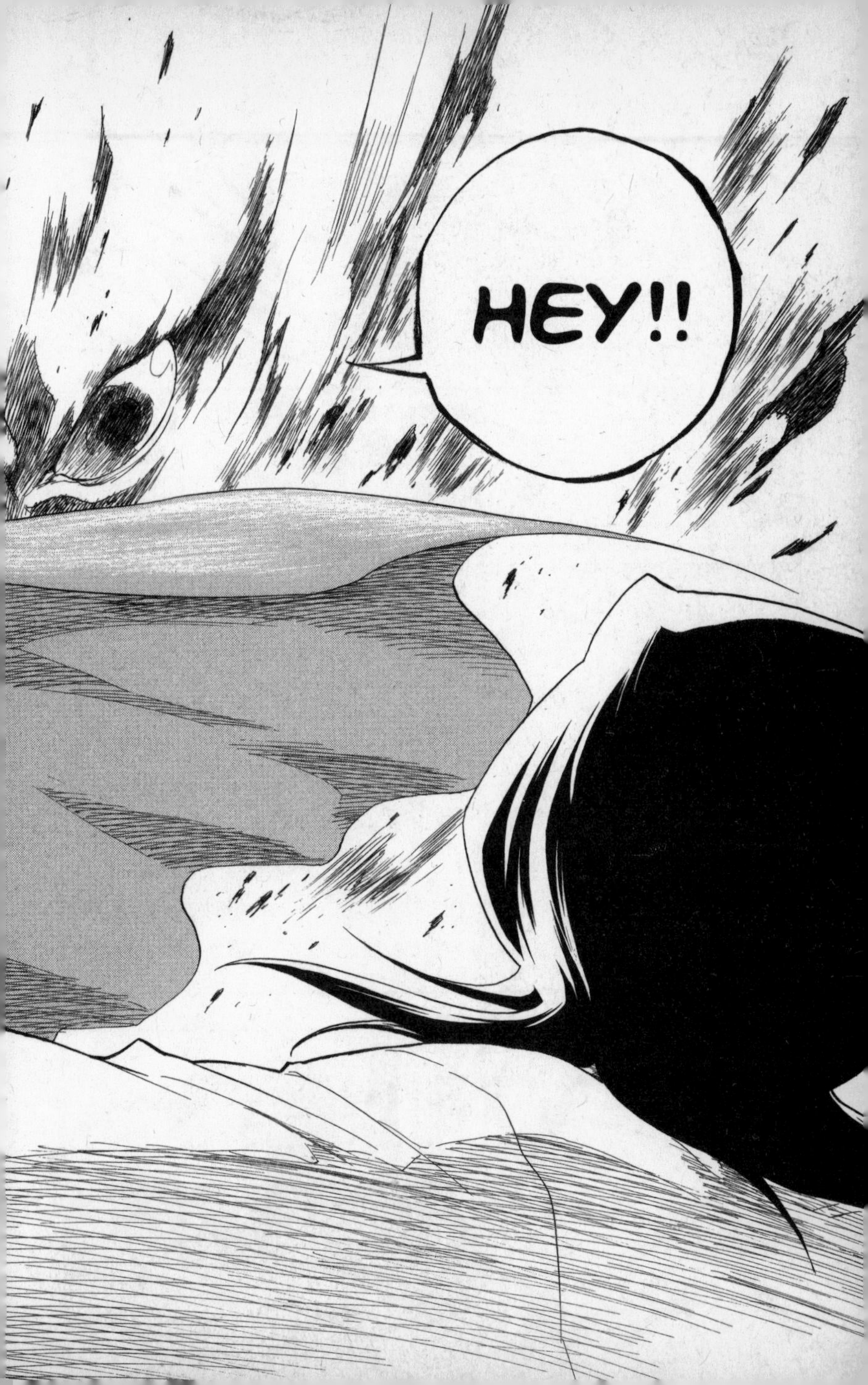
HEY!!

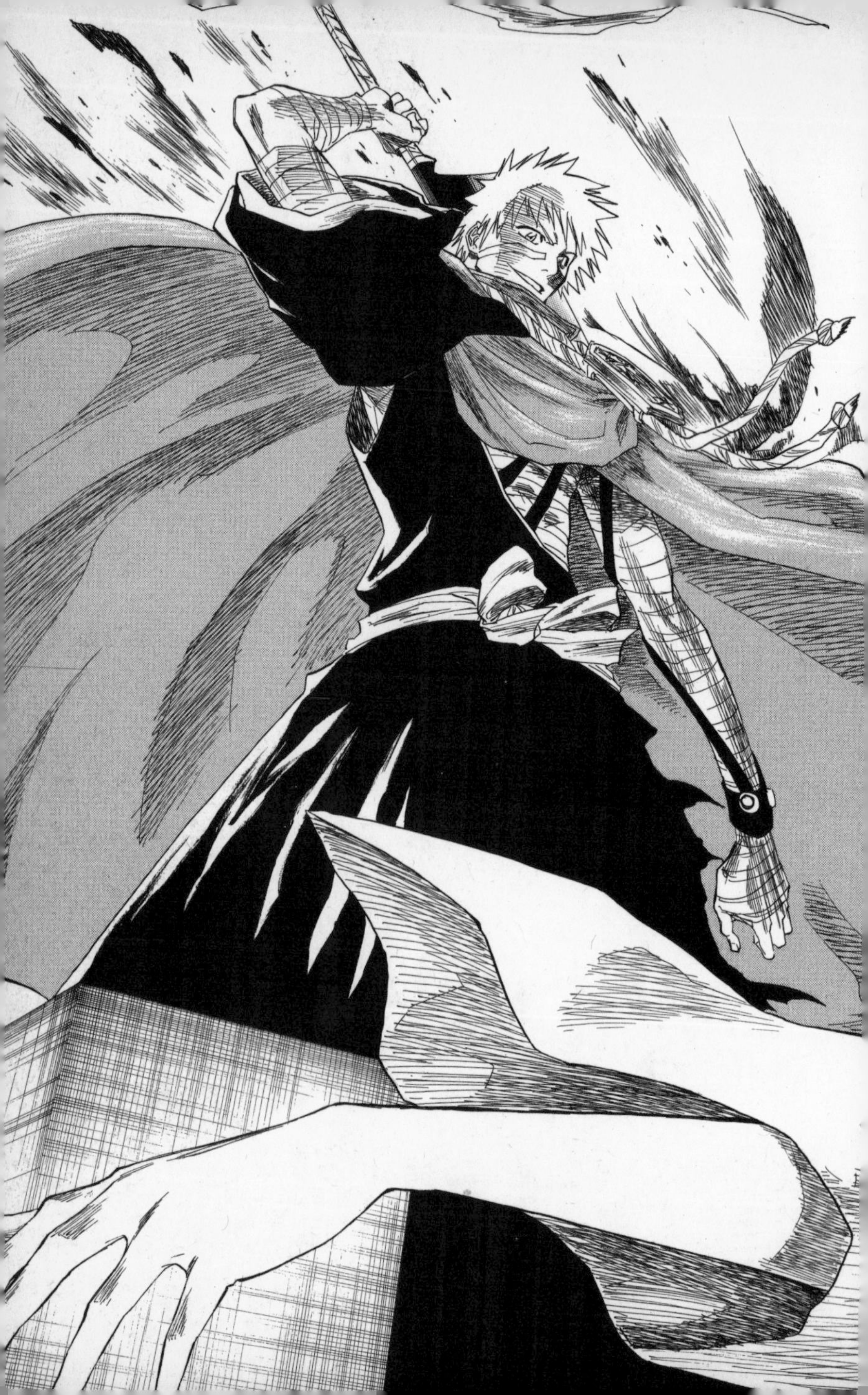

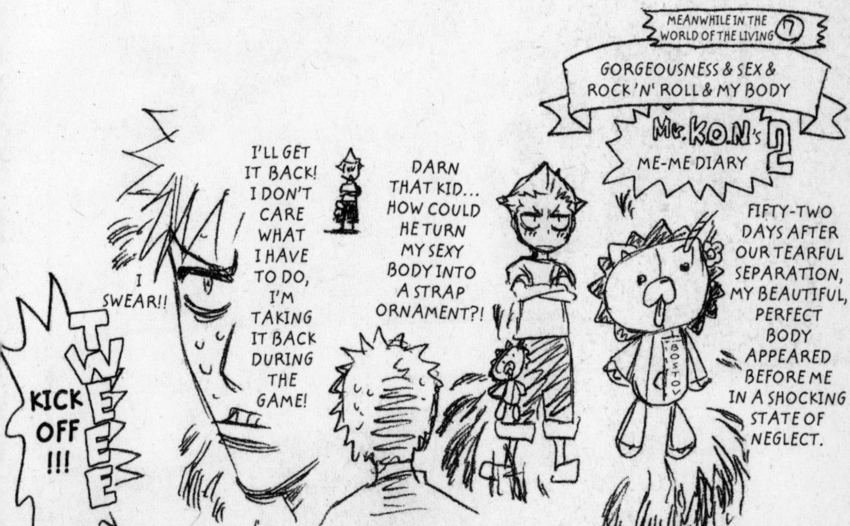
MEANWHILE IN THE WORLD OF THE LIVING 7
GORGEOUSNESS & SEX & ROCK 'N' ROLL & MY BODY
Mr. KO.N's ME-ME DIARY 2
FIFTY-TWO DAYS AFTER OUR TEARFUL SEPARATION, MY BEAUTIFUL, PERFECT BODY APPEARED BEFORE ME IN A SHOCKING STATE OF NEGLECT.
BOSTOV
DARN THAT KID... HOW COULD HE TURN MY SEXY BODY INTO A STRAP ORNAMENT?!
I'LL GET IT BACK! I DON'T CARE WHAT I HAVE TO DO, I'M TAKING IT BACK DURING THE GAME!
I SWEAR!!
TWEEEE
KICK OFF !!!

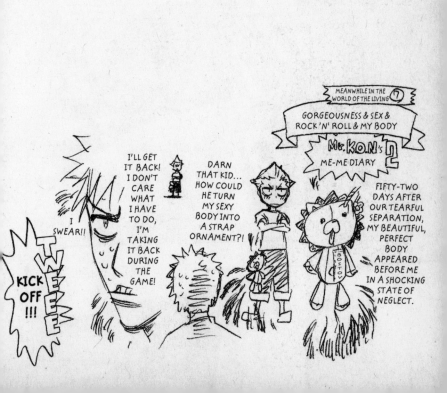

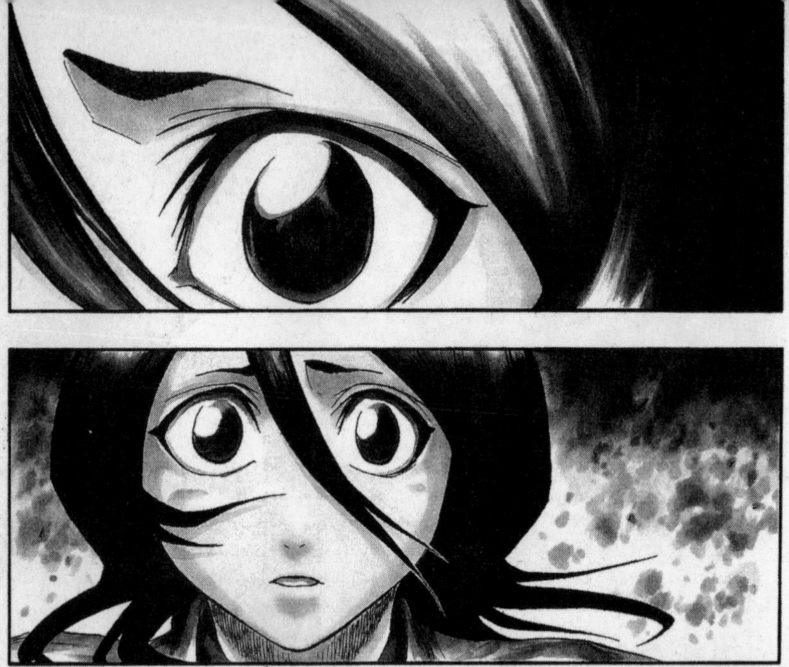

151. Deathberry Returns

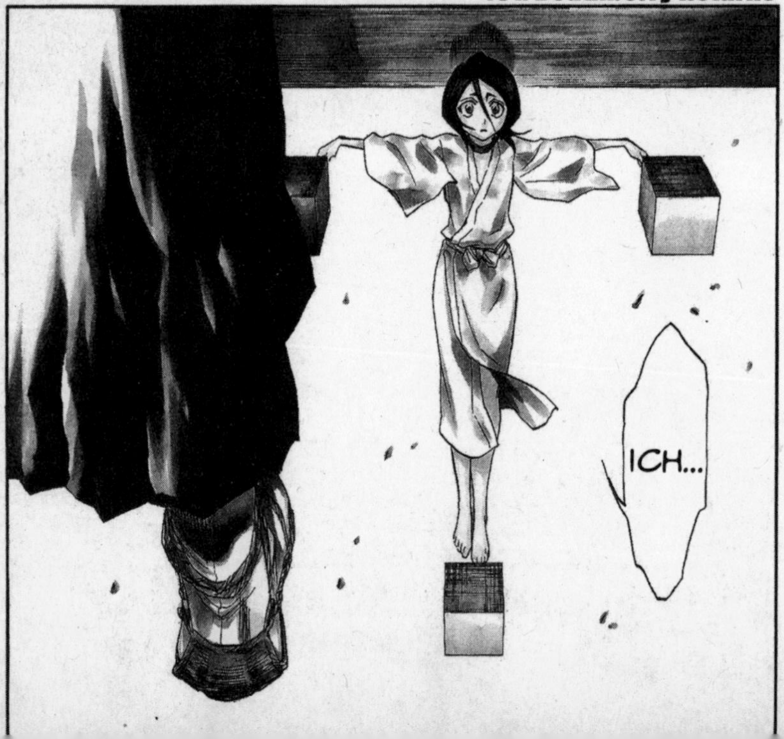
ICH...

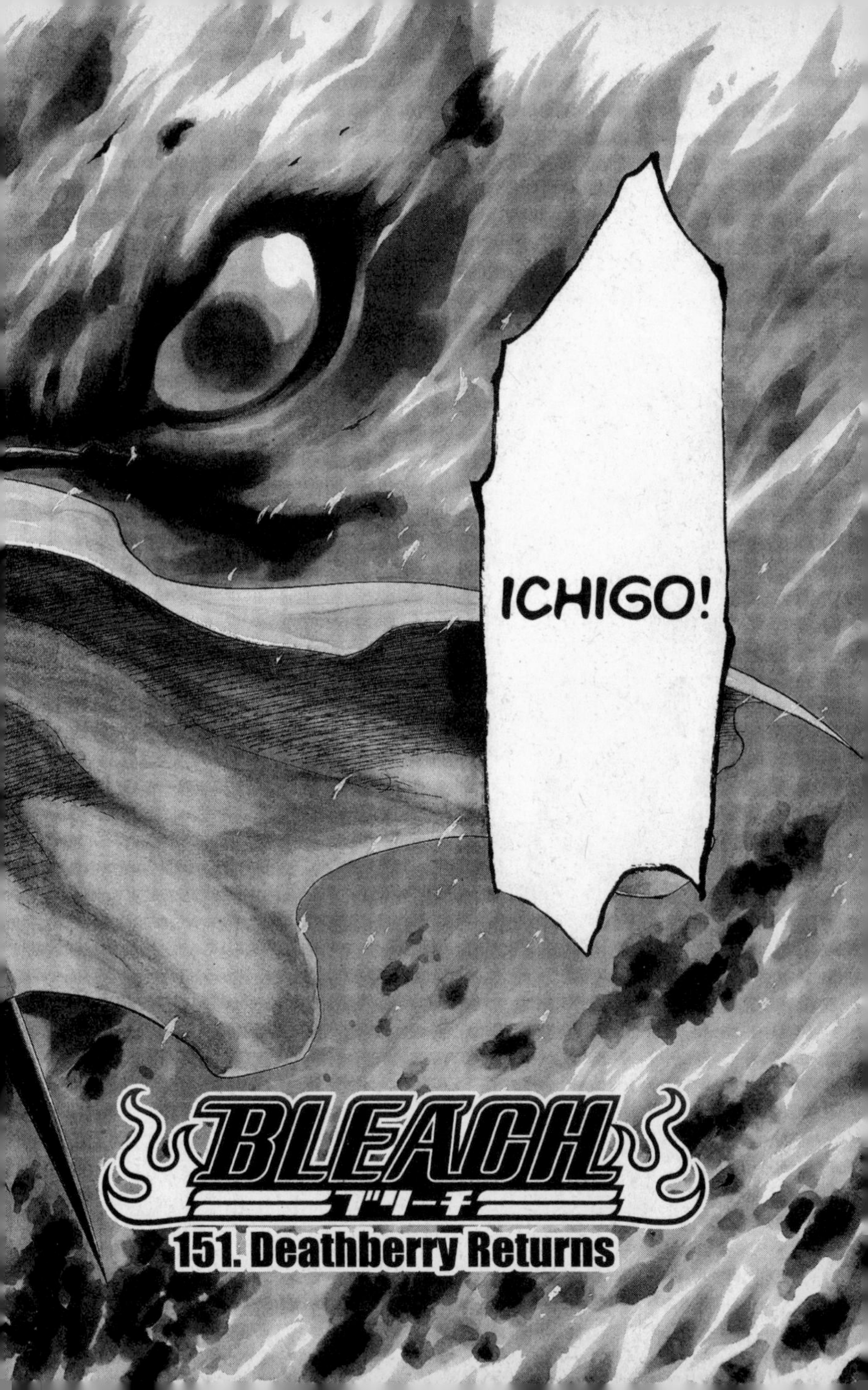
ICHIGO!
BLEACH
ブリーチ
151. Deathberry Returns

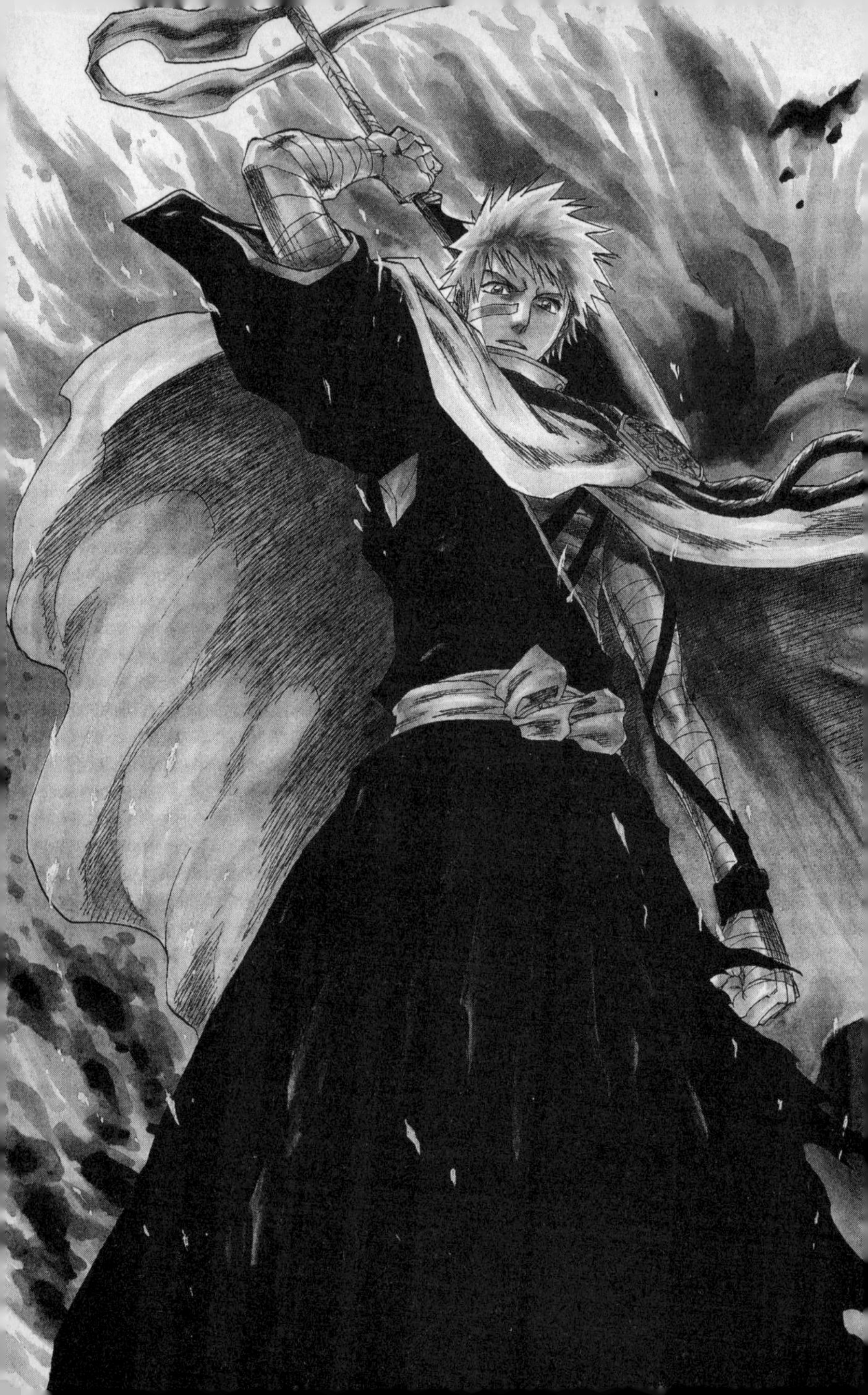

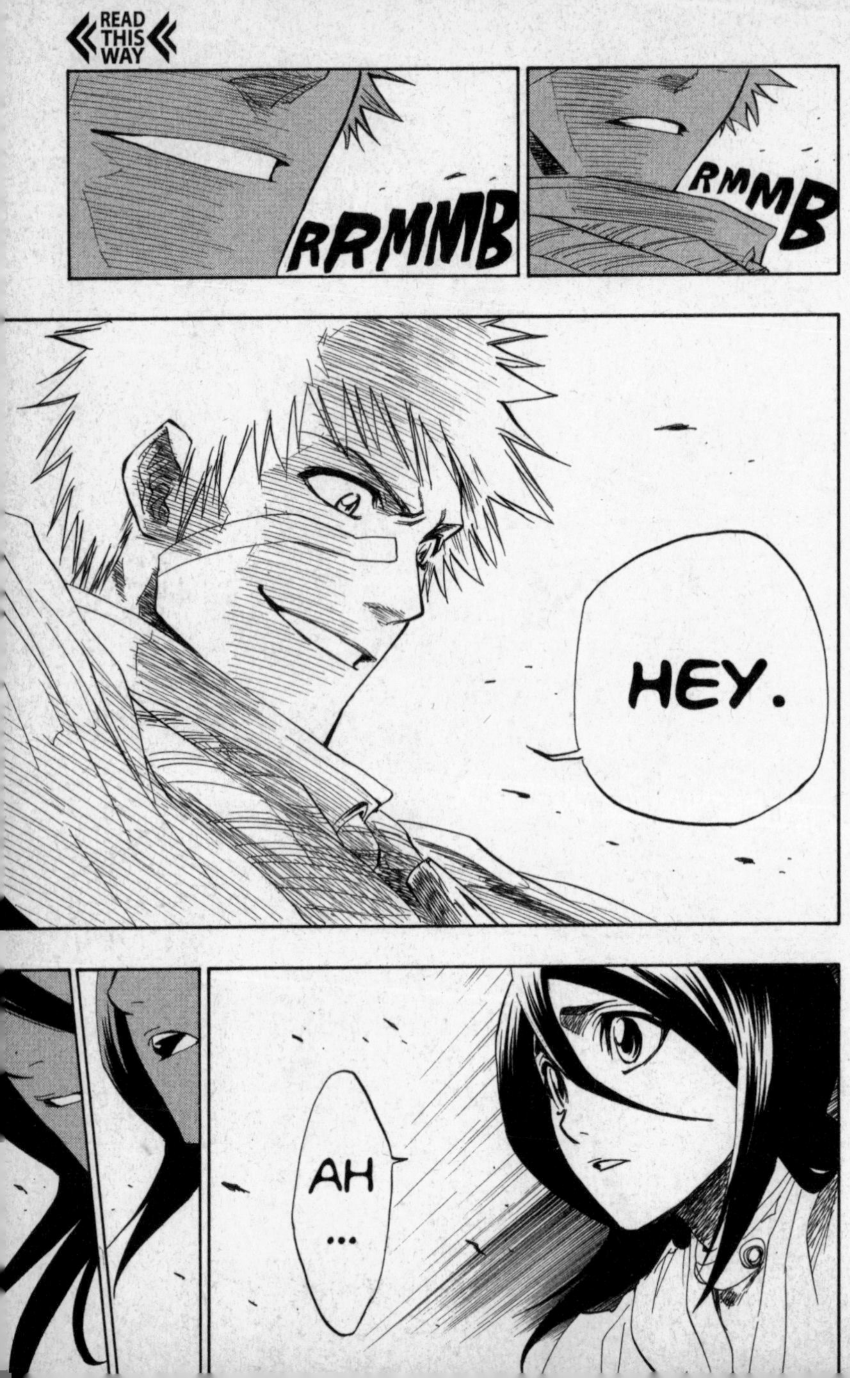
READ THIS WAY
RMMB
RRMMB
HEY.
AH ...

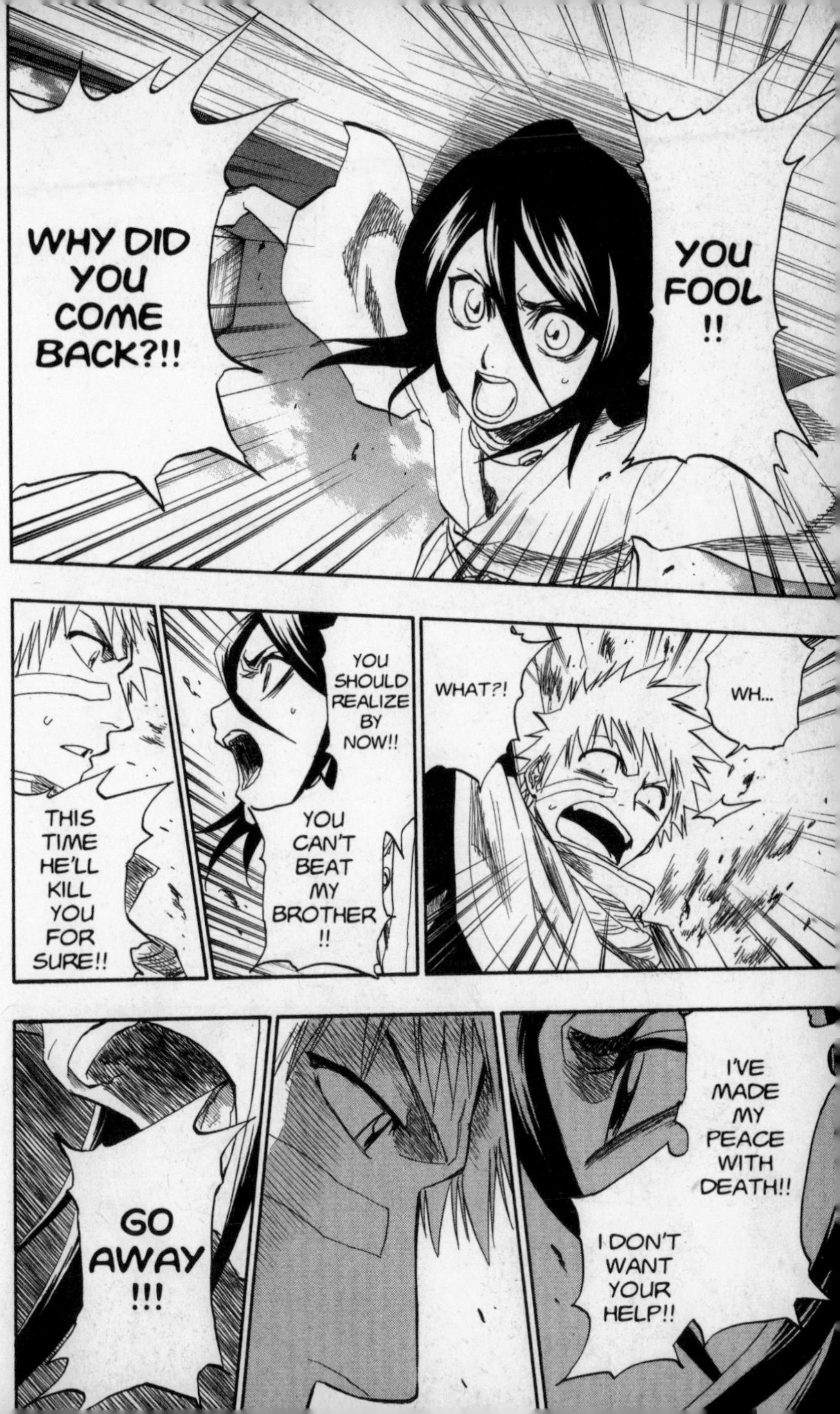
YOU FOOL!!
WHY DID YOU COME BACK?!!
WH...
WHAT?!
YOU SHOULD REALIZE BY NOW!!
YOU CAN'T BEAT MY BROTHER!!
THIS TIME HE'LL KILL YOU FOR SURE!!
I'VE MADE MY PEACE WITH DEATH!!
I DON'T WANT YOUR HELP!!
GO AWAY!!!

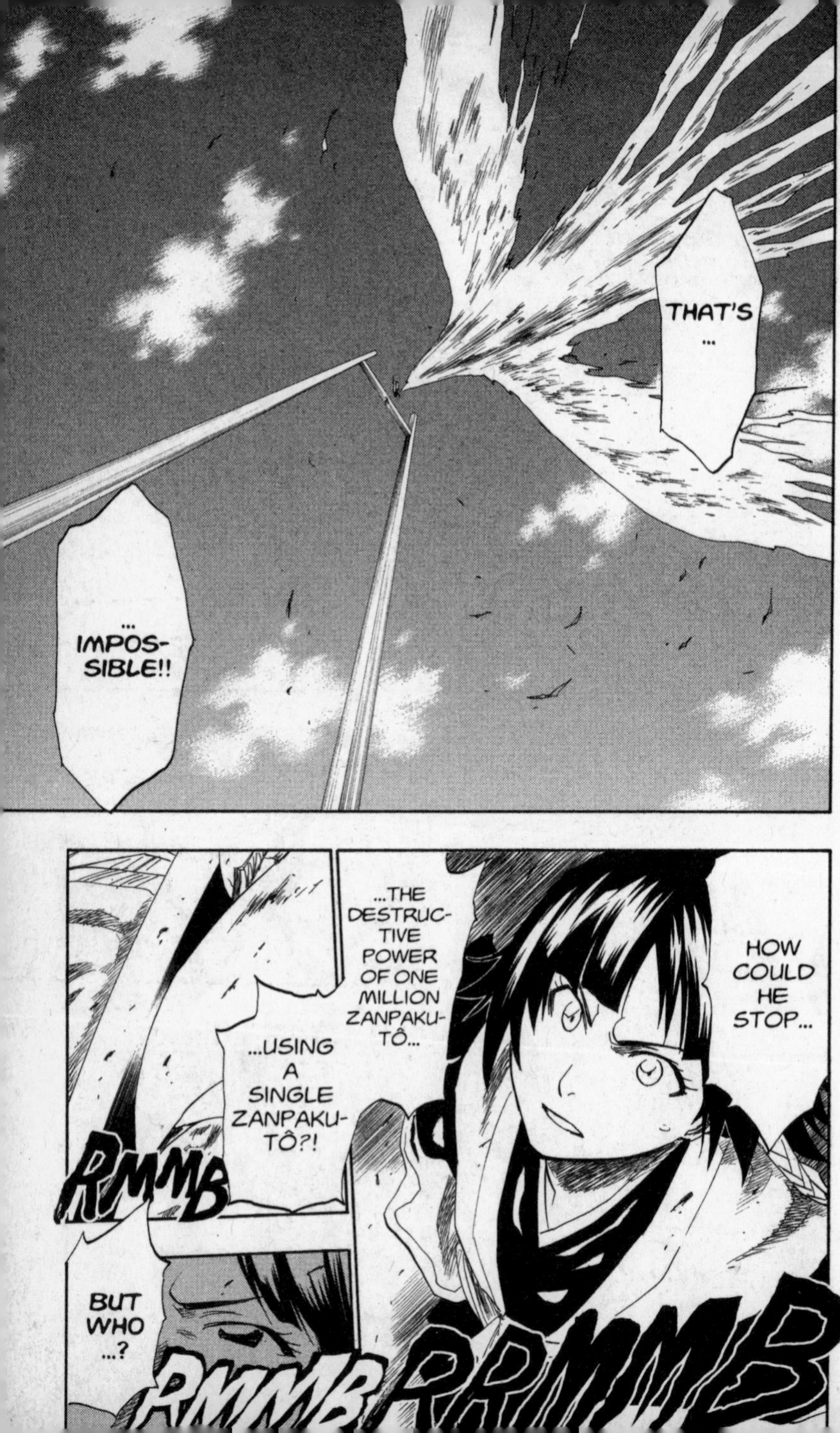
THAT'S ...
... IMPOSSIBLE!!
HOW COULD HE STOP...
...THE DESTRUCTIVE POWER OF ONE MILLION ZANPAKUTÔ...
...USING A SINGLE ZANPAKUTÔ?!
RMMB
BUT WHO ...?
RMMB RRMMMB

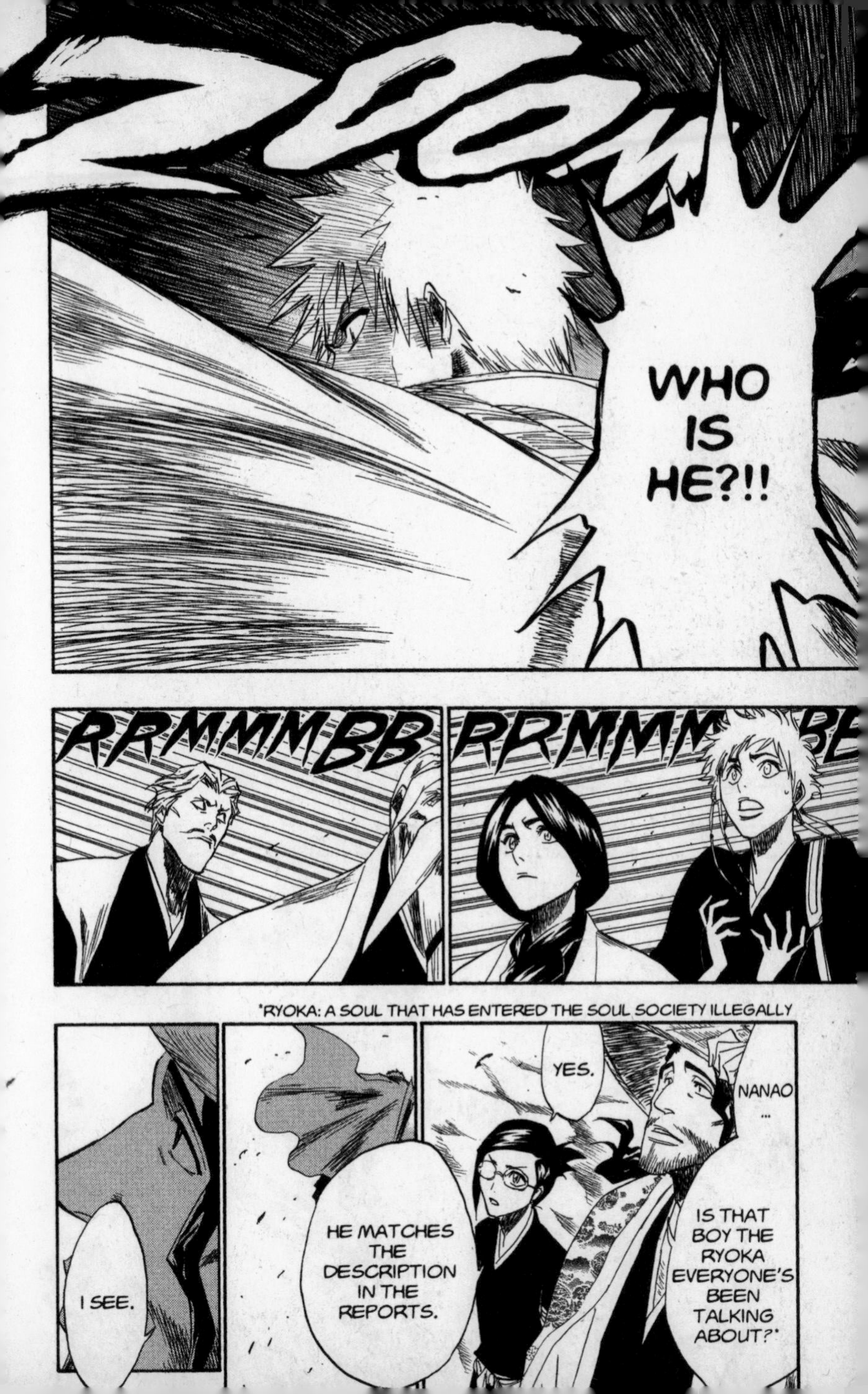
WHO IS HE?!!
RRMMMBB
RRMMMBB
*RYOKA: A SOUL THAT HAS ENTERED THE SOUL SOCIETY ILLEGALLY
NANAO ...
IS THAT BOY THE RYOKA EVERYONE'S BEEN TALKING ABOUT?*
YES.
HE MATCHES THE DESCRIPTION IN THE REPORTS.
I SEE.

READ THIS WAY

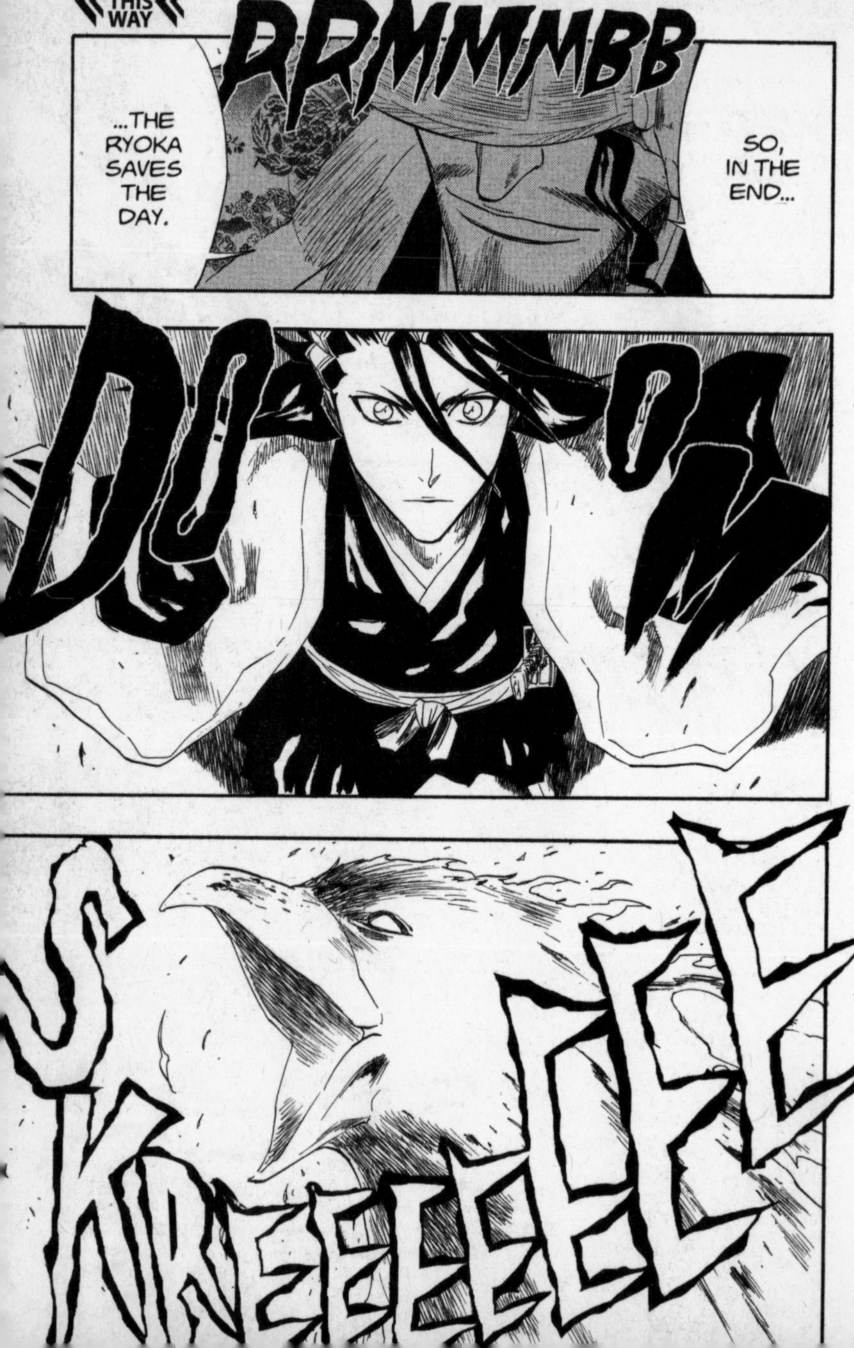
DRMMMBB
SO, IN THE END...
...THE RYOKA SAVES THE DAY.
DOOM
SKREEEEEEE

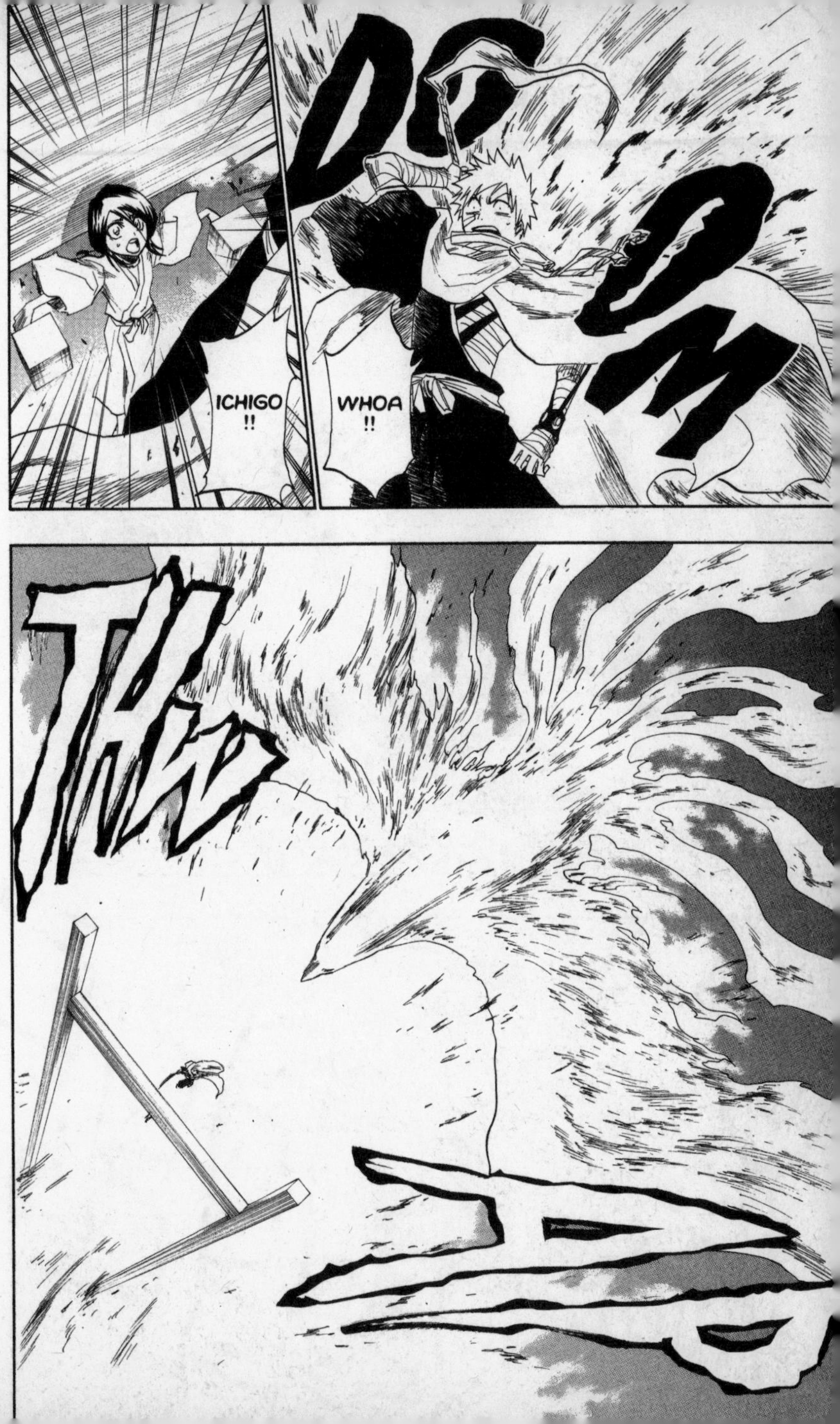
DOOM
WHOA!!
ICHIGO!!

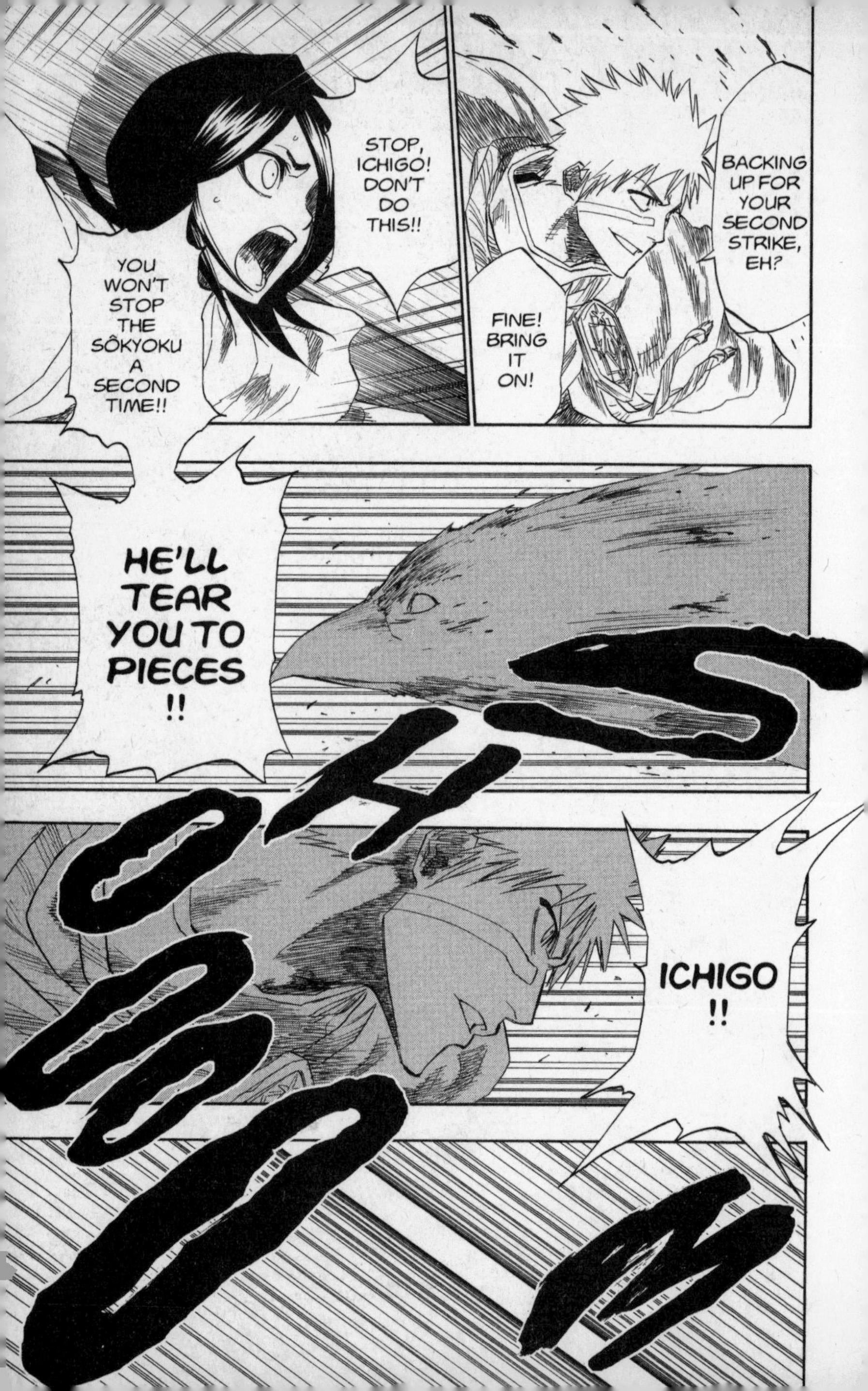
BACKING UP FOR YOUR SECOND STRIKE, EH?
FINE! BRING IT ON!
STOP, ICHIGO! DON'T DO THIS!!
YOU WON'T STOP THE SÔKYOKU A SECOND TIME!!
HE'LL TEAR YOU TO PIECES!!
ICHIGO!!
SHOOOOM

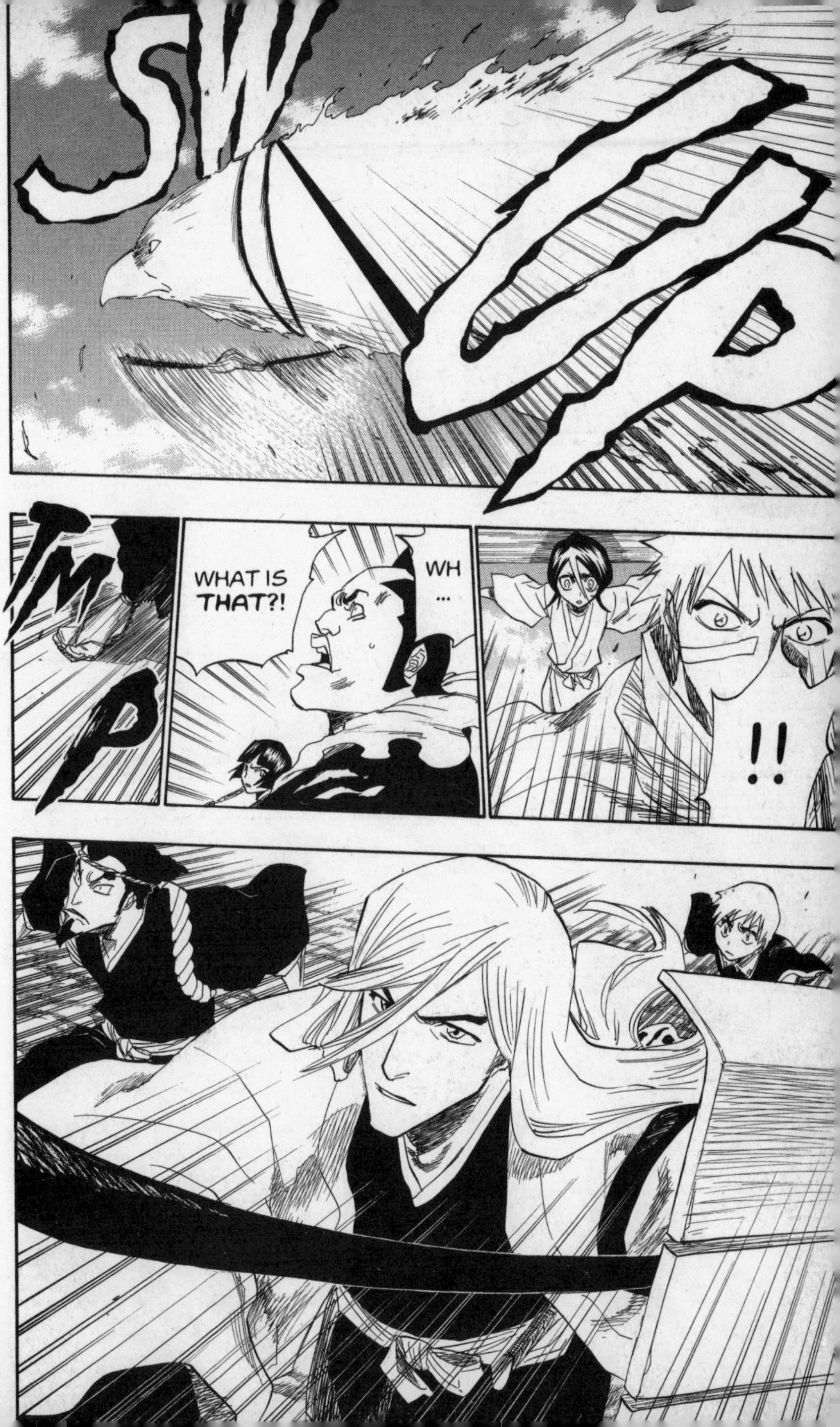
SWOOP
!!
WH ...
WHAT IS THAT?!
TMP

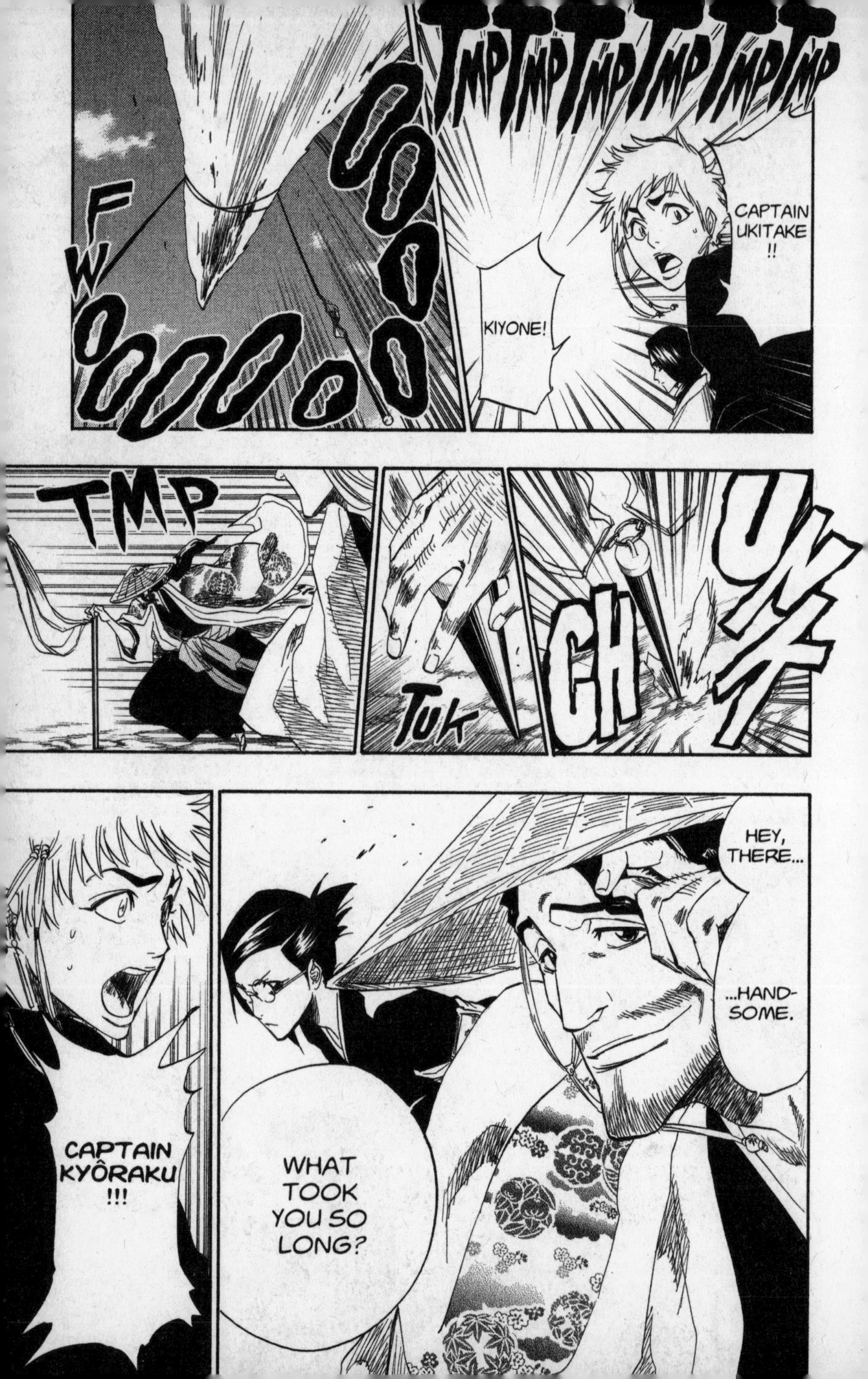
TMPTMPTMPTMPTMPTMP
CAPTAIN UKITAKE !!
KIYONE!
FWOOOOOOOOOOO
CHUNK
TUK
TMP
HEY, THERE...
...HAND-SOME.
WHAT TOOK YOU SO LONG?
CAPTAIN KYÔRAKU !!!

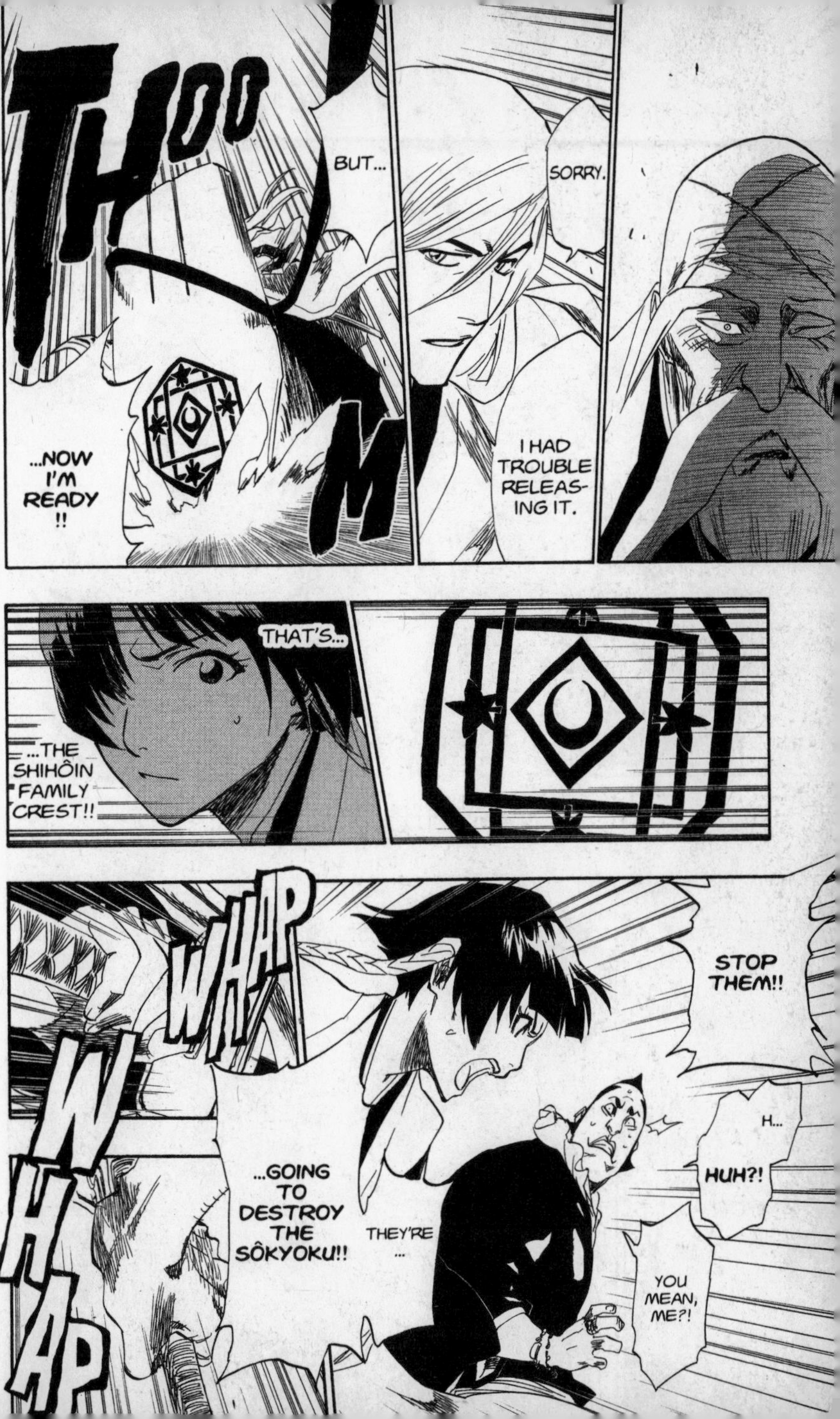
SORRY.
I HAD TROUBLE RELEASING IT.
BUT...
THOOOM
...NOW I'M READY!!
THAT'S...
...THE SHIHÔIN FAMILY CREST!!
STOP THEM!!
H...
HUH?!
YOU MEAN, ME?!
WHAP
THEY'RE...
...GOING TO DESTROY THE SÔKYOKU!!
WHAP

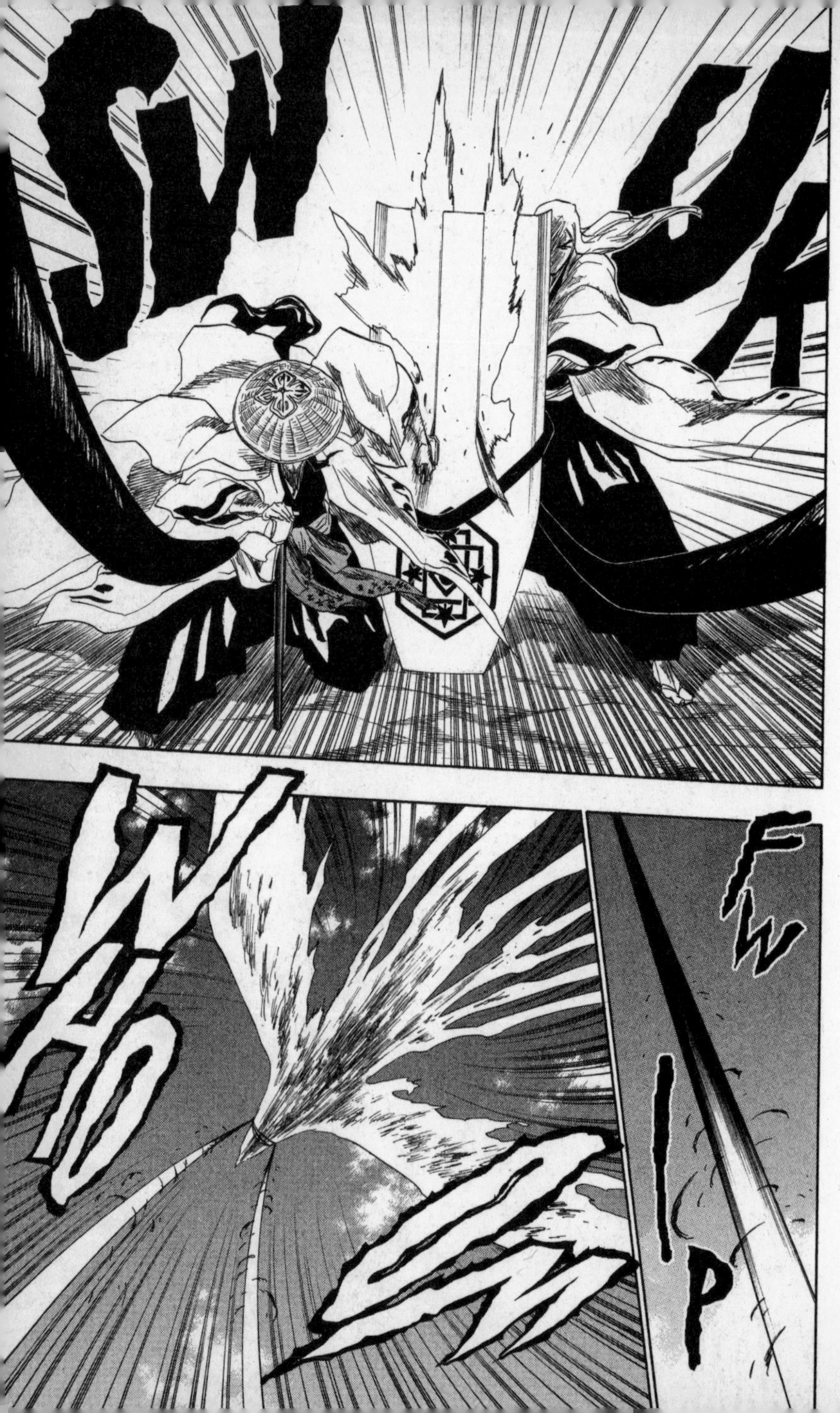
FWIP

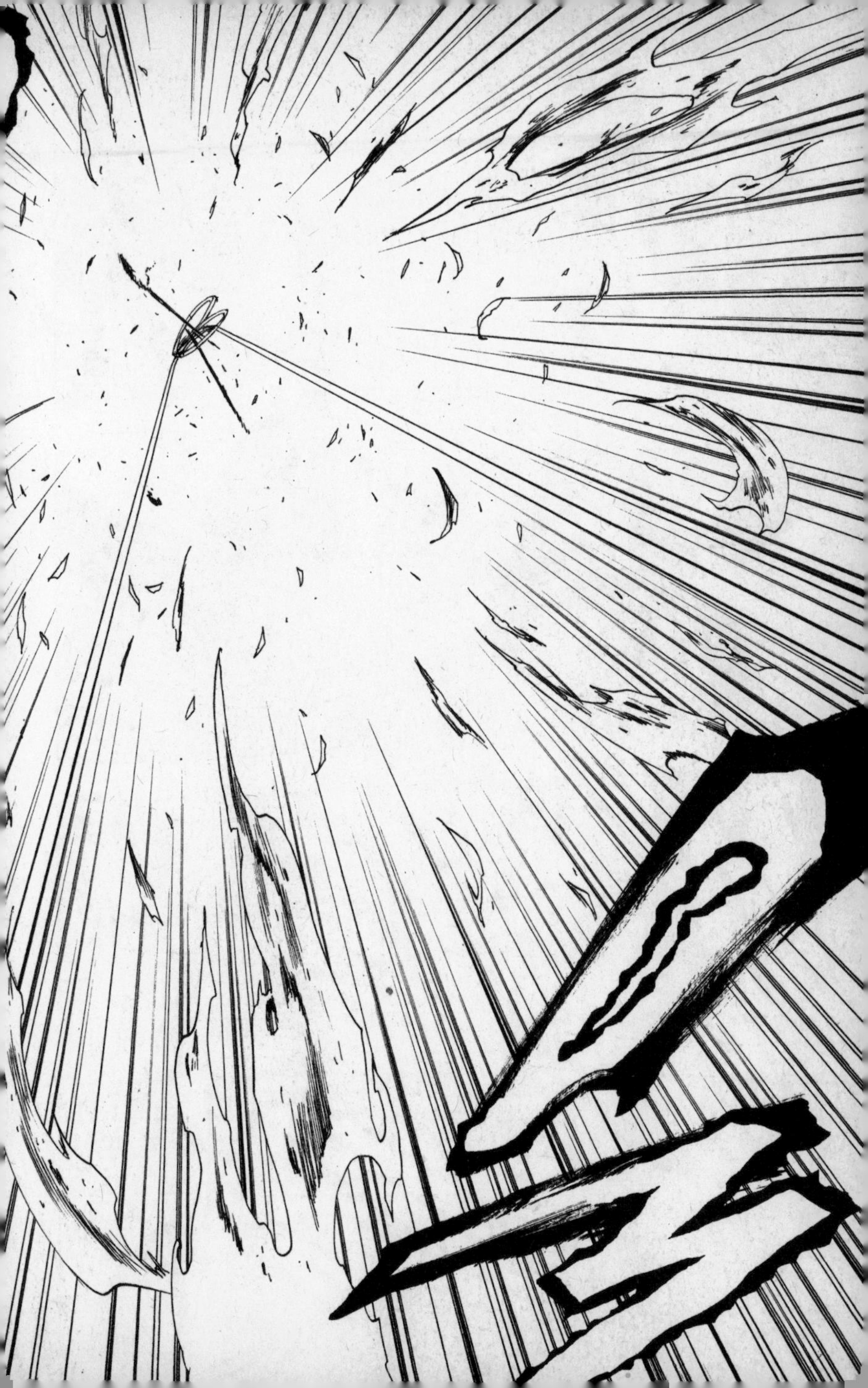

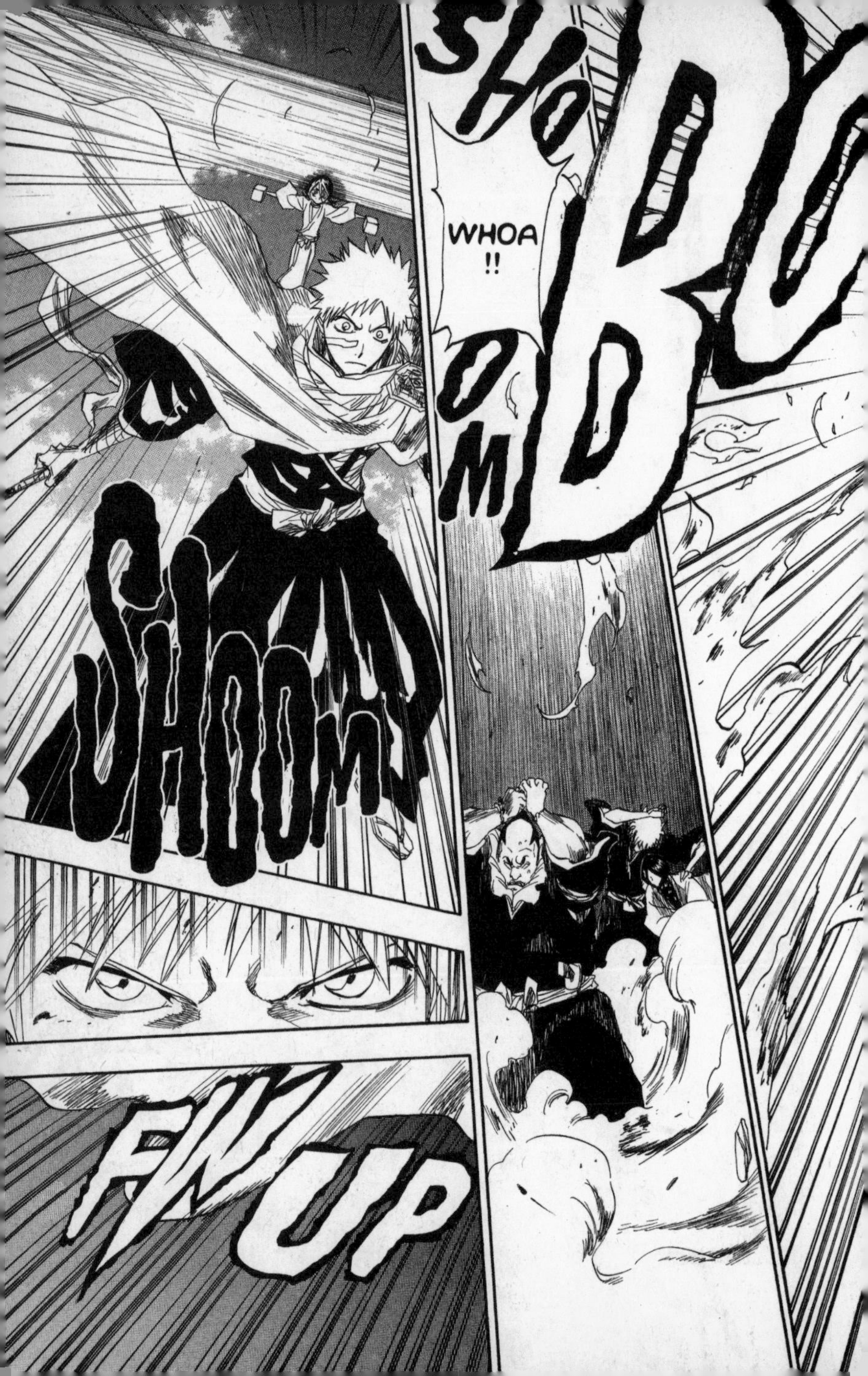
SHOOOM
WHOA !!
SHOOM
FWUP

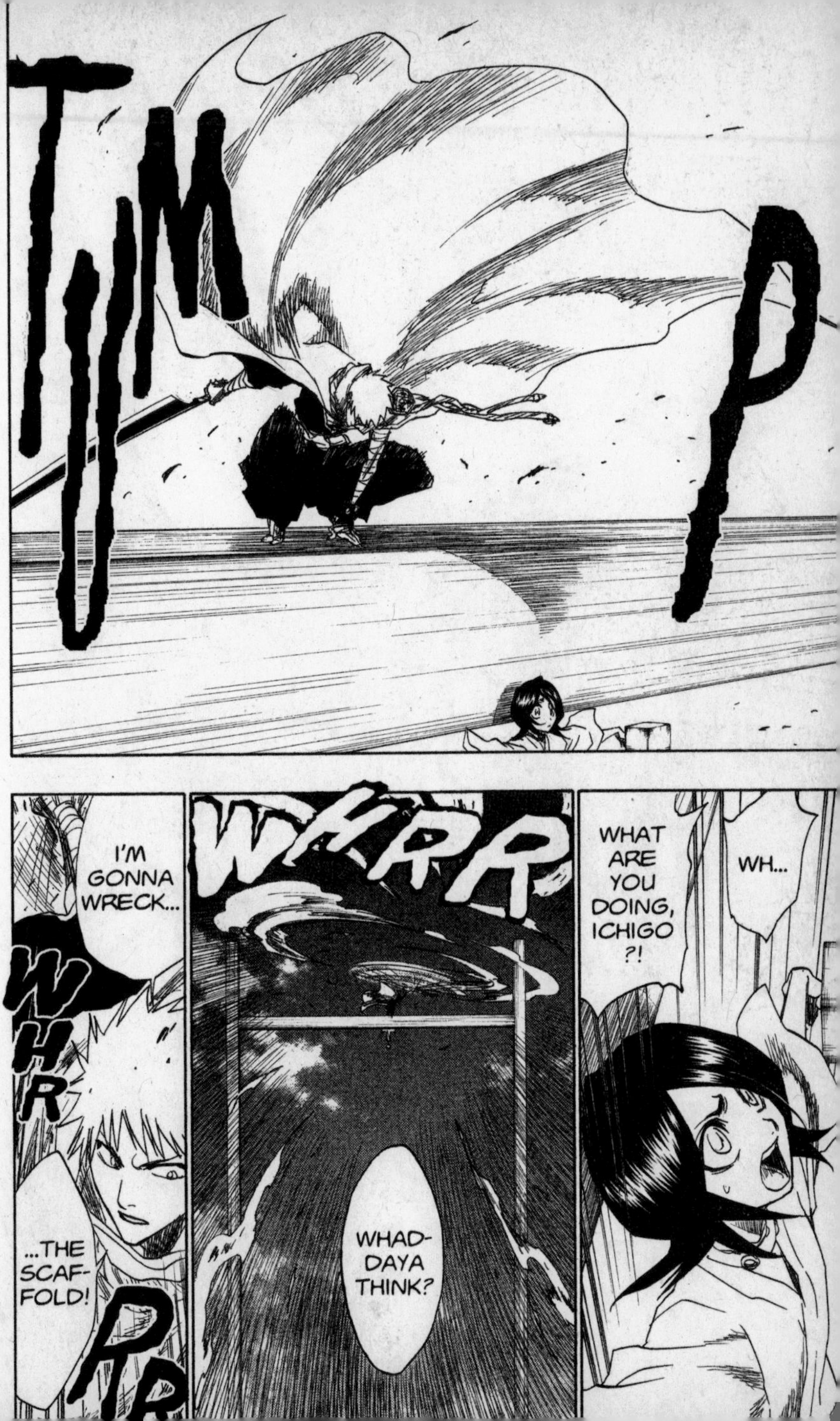
TUMP
WH...
WHAT ARE YOU DOING, ICHIGO?!
WHRR
WHAD-DAYA THINK?
I'M GONNA WRECK...
WHR
...THE SCAFFOLD!

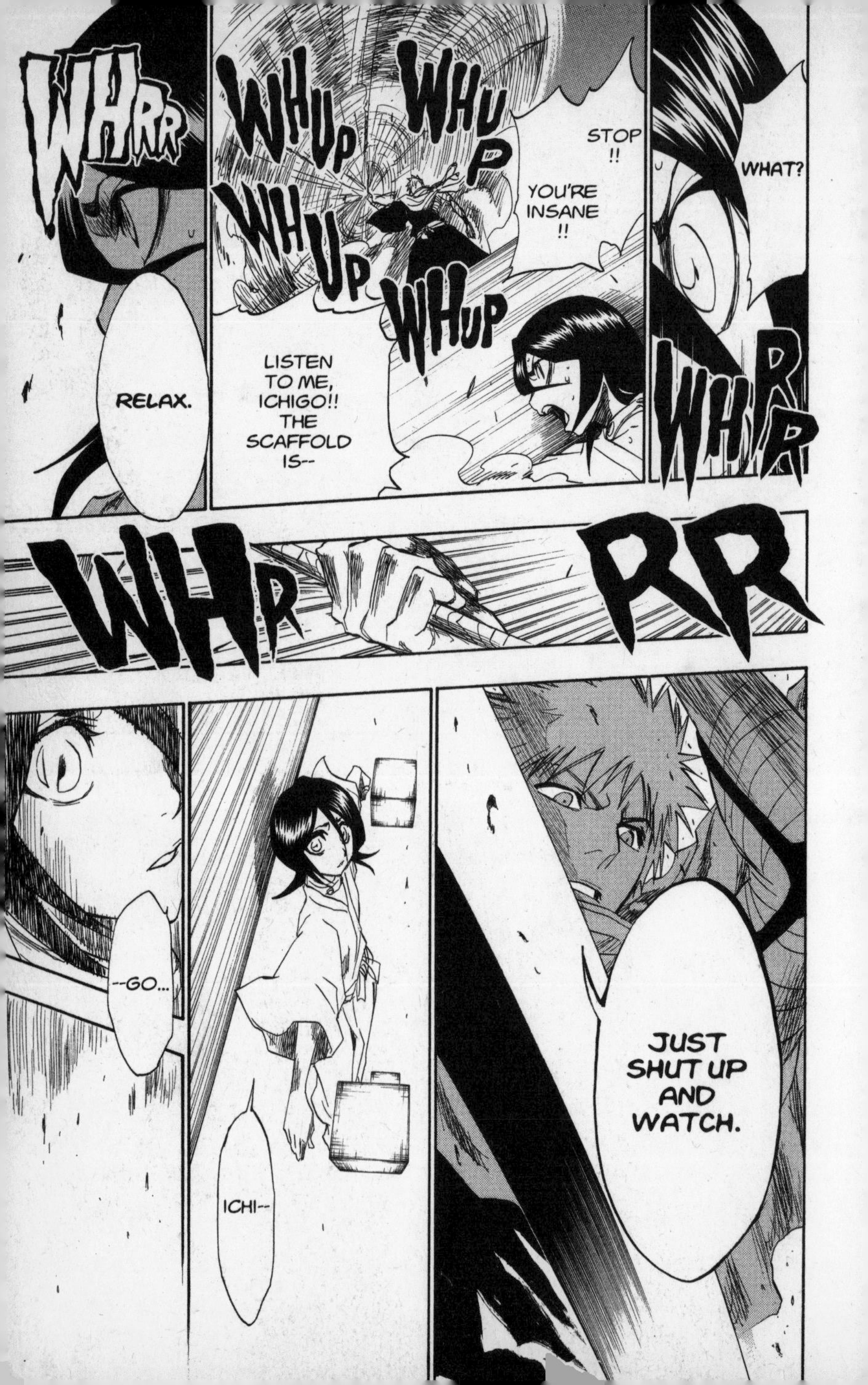
WHAT?
WHRR
STOP!!
YOU'RE INSANE!!
WHUP WHUP
WHUP WHUP
WHUP
LISTEN TO ME, ICHIGO!! THE SCAFFOLD IS--
WHRR
RELAX.
WHR RR
JUST SHUT UP AND WATCH.
ICHI--
--GO...

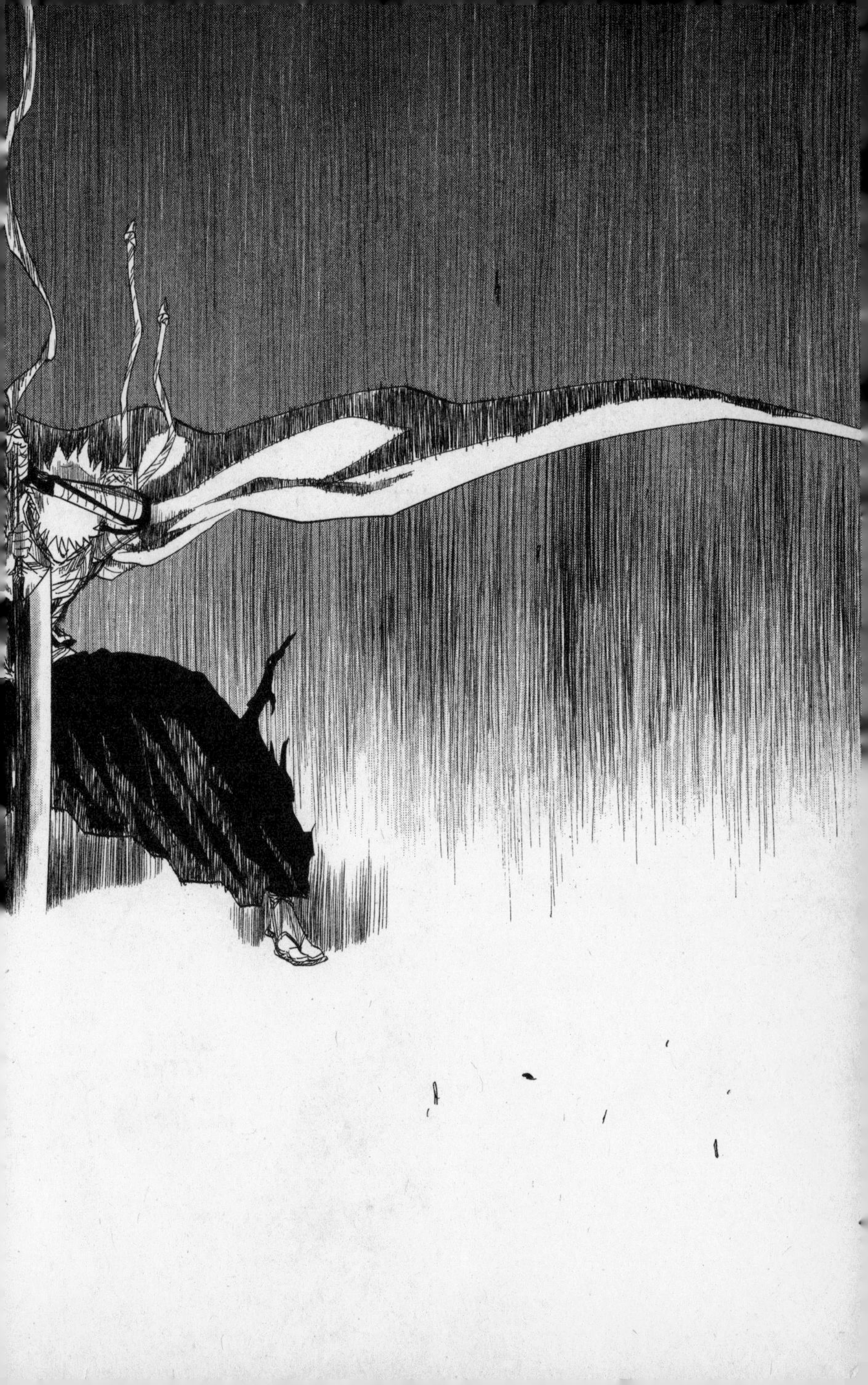

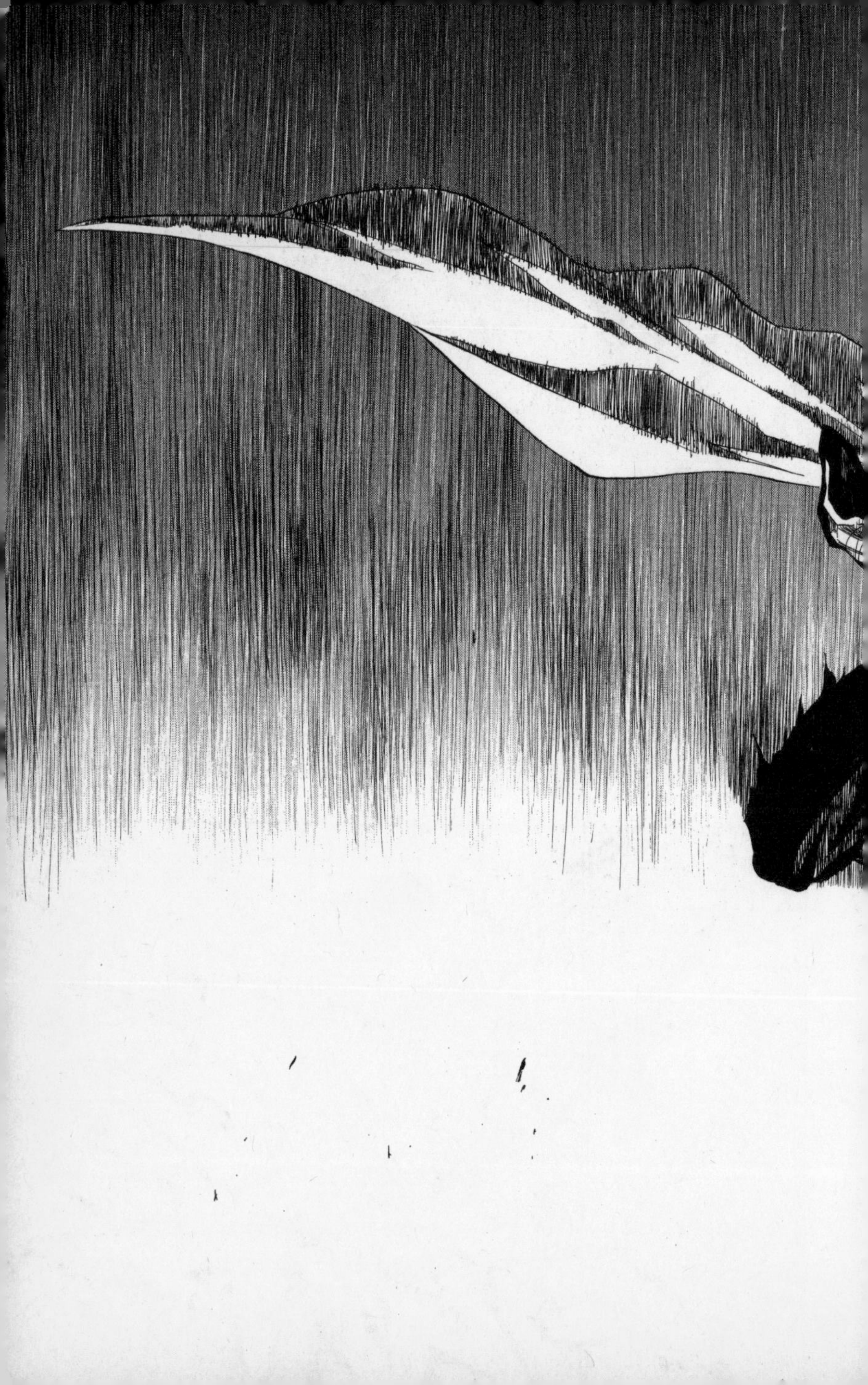

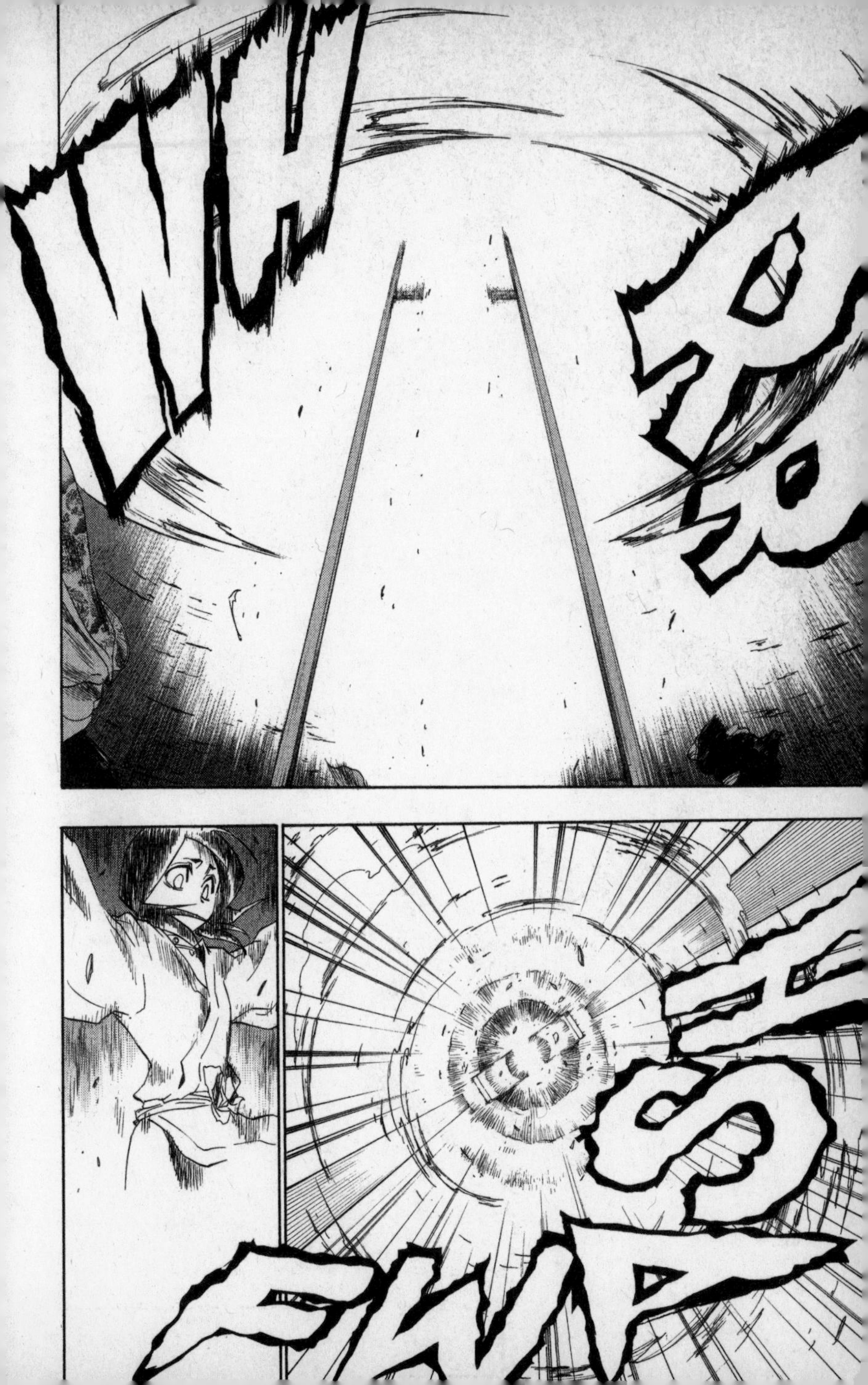

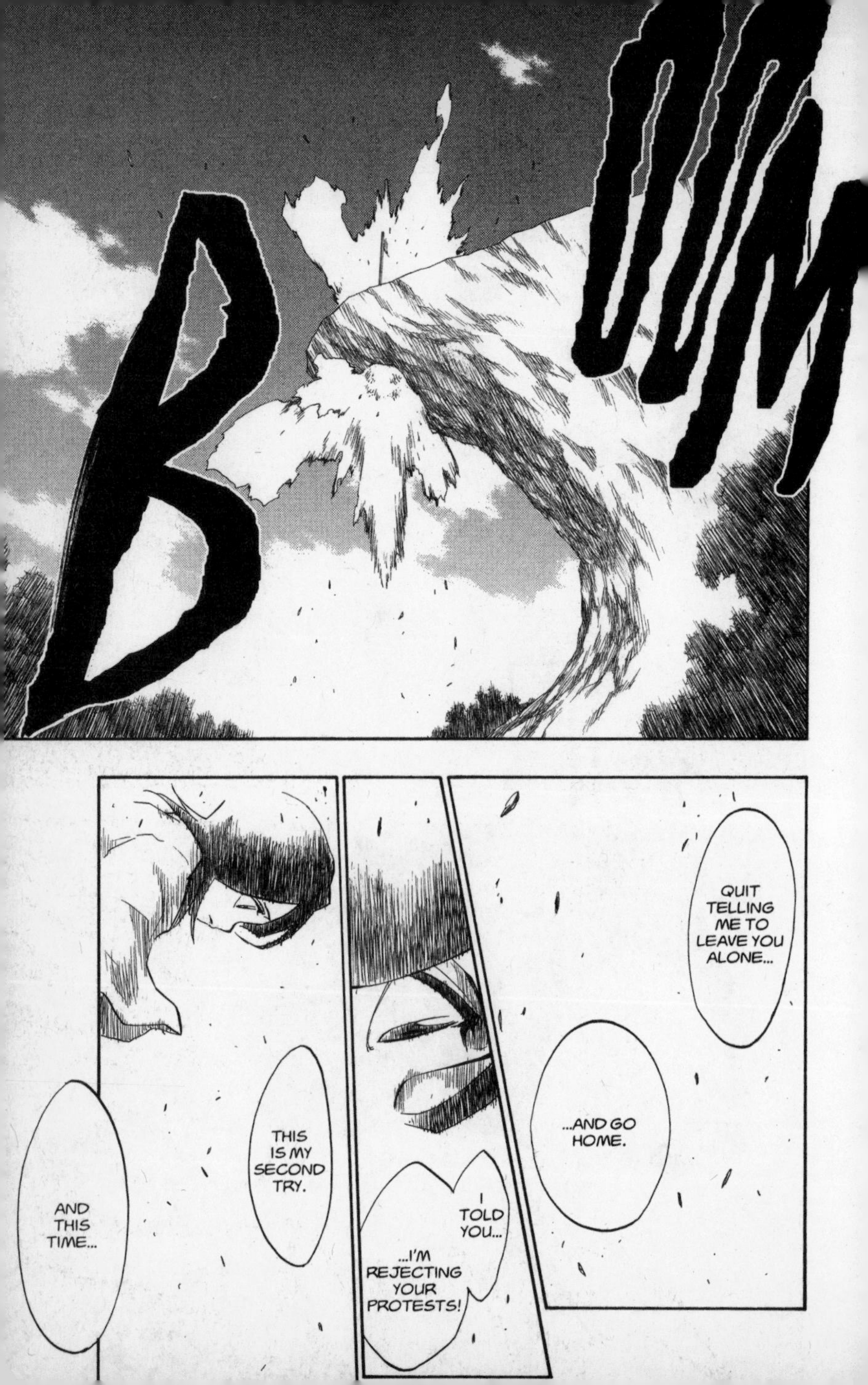

BOOM
QUIT TELLING ME TO LEAVE YOU ALONE...
...AND GO HOME.
I TOLD YOU...
...I'M REJECTING YOUR PROTESTS!
THIS IS MY SECOND TRY.
AND THIS TIME...

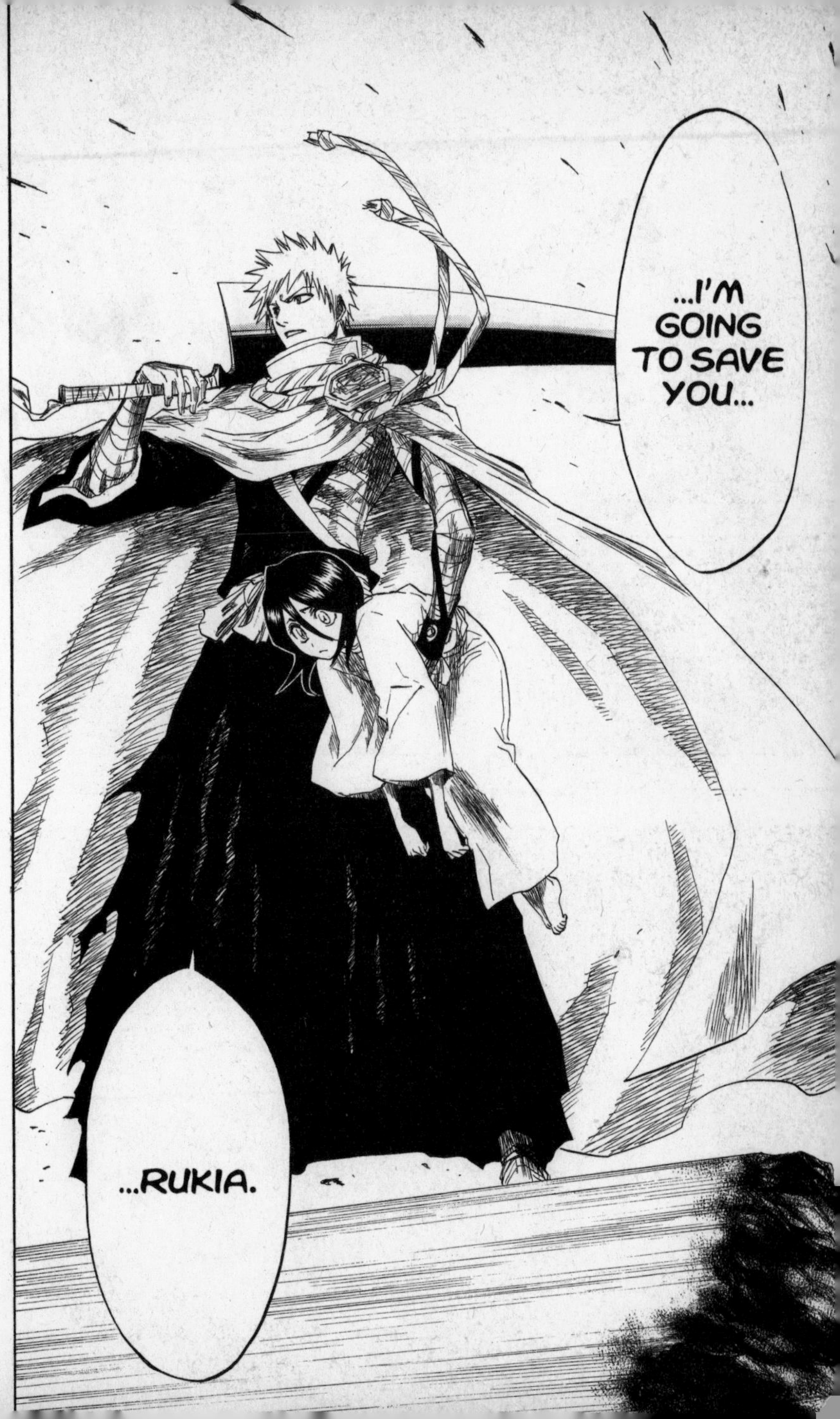
...I'M GOING TO SAVE YOU...
...RUKIA.

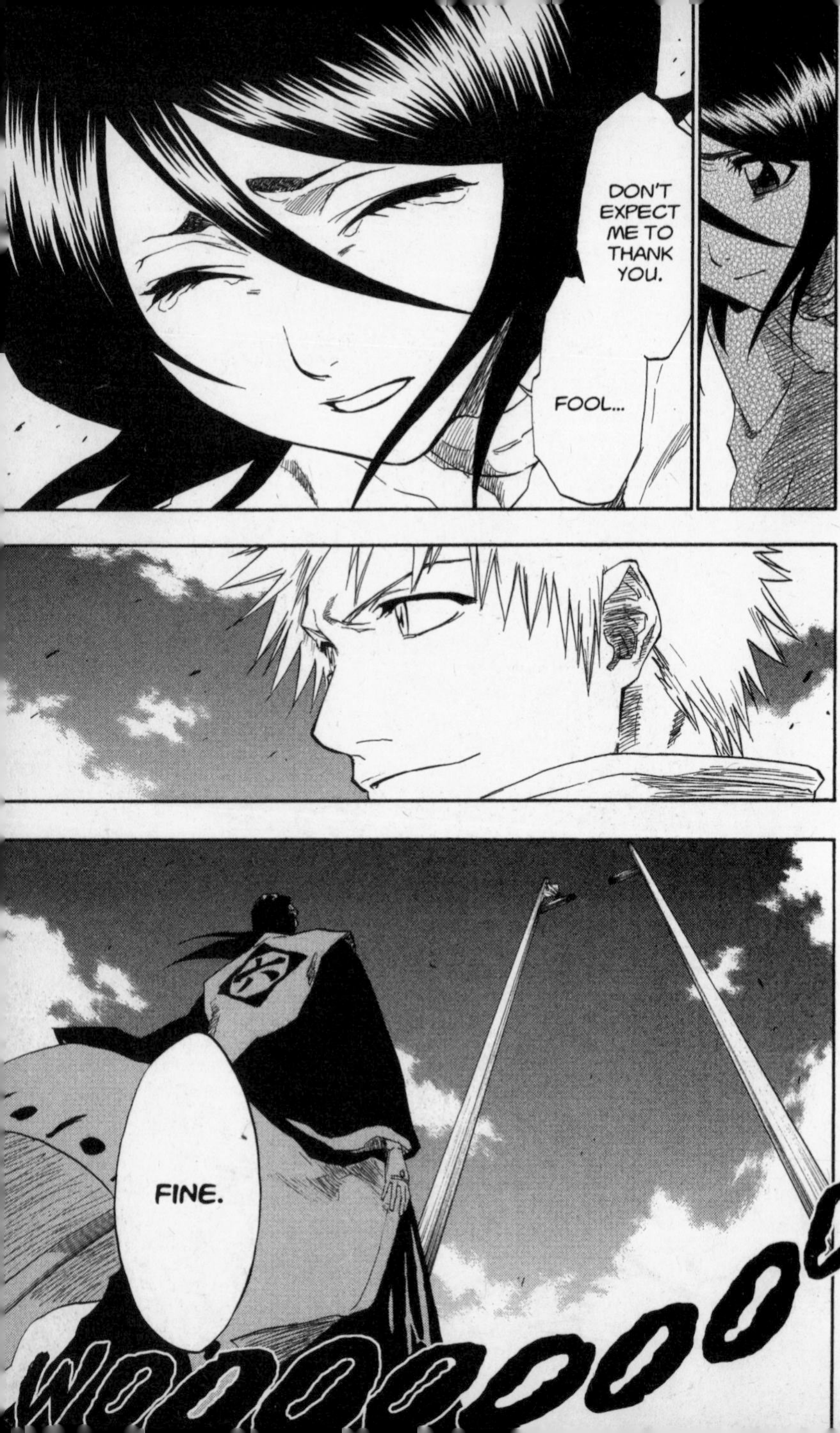
DON'T EXPECT ME TO THANK YOU.
FOOL...
FINE.
WOOOOOOOOOO

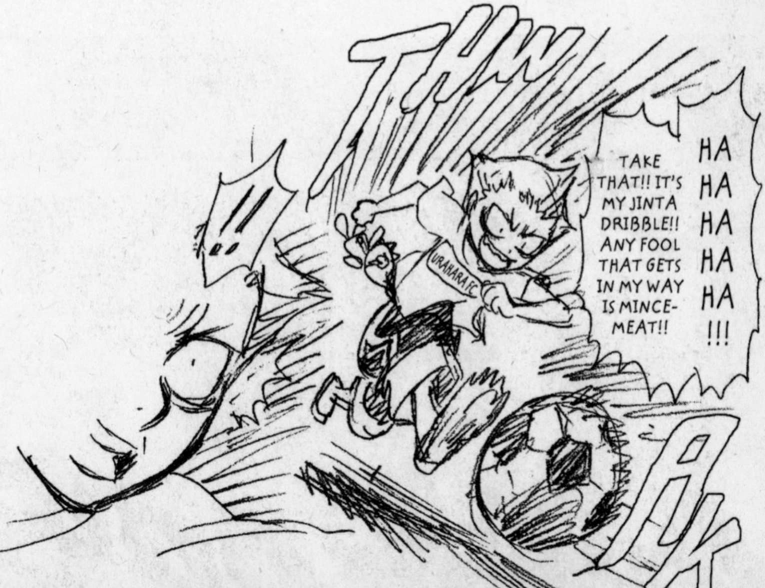
THWAK
HA HA HA HA HA!!!
TAKE THAT!! IT'S MY JINTA DRIBBLE!! ANY FOOL THAT GETS IN MY WAY IS MINCE-MEAT!!
URAHARA FC
!!

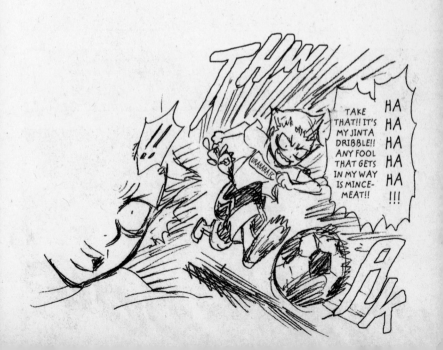

152. The Speed Phantom

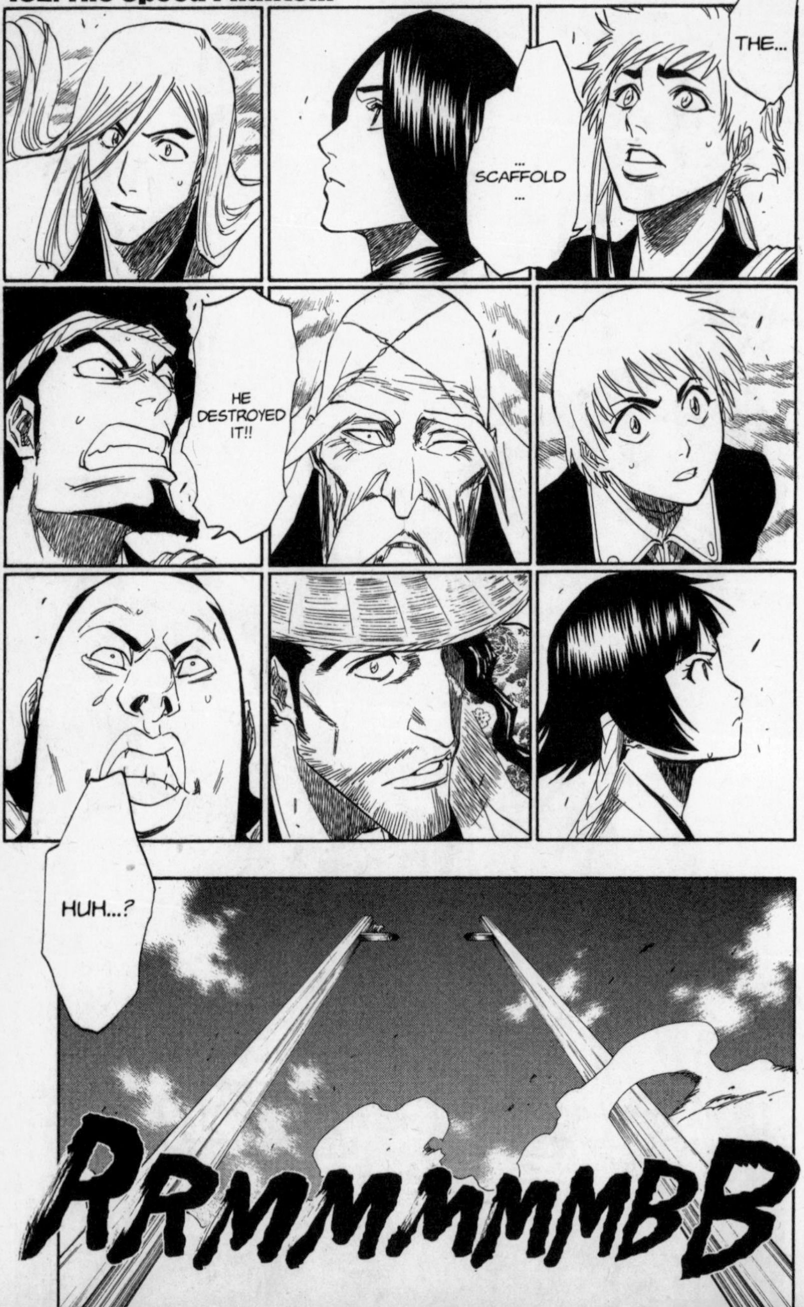
THE...
... SCAFFOLD ...
HE DESTROYED IT!!
HUH...?
RRMMMMMBB

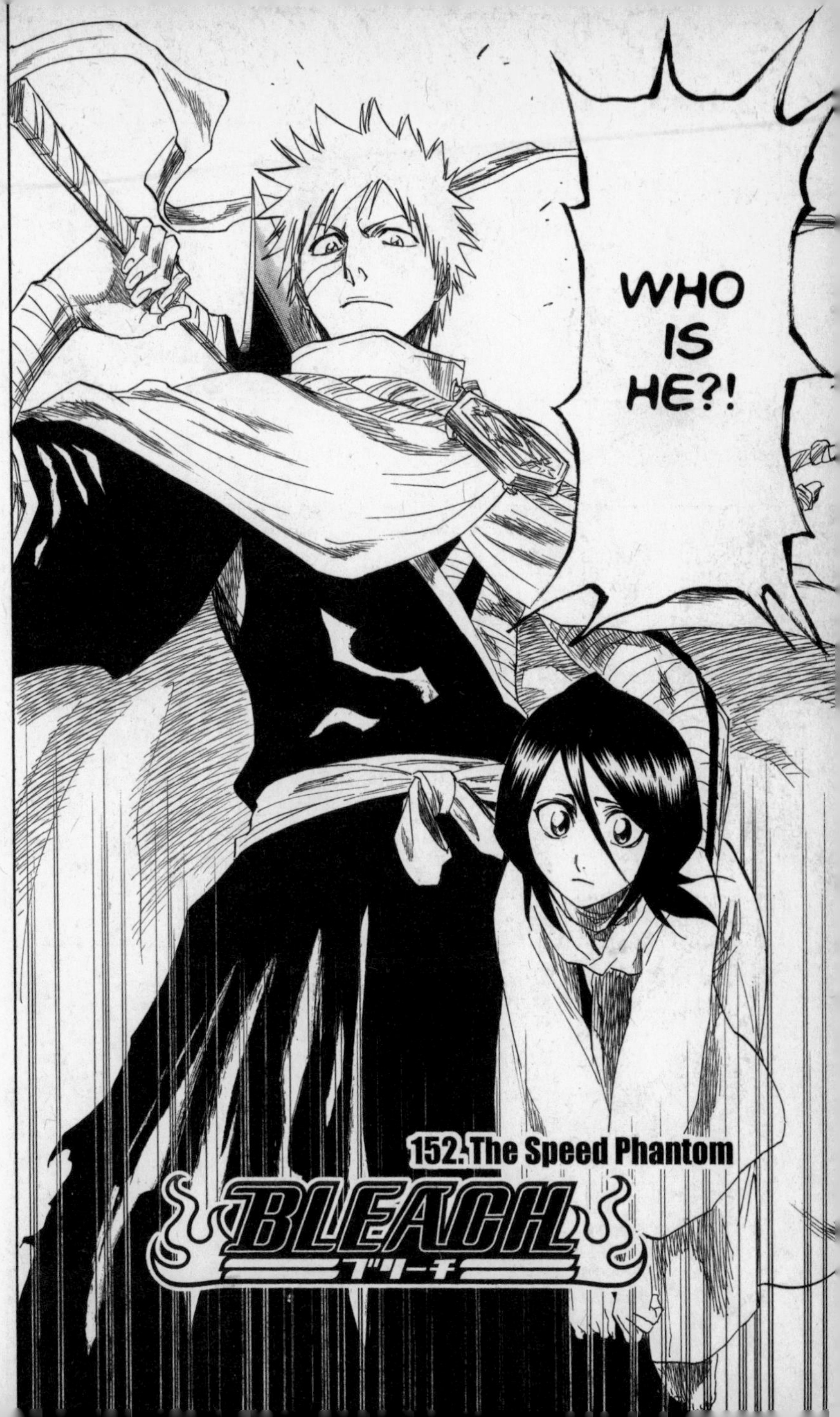
WHO IS HE?!
152. The Speed Phantom
BLEACH
ブリーチ

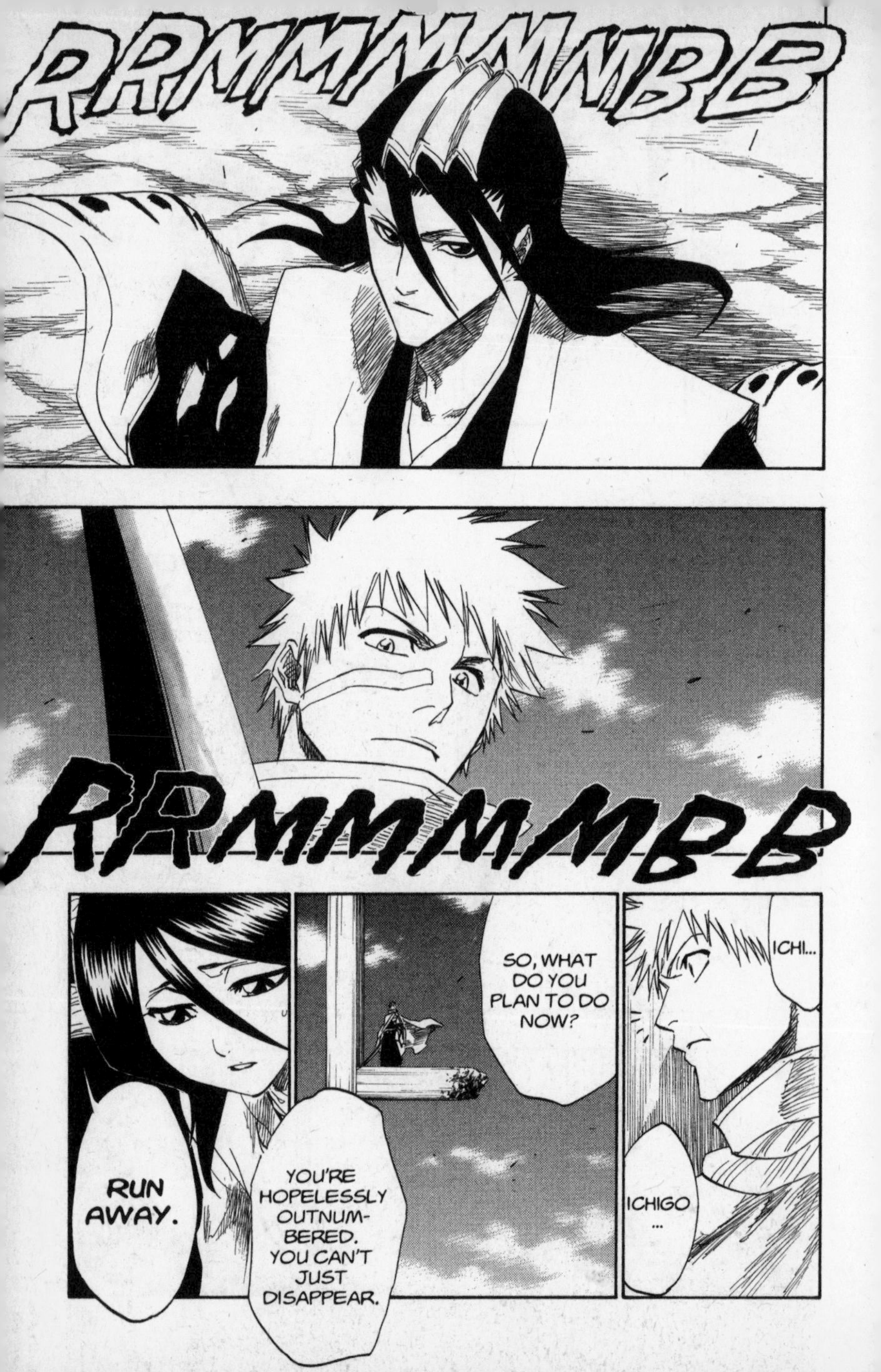
RRMMMMMBB
RRMMMMMBB
ICHI...
ICHIGO ...
SO, WHAT DO YOU PLAN TO DO NOW?
YOU'RE HOPELESSLY OUTNUMBERED. YOU CAN'T JUST DISAPPEAR.
RUN AWAY.

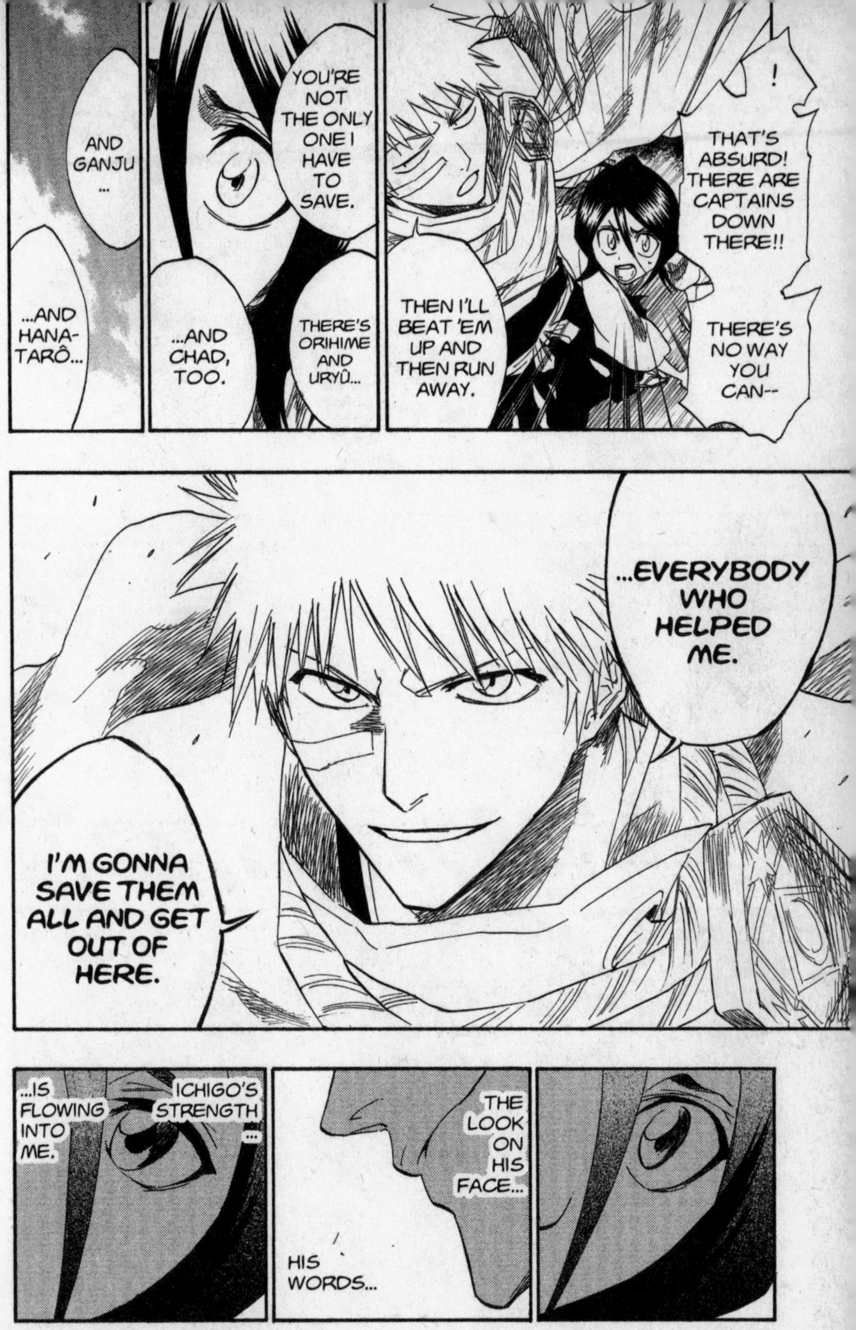
!
THAT'S ABSURD! THERE ARE CAPTAINS DOWN THERE!!
THERE'S NO WAY YOU CAN--
THEN I'LL BEAT 'EM UP AND THEN RUN AWAY.
YOU'RE NOT THE ONLY ONE I HAVE TO SAVE.
THERE'S ORIHIME AND URYÛ...
...AND CHAD, TOO.
AND GANJU...
...AND HANA-TARÔ...
...EVERYBODY WHO HELPED ME.
I'M GONNA SAVE THEM ALL AND GET OUT OF HERE.
THE LOOK ON HIS FACE...
HIS WORDS...
ICHIGO'S STRENGTH...
...IS FLOWING INTO ME.

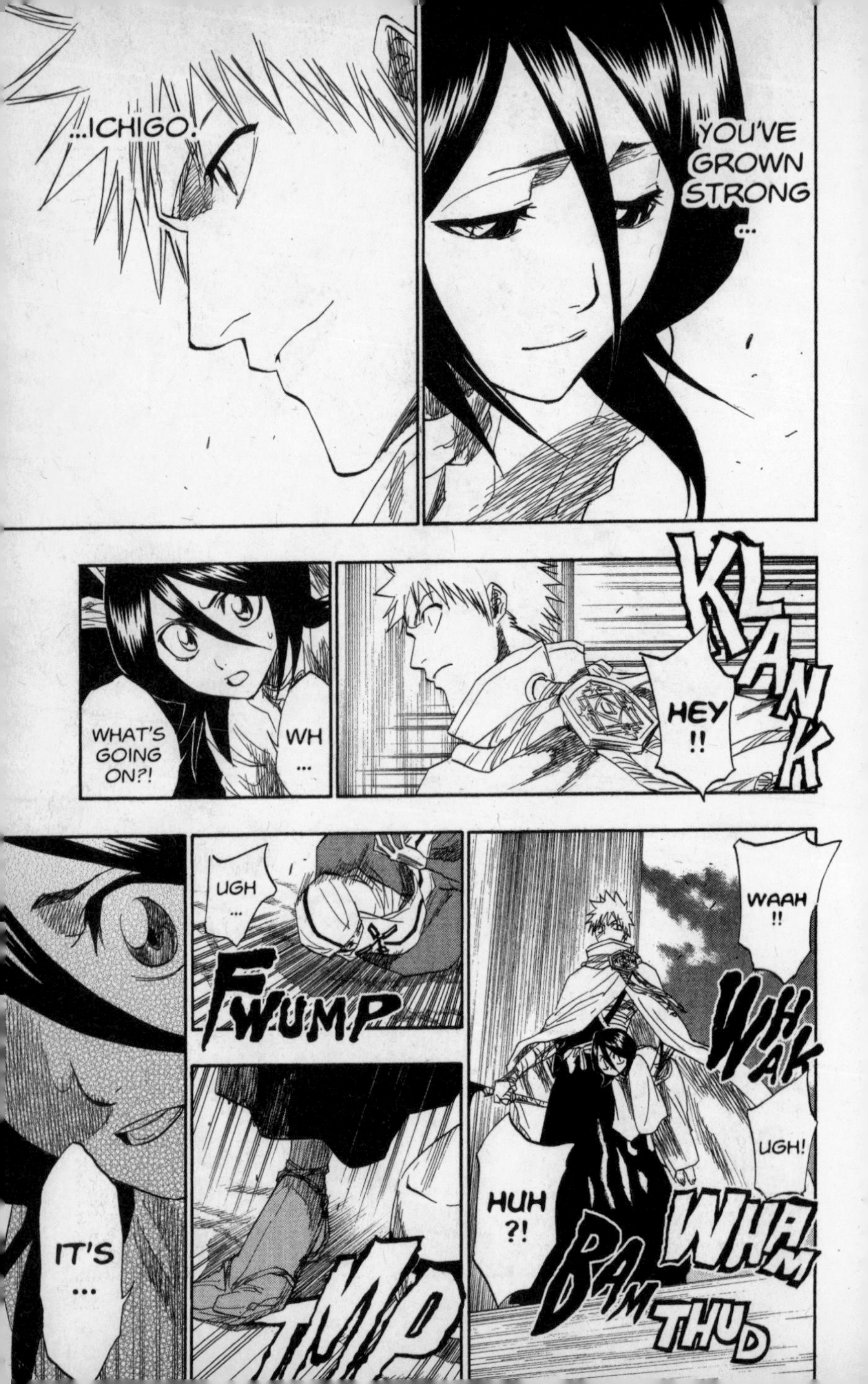
YOU'VE GROWN STRONG ...
...ICHIGO!
KLANK
HEY !!
WH ...
WHAT'S GOING ON?!
WAAH !!
WHAK
UGH!
HUH ?!
WHAM
BAM
THUD
UGH ...
FWUMP
TMP
IT'S ...

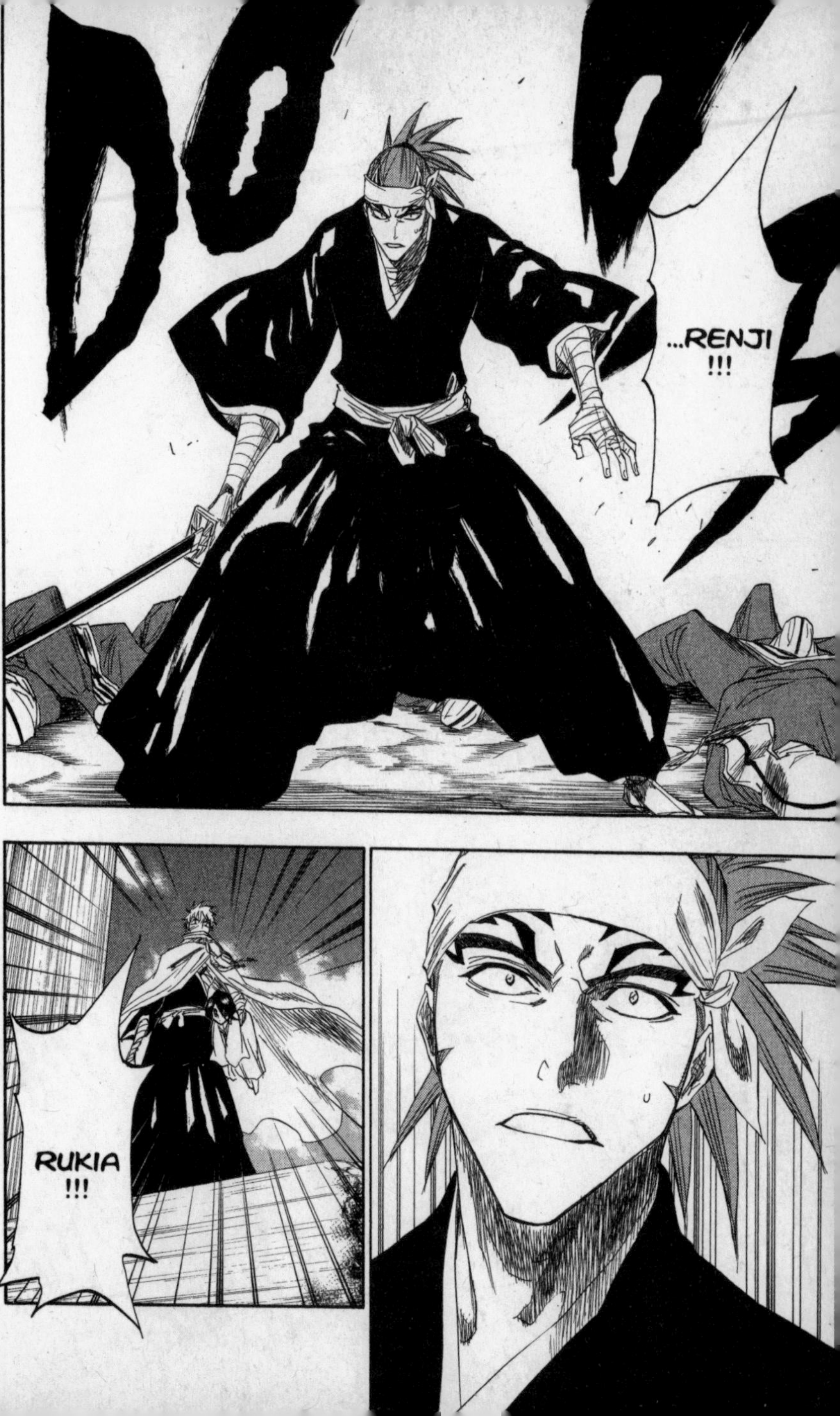
...RENJI !!!
RUKIA !!!

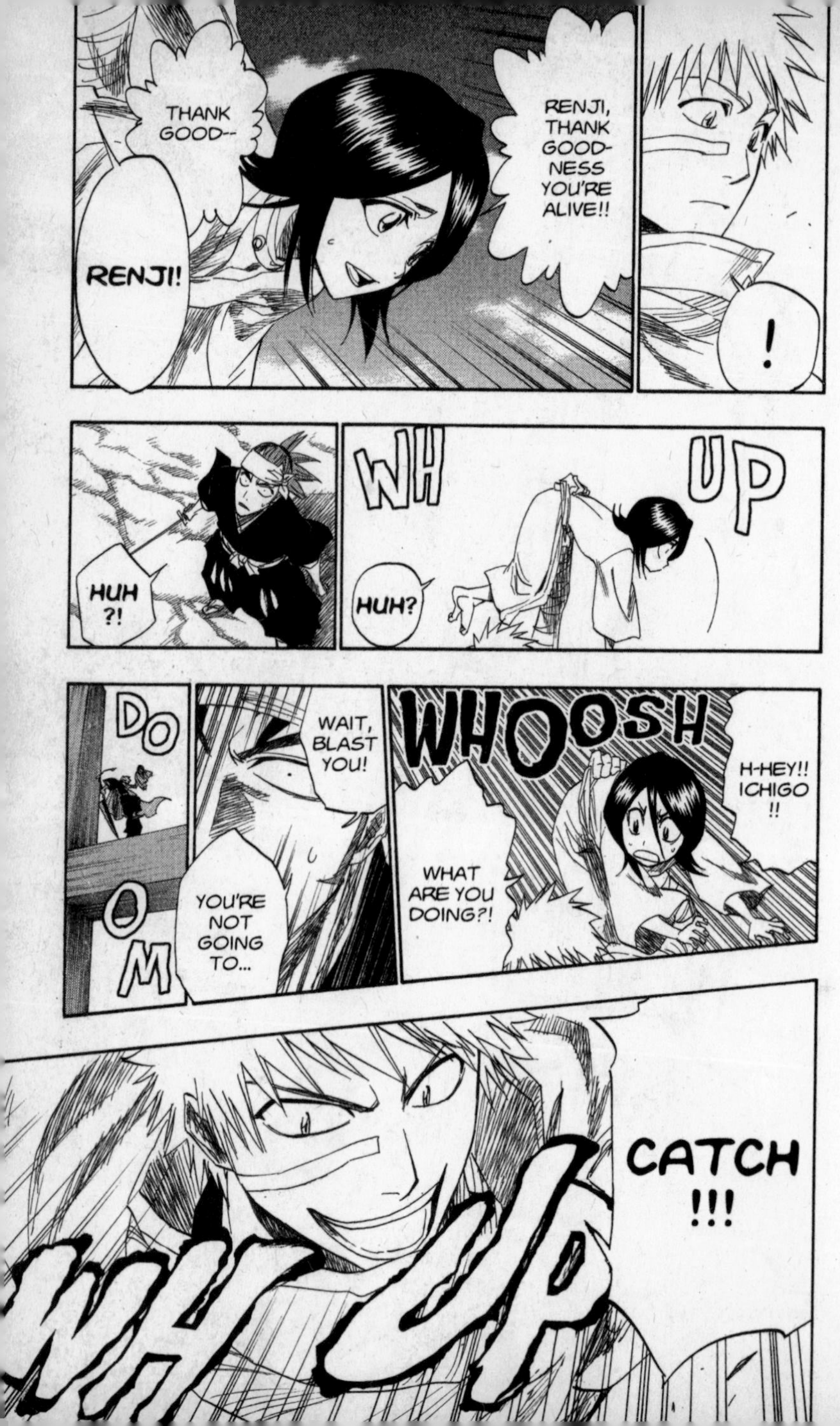
!
RENJI, THANK GOODNESS YOU'RE ALIVE!!
THANK GOOD--
RENJI!
WH UP
HUH?
HUH ?!
WHOOSH
H-HEY!! ICHIGO !!
WHAT ARE YOU DOING?!
WAIT, BLAST YOU!
YOU'RE NOT GOING TO...
DOOM
CATCH !!!
WHUP

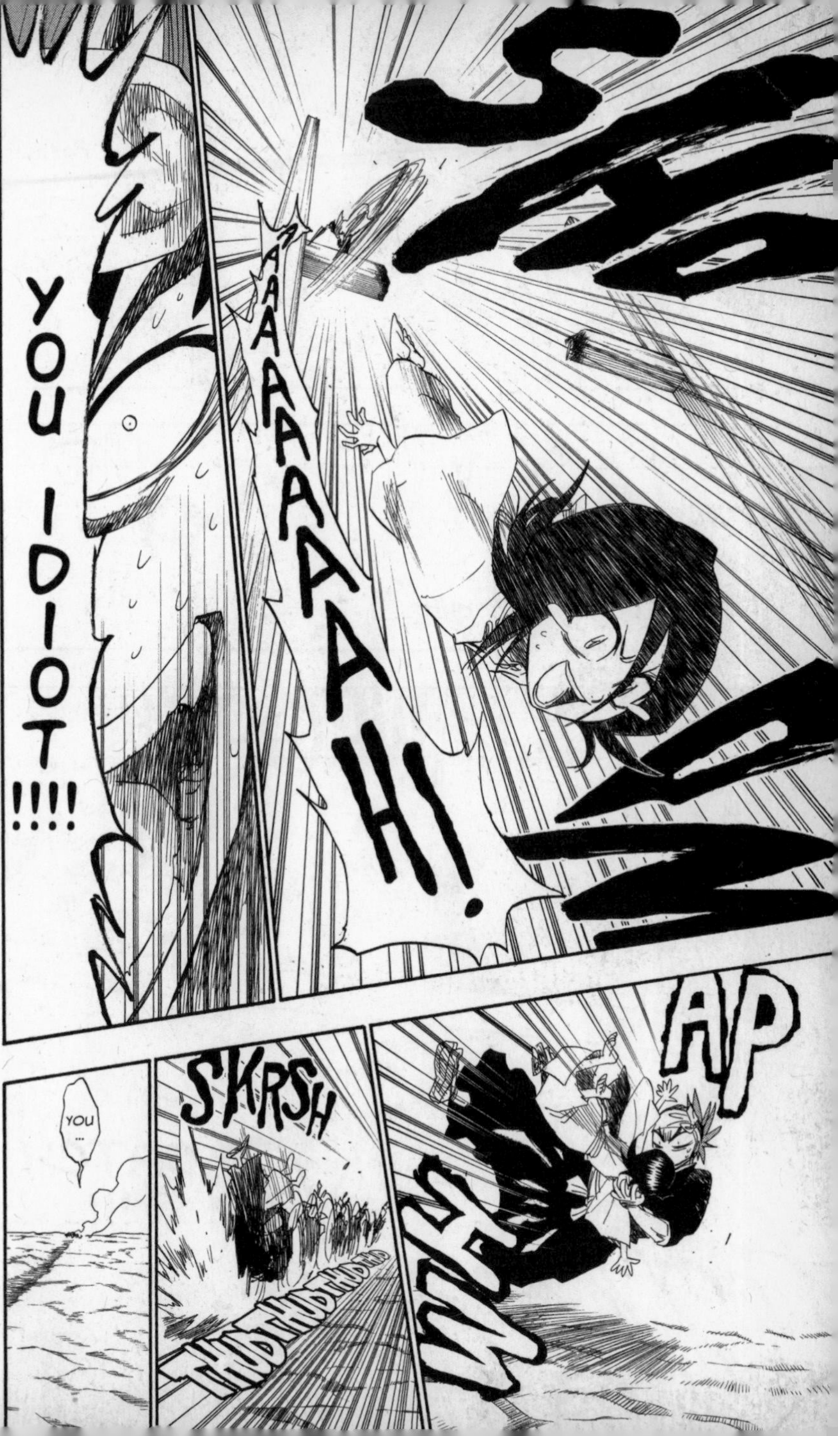
AAAAAAAAAH!
YOU IDIOT!!!!
AP
SKRSH
THUDTHUDTHUD
YOU...

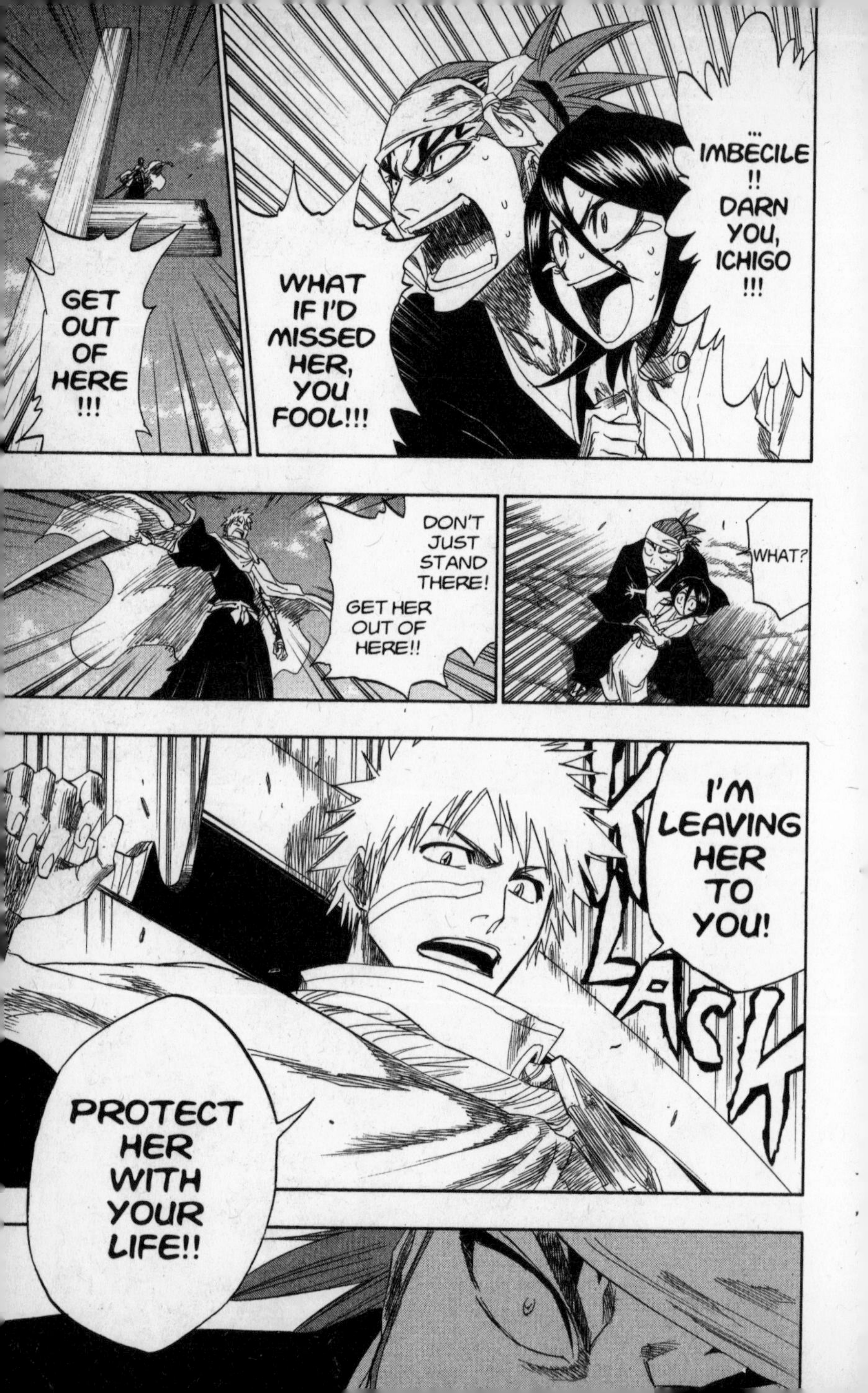
...IMBECILE!! DARN YOU, ICHIGO!!!
WHAT IF I'D MISSED HER, YOU FOOL!!!
GET OUT OF HERE!!!
WHAT?
DON'T JUST STAND THERE!
GET HER OUT OF HERE!!
I'M LEAVING HER TO YOU!
PROTECT HER WITH YOUR LIFE!!

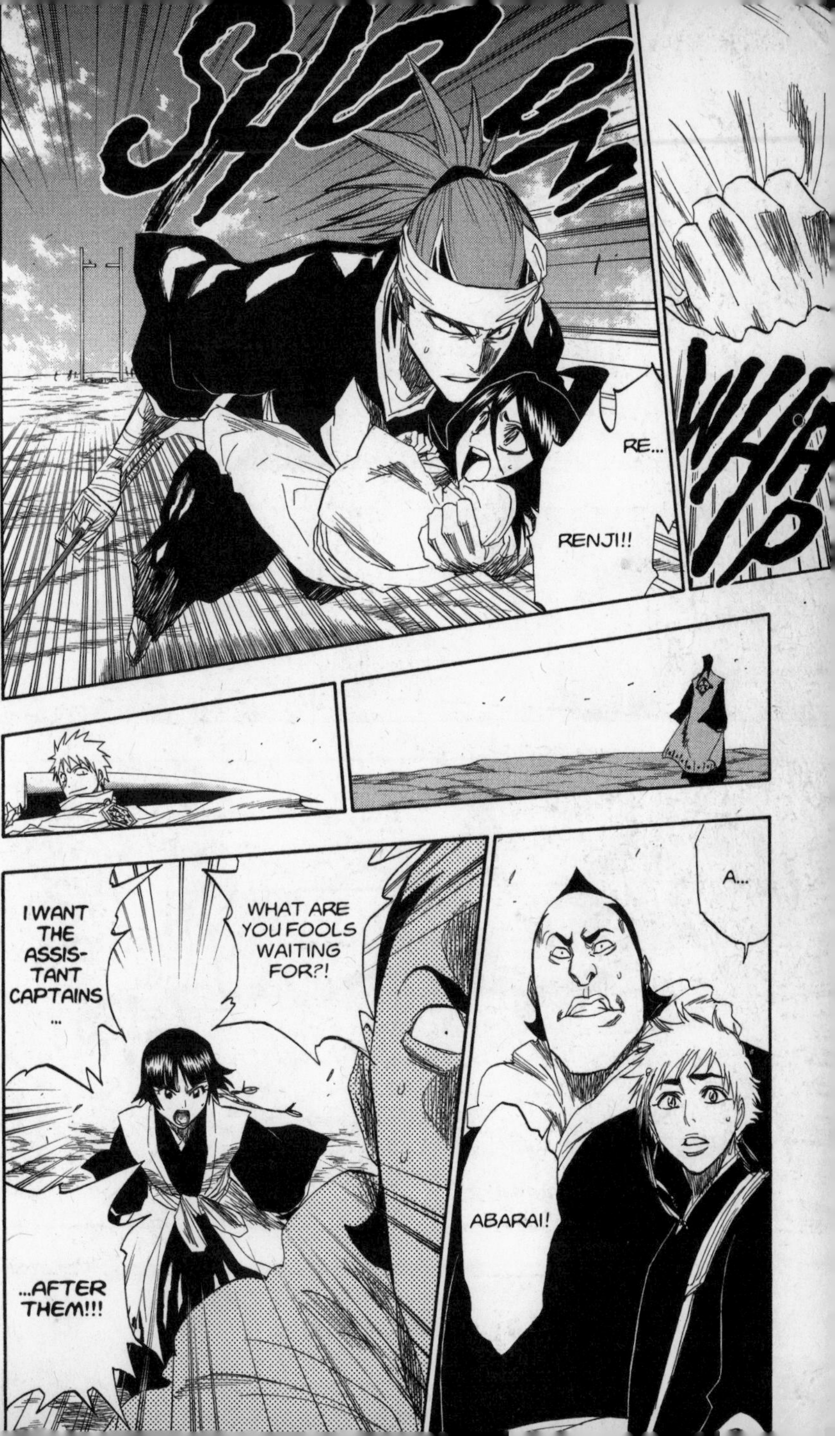
WHAP
SHOM
RE...
RENJI!!
A...
ABARAI!
WHAT ARE YOU FOOLS WAITING FOR?!
I WANT THE ASSIS-TANT CAPTAINS...
...AFTER THEM!!!

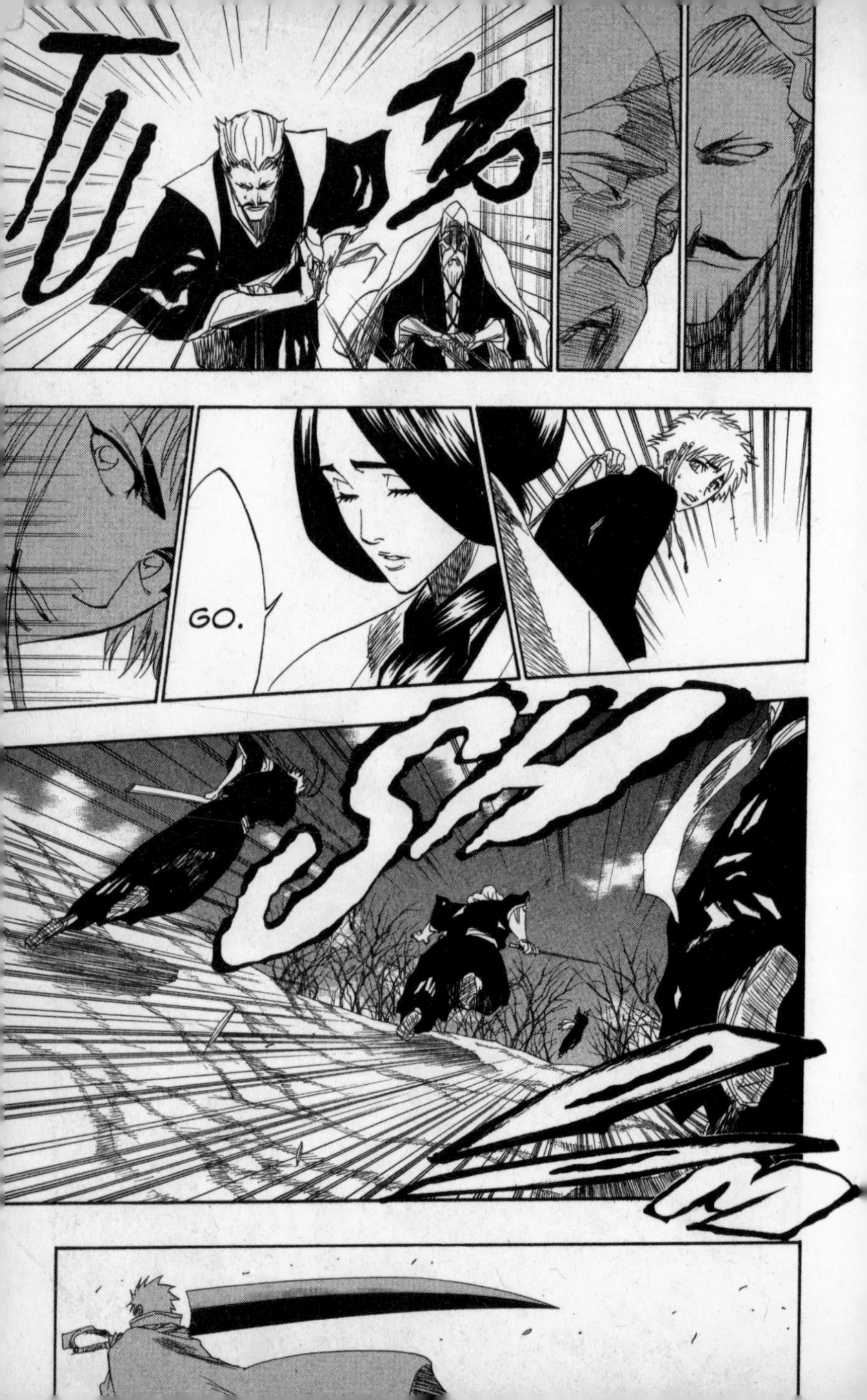
GO.

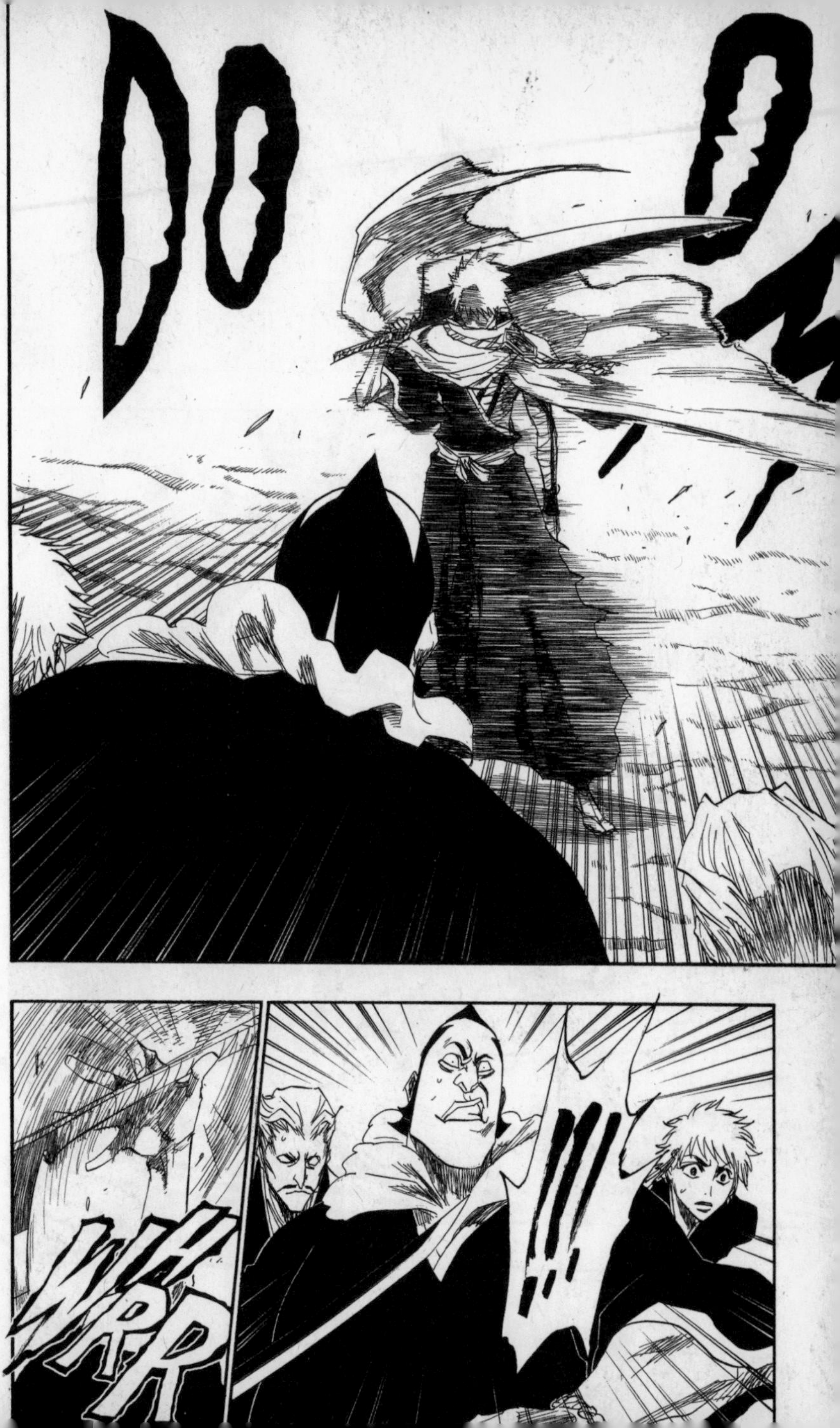
DOOM
!!
WHRR

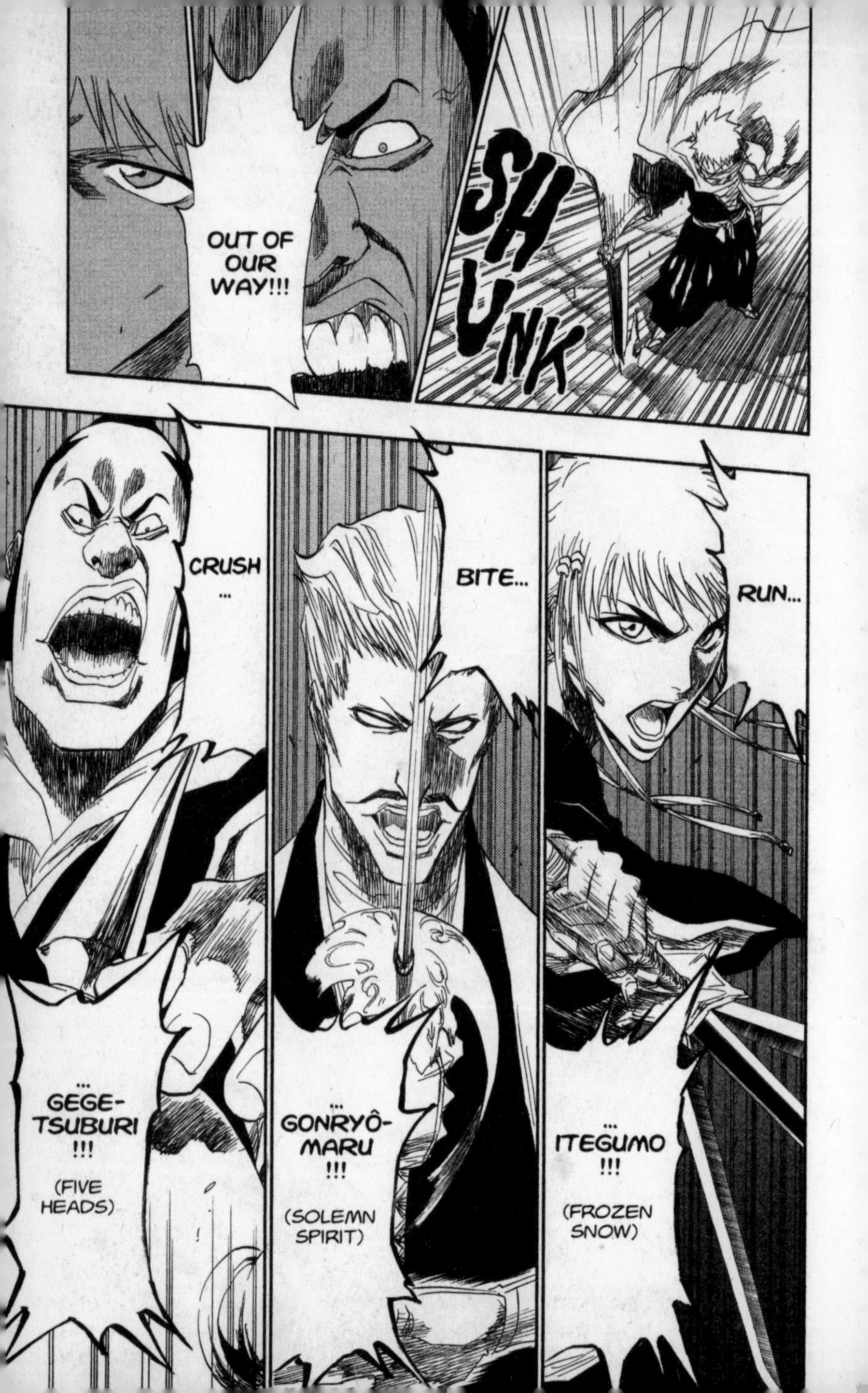
SHUNK
OUT OF OUR WAY!!!
RUN...
... ITEGUMO !!!
(FROZEN SNOW)
BITE...
... GONRYÔ-MARU !!!
(SOLEMN SPIRIT)
CRUSH ...
... GEGE-TSUBURI !!!
(FIVE HEADS)

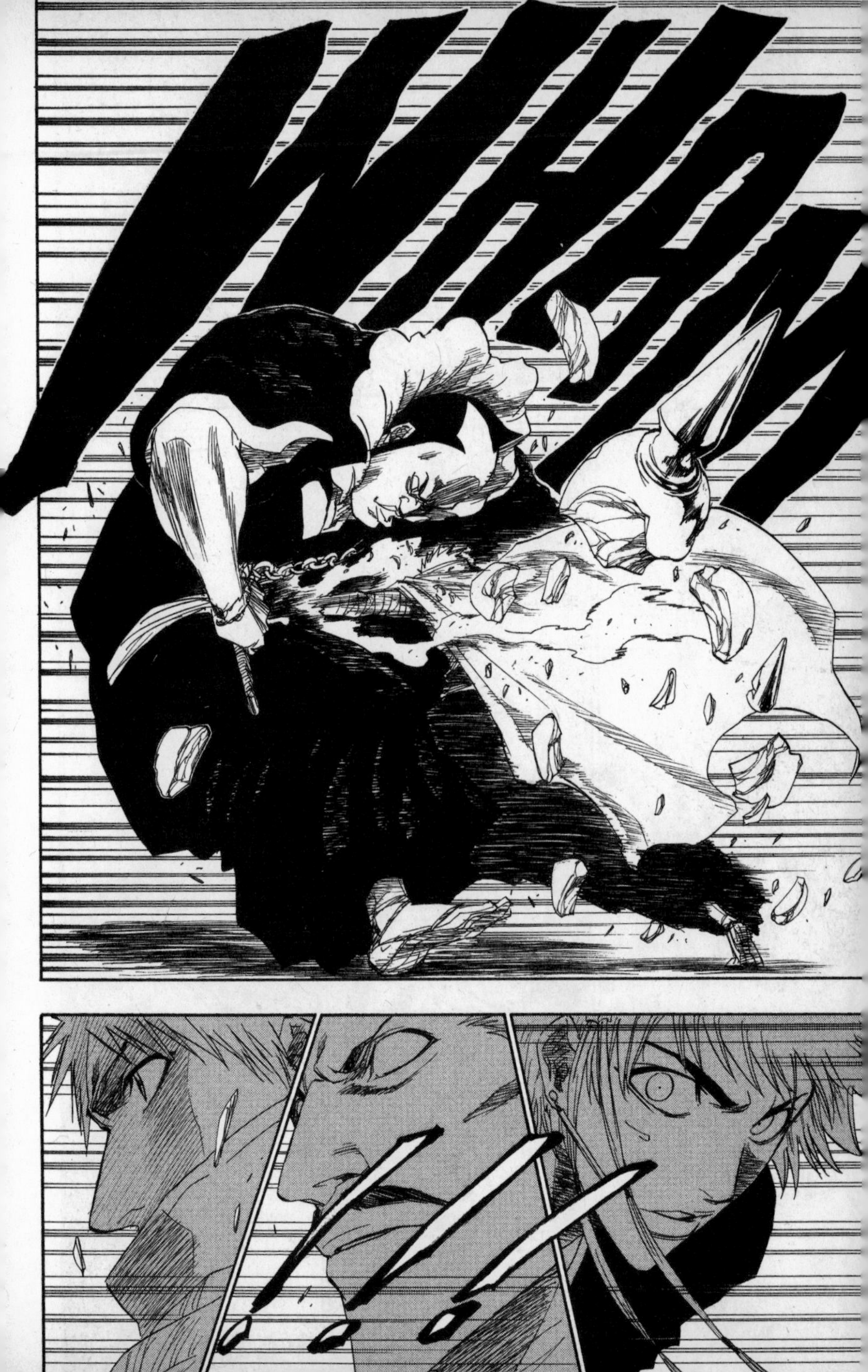
WHAM

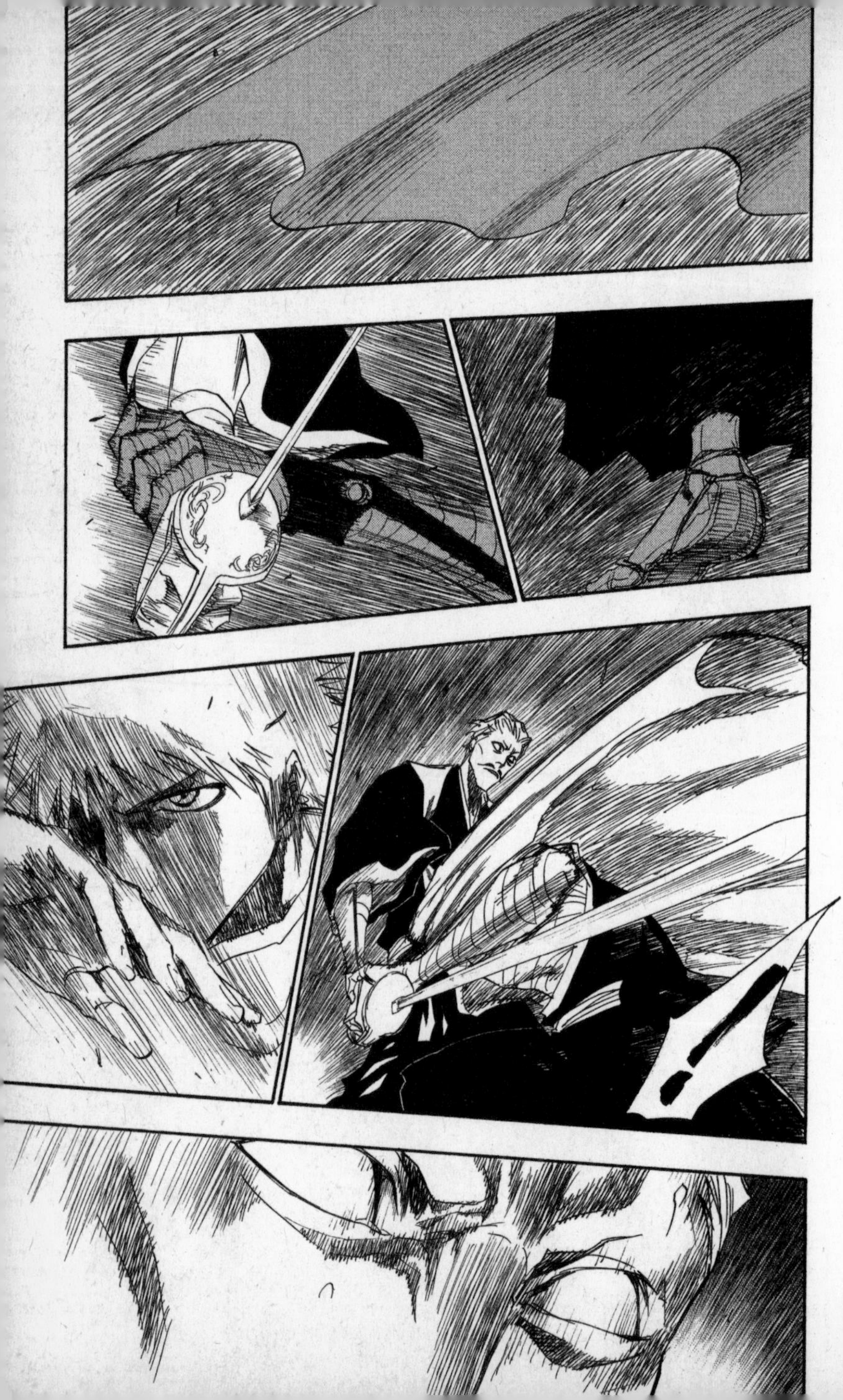

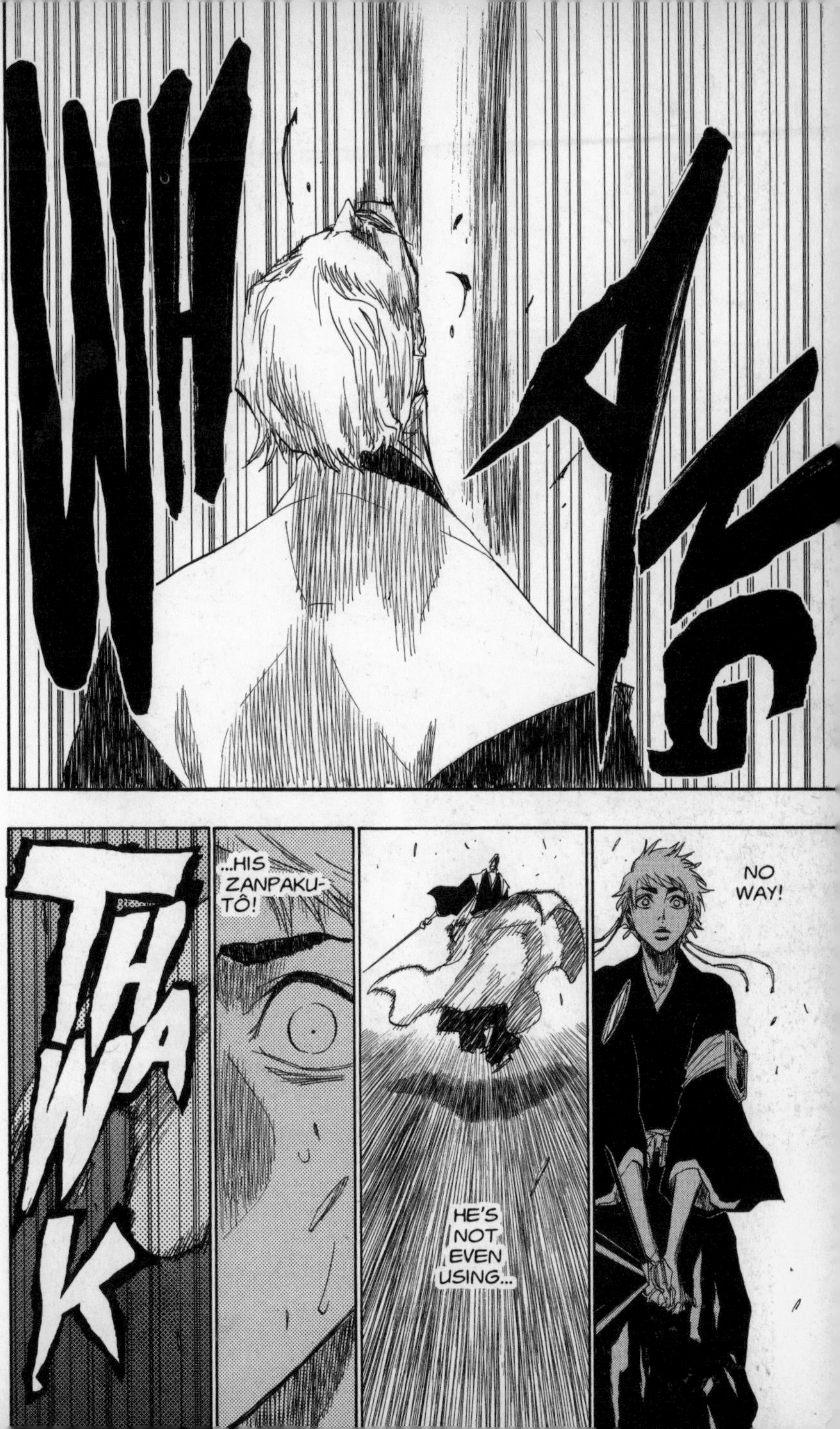
WHAANG
NO WAY!
HE'S NOT EVEN USING...
...HIS ZANPAKU-TÔ!
THWAK

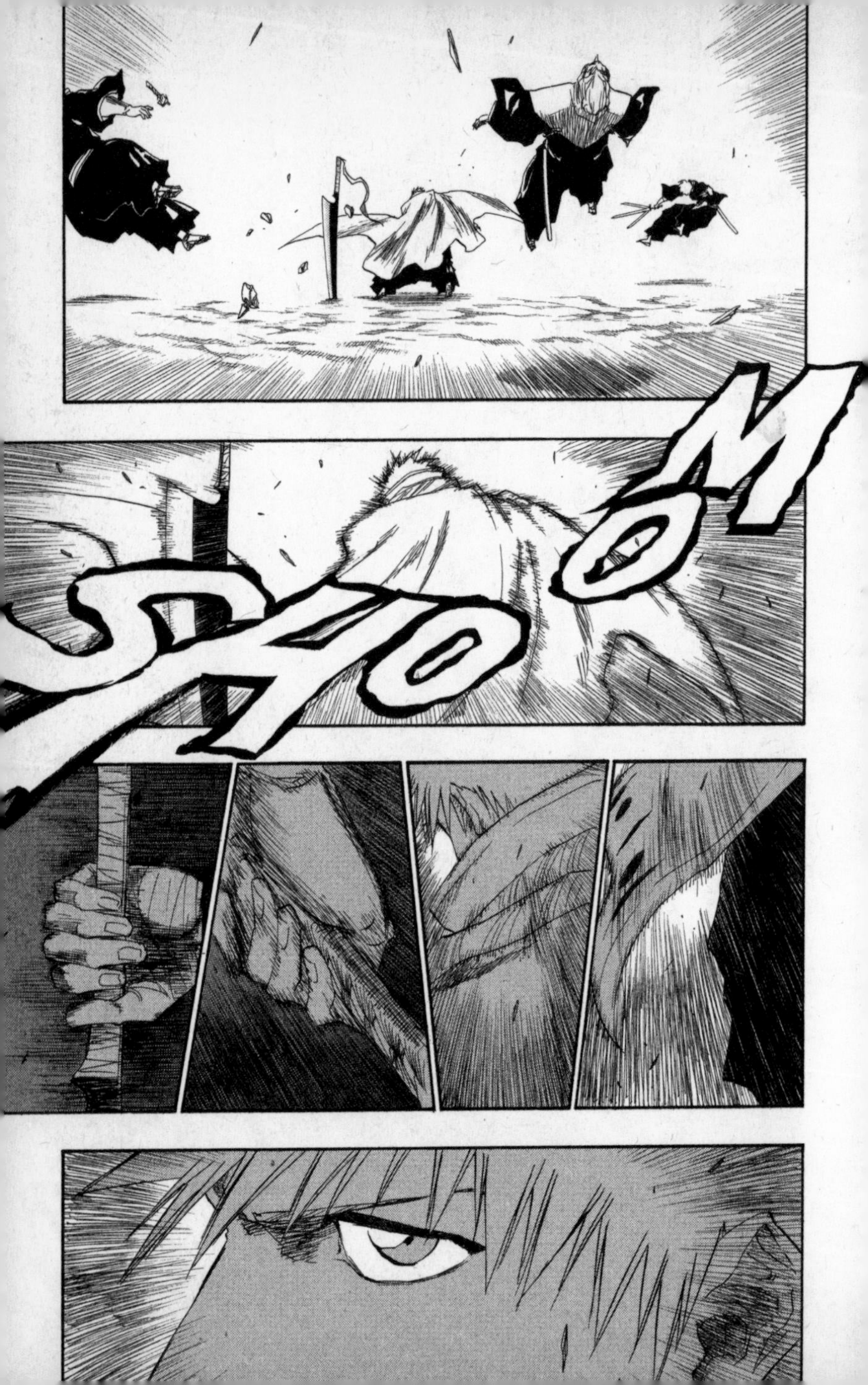
SHOOM

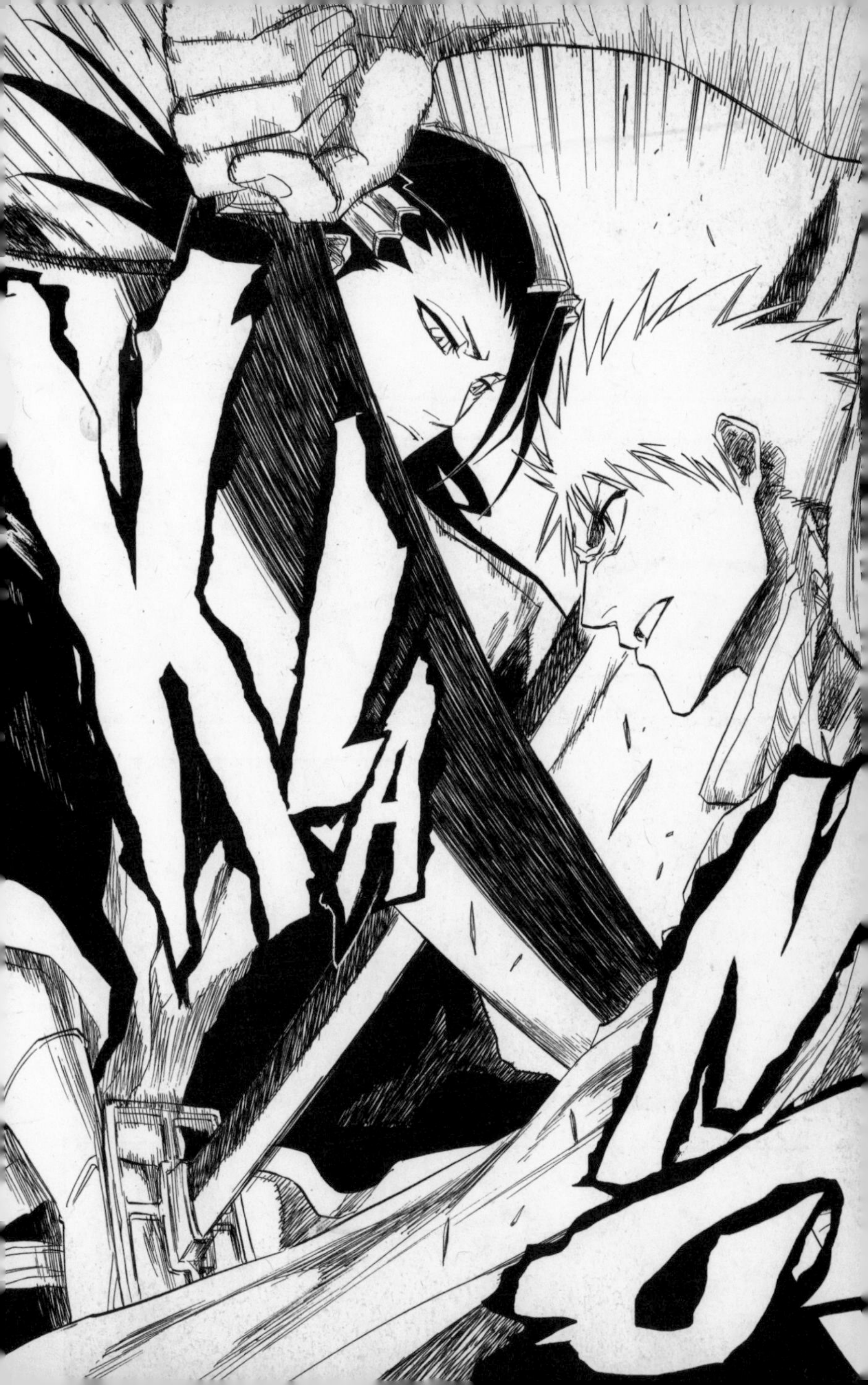

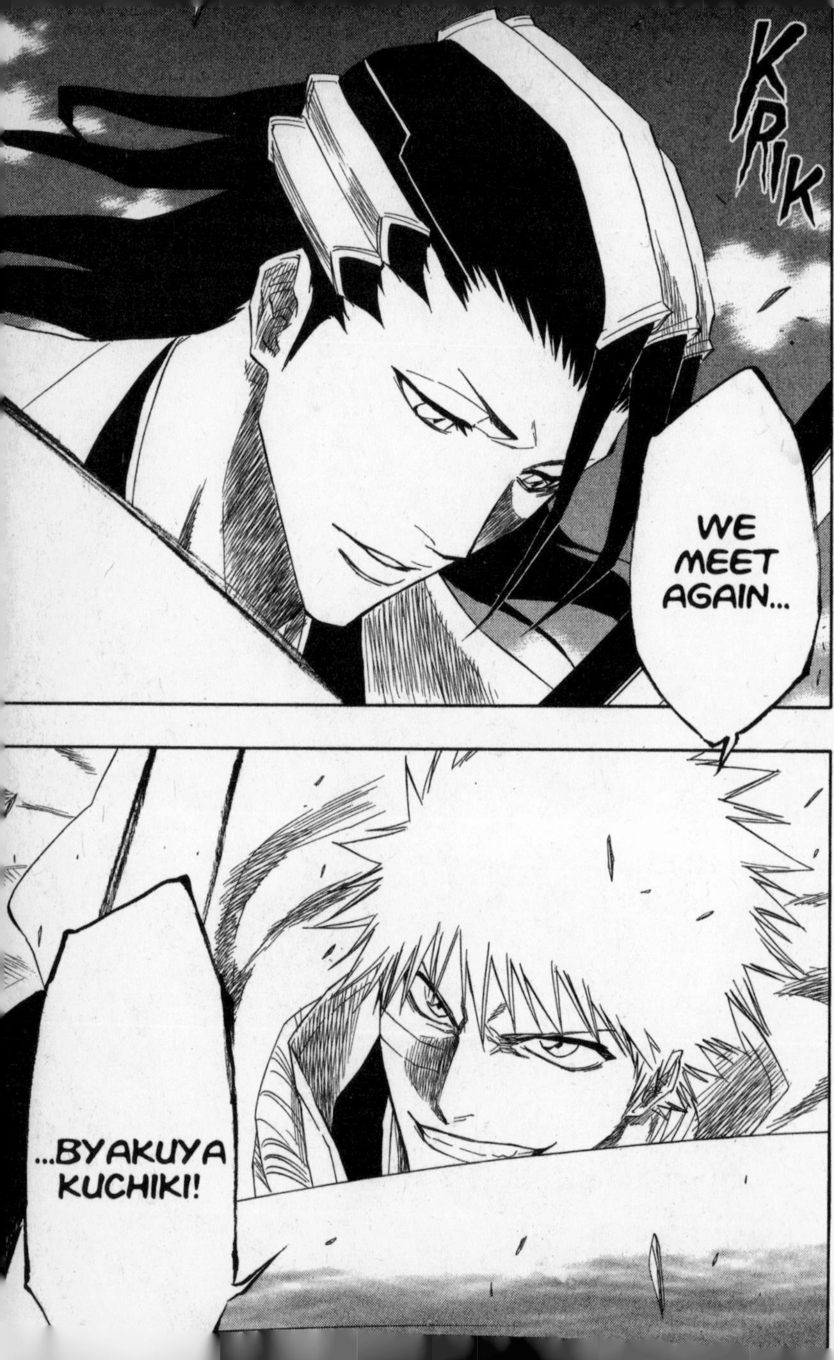
KRIK
WE MEET AGAIN...
...BYAKUYA KUCHIKI!

KILL!
JUMP
WHOA !!
BOOM
WHAT'RE THEY DOING ?!
THAT'S A RED CARD!
WHAT?! IT'S NOT A FOUL?!
WAIT, YOU'RE THE REF?!

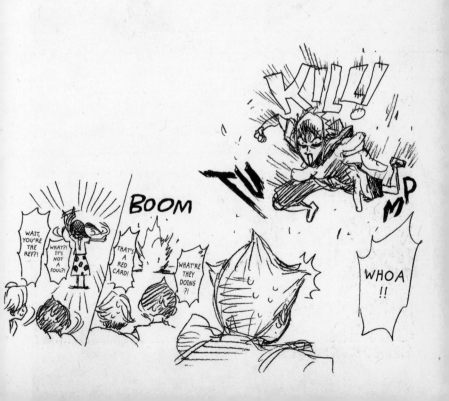

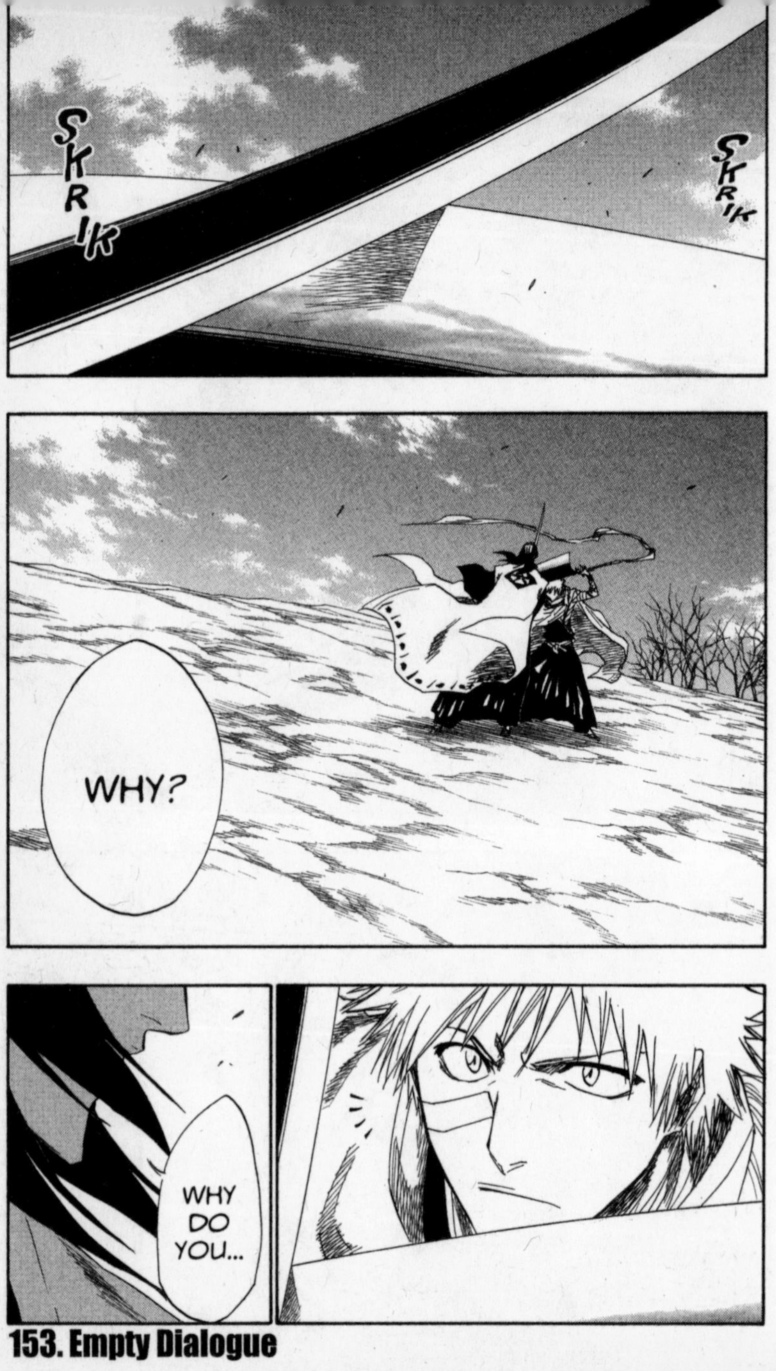
SKRIK
SKRIK
WHY?
WHY DO YOU...

153. Empty Dialogue

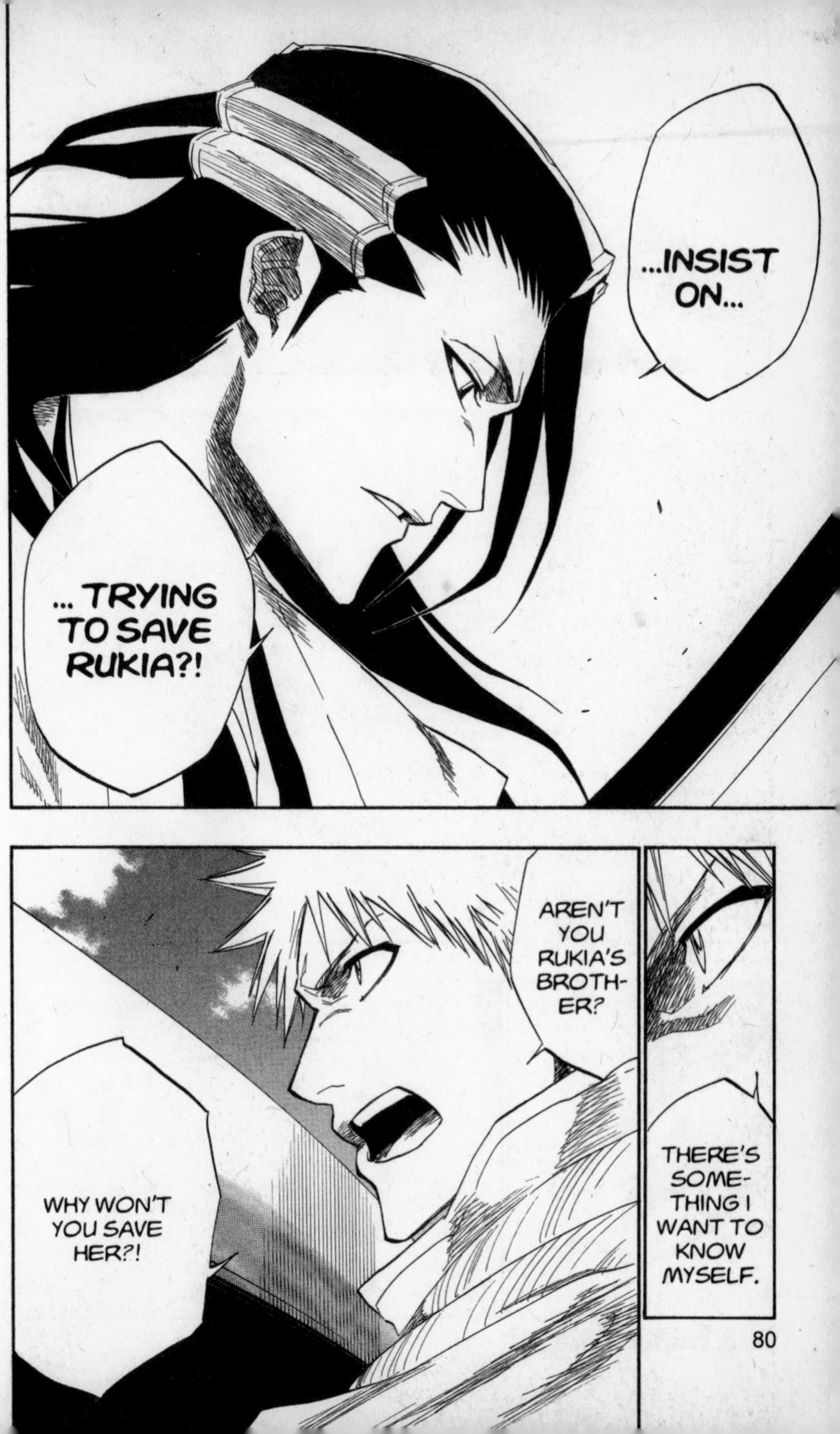
...INSIST ON...
... TRYING TO SAVE RUKIA?!
THERE'S SOME-THING I WANT TO KNOW MYSELF.
AREN'T YOU RUKIA'S BROTH-ER?
WHY WON'T YOU SAVE HER?!

READ THIS WAY

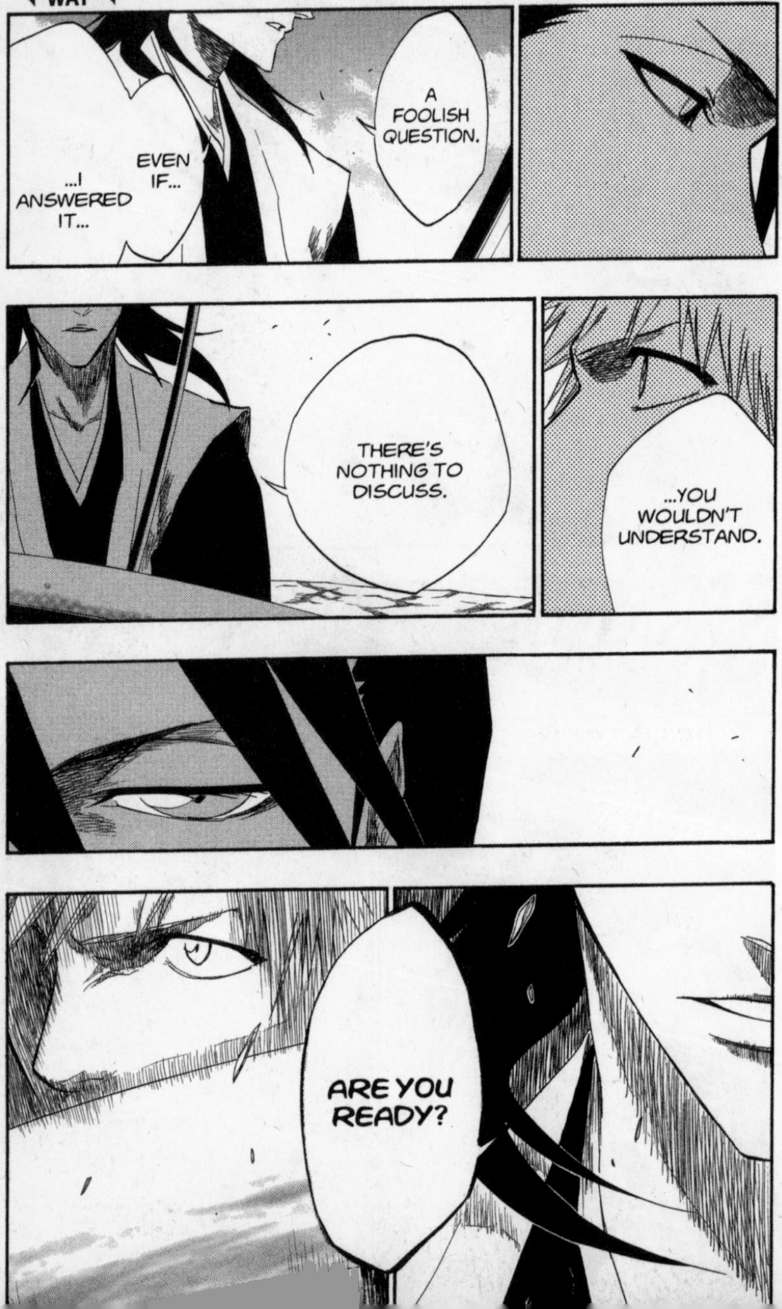
A FOOLISH QUESTION.
EVEN IF...
...I ANSWERED IT...
...YOU WOULDN'T UNDERSTAND.
THERE'S NOTHING TO DISCUSS.
ARE YOU READY?

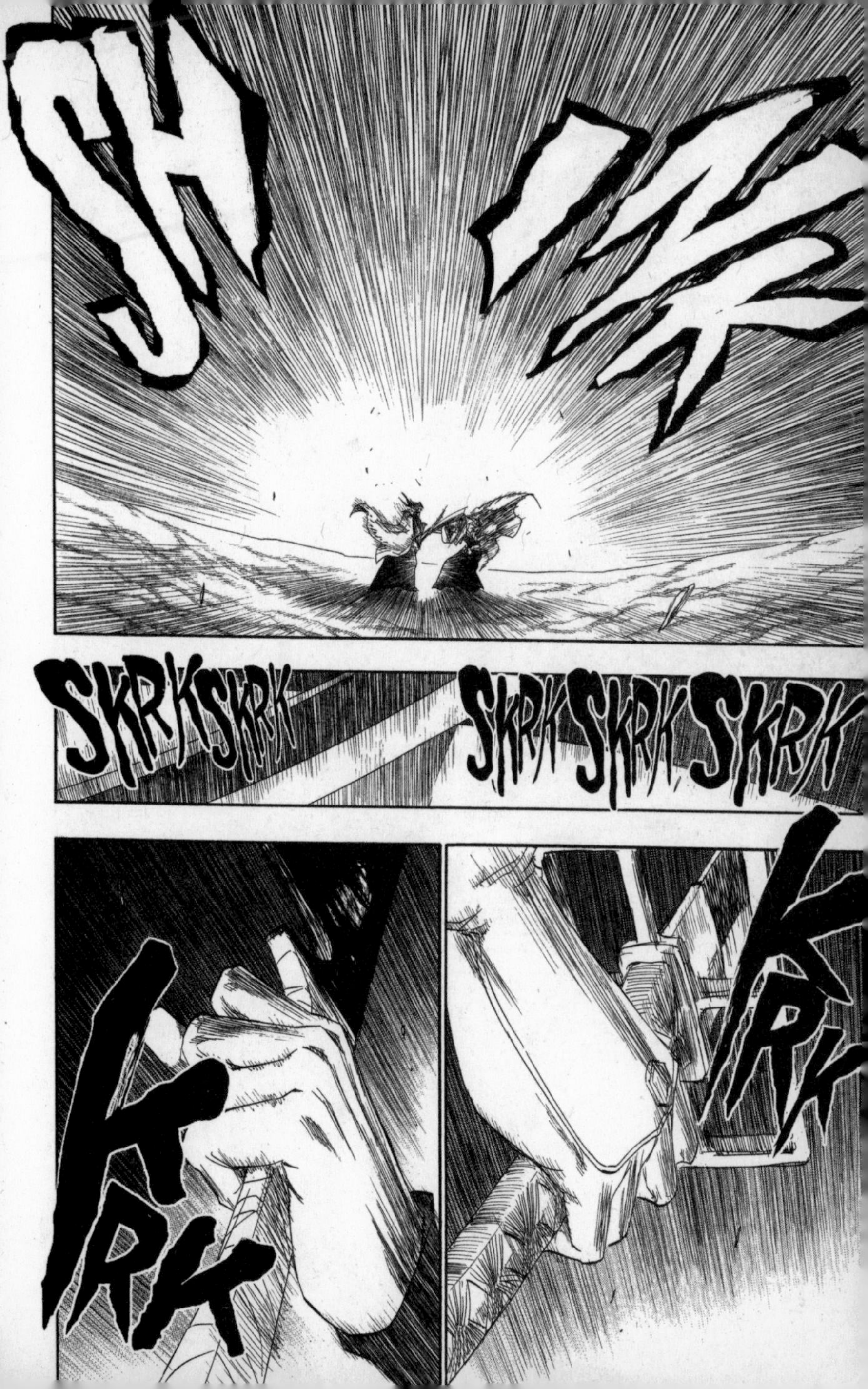
SKRK SKRK SKRK
SKRK SKRK
KRK
KRK

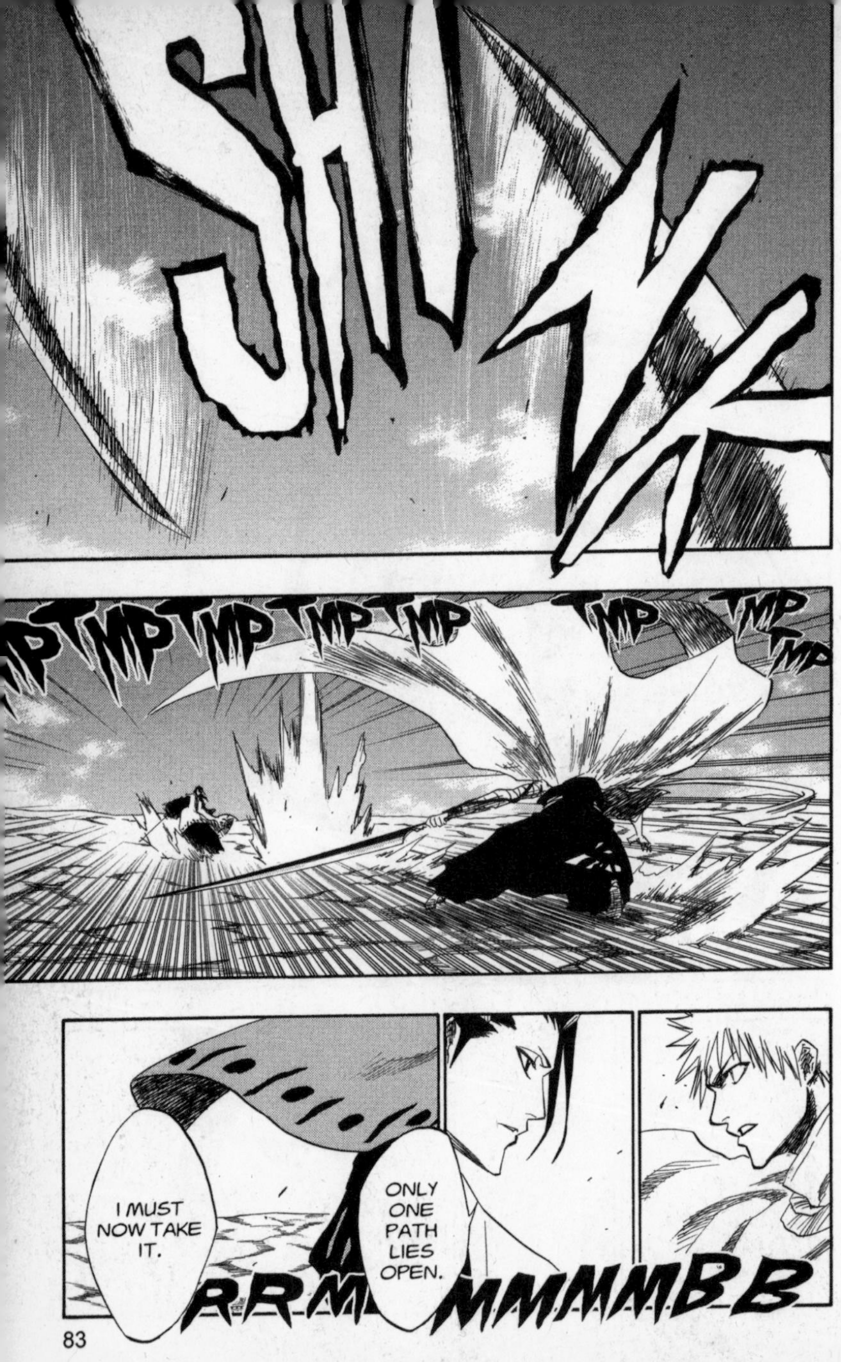
SHUNK
MP TMP TMP TMP TMP TMP TMP MP
ONLY ONE PATH LIES OPEN.
I MUST NOW TAKE IT.
RRM MMMMMBB

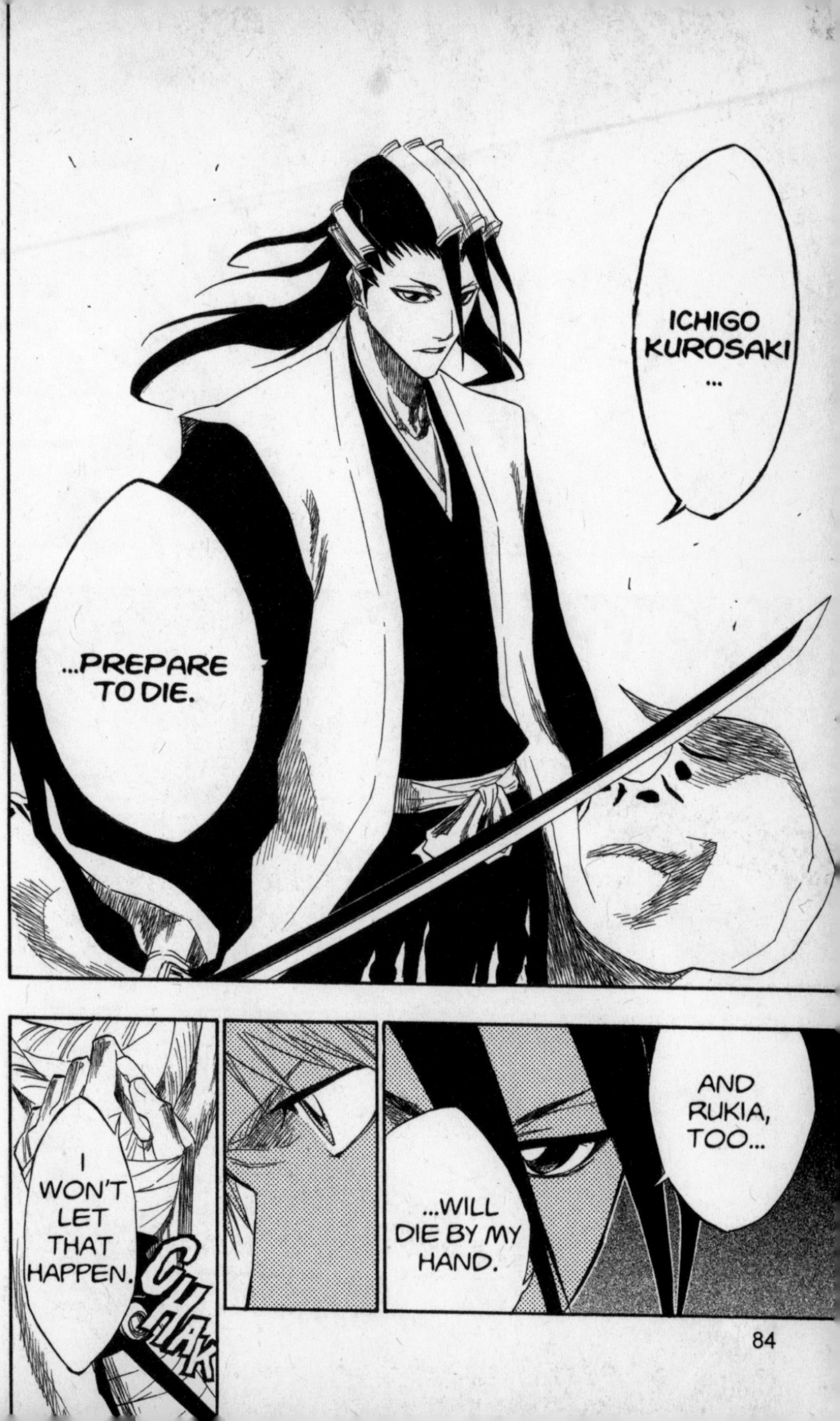
ICHIGO KUROSAKI ...
...PREPARE TO DIE.
AND RUKIA, TOO...
...WILL DIE BY MY HAND.
I WON'T LET THAT HAPPEN.
CHAK

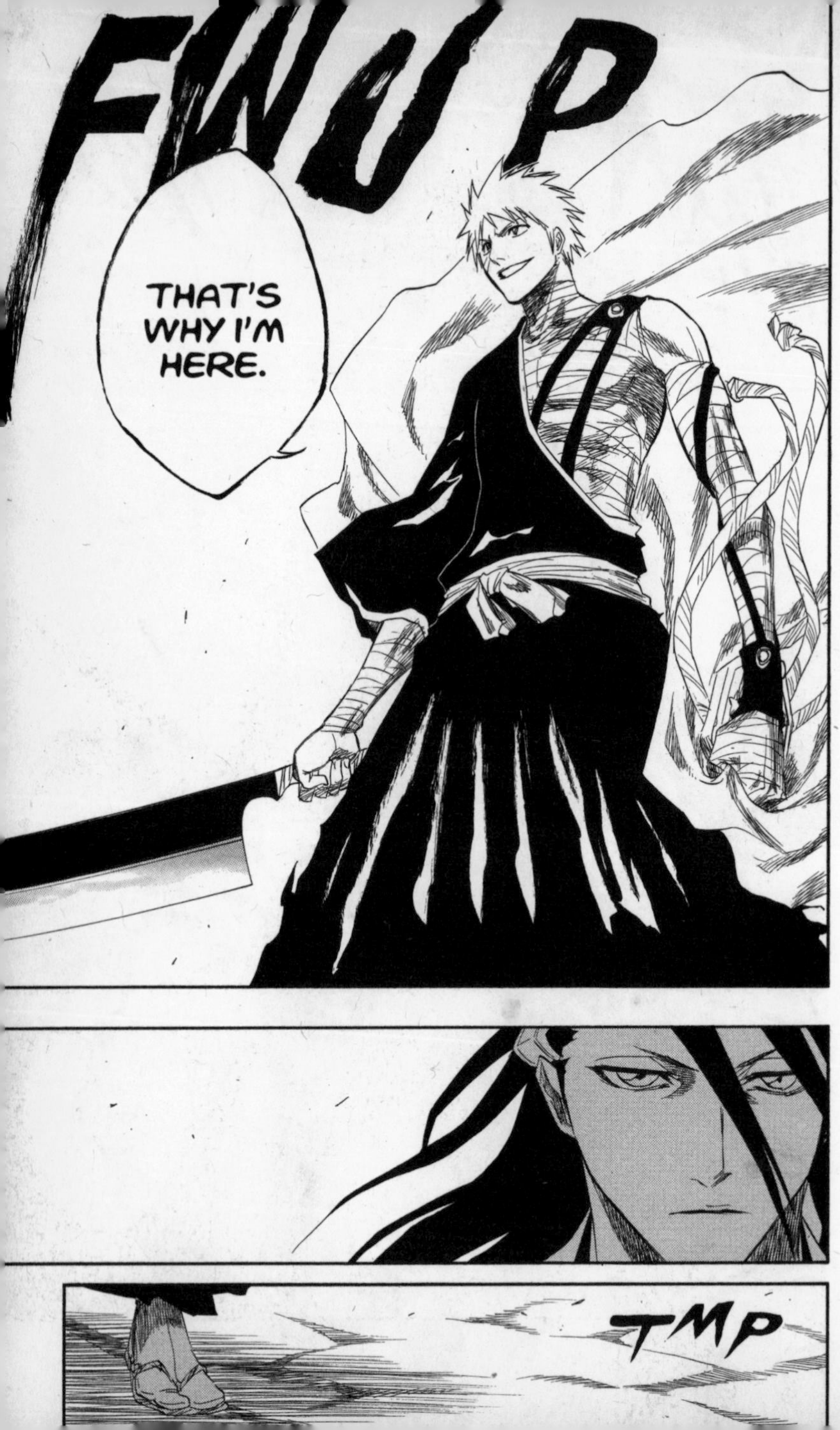
FWUP
THAT'S WHY I'M HERE.
TMP

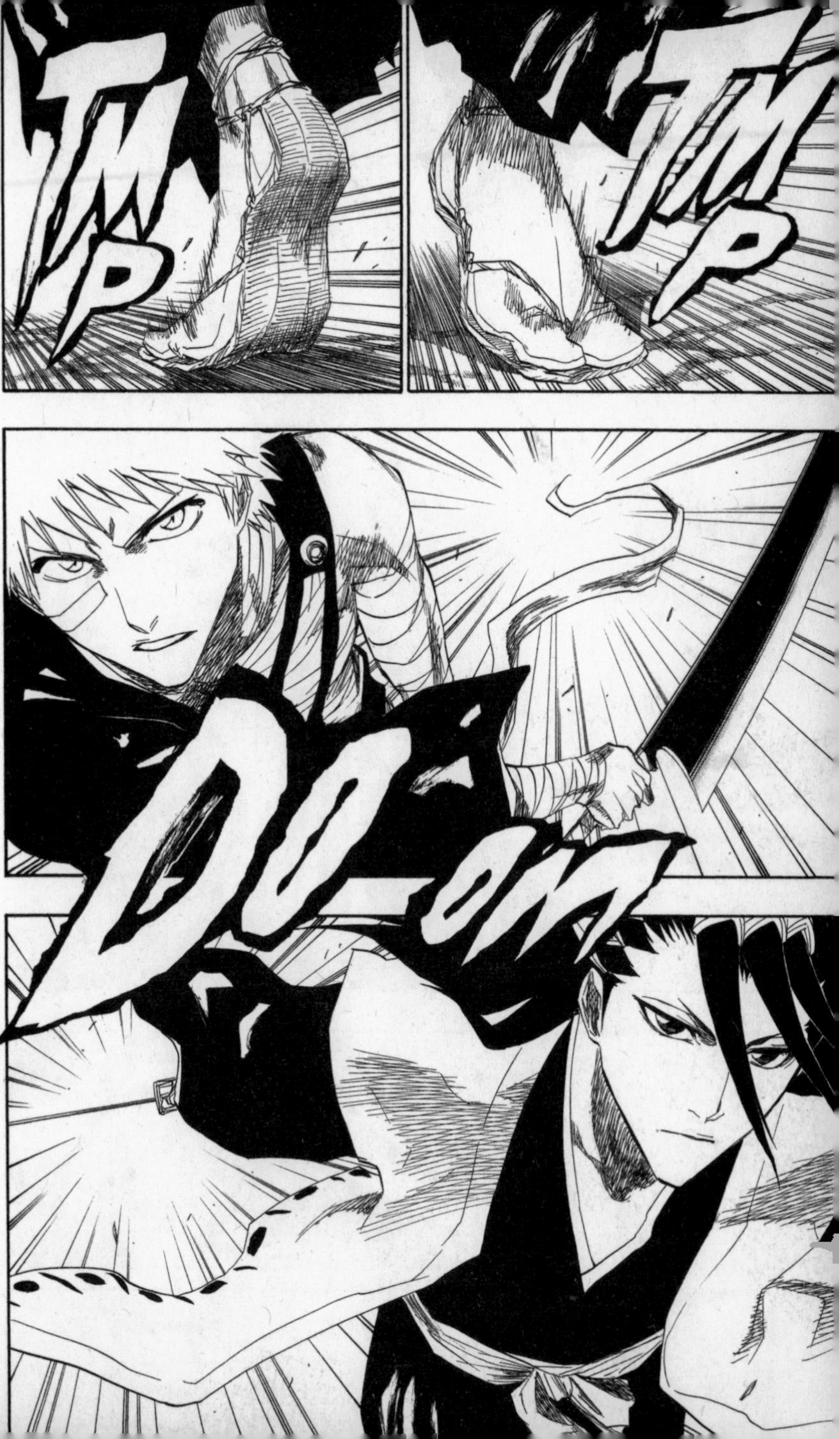
TMP
TMP
DOOM

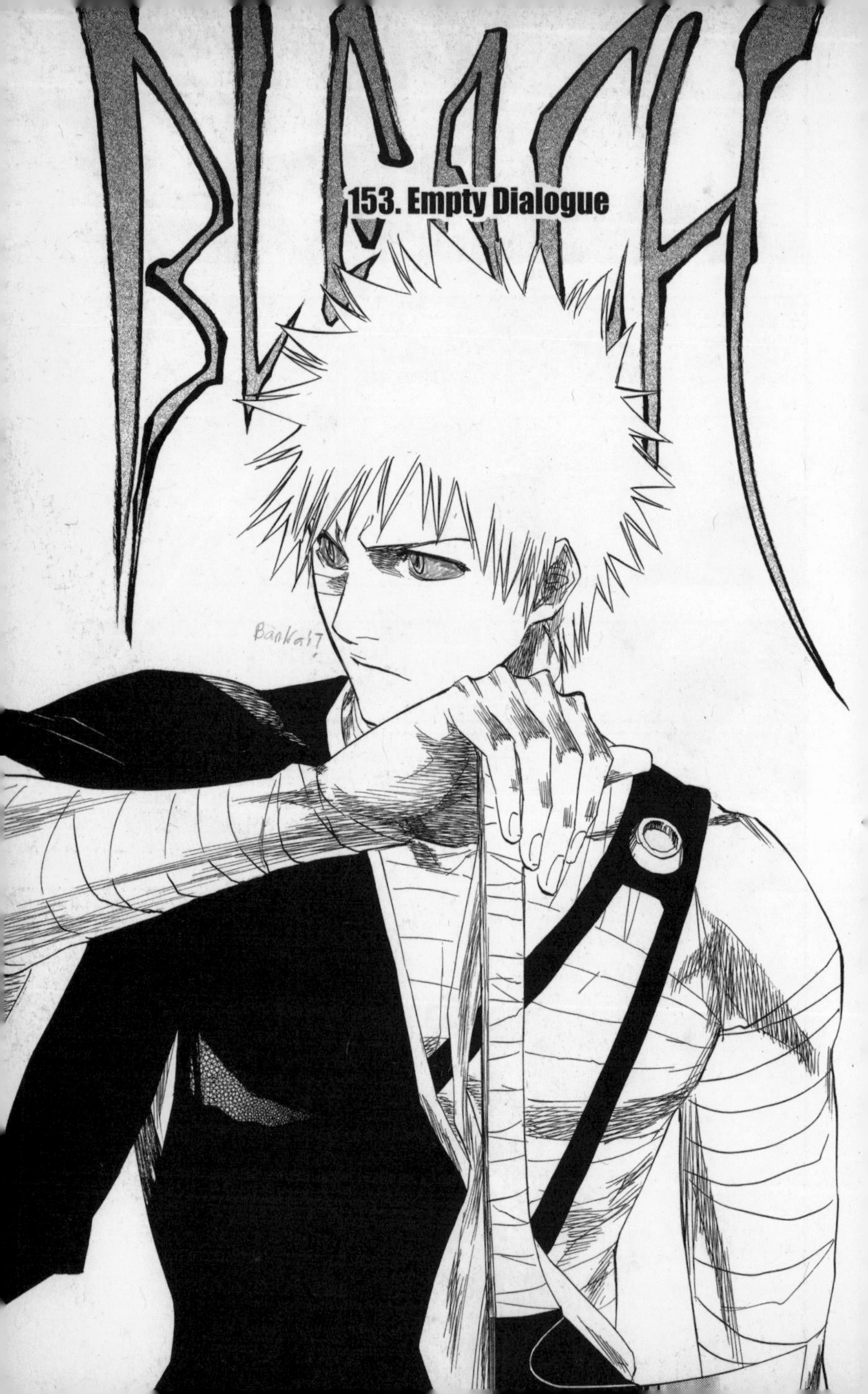
BLEACH
153. Empty Dialogue

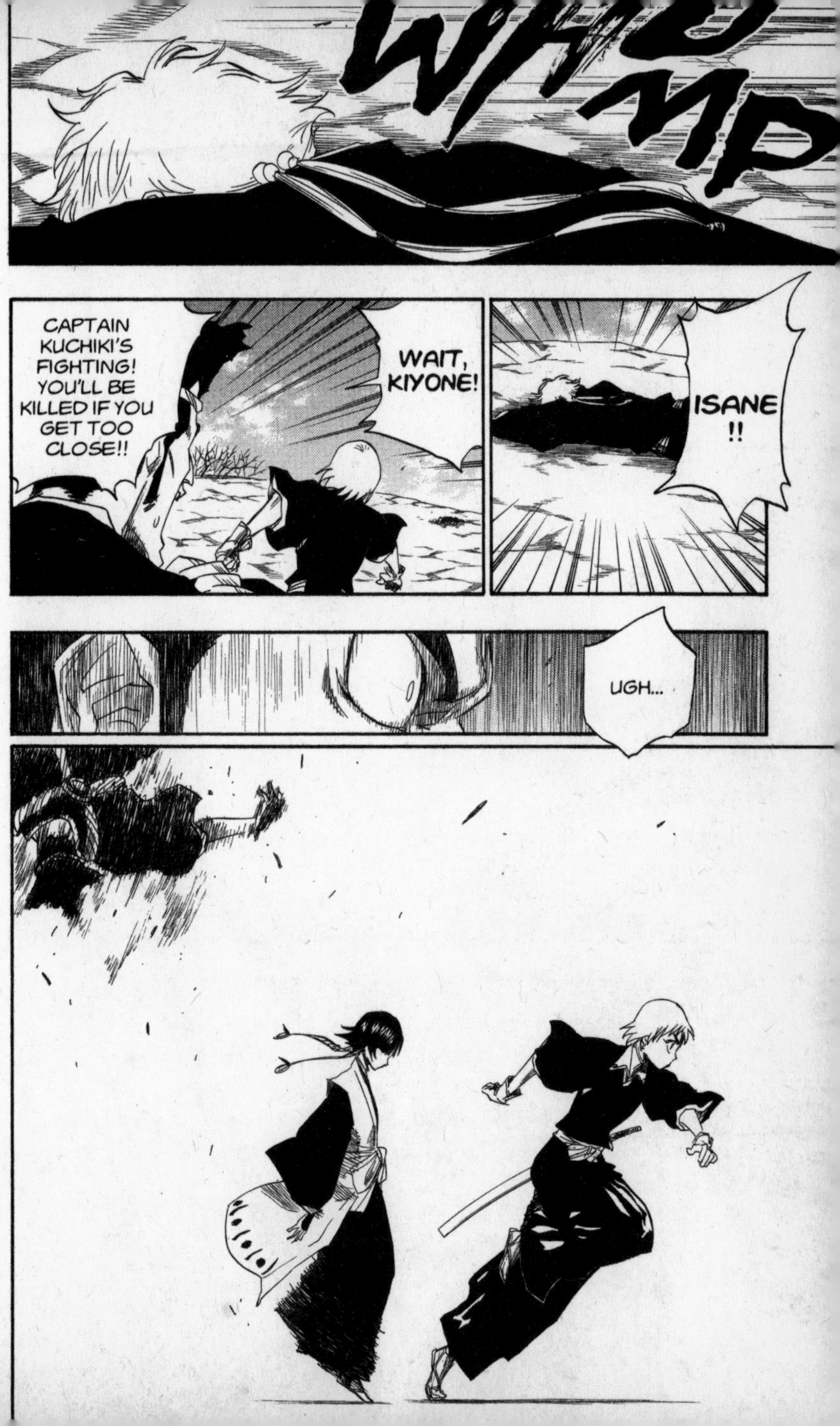
WHUMP
ISANE!!
WAIT, KIYONE!
CAPTAIN KUCHIKI'S FIGHTING! YOU'LL BE KILLED IF YOU GET TOO CLOSE!!
UGH...

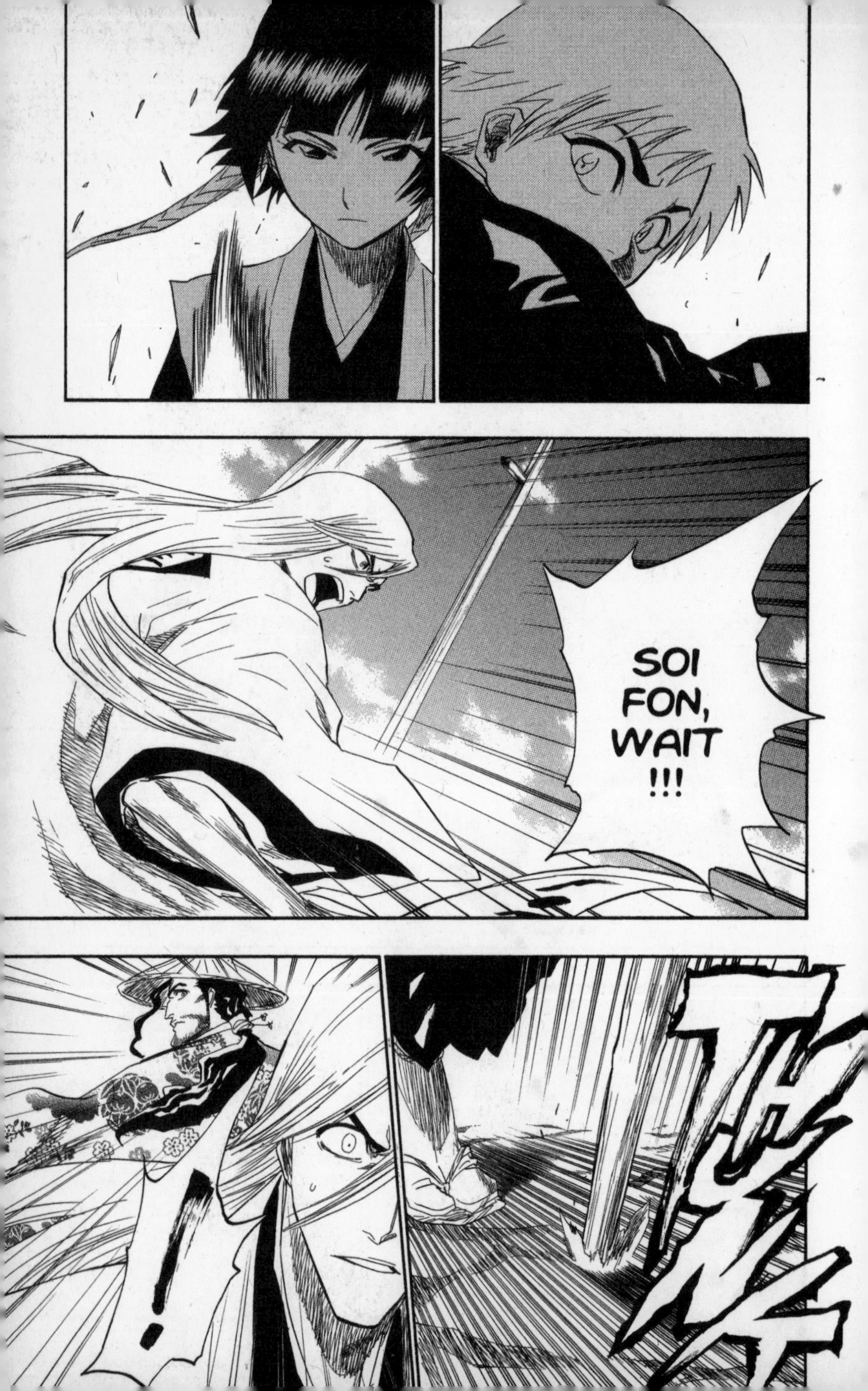
SOI FON, WAIT !!!
!

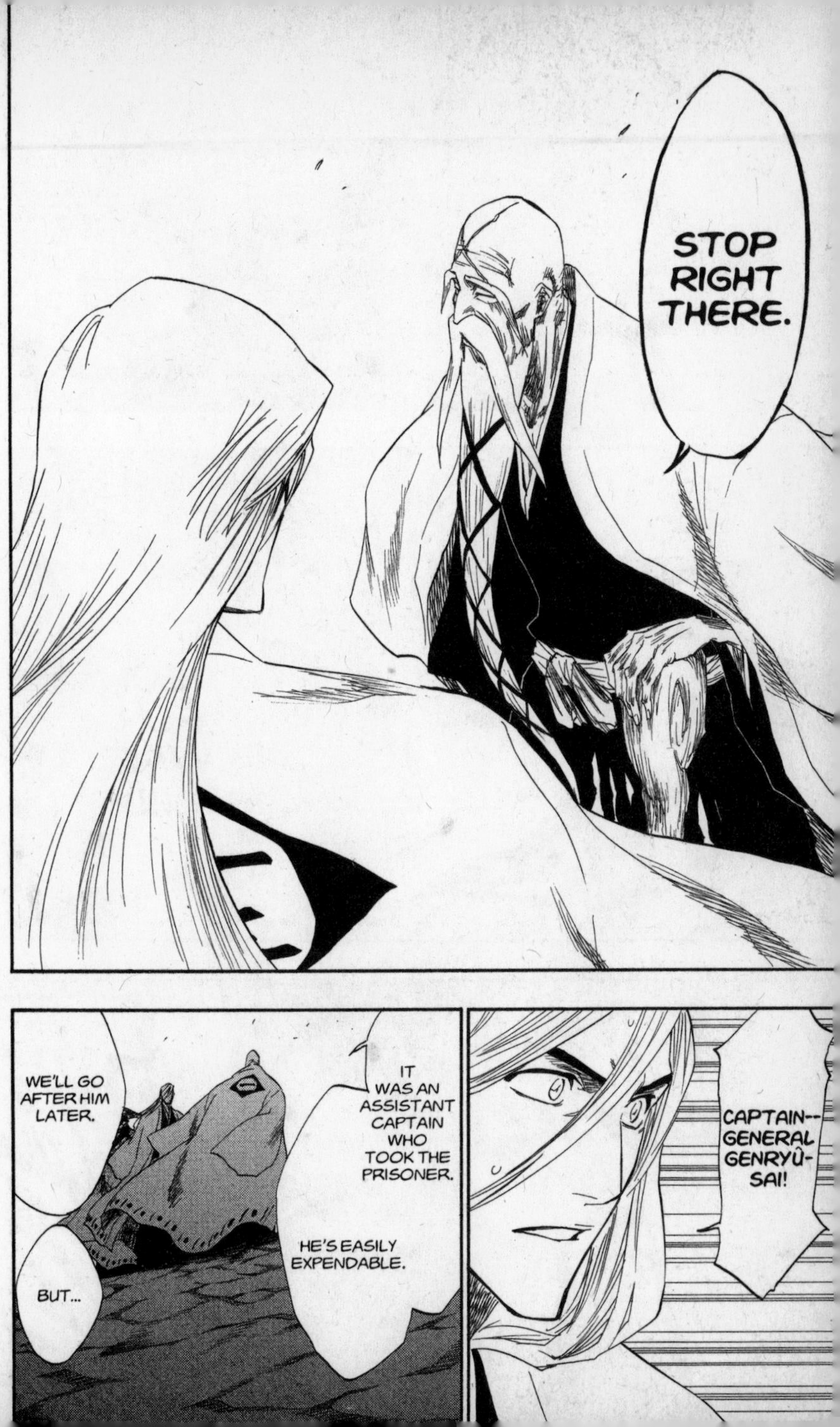
STOP RIGHT THERE.
CAPTAIN--GENERAL GENRYÛ-SAI!
IT WAS AN ASSISTANT CAPTAIN WHO TOOK THE PRISONER.
HE'S EASILY EXPENDABLE.
WE'LL GO AFTER HIM LATER.
BUT...

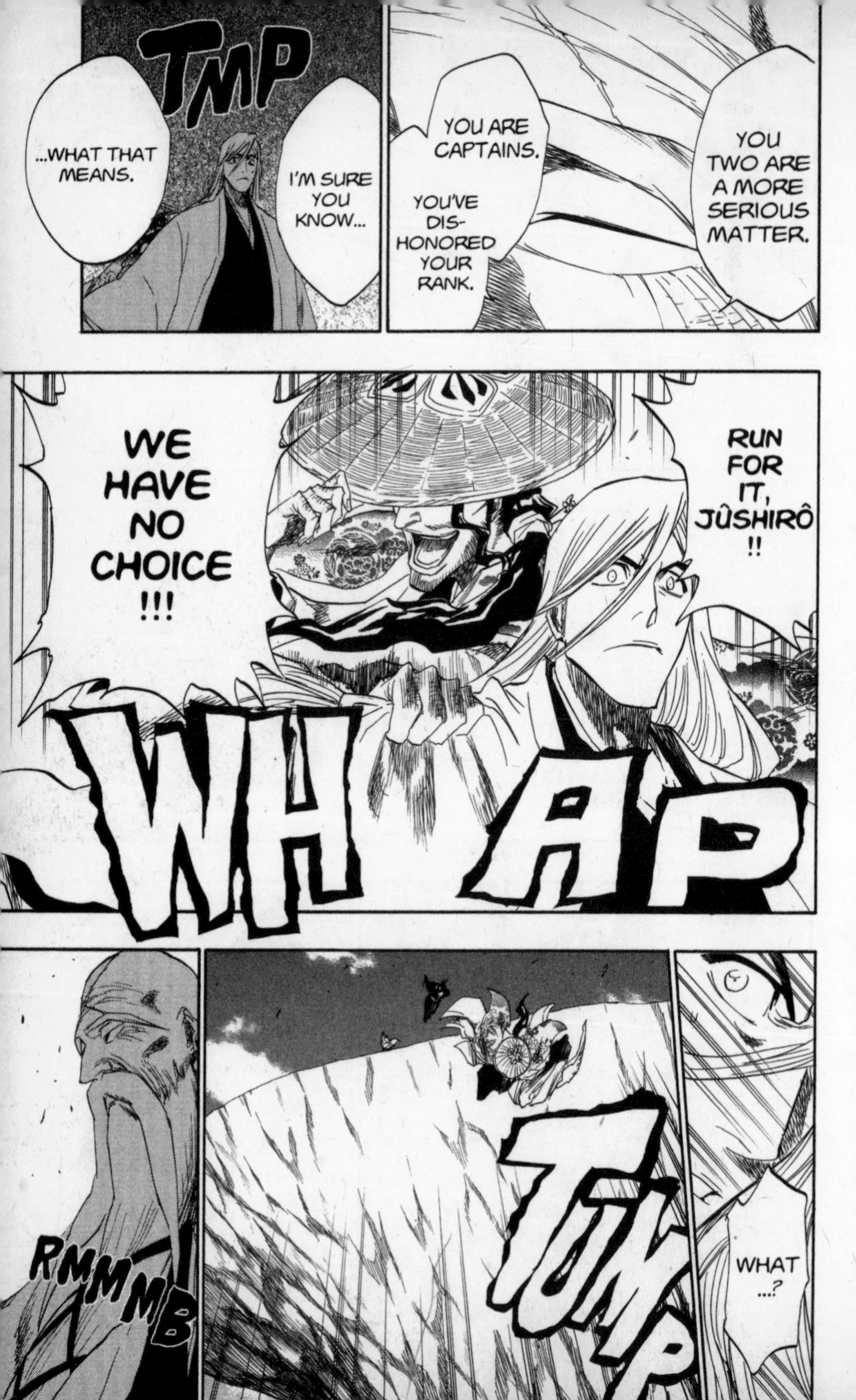
YOU TWO ARE A MORE SERIOUS MATTER.
YOU ARE CAPTAINS.
YOU'VE DIS-HONORED YOUR RANK.
TMP
I'M SURE YOU KNOW...
...WHAT THAT MEANS.
RUN FOR IT, JÛSHIRÔ!!
WE HAVE NO CHOICE!!!
WHAP
WHAT ...?
TUMP
RMMMB

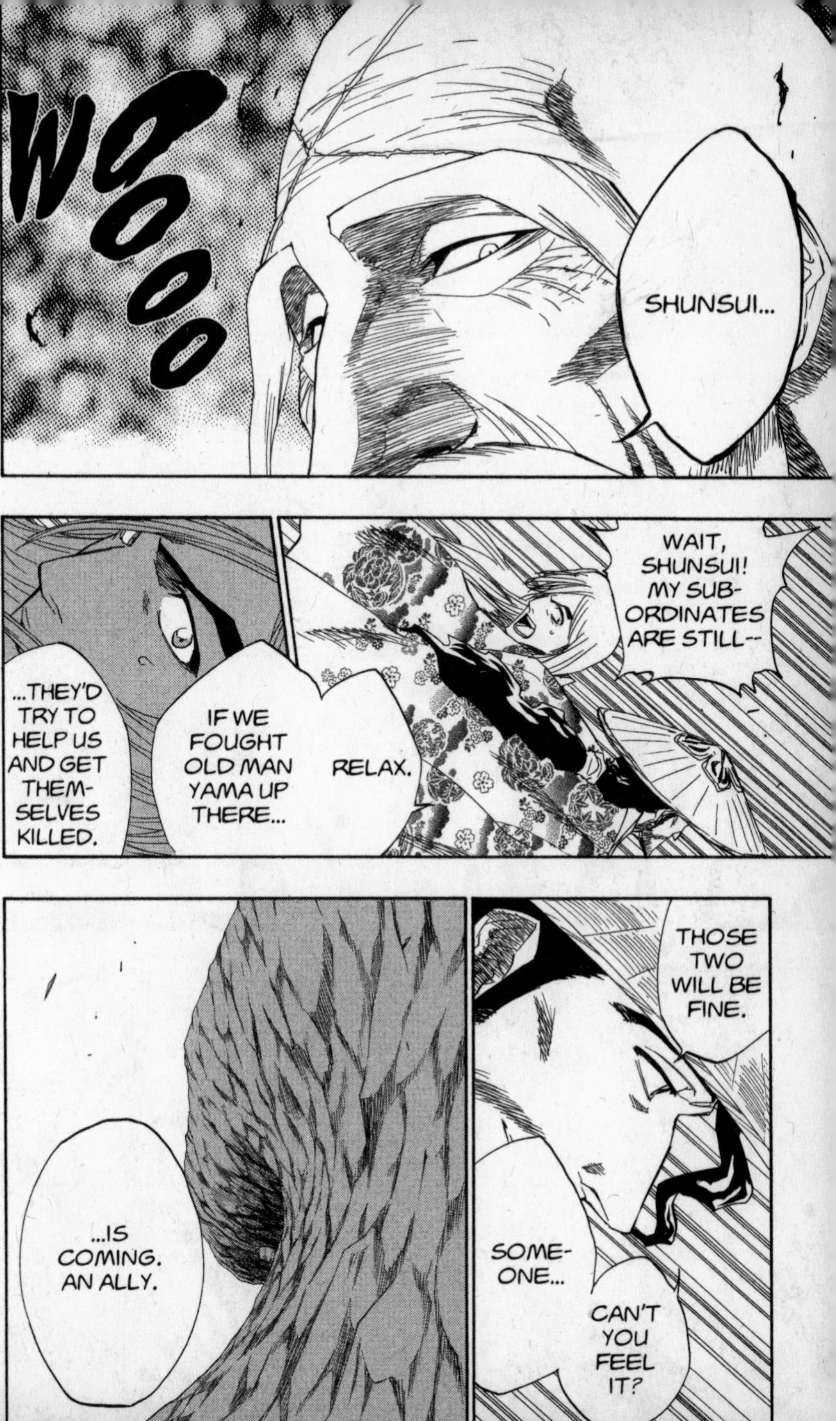
SHUNSUI...
WOOOOO
WAIT, SHUNSUI! MY SUB-ORDINATES ARE STILL--
RELAX.
IF WE FOUGHT OLD MAN YAMA UP THERE...
...THEY'D TRY TO HELP US AND GET THEM-SELVES KILLED.
THOSE TWO WILL BE FINE.
CAN'T YOU FEEL IT?
SOME-ONE...
...IS COMING. AN ALLY.

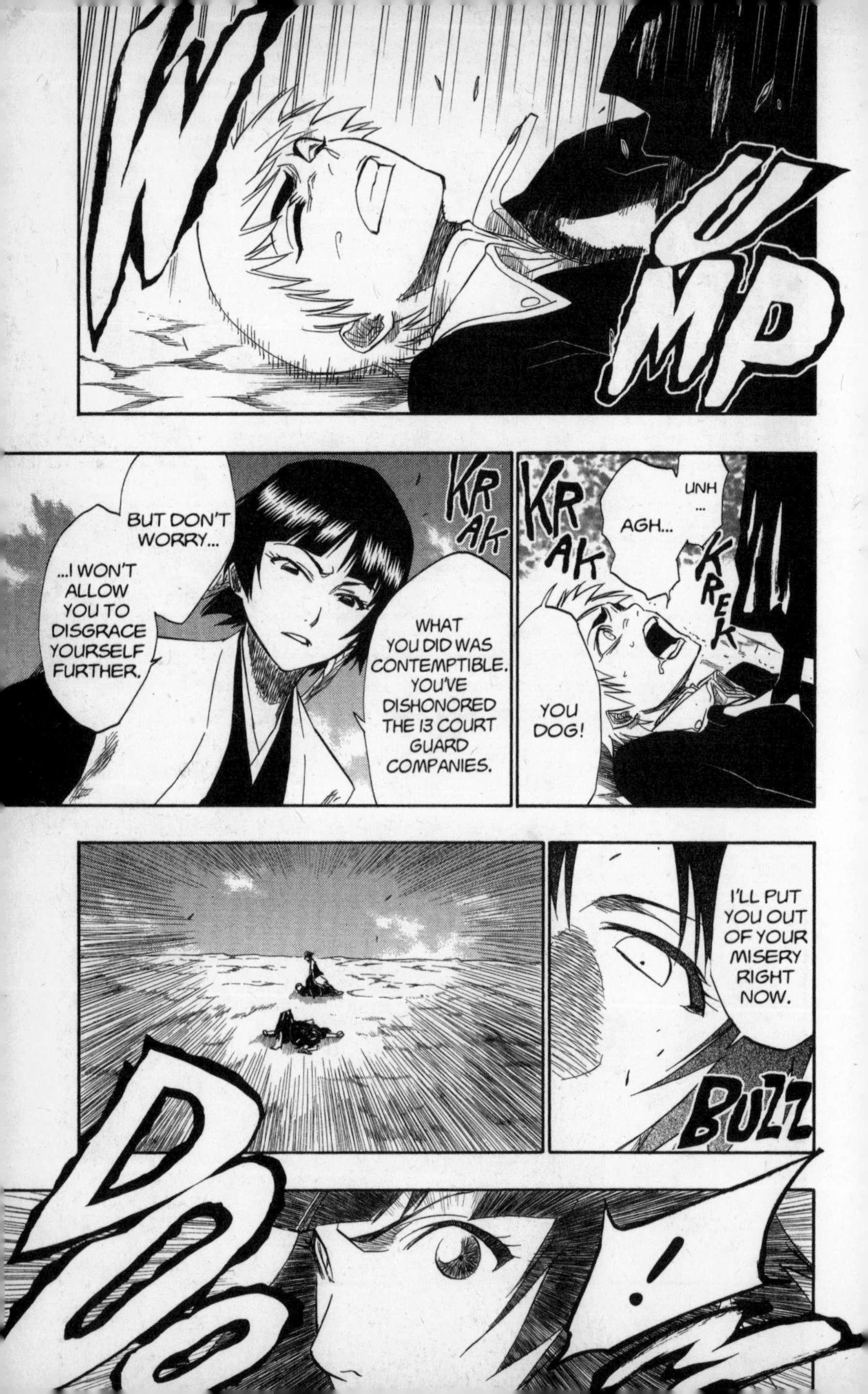
WUMP
UNH ...
AGH...
KRAK
KREK
YOU DOG!
KRAK
WHAT YOU DID WAS CONTEMPTIBLE. YOU'VE DISHONORED THE 13 COURT GUARD COMPANIES.
BUT DON'T WORRY...
...I WON'T ALLOW YOU TO DISGRACE YOURSELF FURTHER.
I'LL PUT YOU OUT OF YOUR MISERY RIGHT NOW.
BUZZ
!

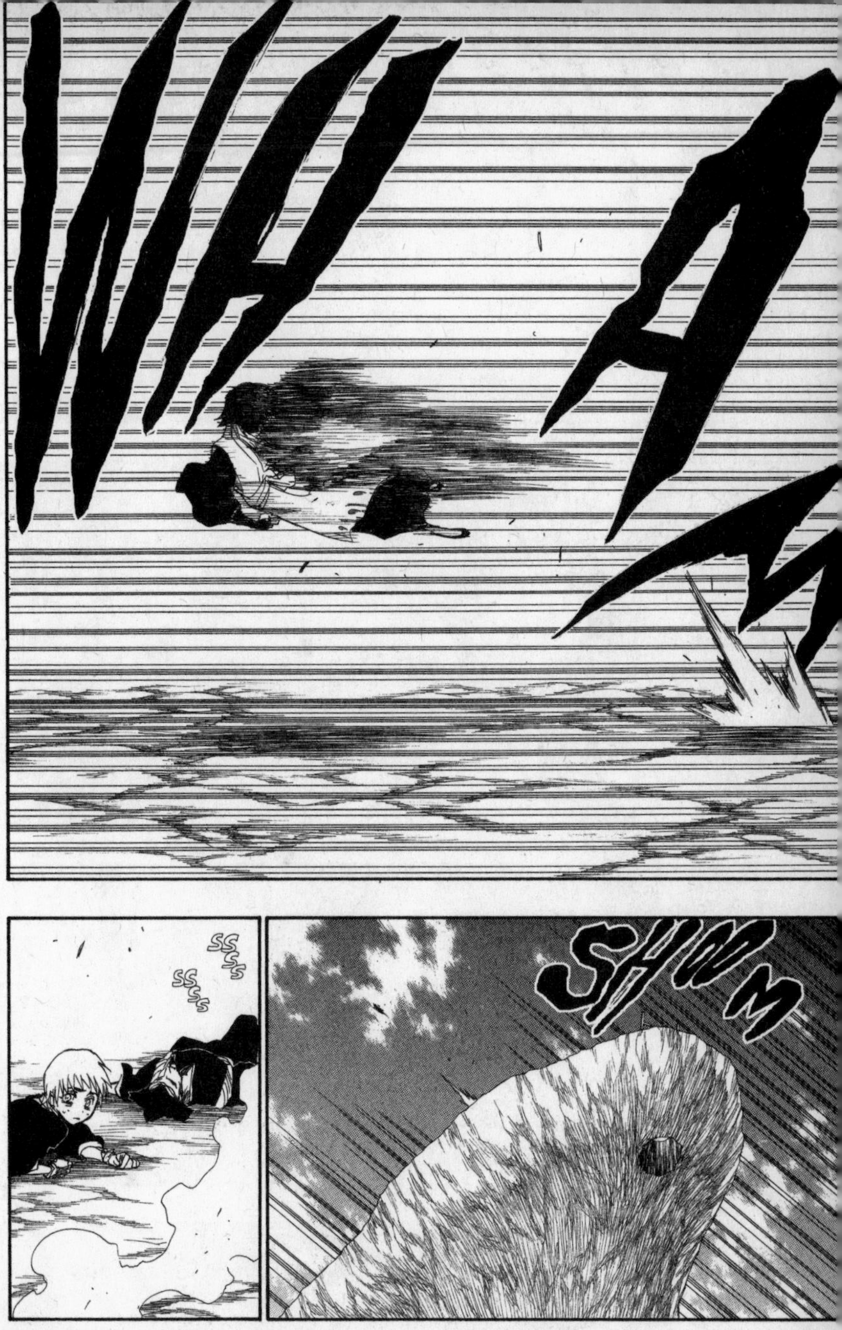
WHAM
SHOOM
SSSS
SSSS

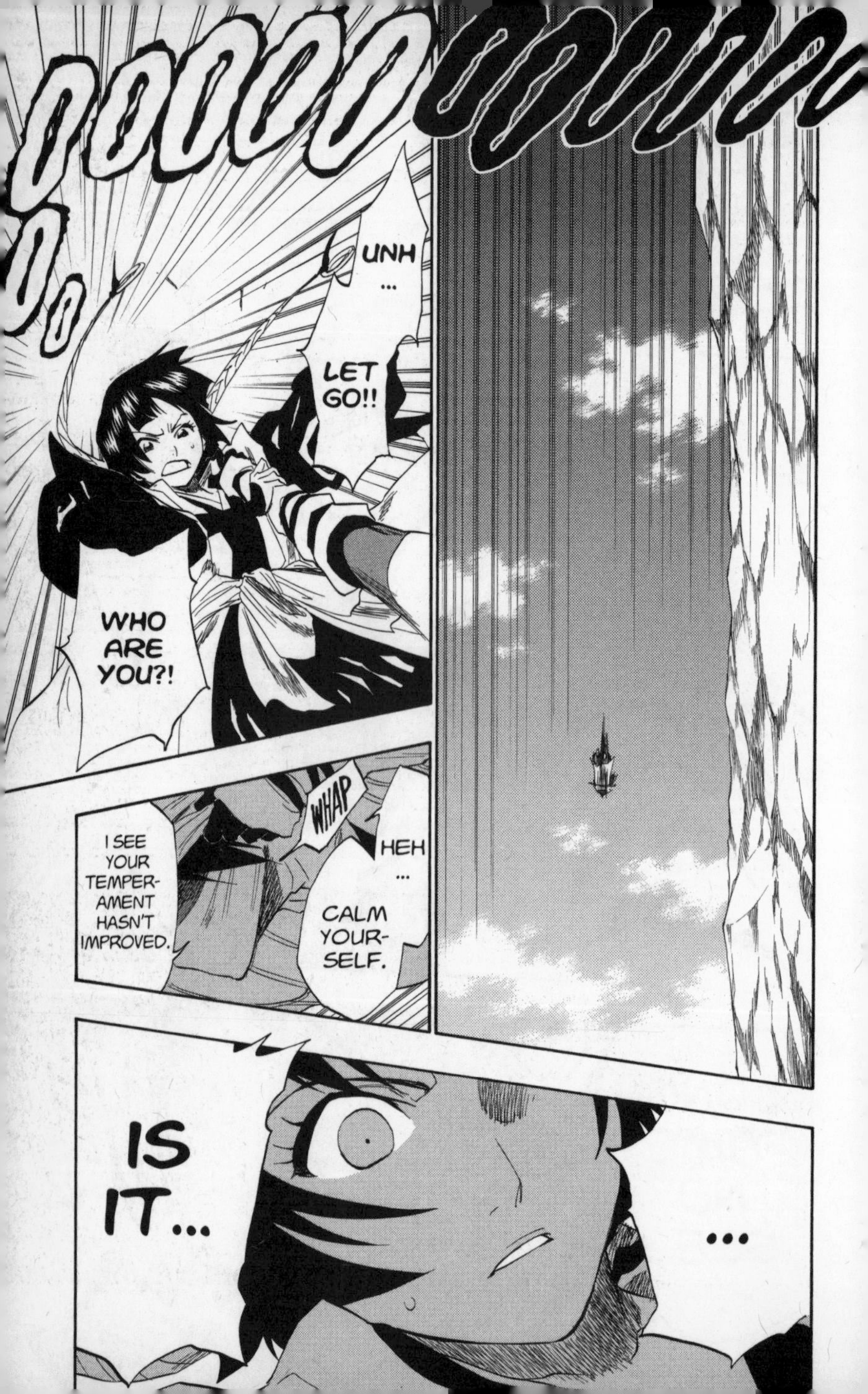
UNH ...
LET GO!!
WHO ARE YOU?!
WHAP
HEH ...
CALM YOURSELF.
I SEE YOUR TEMPERAMENT HASN'T IMPROVED.
...
IS IT...

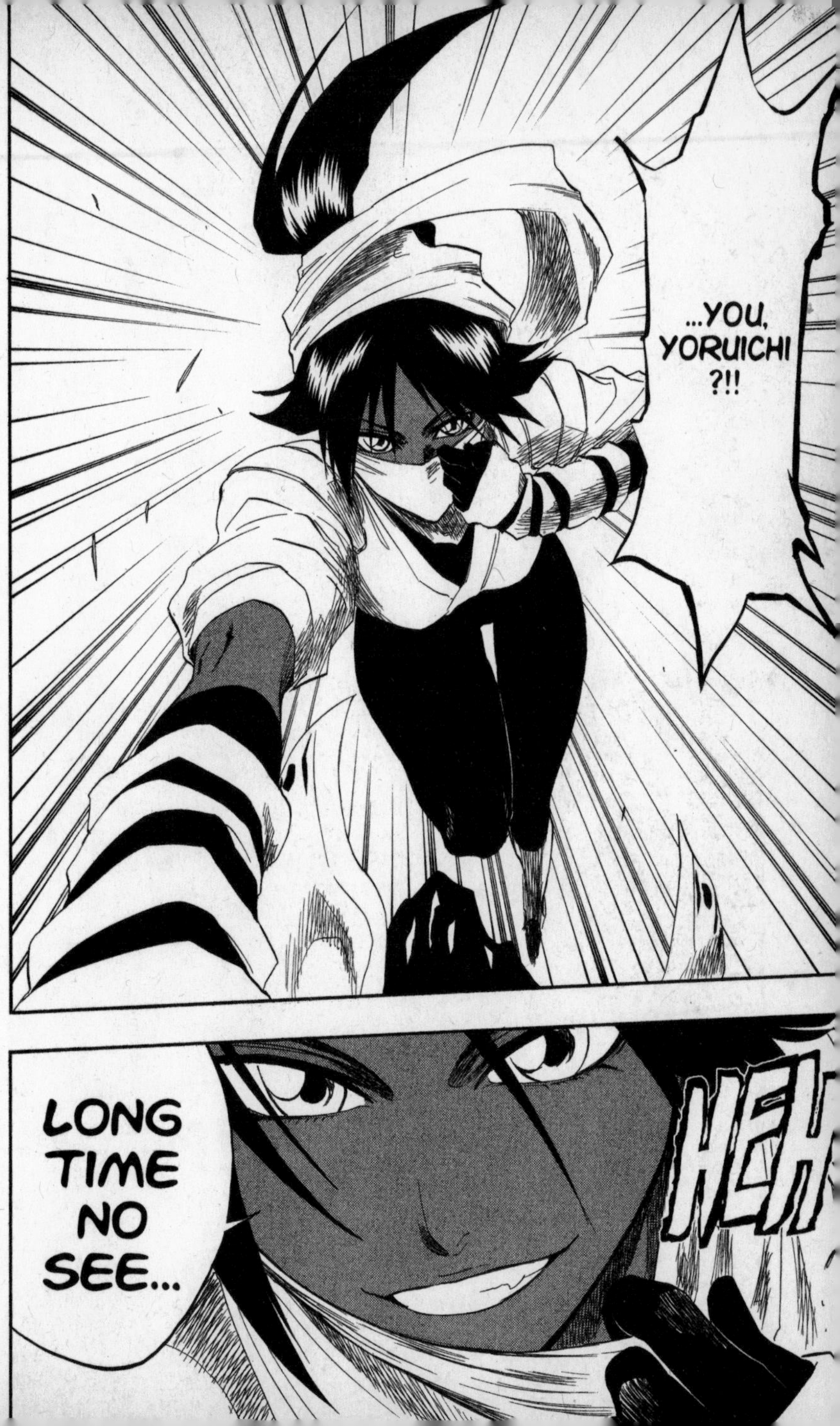
...YOU, YORUICHI ?!!
HEH
LONG TIME NO SEE...

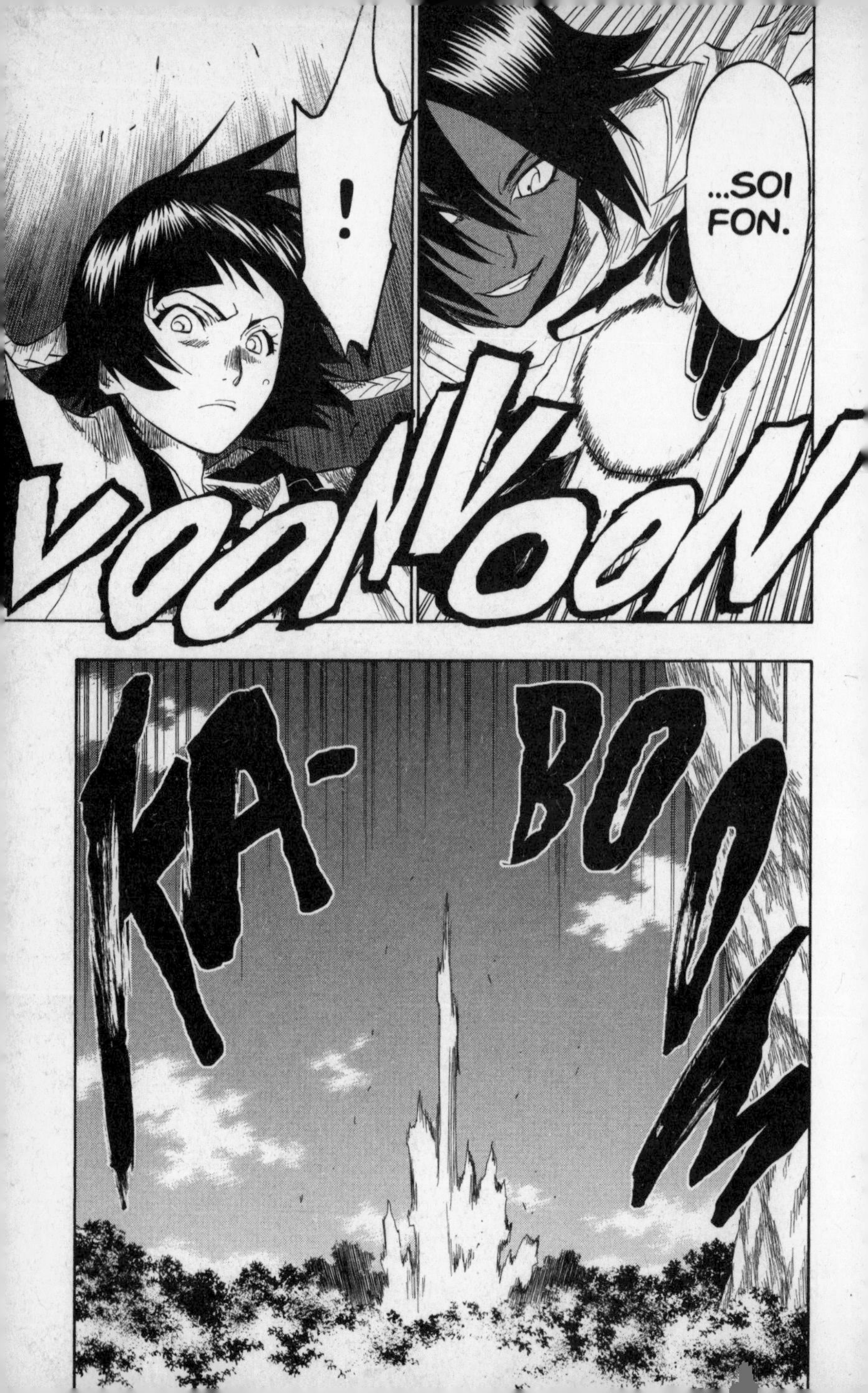
...SOI FON.
!
VOON VOON
KA-BOOM

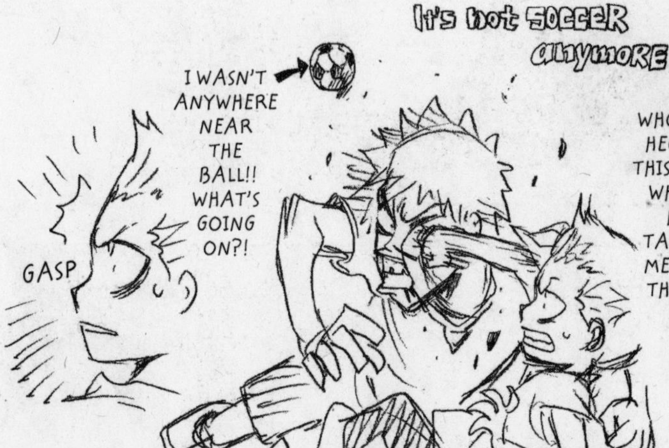
It's not SOCCER anymore.
WHO THE HECK IS THIS GUY? WHY'D HE TACKLE ME LIKE THAT?
I WASN'T ANYWHERE NEAR THE BALL!! WHAT'S GOING ON?!
GASP

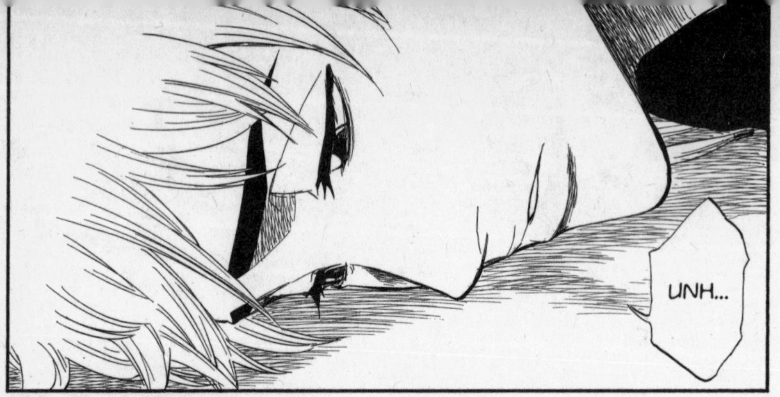
UNH...

154. "Flash Master"

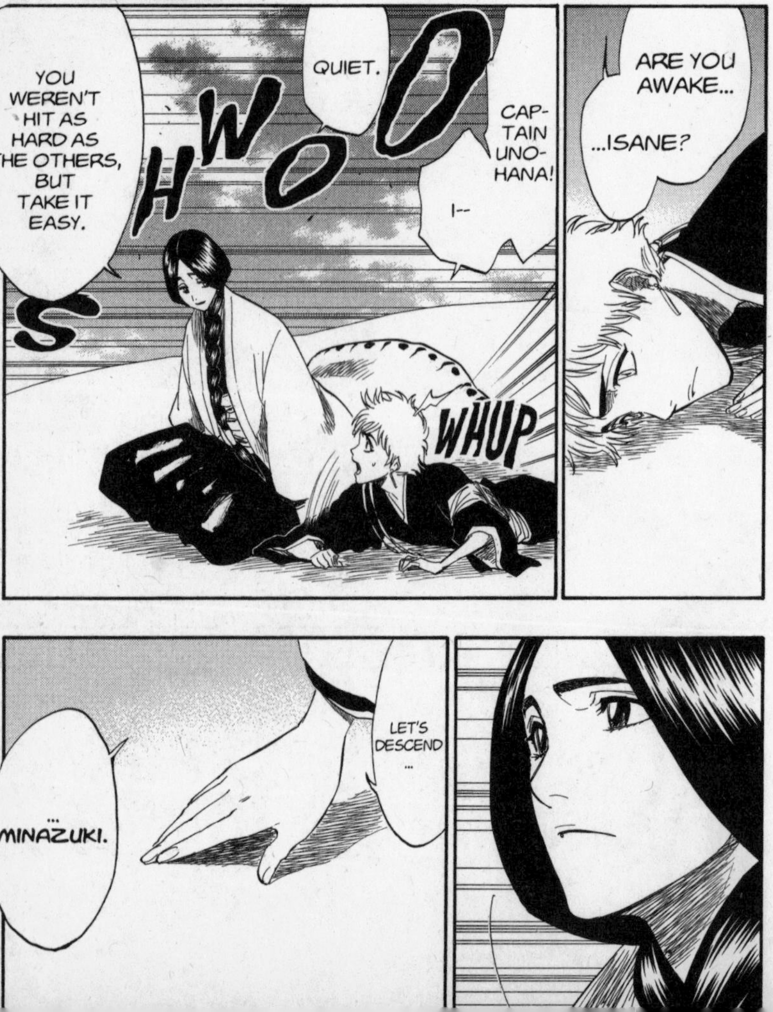
ARE YOU AWAKE...
...ISANE?
CAPTAIN UNOHANA!
I--
WHUP
WHOO
QUIET.
YOU WEREN'T HIT AS HARD AS THE OTHERS, BUT TAKE IT EASY.
S
LET'S DESCEND...
...MINAZUKI.

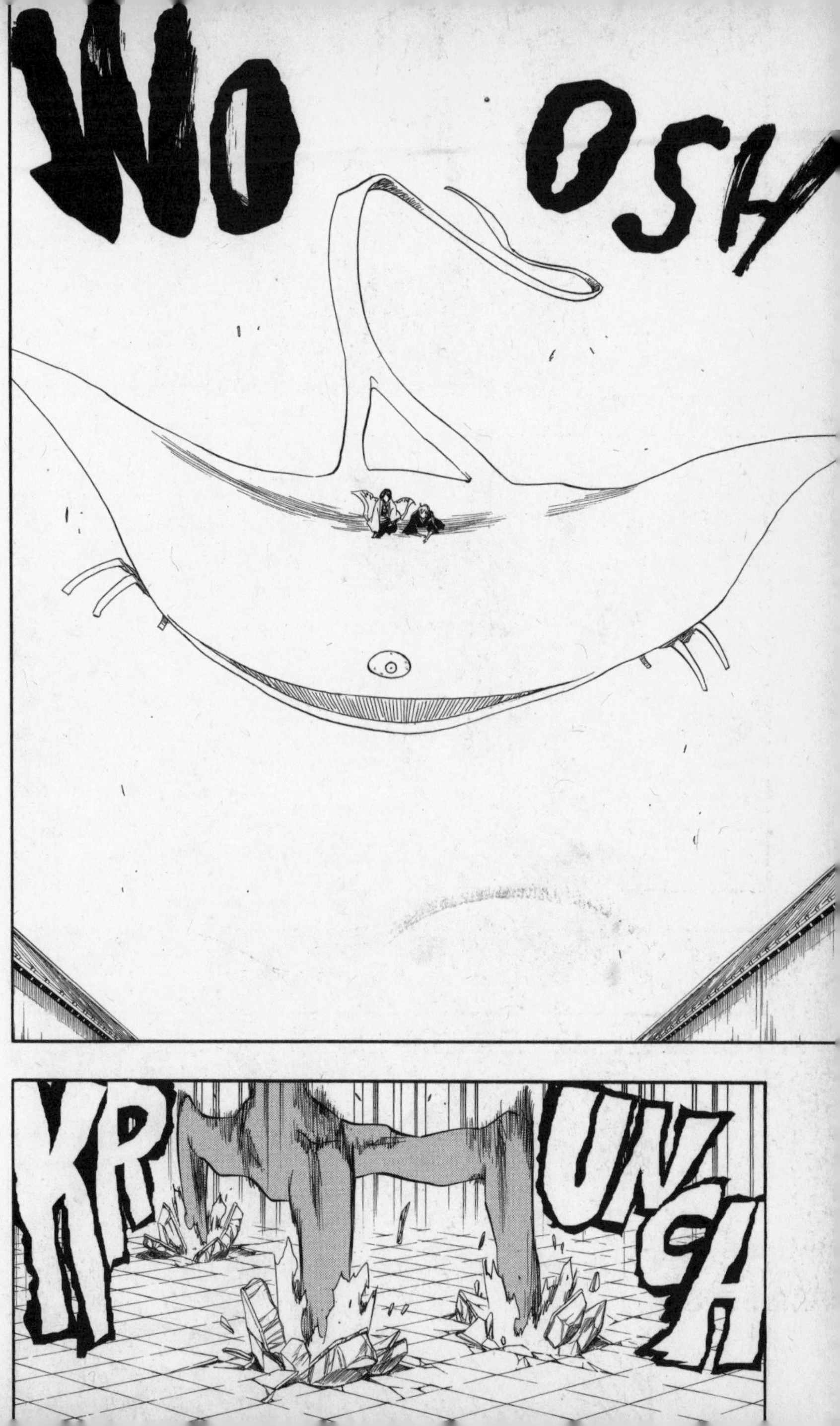
WOOSH
KRUNCH

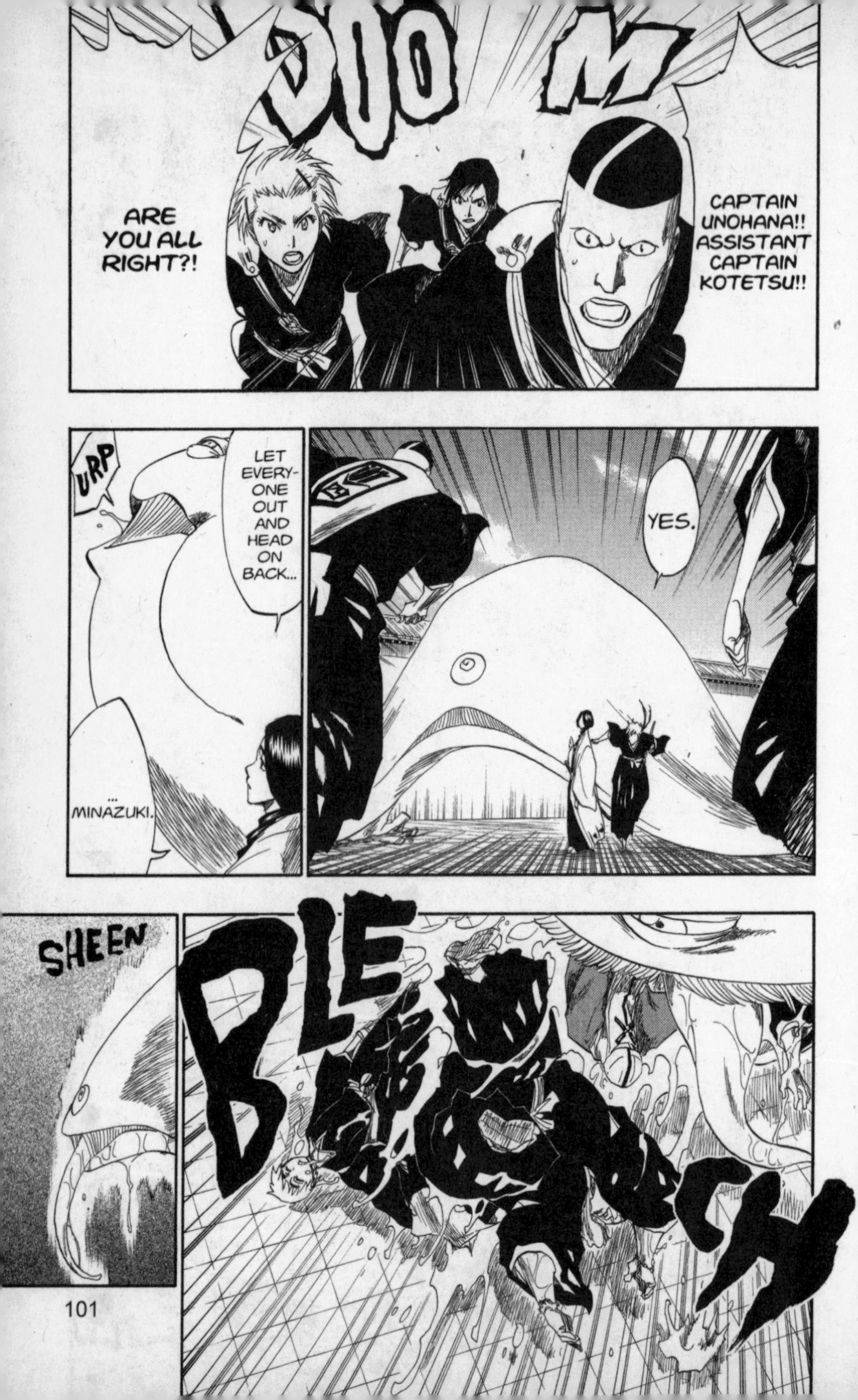
CAPTAIN UNOHANA!! ASSISTANT CAPTAIN KOTETSU!!
ARE YOU ALL RIGHT?!
YES.
LET EVERYONE OUT AND HEAD ON BACK...
URP
...MINAZUKI.
SHEEN

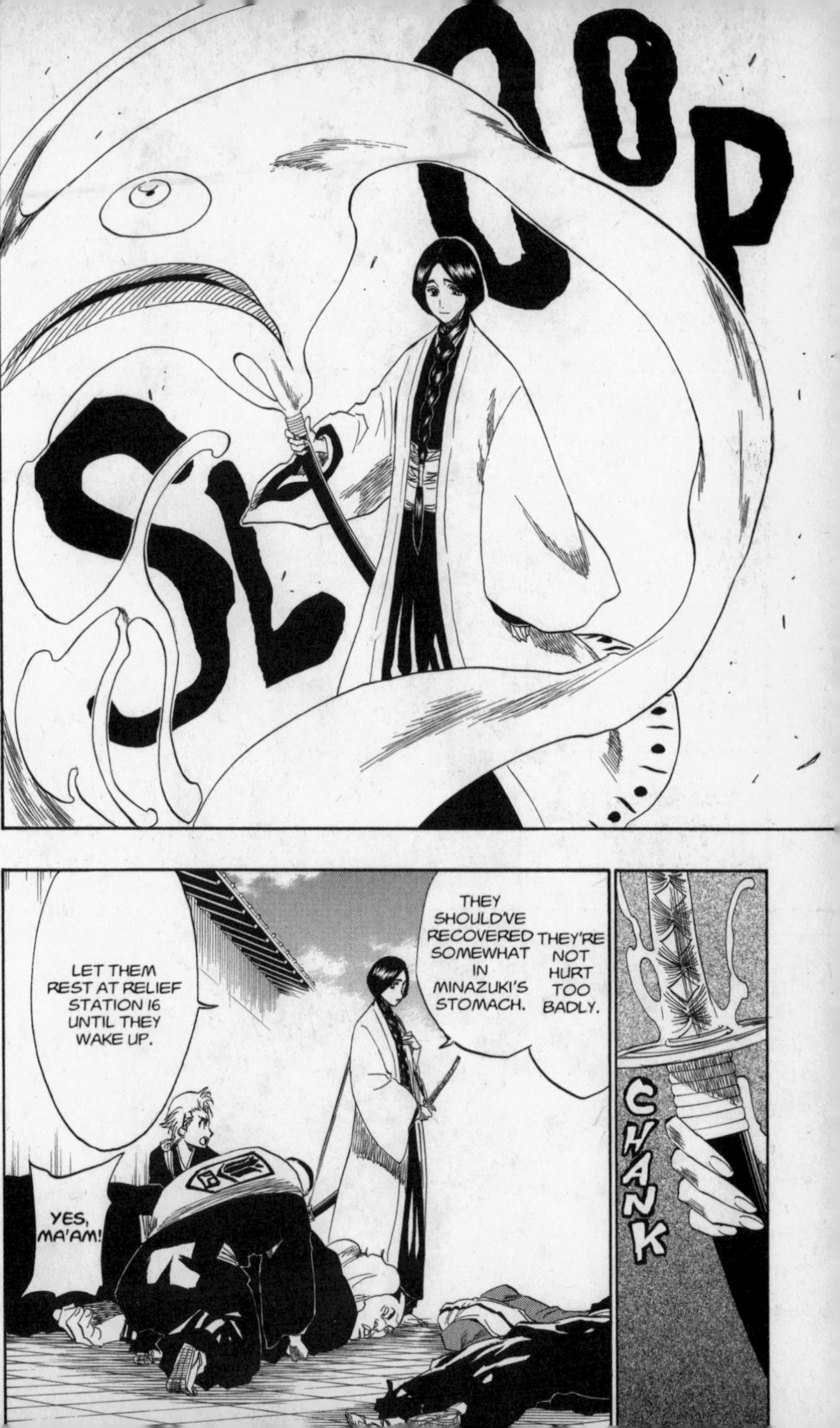
CHANK
THEY'RE NOT HURT TOO BADLY.
THEY SHOULD'VE RECOVERED SOMEWHAT IN MINAZUKI'S STOMACH.
LET THEM REST AT RELIEF STATION 16 UNTIL THEY WAKE UP.
YES, MA'AM!

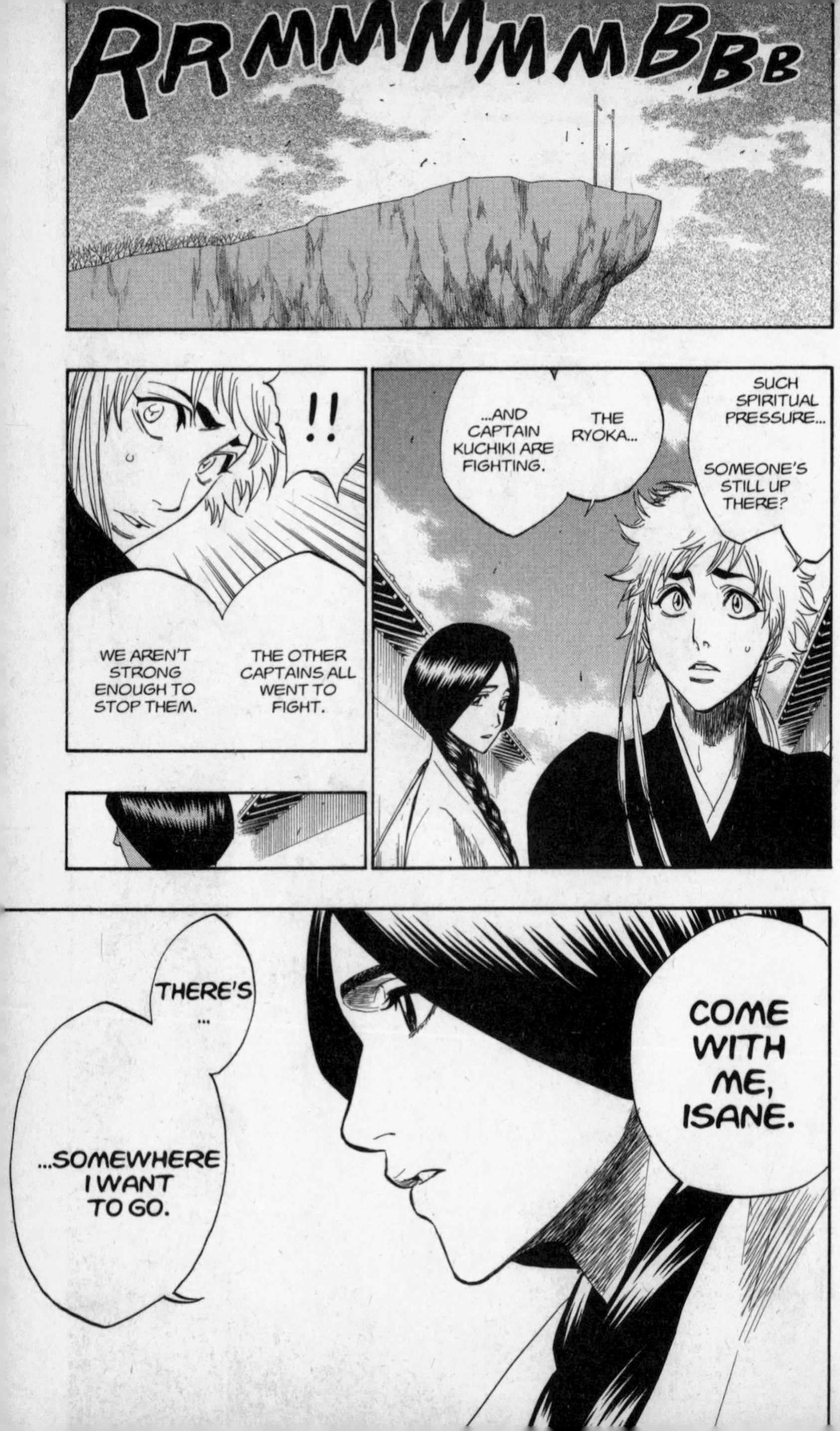
RRMMMMMBBB
SUCH SPIRITUAL PRESSURE...
SOMEONE'S STILL UP THERE?
THE RYOKA...
...AND CAPTAIN KUCHIKI ARE FIGHTING.
!!
THE OTHER CAPTAINS ALL WENT TO FIGHT.
WE AREN'T STRONG ENOUGH TO STOP THEM.
COME WITH ME, ISANE.
THERE'S...
...SOMEWHERE I WANT TO GO.

154. "Flash Master"

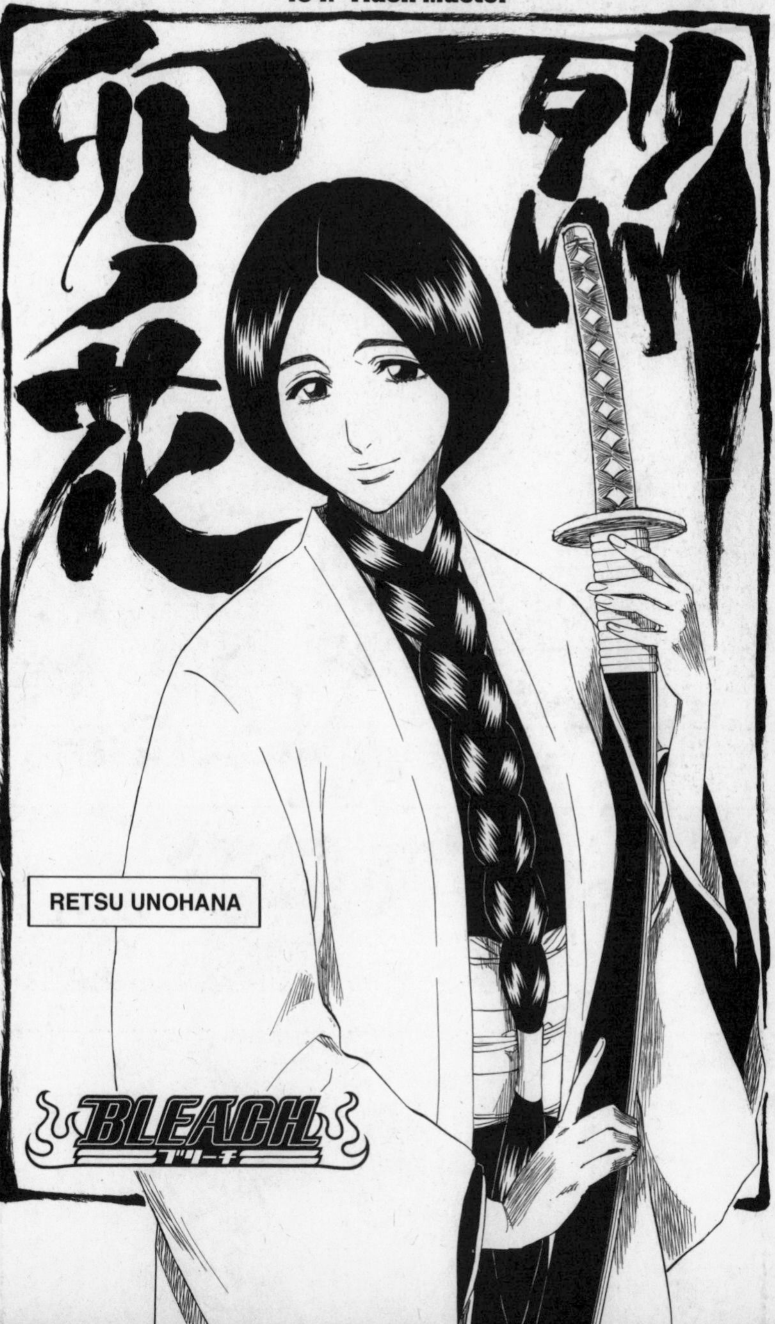
烈
卯ノ花
RETSU UNOHANA
BLEACH
ブリーチ

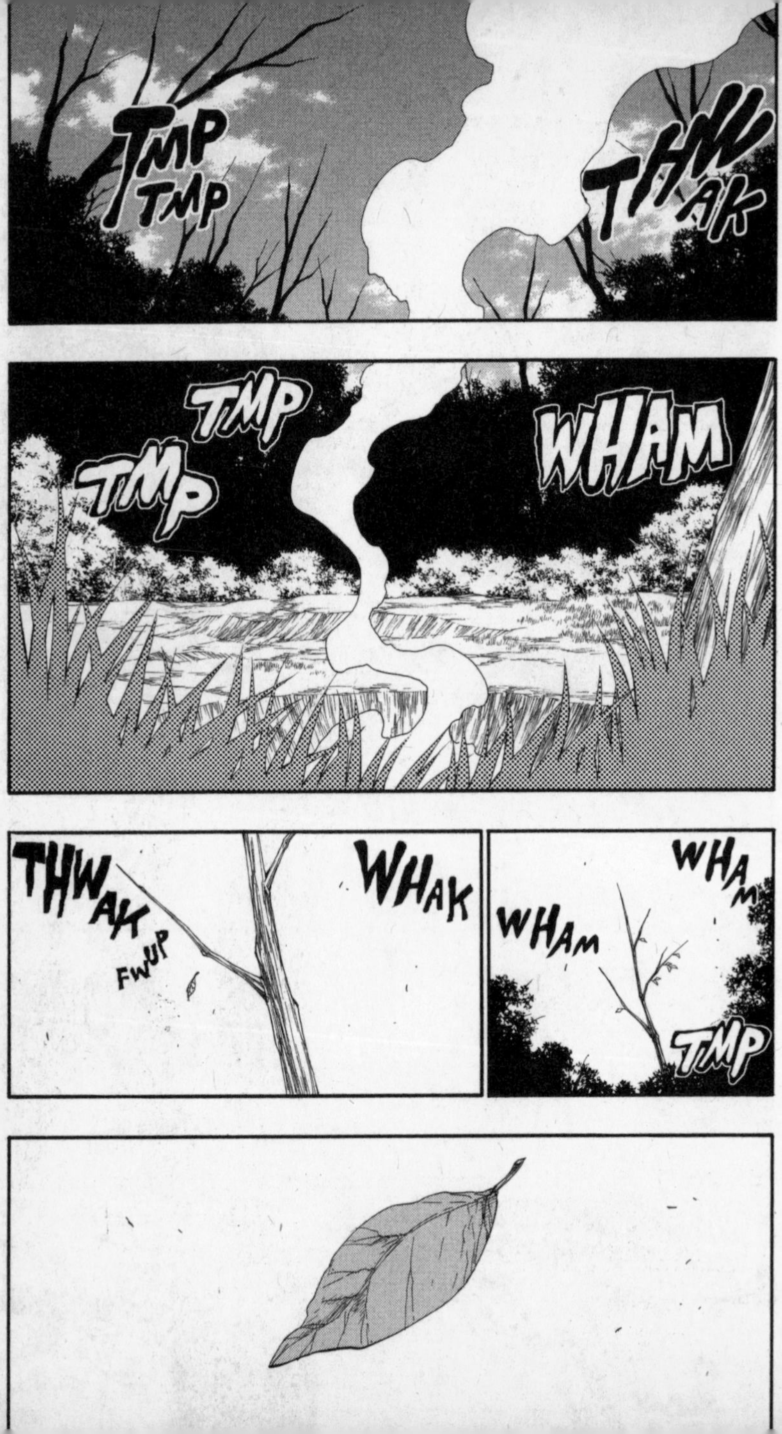
THWAK
TMP TMP
WHAM
TMP
TMP
WHAM
WHAM
TMP
WHAK
THWAK
FWUP

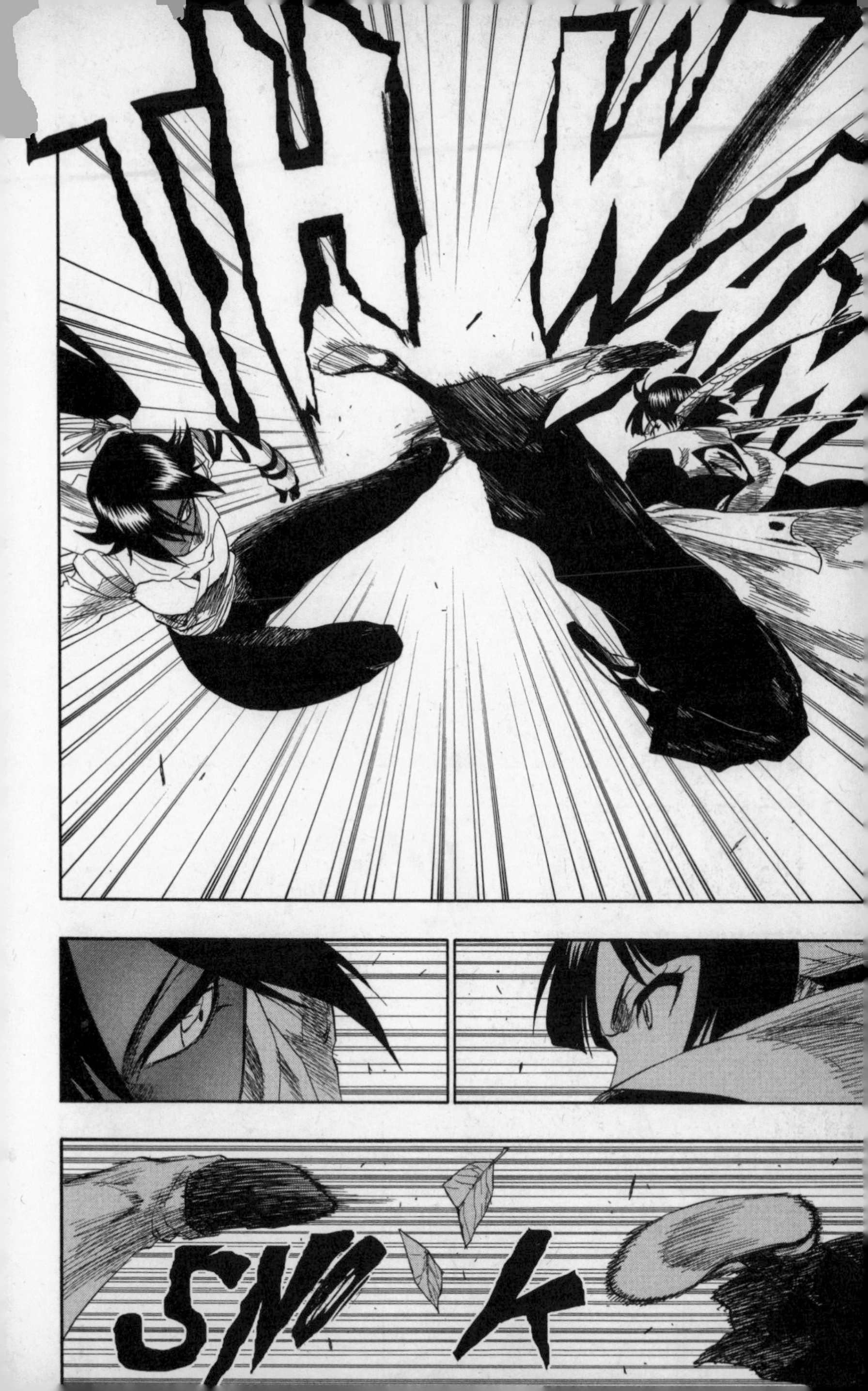

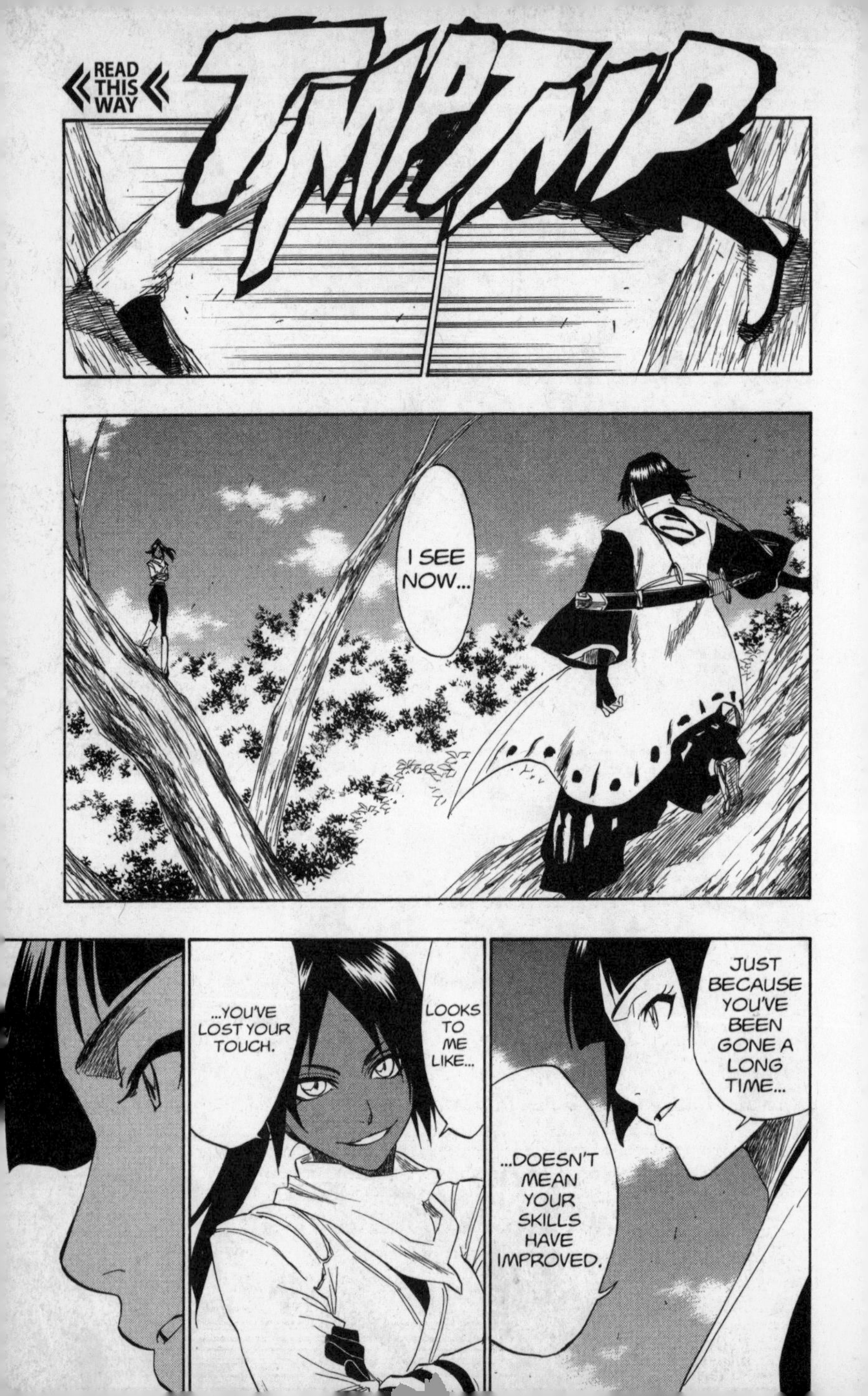
READ THIS WAY
TMPTMP
I SEE NOW...
JUST BECAUSE YOU'VE BEEN GONE A LONG TIME...
...DOESN'T MEAN YOUR SKILLS HAVE IMPROVED.
LOOKS TO ME LIKE...
...YOU'VE LOST YOUR TOUCH.

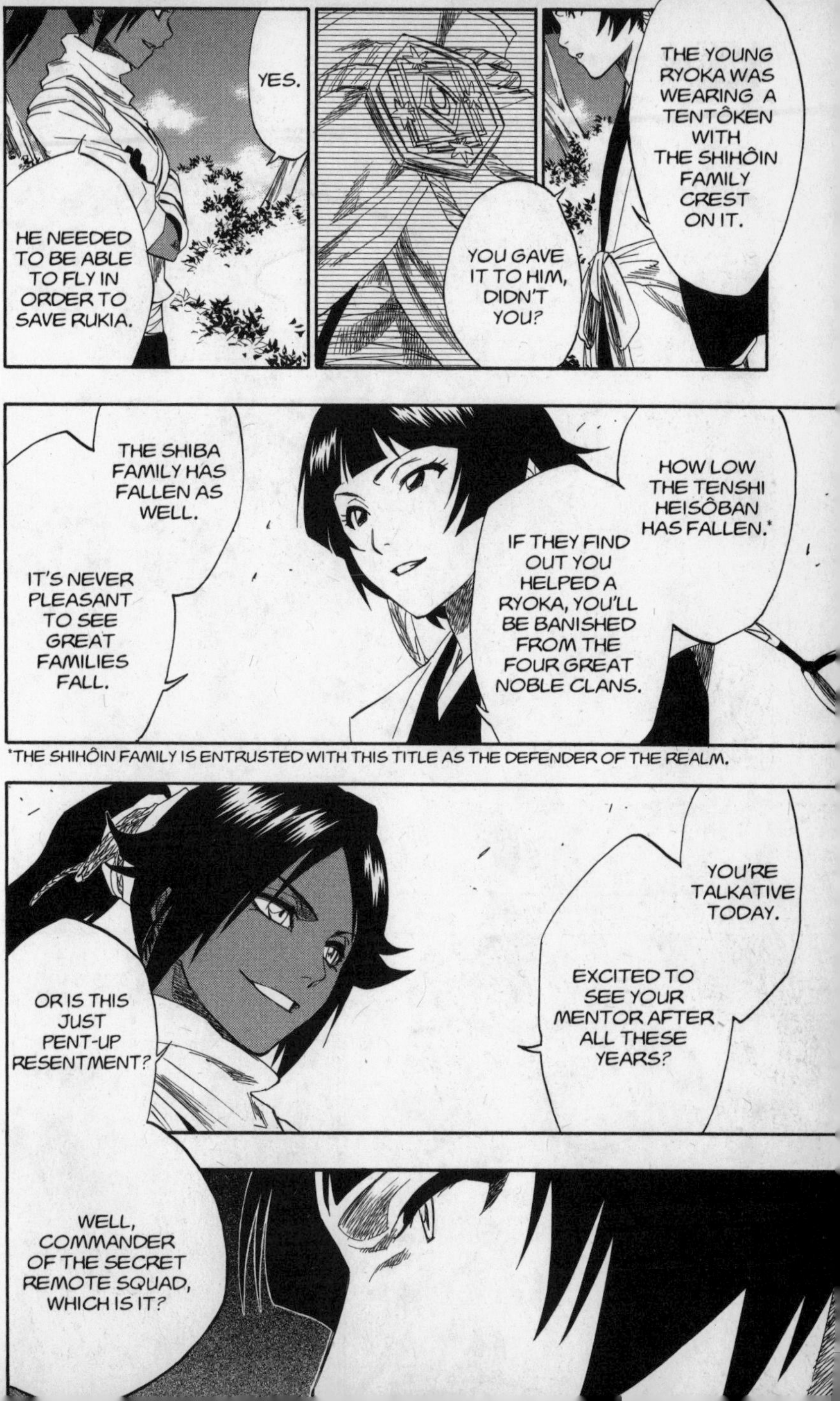
THE YOUNG RYOKA WAS WEARING A TENTÔKEN WITH THE SHIHÔIN FAMILY CREST ON IT.
YOU GAVE IT TO HIM, DIDN'T YOU?
YES.
HE NEEDED TO BE ABLE TO FLY IN ORDER TO SAVE RUKIA.
HOW LOW THE TENSHI HEISÔBAN HAS FALLEN.*
IF THEY FIND OUT YOU HELPED A RYOKA, YOU'LL BE BANISHED FROM THE FOUR GREAT NOBLE CLANS.
THE SHIBA FAMILY HAS FALLEN AS WELL.
IT'S NEVER PLEASANT TO SEE GREAT FAMILIES FALL.
YOU'RE TALKATIVE TODAY.
EXCITED TO SEE YOUR MENTOR AFTER ALL THESE YEARS?
OR IS THIS JUST PENT-UP RESENTMENT?
WELL, COMMANDER OF THE SECRET REMOTE SQUAD, WHICH IS IT?

*THE SHIHÔIN FAMILY IS ENTRUSTED WITH THIS TITLE AS THE DEFENDER OF THE REALM.

READ THIS WAY

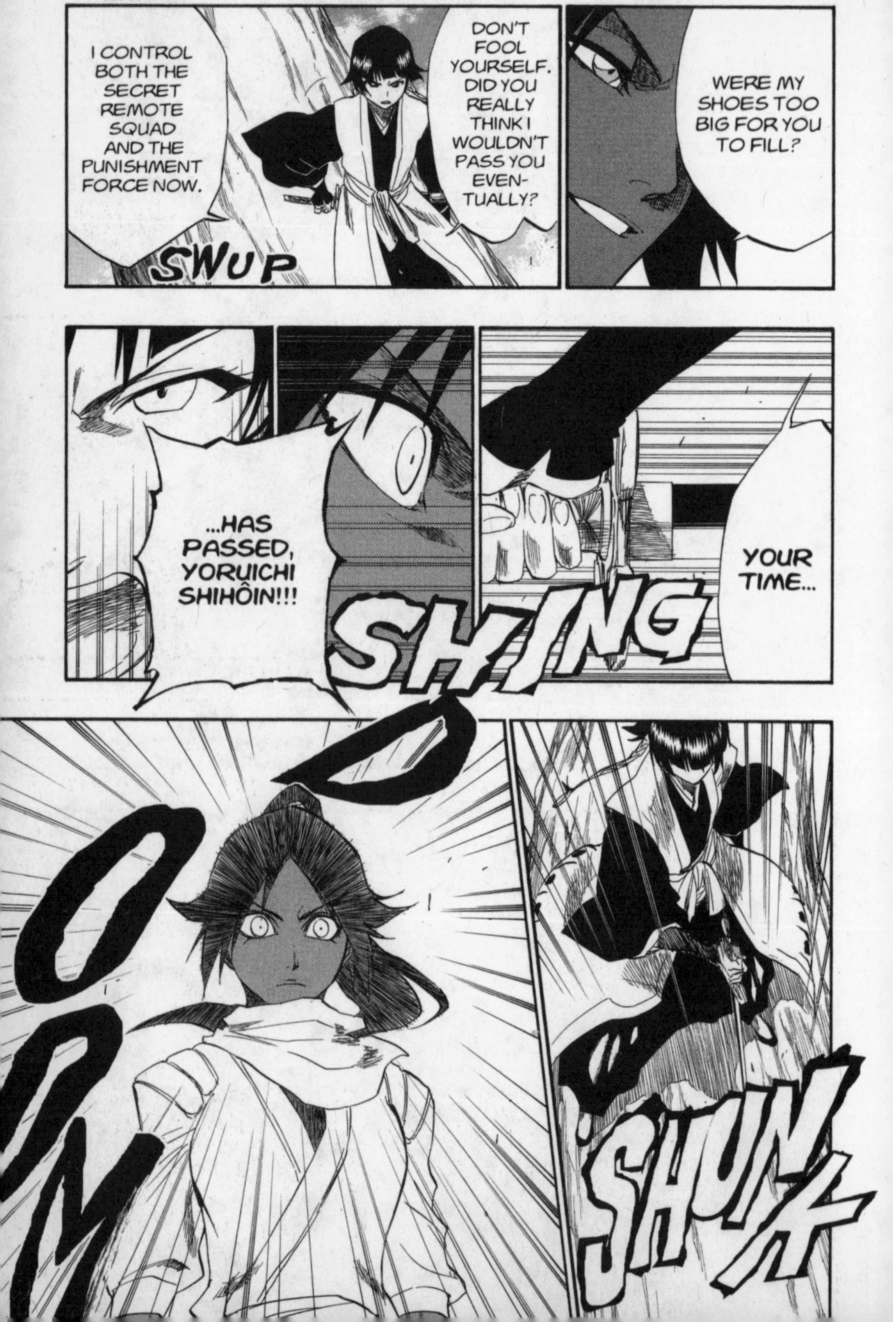
WERE MY SHOES TOO BIG FOR YOU TO FILL?
DON'T FOOL YOURSELF. DID YOU REALLY THINK I WOULDN'T PASS YOU EVEN-TUALLY?
I CONTROL BOTH THE SECRET REMOTE SQUAD AND THE PUNISHMENT FORCE NOW.
SWUP
YOUR TIME...
SHING
...HAS PASSED, YORUICHI SHIHÔIN!!!
SHUNK

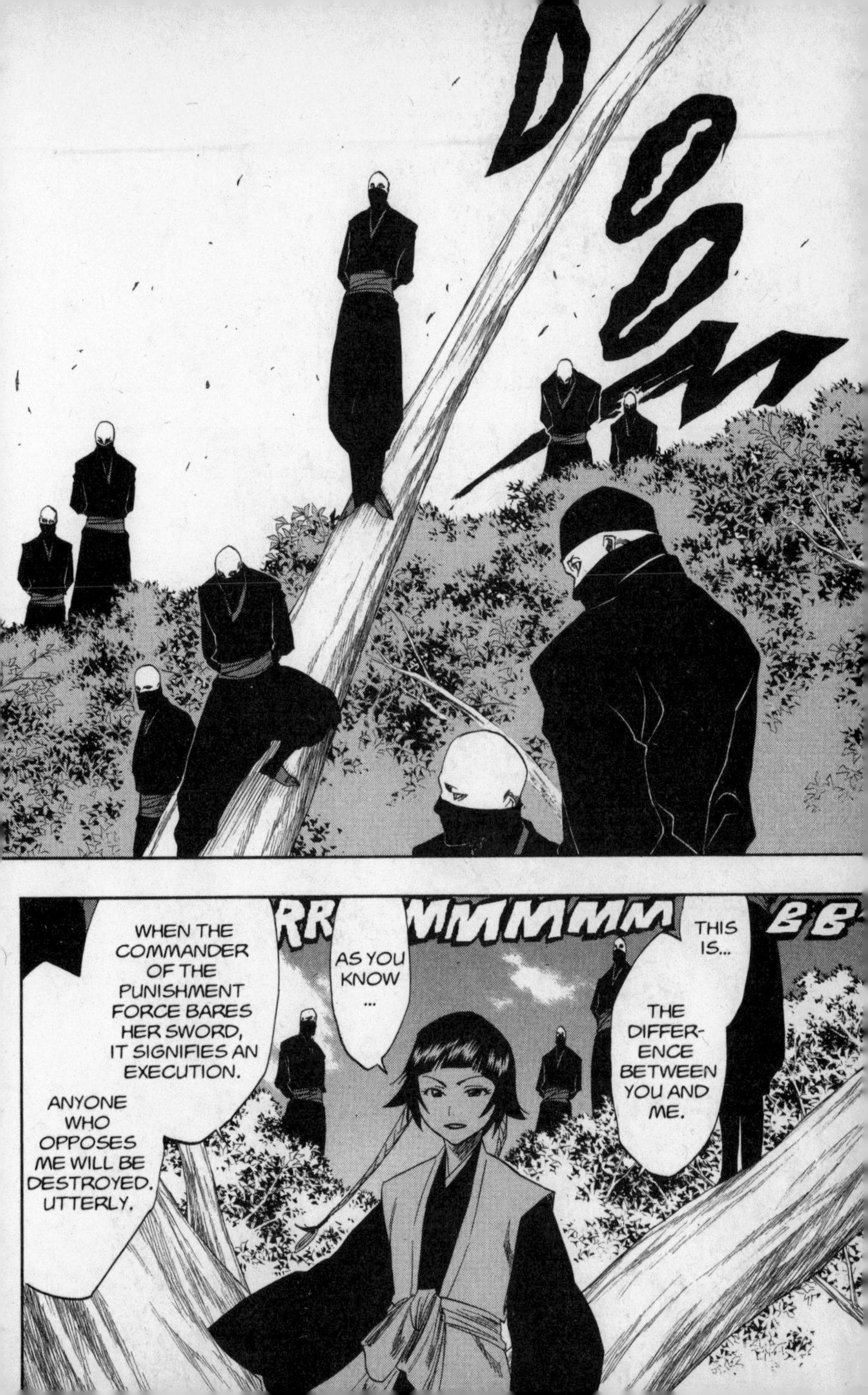
DOOM
RR MMMMMM BB
THIS IS...
THE DIFFERENCE BETWEEN YOU AND ME.
AS YOU KNOW ...
WHEN THE COMMANDER OF THE PUNISHMENT FORCE BARES HER SWORD, IT SIGNIFIES AN EXECUTION.
ANYONE WHO OPPOSES ME WILL BE DESTROYED. UTTERLY.

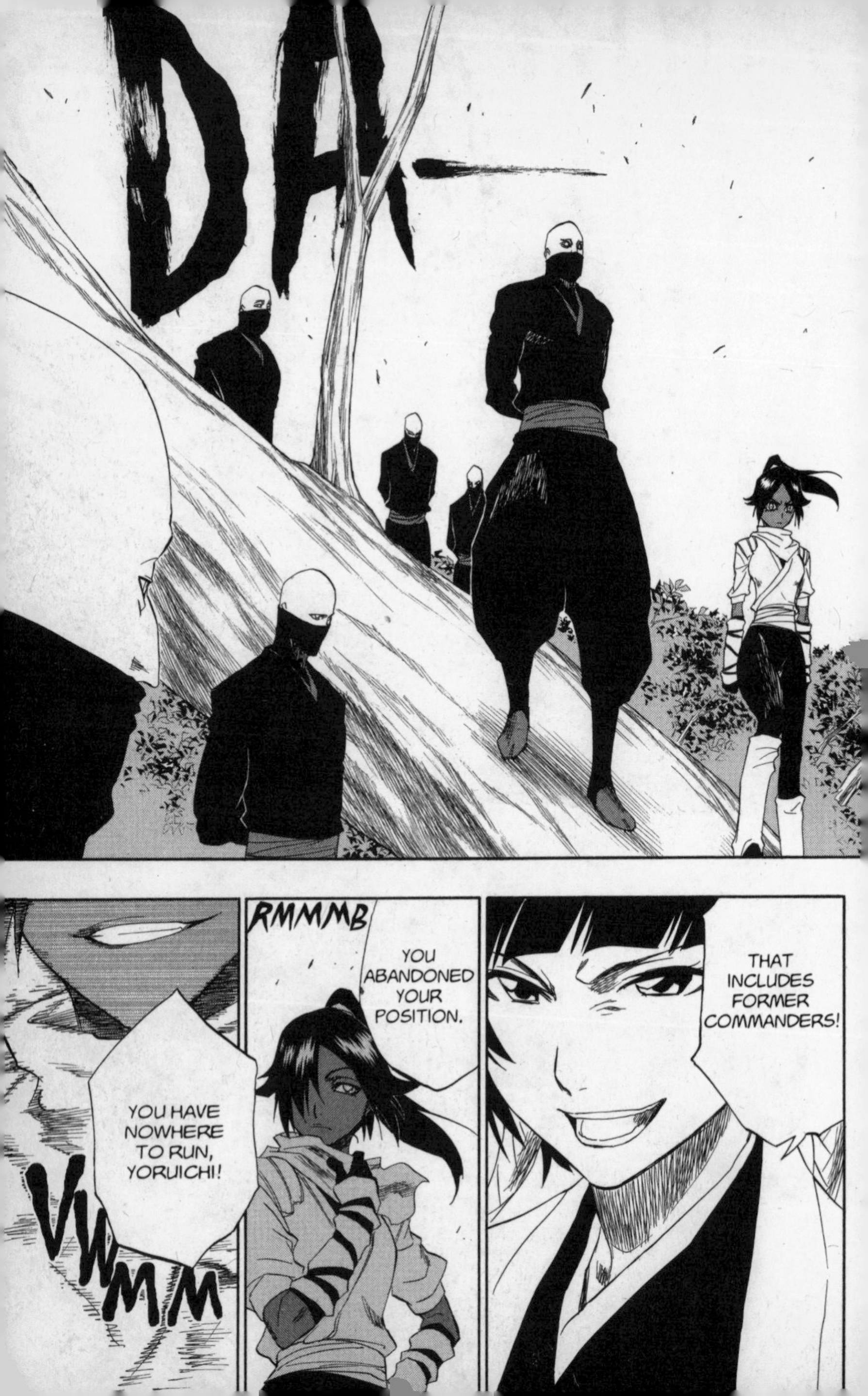
DA
THAT INCLUDES FORMER COMMANDERS!
RMMMB
YOU ABANDONED YOUR POSITION.
YOU HAVE NOWHERE TO RUN, YORUICHI!
VWMM

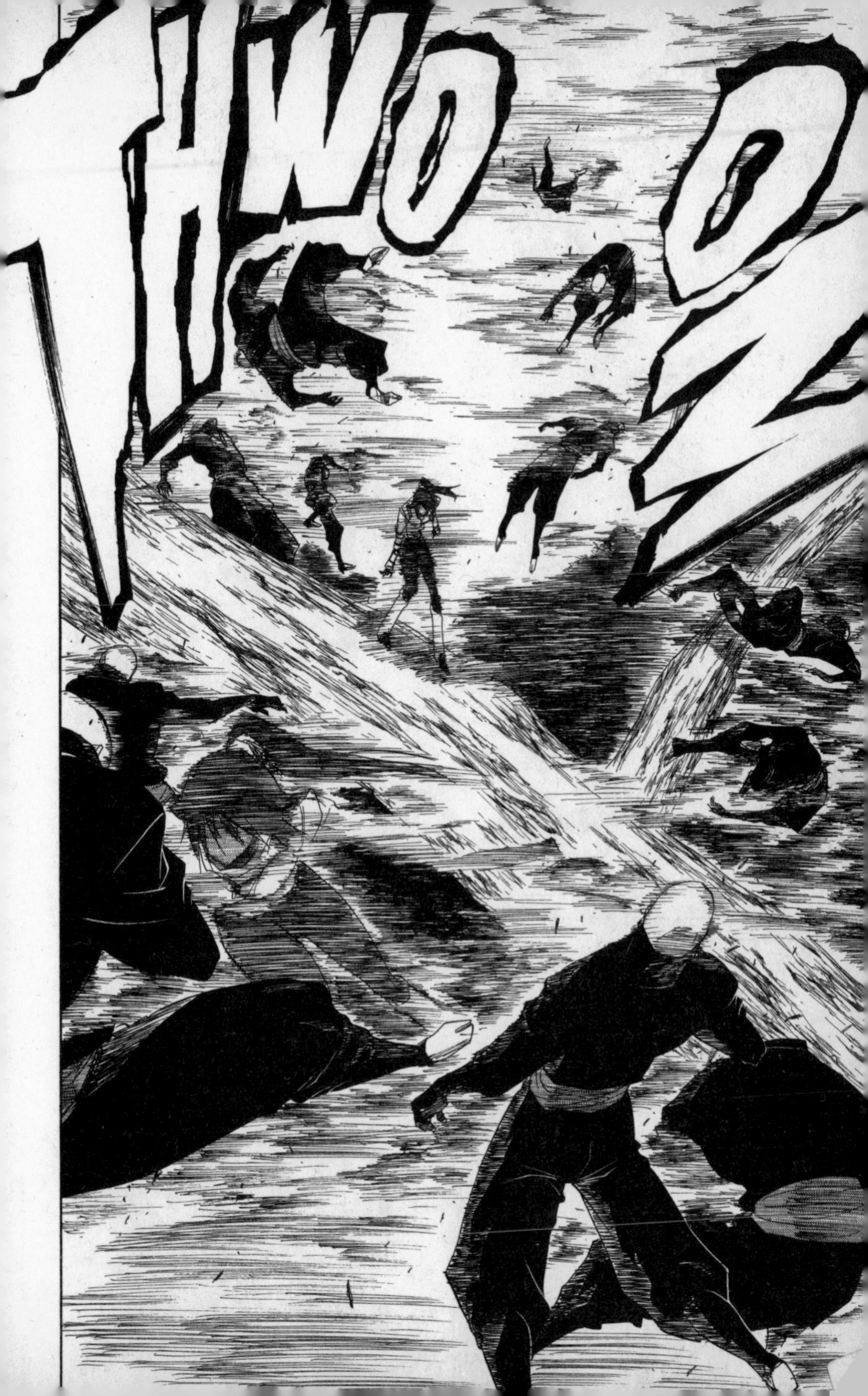

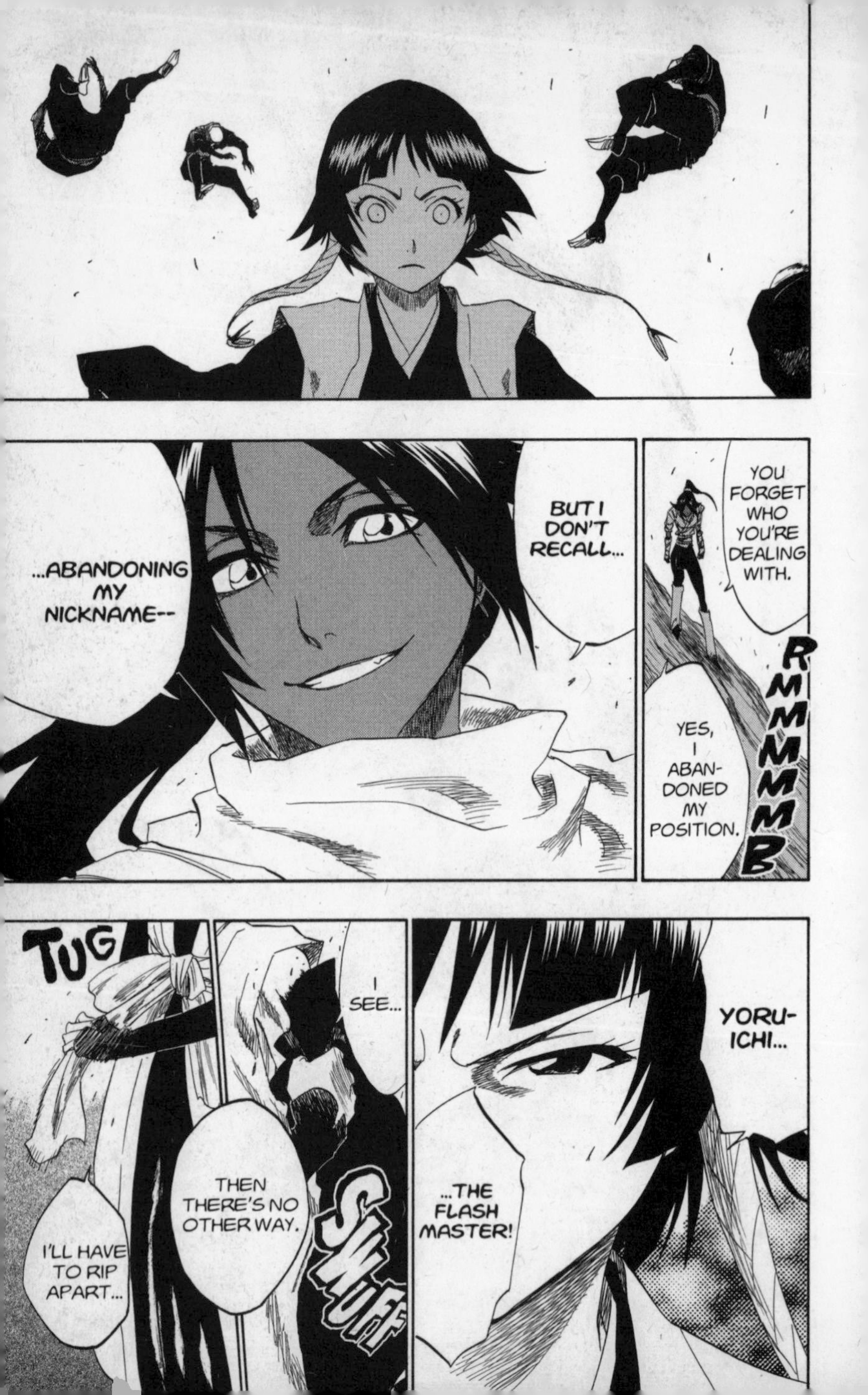
YOU FORGET WHO YOU'RE DEALING WITH.
YES, I ABAN-DONED MY POSITION.
RMMMMMB
BUT I DON'T RECALL...
...ABANDONING MY NICKNAME--
YORU-ICHI...
...THE FLASH MASTER!
I SEE...
THEN THERE'S NO OTHER WAY.
SWUFF
TUG
I'LL HAVE TO RIP APART...

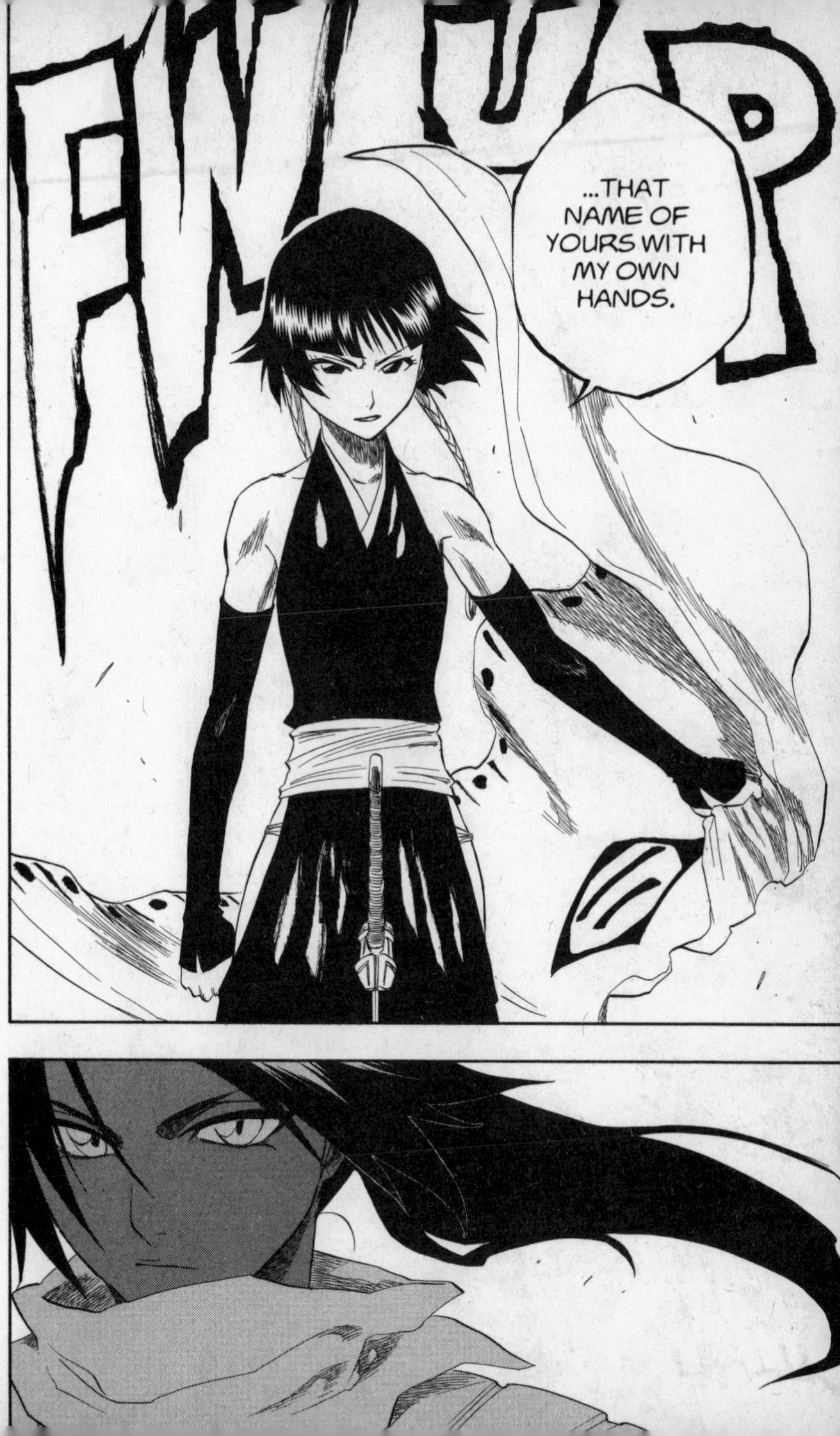
...THAT NAME OF YOURS WITH MY OWN HANDS.

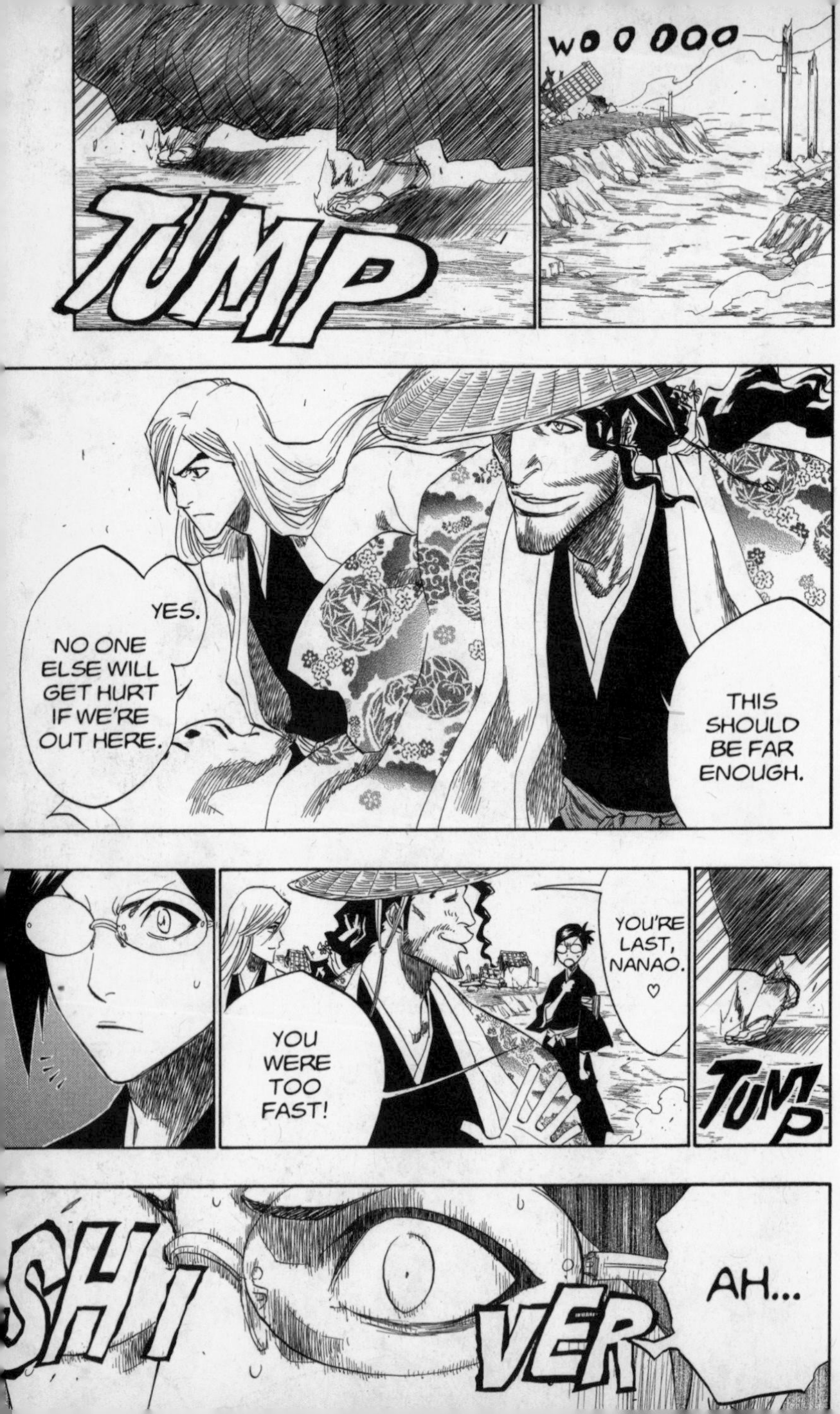
WOOOOO
TUMP
THIS SHOULD BE FAR ENOUGH.
YES. NO ONE ELSE WILL GET HURT IF WE'RE OUT HERE.
TUMP
YOU'RE LAST, NANAO. ♡
YOU WERE TOO FAST!
AH...
SHIVER

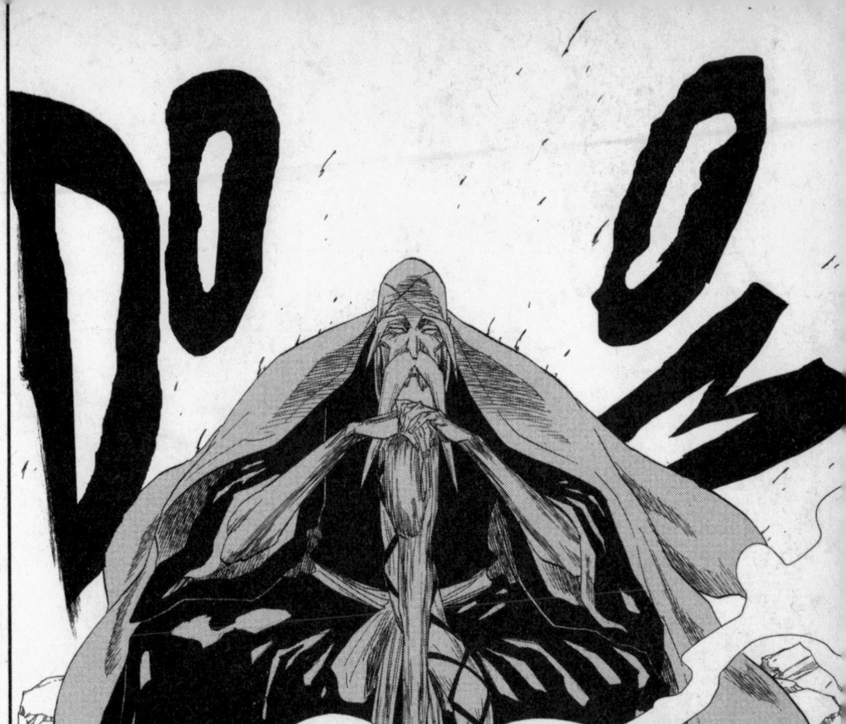
DOOM
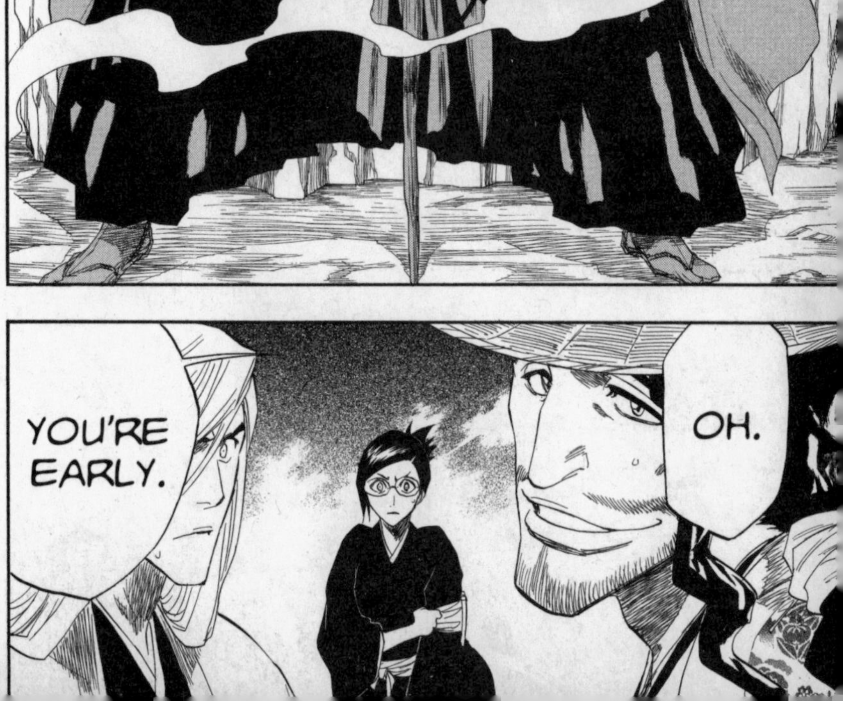
OH.
YOU'RE EARLY.

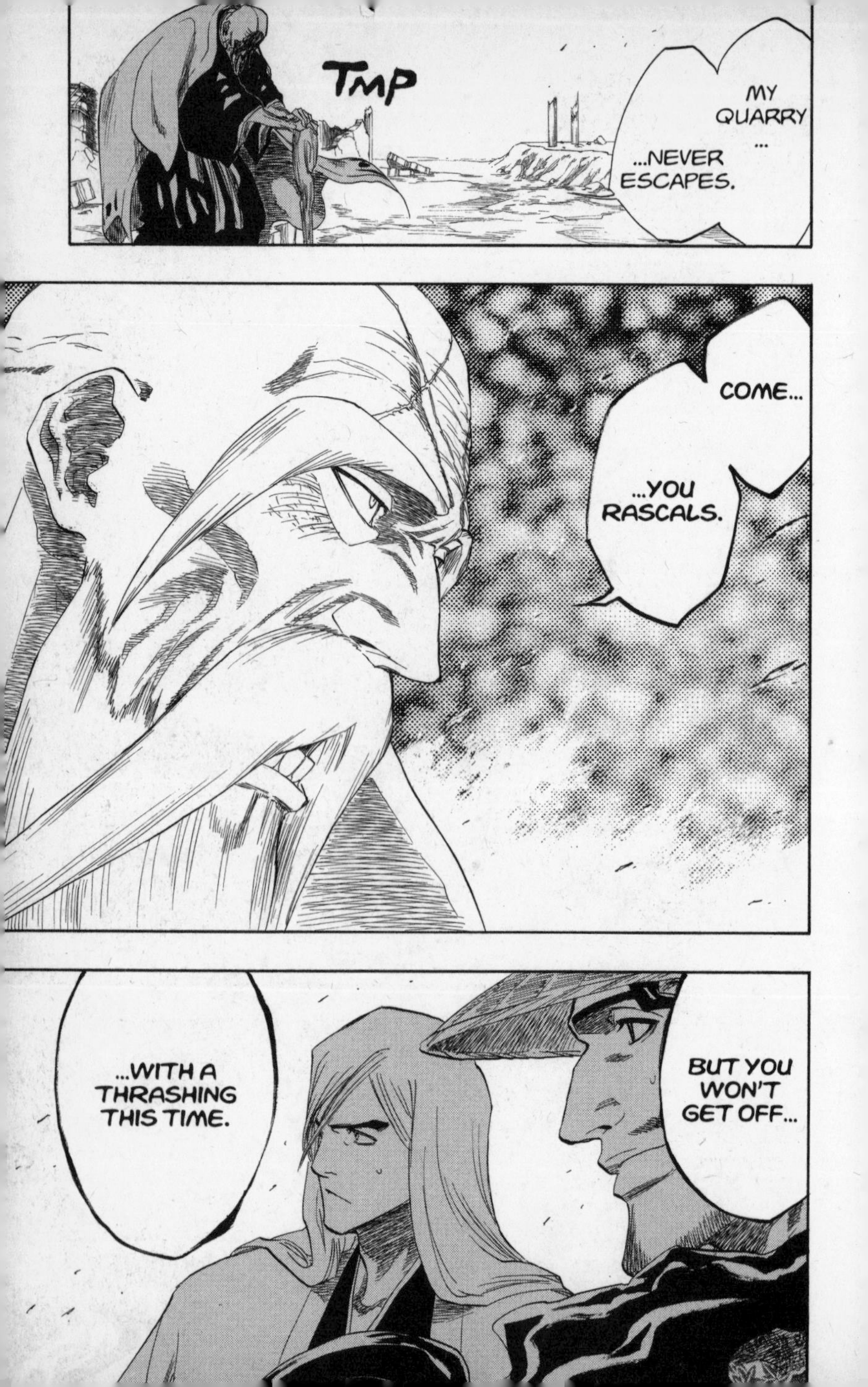
MY QUARRY ...
...NEVER ESCAPES.
TMP
COME...
...YOU RASCALS.
BUT YOU WON'T GET OFF...
...WITH A THRASHING THIS TIME.

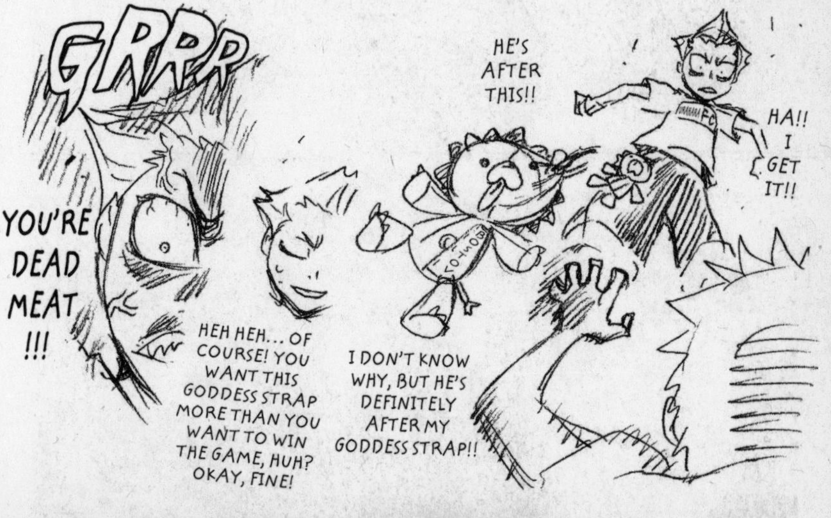
HA!! I GET IT!!
HE'S AFTER THIS!!
GRRR
I DON'T KNOW WHY, BUT HE'S DEFINITELY AFTER MY GODDESS STRAP!!
HEH HEH... OF COURSE! YOU WANT THIS GODDESS STRAP MORE THAN YOU WANT TO WIN THE GAME, HUH? OKAY, FINE!
YOU'RE DEAD MEAT!!!

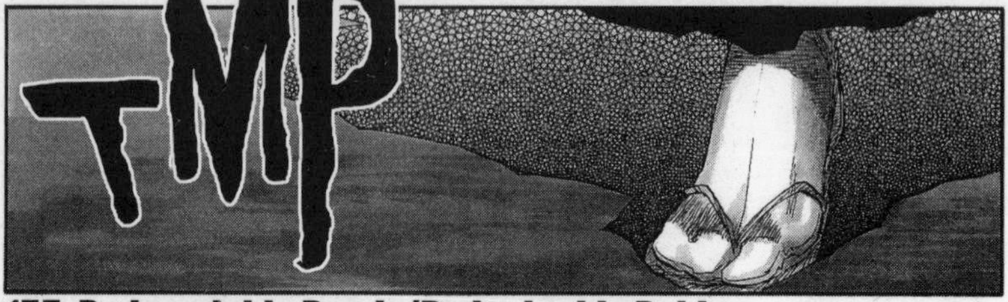
TMP

155: Redoundable Deeds/Redoubtable Babies

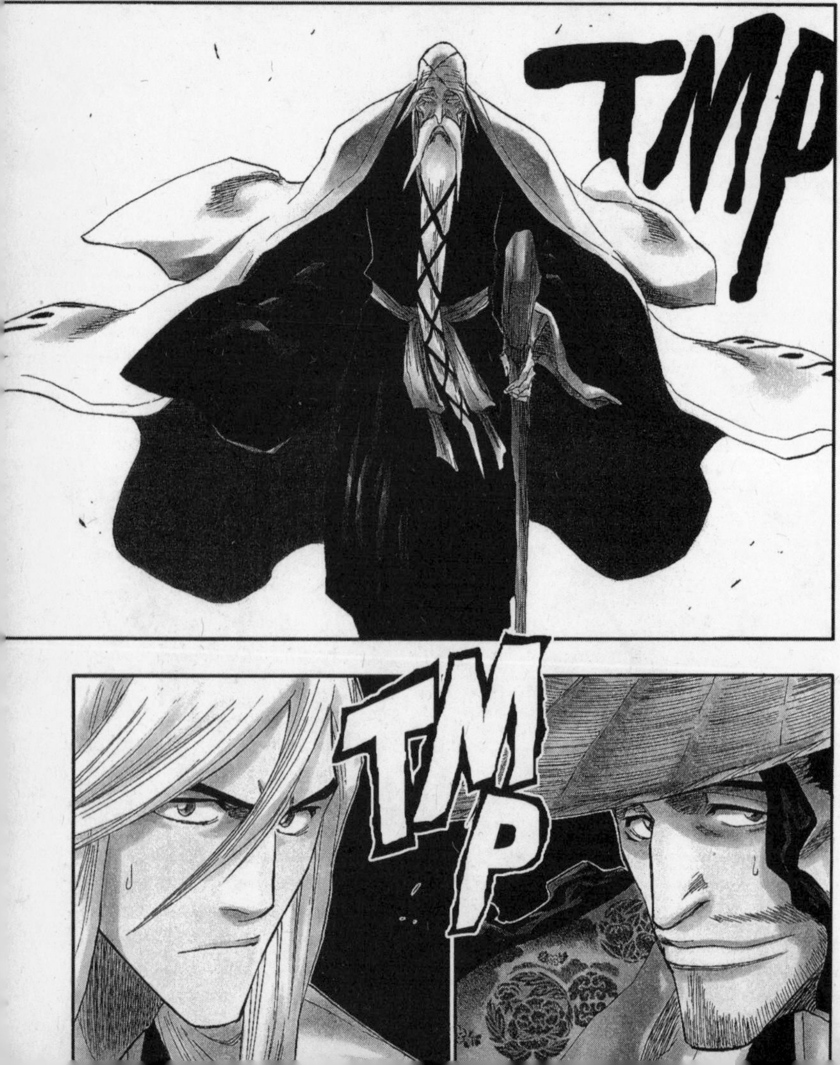
TMP
TMP

Redoundable Deeds/ Redoubtable Babies

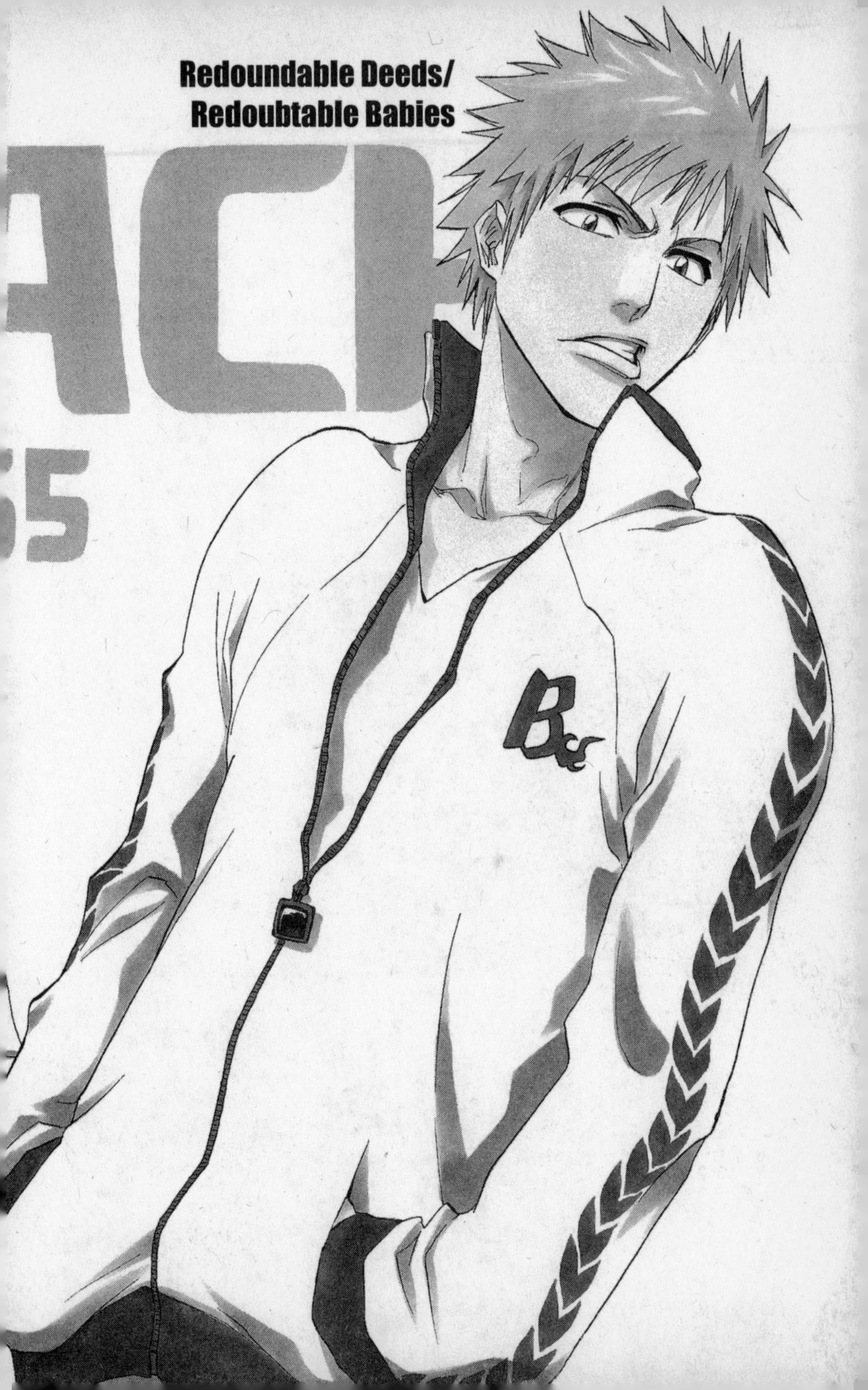

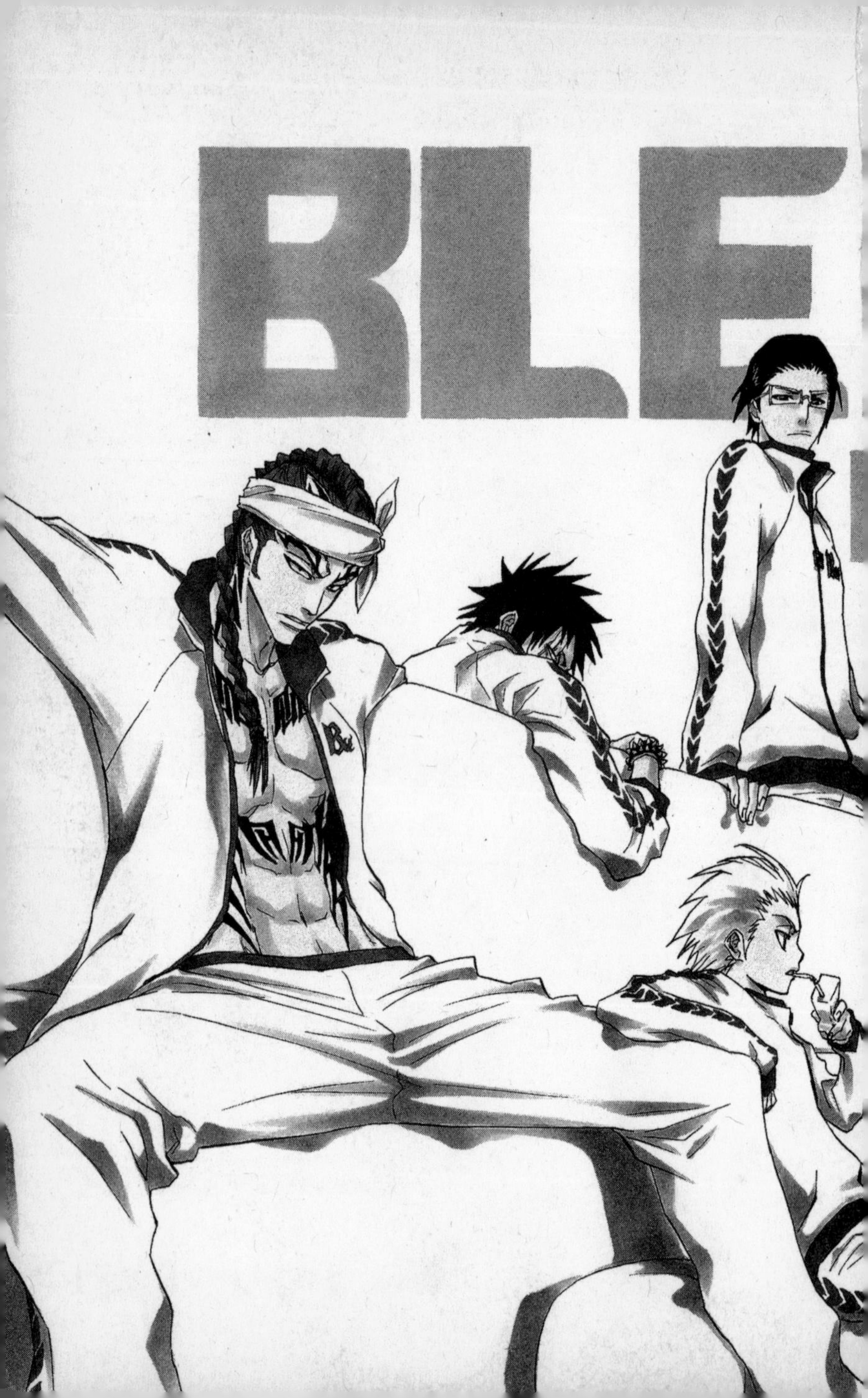
BLE

BLEACH
ブリーチ

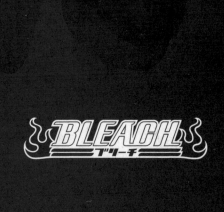

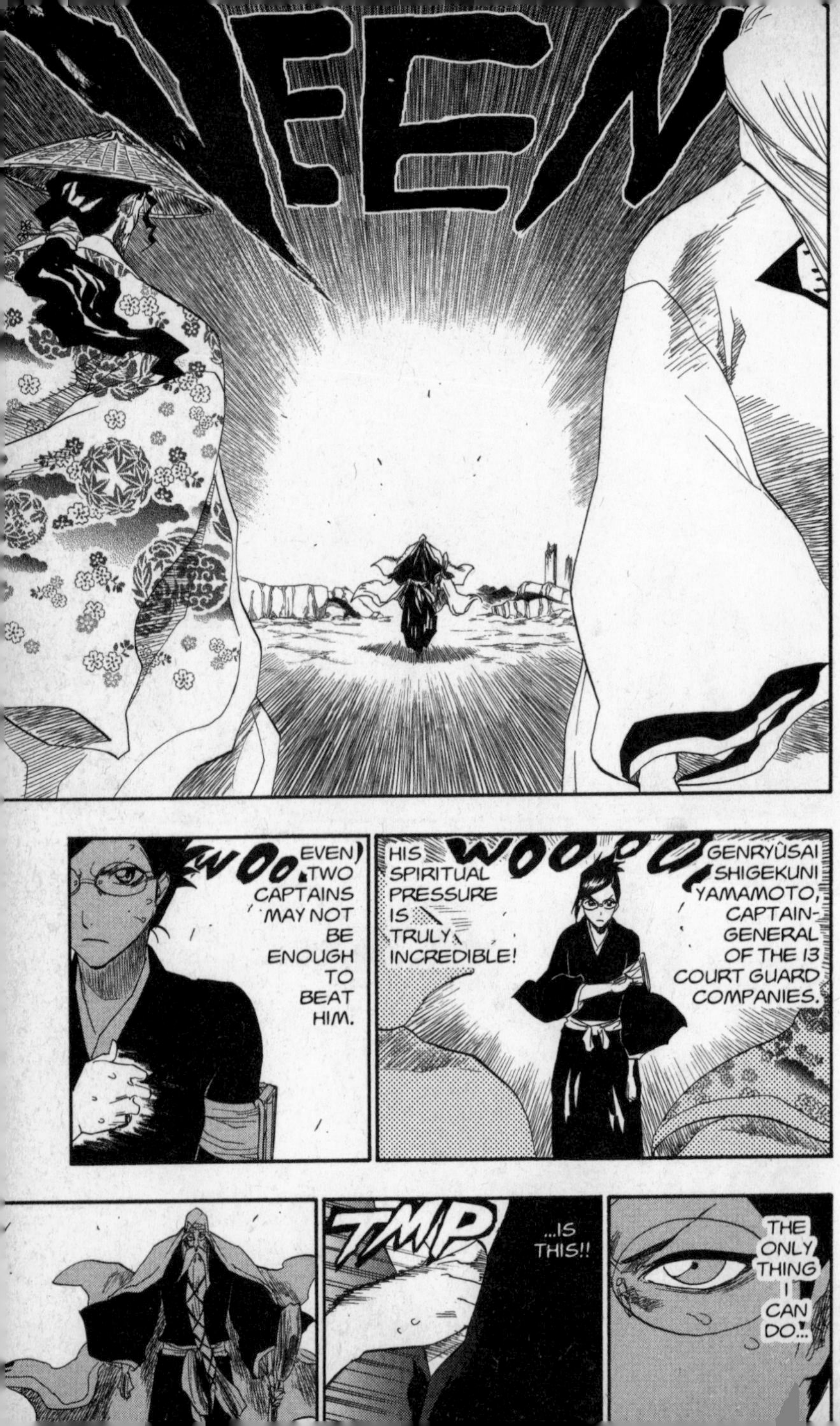
EEN
WOOOO
GENRYÛSAI SHIGEKUNI YAMAMOTO, CAPTAIN-GENERAL OF THE 13 COURT GUARD COMPANIES.
HIS SPIRITUAL PRESSURE IS TRULY INCREDIBLE!
WOO
EVEN TWO CAPTAINS MAY NOT BE ENOUGH TO BEAT HIM.
THE ONLY THING I CAN DO...
TMP
...IS THIS!!

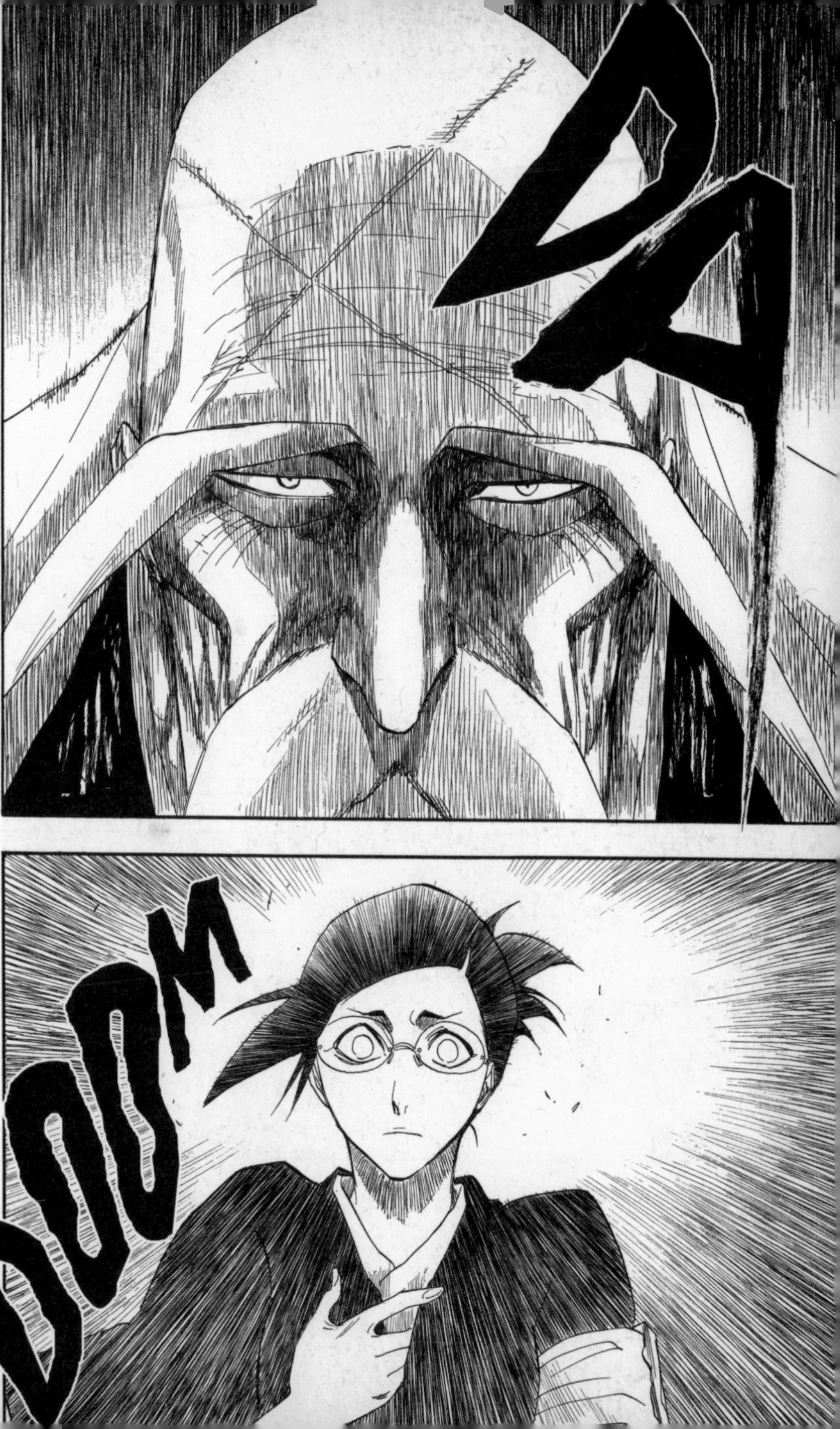
DA
DOOM

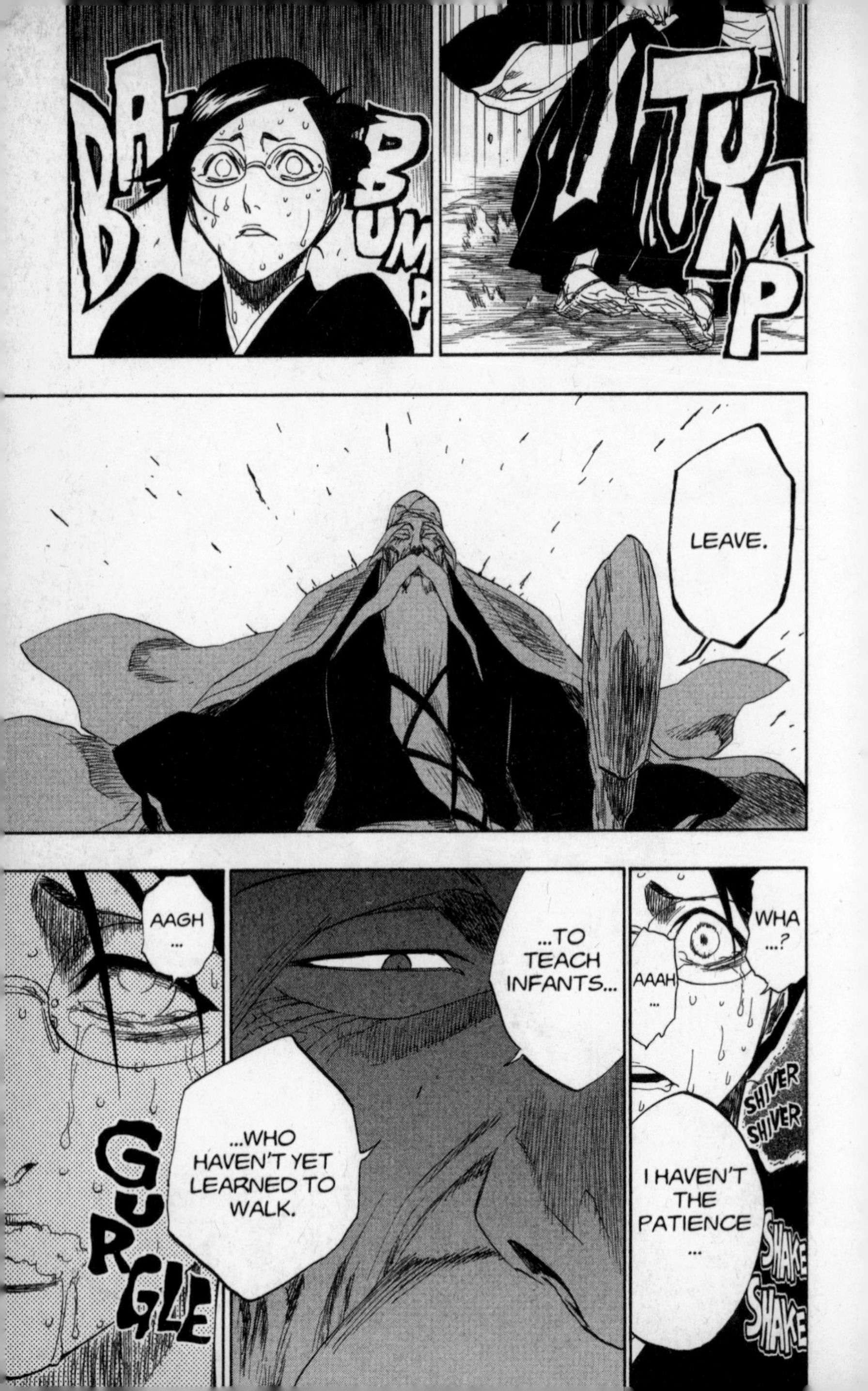
TUMP
BUMP
LEAVE.
WHA ...?
AAAH ...
I HAVEN'T THE PATIENCE ...
SHIVER SHIVER
SHAKE SHAKE
...TO TEACH INFANTS...
...WHO HAVEN'T YET LEARNED TO WALK.
AAGH ...
GURGLE

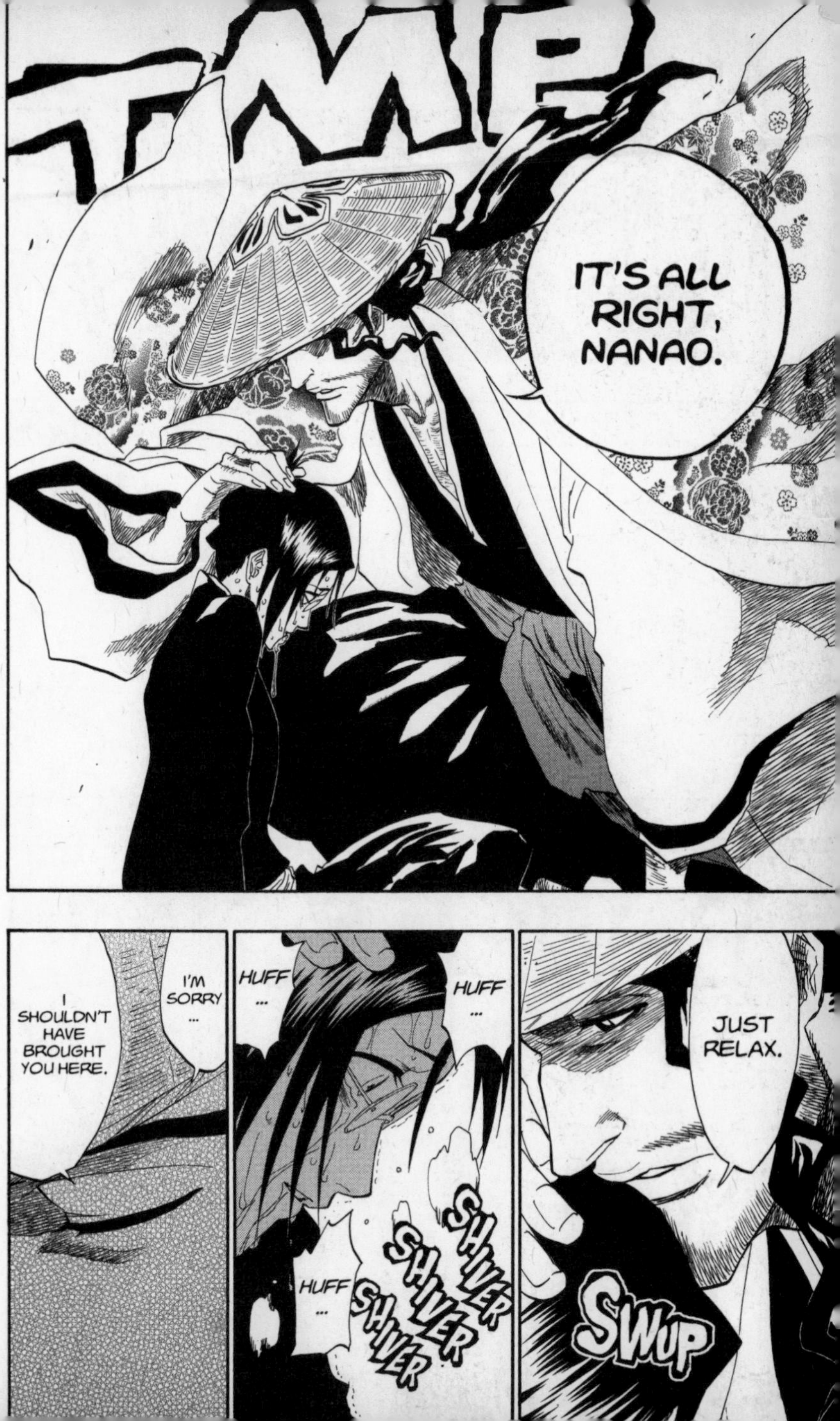
TMP
IT'S ALL RIGHT, NANAO.
JUST RELAX.
SWUP
HUFF ...
HUFF ...
SHIVER SHIVER SHIVER
HUFF ...
I'M SORRY ...
I SHOULDN'T HAVE BROUGHT YOU HERE.

READ THIS WAY

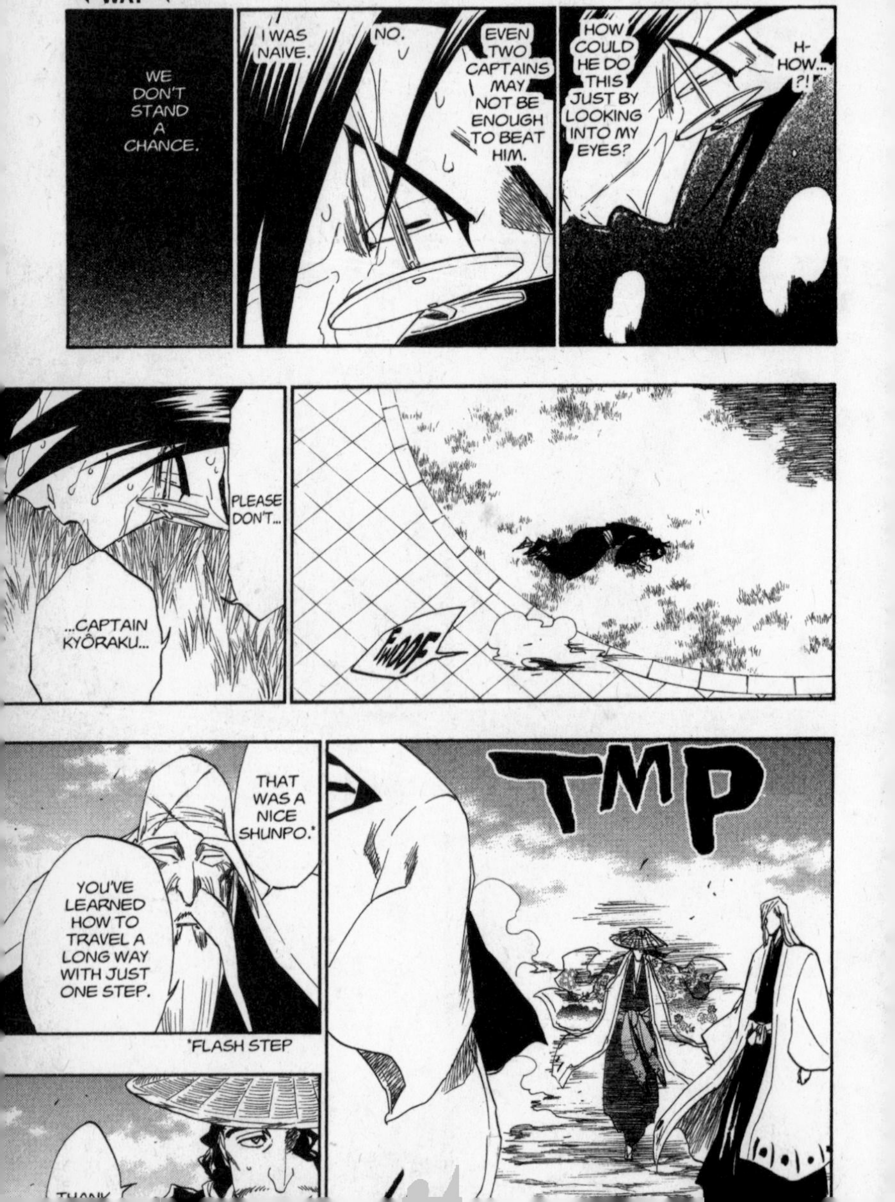

H-HOW...?!
HOW COULD HE DO THIS JUST BY LOOKING INTO MY EYES?
EVEN TWO CAPTAINS MAY NOT BE ENOUGH TO BEAT HIM.
NO.
I WAS NAIVE.
WE DON'T STAND A CHANCE.
FWOOF
PLEASE DON'T...
...CAPTAIN KYÔRAKU...
TMP
THAT WAS A NICE SHUNPO.*
YOU'VE LEARNED HOW TO TRAVEL A LONG WAY WITH JUST ONE STEP.
*FLASH STEP
THANK

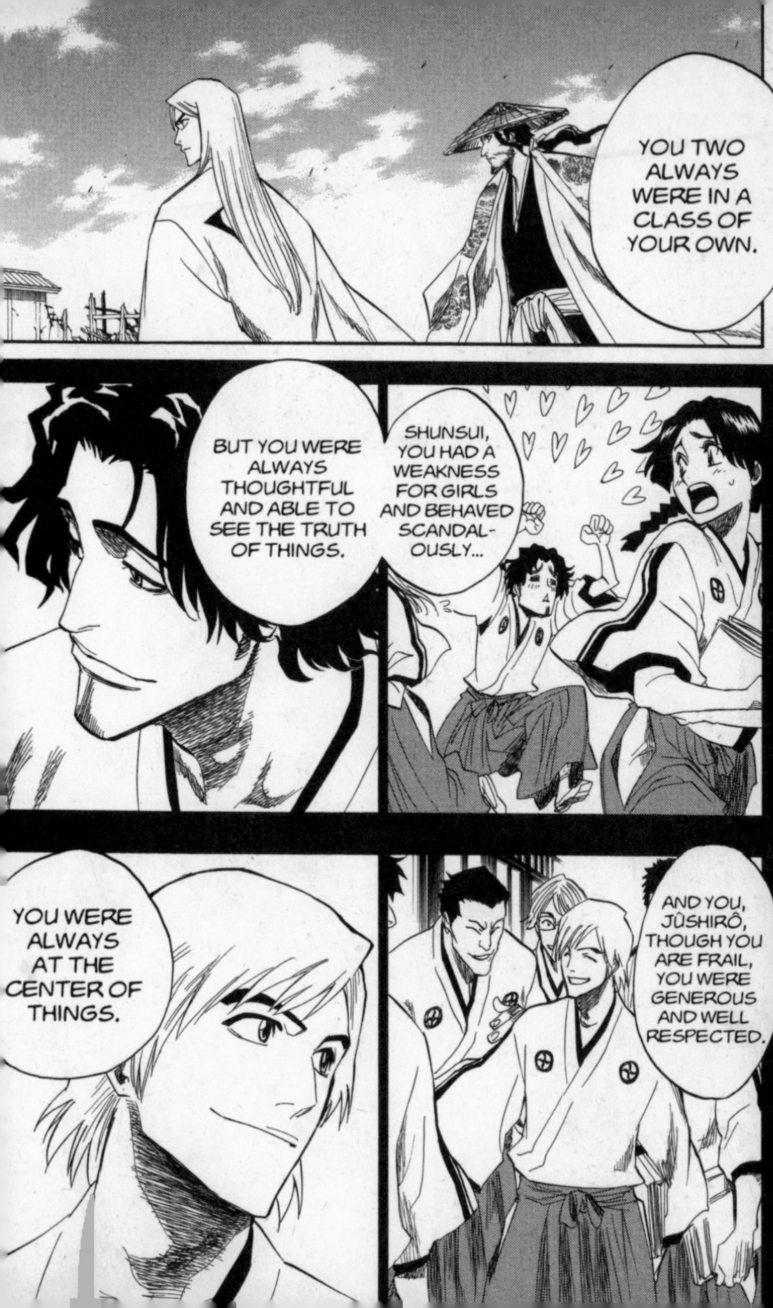
YOU TWO ALWAYS WERE IN A CLASS OF YOUR OWN.
SHUNSUI, YOU HAD A WEAKNESS FOR GIRLS AND BEHAVED SCANDAL-OUSLY...
BUT YOU WERE ALWAYS THOUGHTFUL AND ABLE TO SEE THE TRUTH OF THINGS.
AND YOU, JÛSHIRÔ, THOUGH YOU ARE FRAIL, YOU WERE GENEROUS AND WELL RESPECTED.
YOU WERE ALWAYS AT THE CENTER OF THINGS.

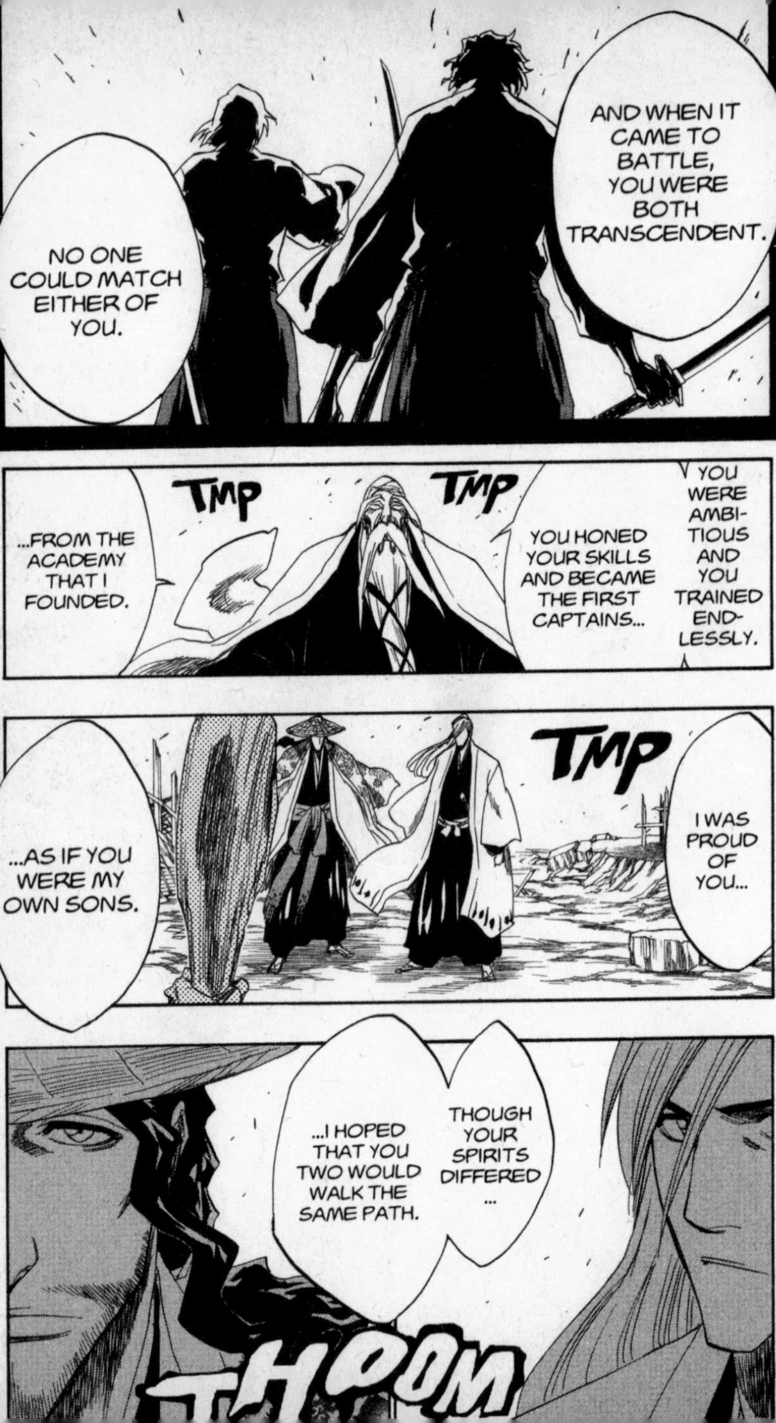
AND WHEN IT CAME TO BATTLE, YOU WERE BOTH TRANSCENDENT.
NO ONE COULD MATCH EITHER OF YOU.
YOU WERE AMBI-TIOUS AND YOU TRAINED END-LESSLY.
TMP
YOU HONED YOUR SKILLS AND BECAME THE FIRST CAPTAINS...
TMP
...FROM THE ACADEMY THAT I FOUNDED.
TMP
I WAS PROUD OF YOU...
...AS IF YOU WERE MY OWN SONS.
THOUGH YOUR SPIRITS DIFFERED ...
...I HOPED THAT YOU TWO WOULD WALK THE SAME PATH.
THOOM

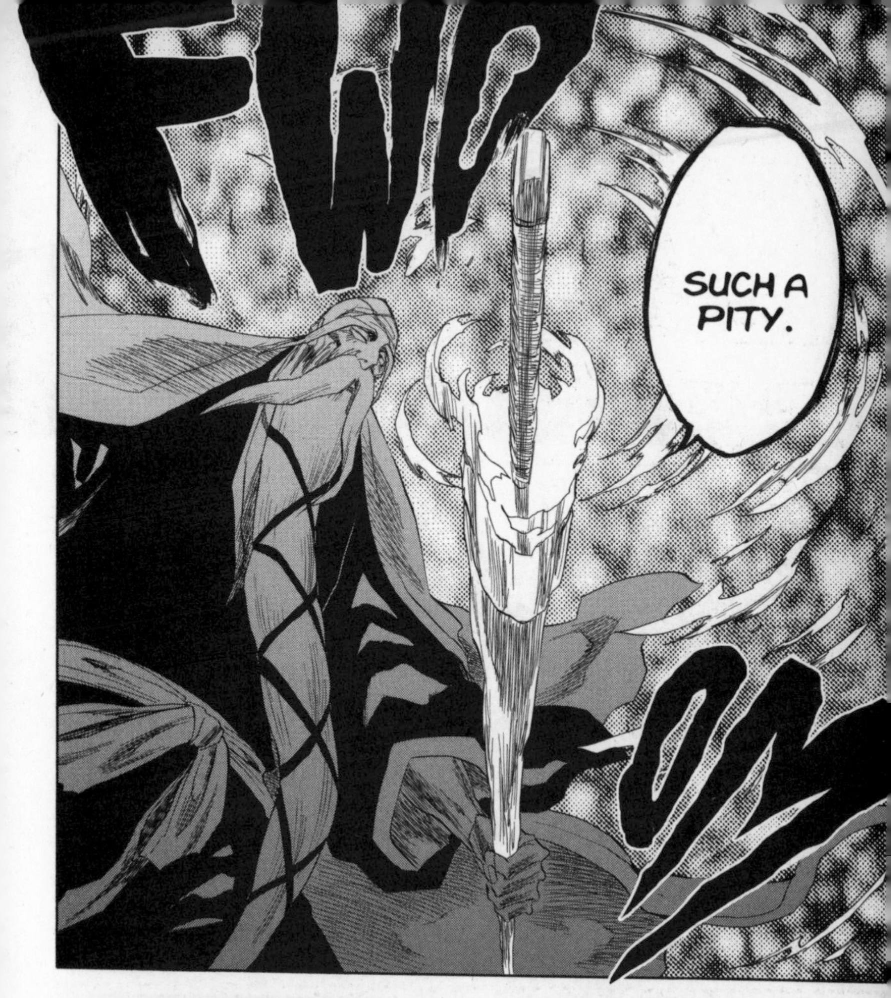
SUCH A PITY.

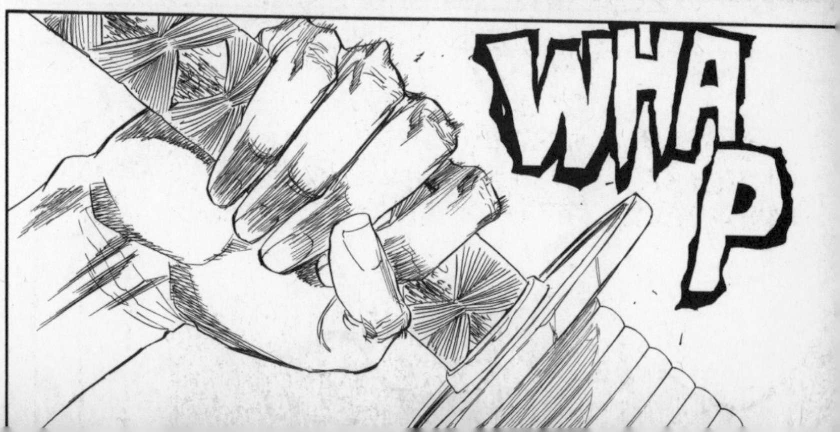
WHAP

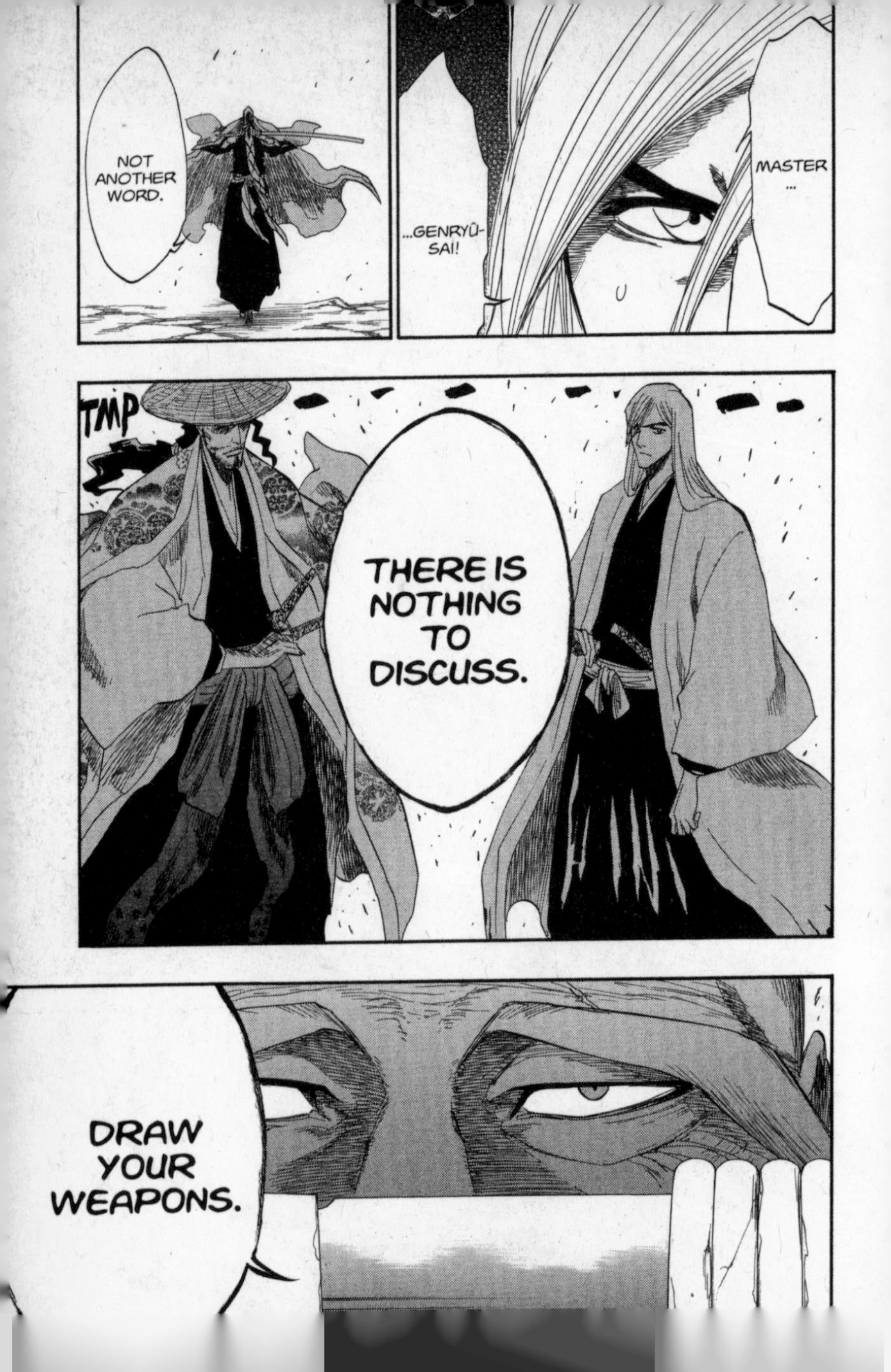
MASTER ...
...GENRYÛ-SAI!
NOT ANOTHER WORD.
THERE IS NOTHING TO DISCUSS.
TMP
DRAW YOUR WEAPONS.

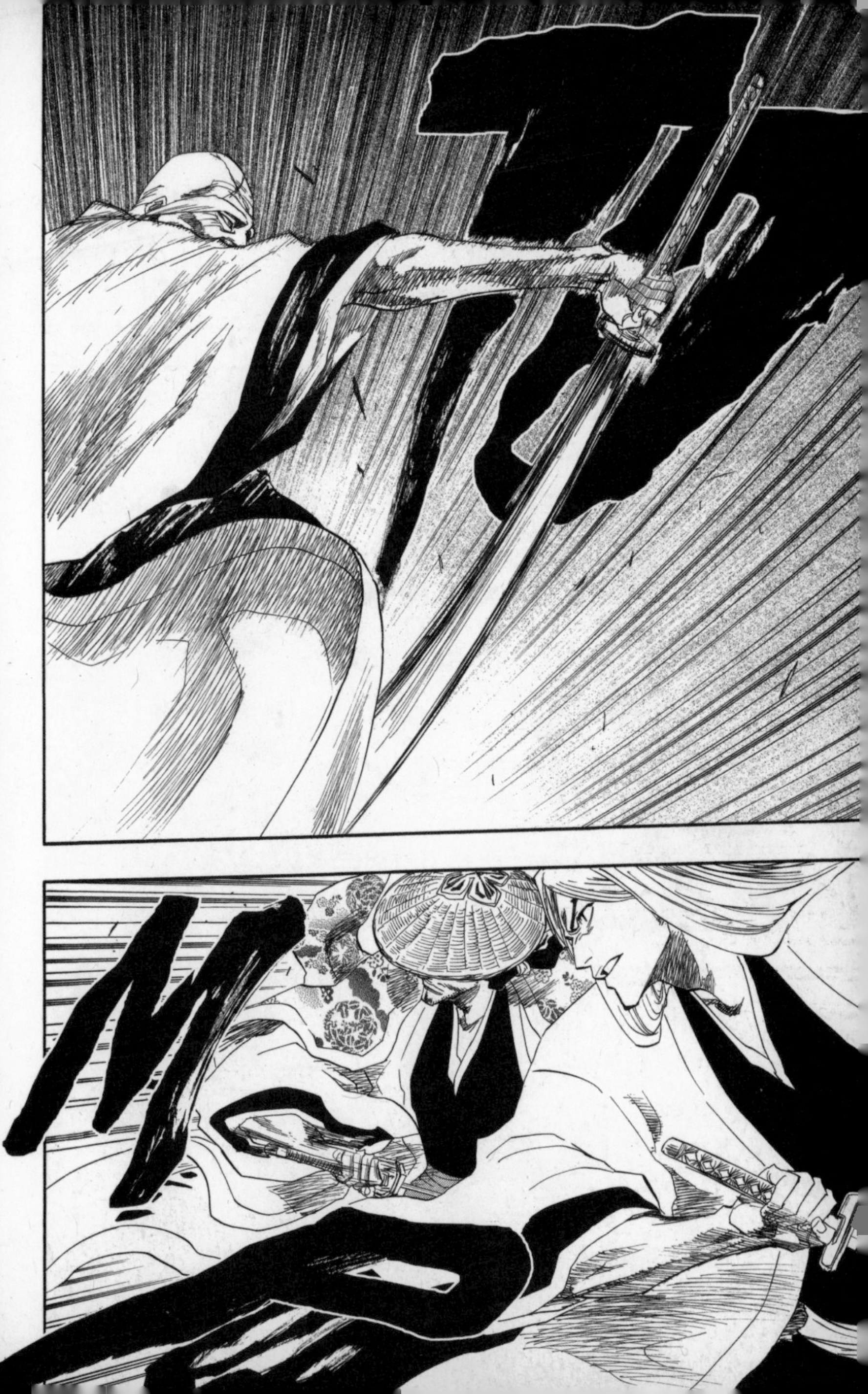

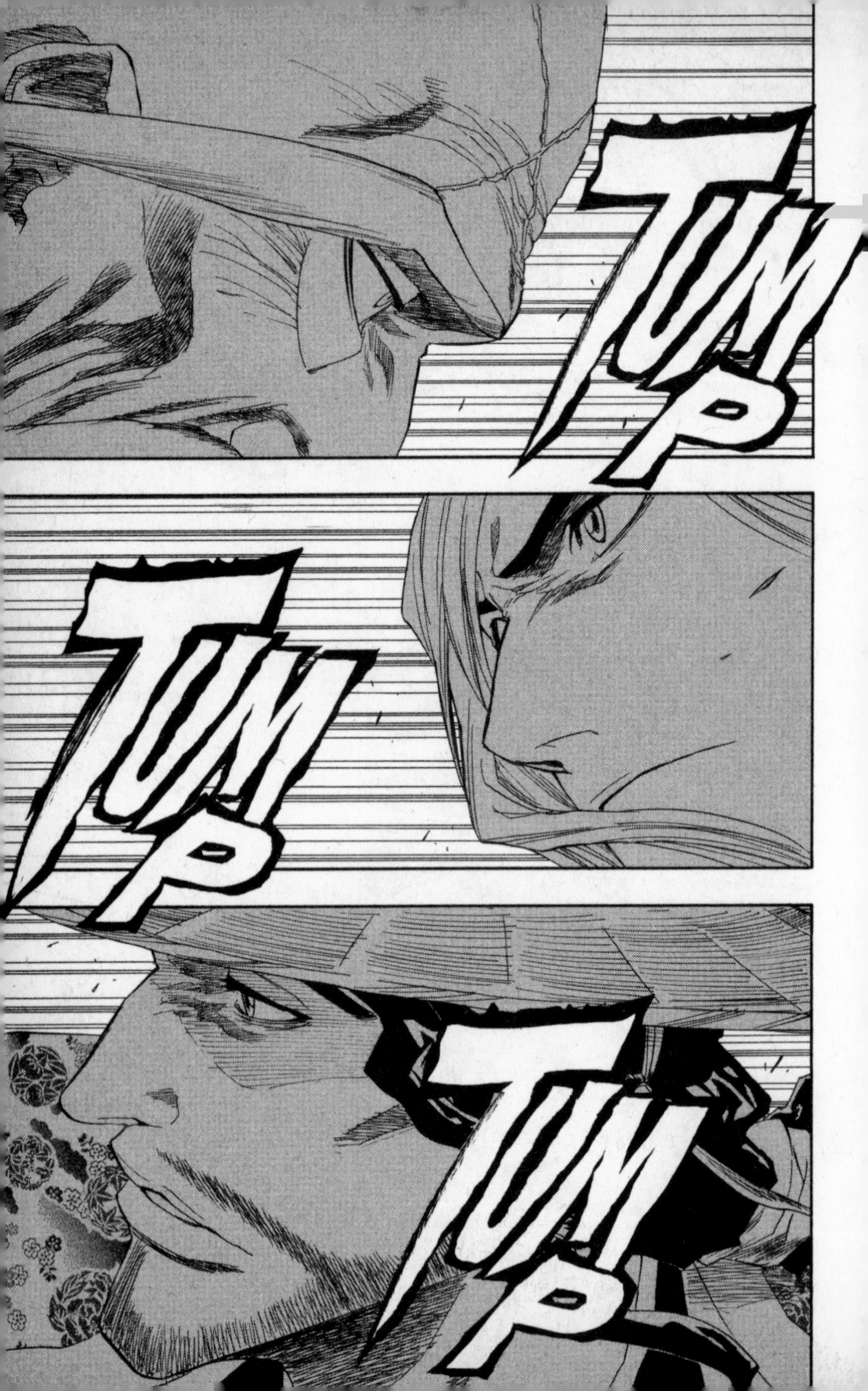
TUMP
TUMP
TUMP

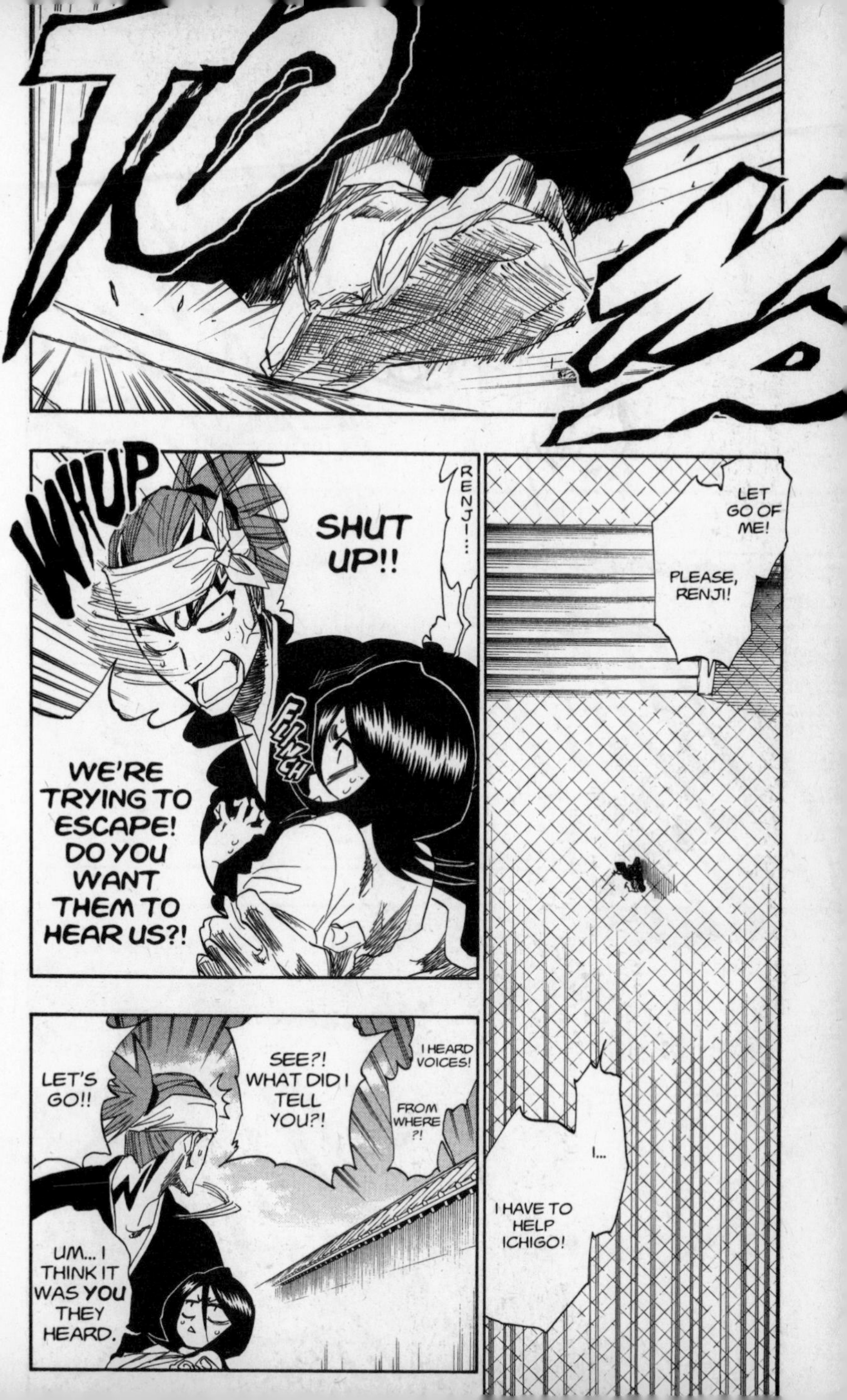
LET GO OF ME!
PLEASE, RENJI!
I...
I HAVE TO HELP ICHIGO!
RENJI...
SHUT UP!!
WHUP
FLINCH
WE'RE TRYING TO ESCAPE! DO YOU WANT THEM TO HEAR US?!
I HEARD VOICES!
FROM WHERE?!
SEE?! WHAT DID I TELL YOU?!
LET'S GO!!
UM... I THINK IT WAS YOU THEY HEARD.

...ICHIGO.

THAT JERK...

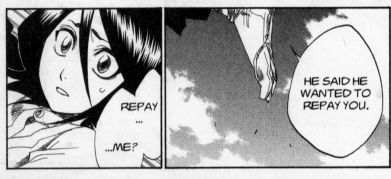

REPAY ... ...ME?

HE SAID HE WANTED TO REPAY YOU.

HE SAID, "RUKIA...

RUKIA SAVED MY LIFE.

YEAH.

"I BECAME A SOUL REAPER BECAUSE OF HER."

"CHANGED ...

"...MY FATE.

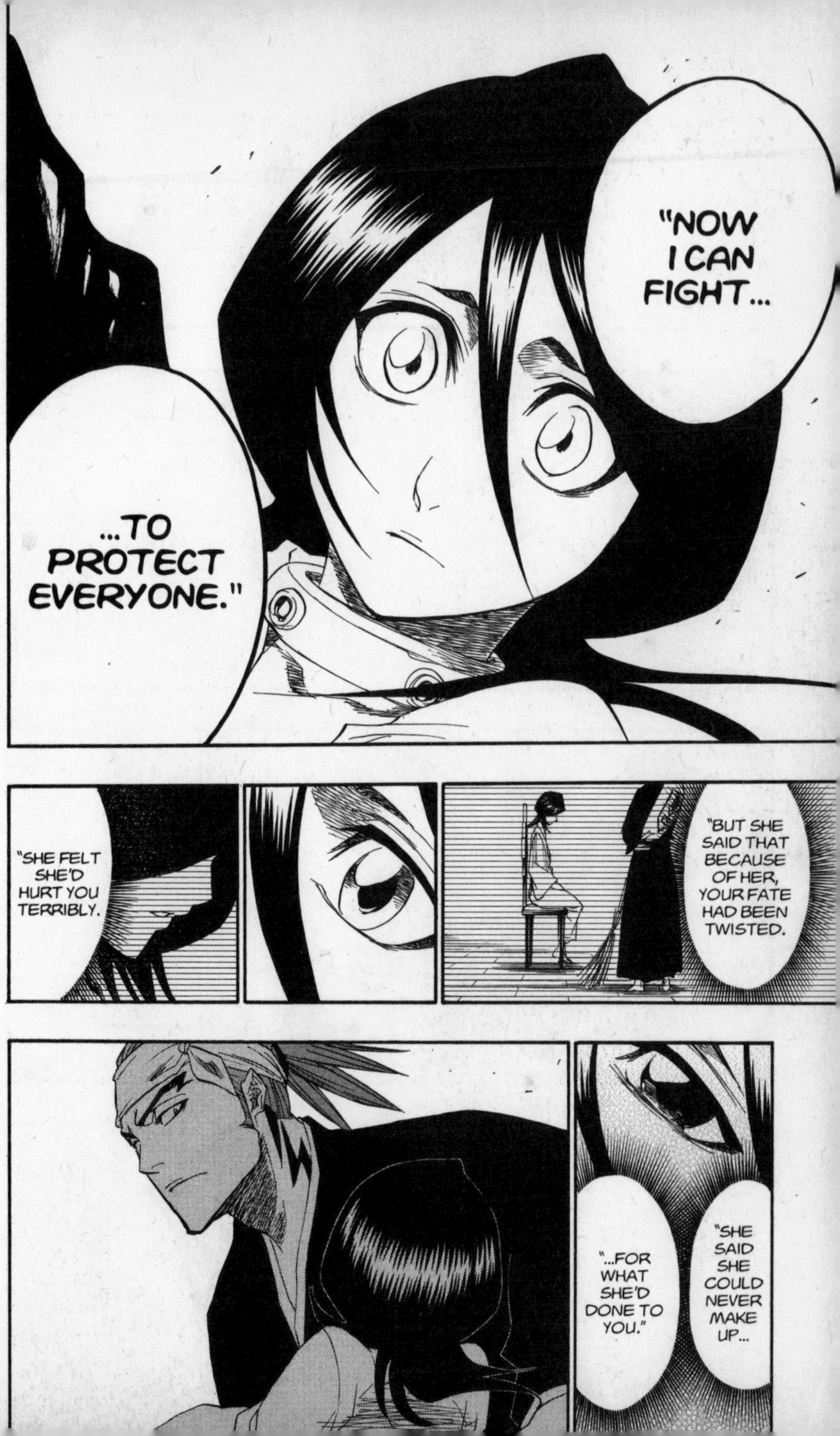
"NOW I CAN FIGHT...
...TO PROTECT EVERYONE."
"BUT SHE SAID THAT BECAUSE OF HER, YOUR FATE HAD BEEN TWISTED.
"SHE FELT SHE'D HURT YOU TERRIBLY.
"SHE SAID SHE COULD NEVER MAKE UP...
"...FOR WHAT SHE'D DONE TO YOU."

READ THIS WAY

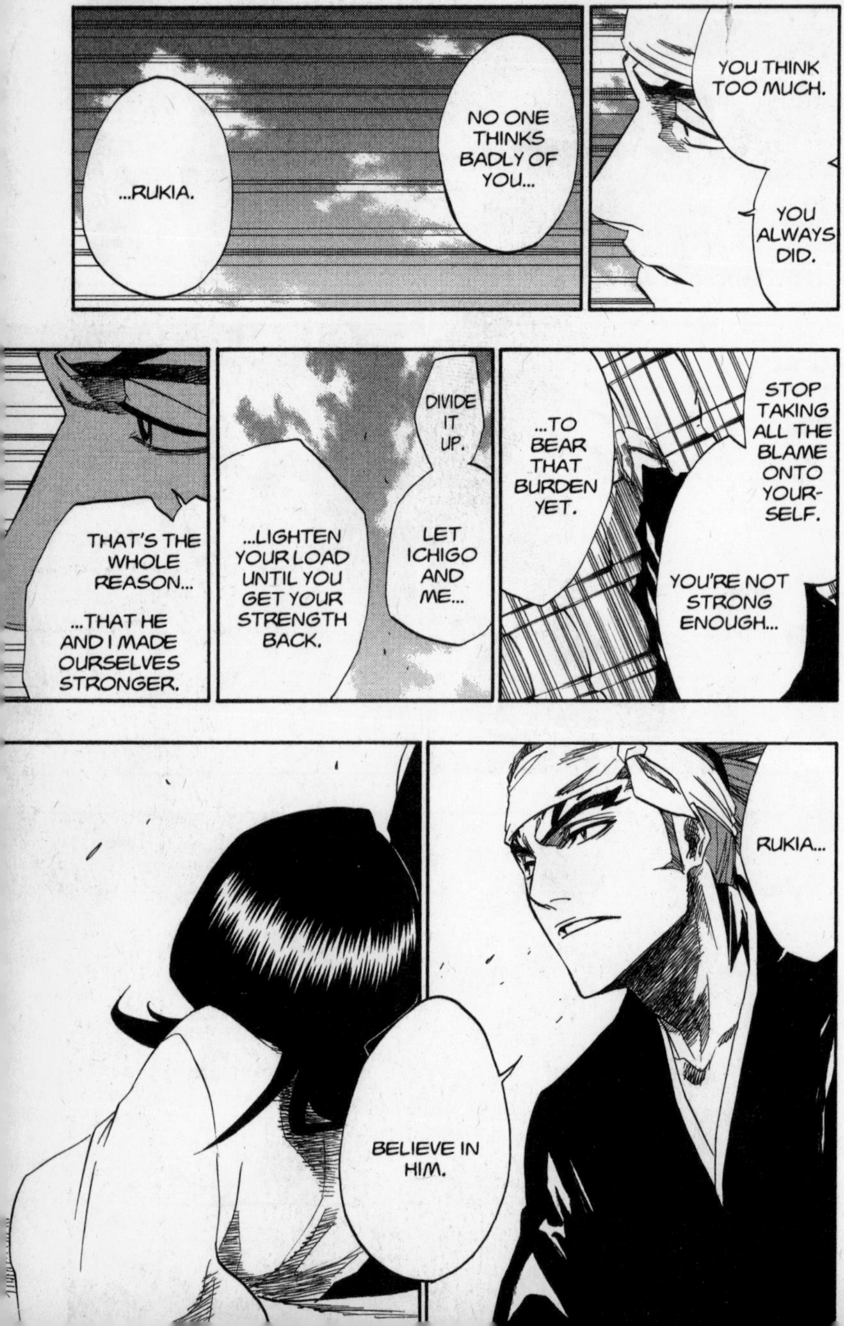
YOU THINK TOO MUCH.
YOU ALWAYS DID.
NO ONE THINKS BADLY OF YOU...
...RUKIA.
STOP TAKING ALL THE BLAME ONTO YOURSELF.
YOU'RE NOT STRONG ENOUGH...
...TO BEAR THAT BURDEN YET.
DIVIDE IT UP.
LET ICHIGO AND ME...
...LIGHTEN YOUR LOAD UNTIL YOU GET YOUR STRENGTH BACK.
THAT'S THE WHOLE REASON...
...THAT HE AND I MADE OURSELVES STRONGER.
RUKIA...
BELIEVE IN HIM.

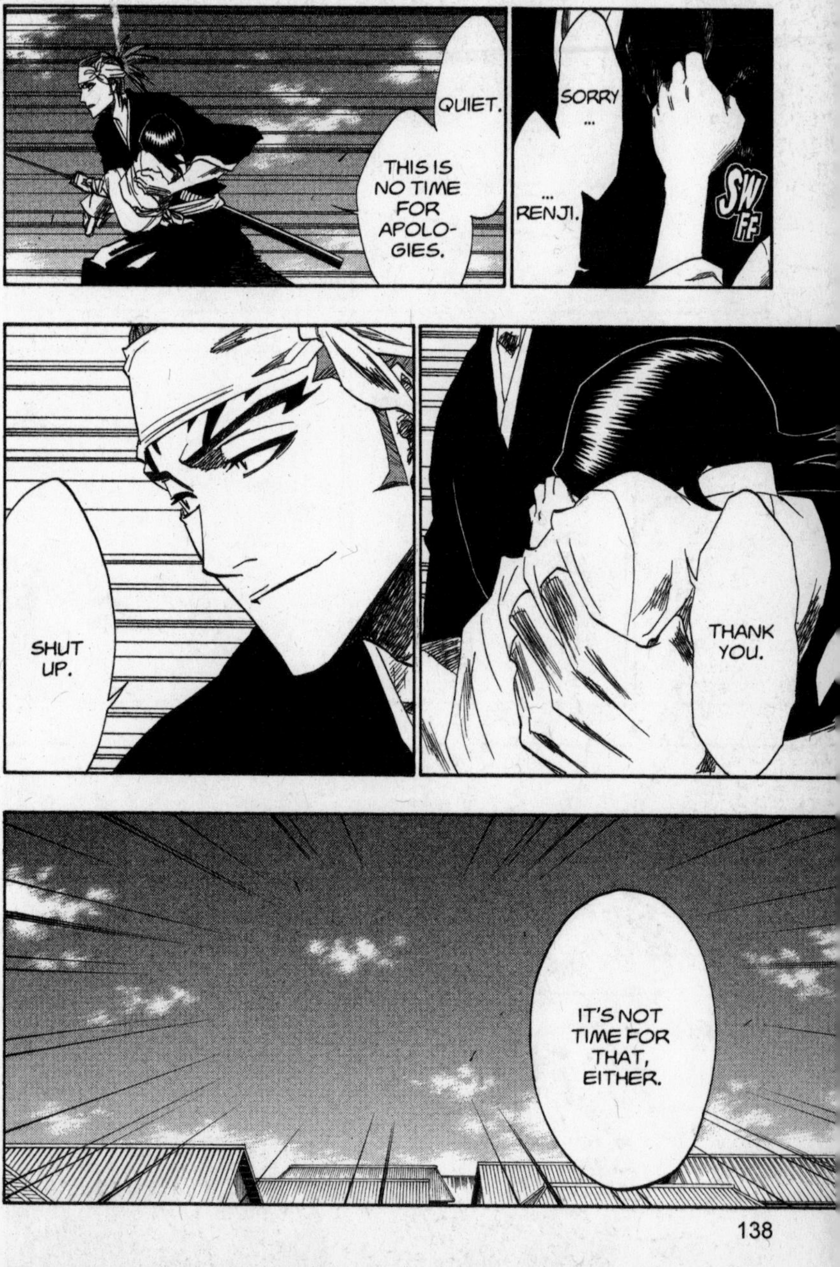
SORRY ...
... RENJI.
SWFF
QUIET.
THIS IS NO TIME FOR APOLOGIES.
THANK YOU.
SHUT UP.
IT'S NOT TIME FOR THAT, EITHER.

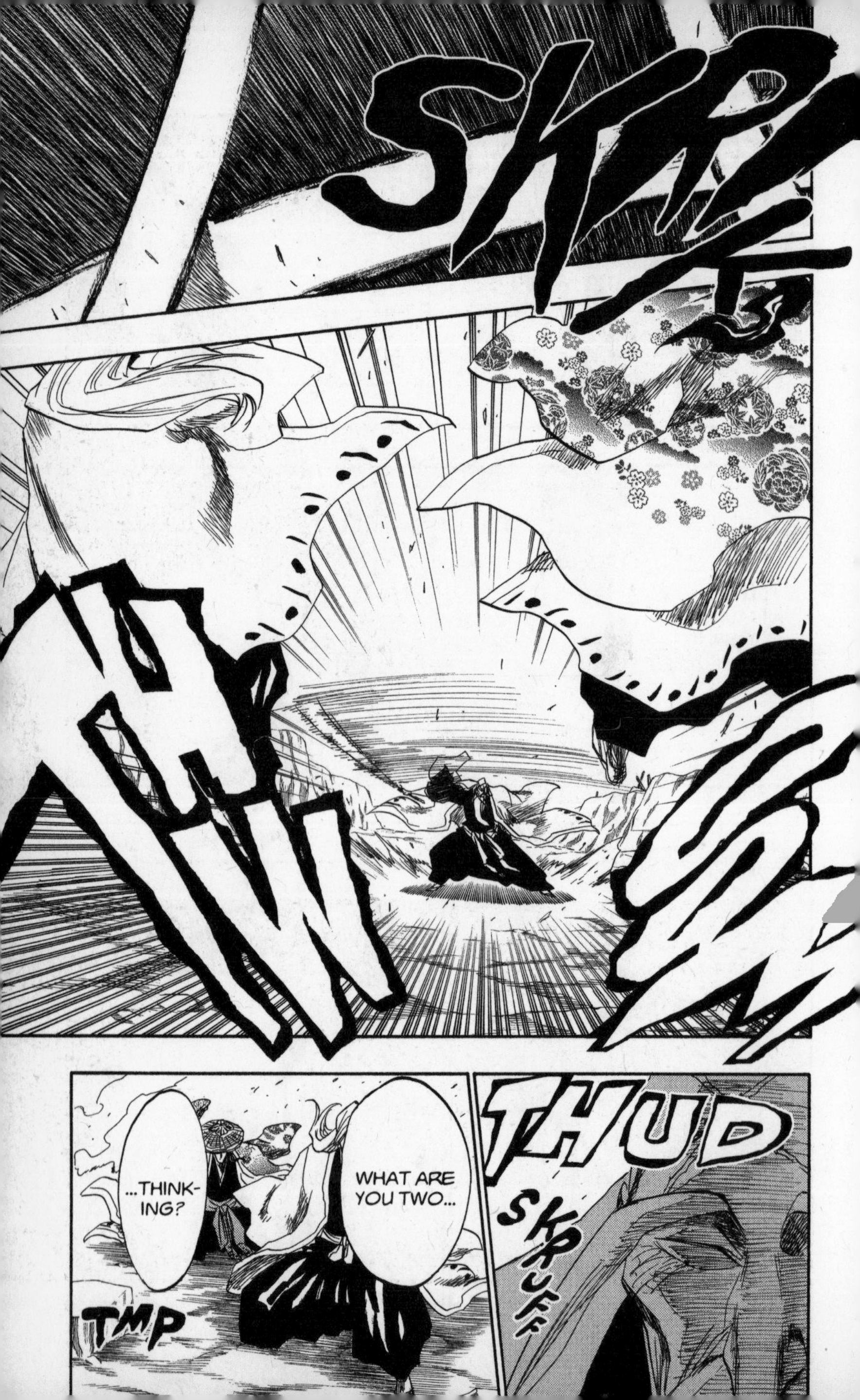
THUD
SKRUFF
WHAT ARE YOU TWO...
...THINK-
ING?
TMP

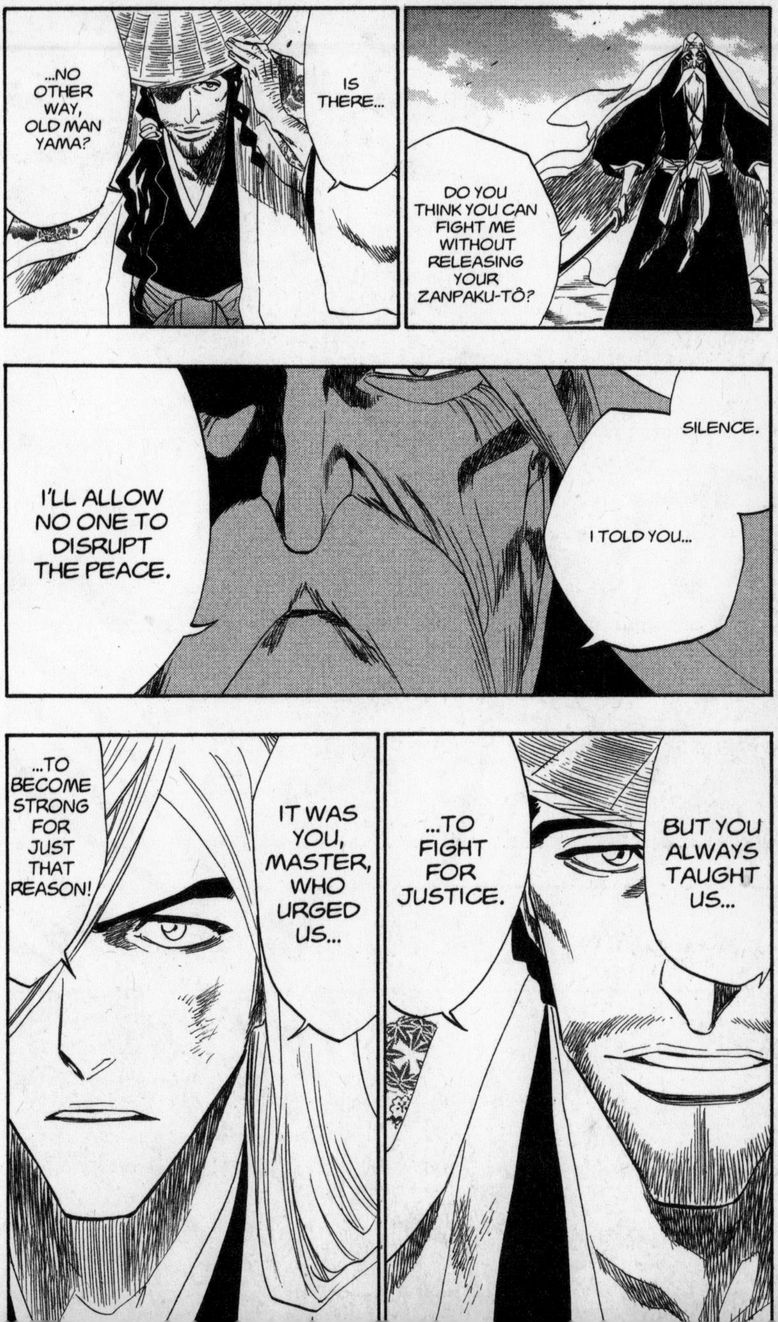
DO YOU THINK YOU CAN FIGHT ME WITHOUT RELEASING YOUR ZANPAKU-TÔ?
IS THERE...
...NO OTHER WAY, OLD MAN YAMA?
SILENCE.
I TOLD YOU...
I'LL ALLOW NO ONE TO DISRUPT THE PEACE.
BUT YOU ALWAYS TAUGHT US...
...TO FIGHT FOR JUSTICE.
IT WAS YOU, MASTER, WHO URGED US...
...TO BECOME STRONG FOR JUST THAT REASON!

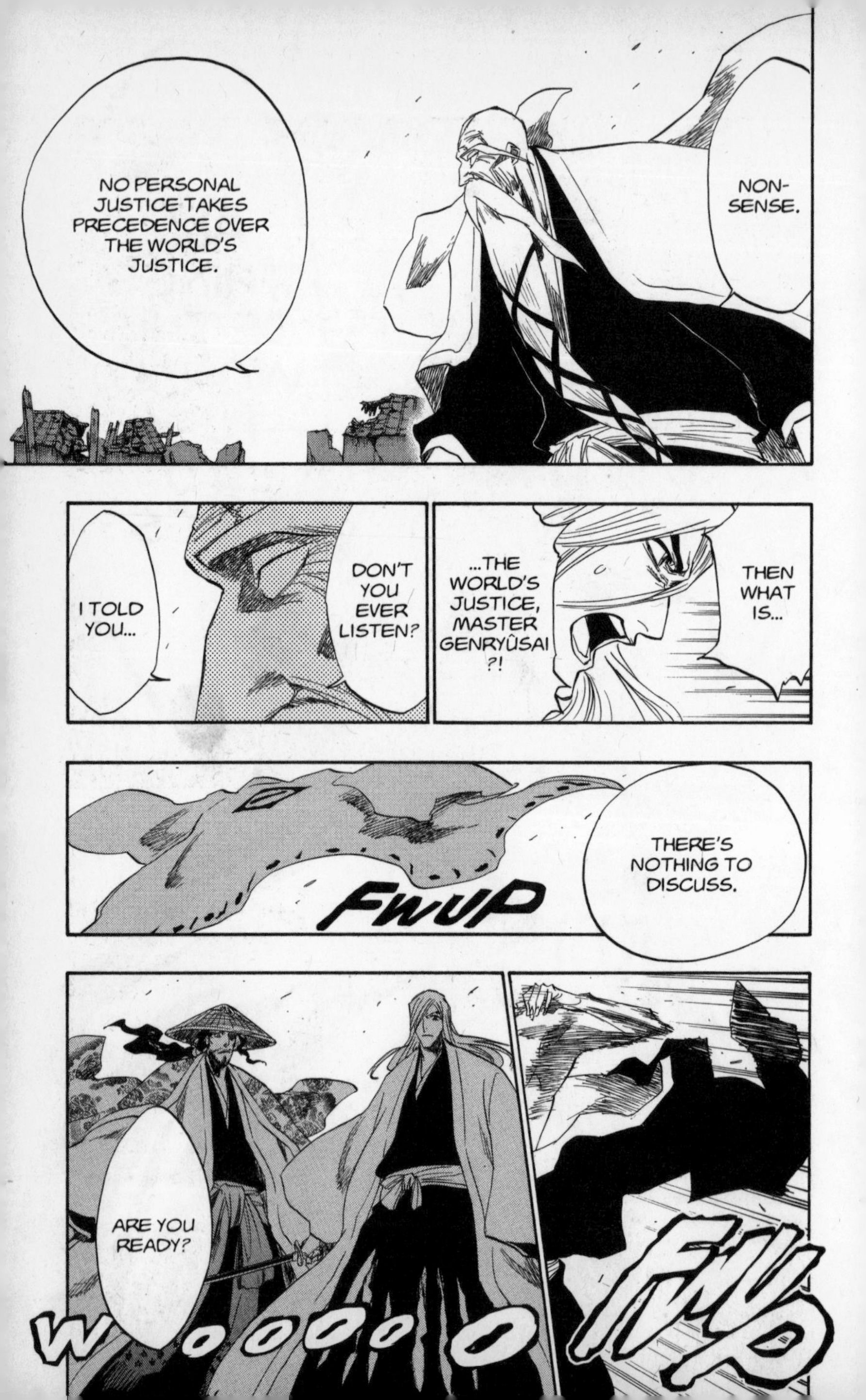
NON-SENSE.
NO PERSONAL JUSTICE TAKES PRECEDENCE OVER THE WORLD'S JUSTICE.
THEN WHAT IS...
...THE WORLD'S JUSTICE, MASTER GENRYÛSAI?!
DON'T YOU EVER LISTEN?
I TOLD YOU...
THERE'S NOTHING TO DISCUSS.
FWUP
FWUP
ARE YOU READY?
WOOOOOO

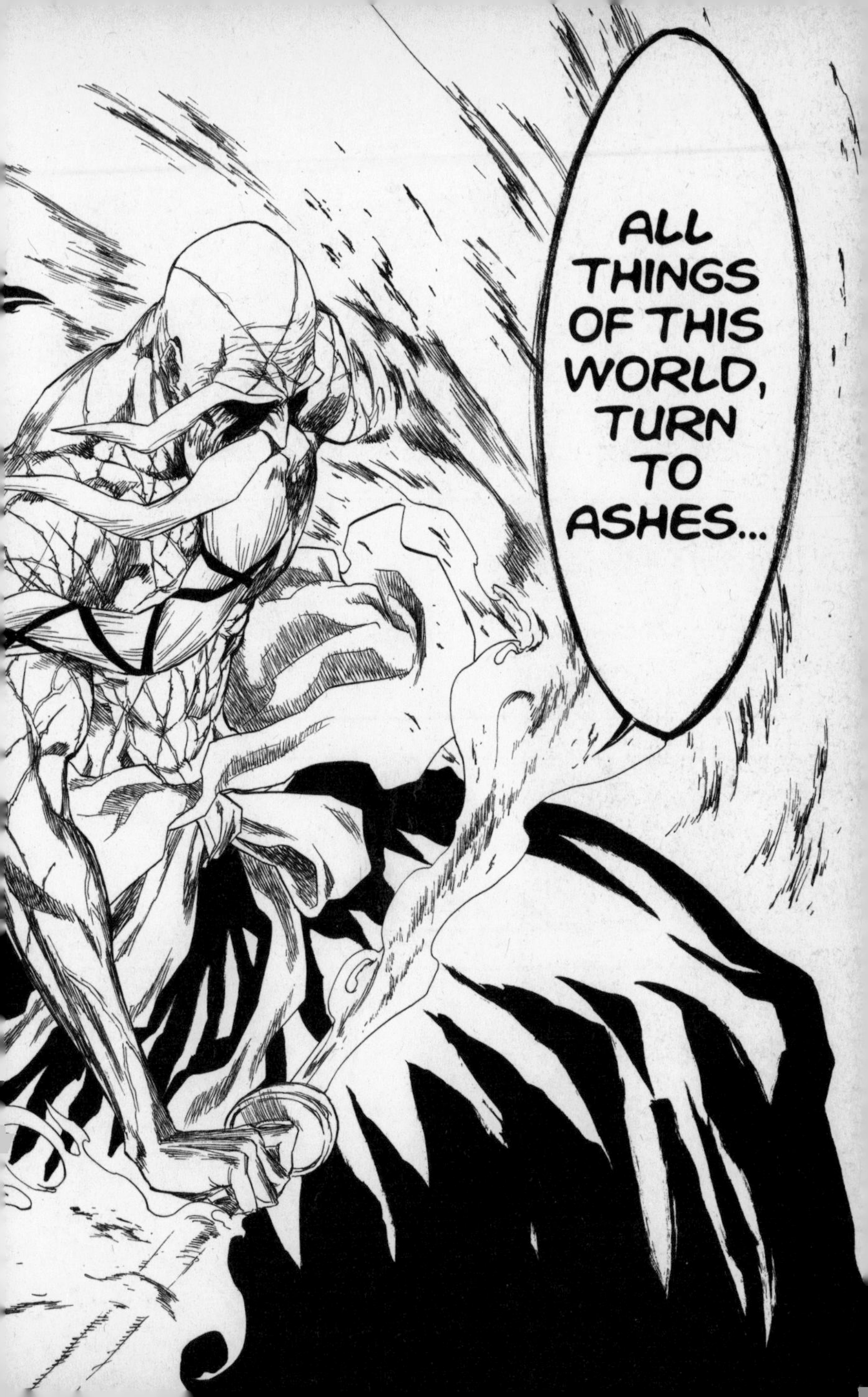
ALL THINGS OF THIS WORLD, TURN TO ASHES...

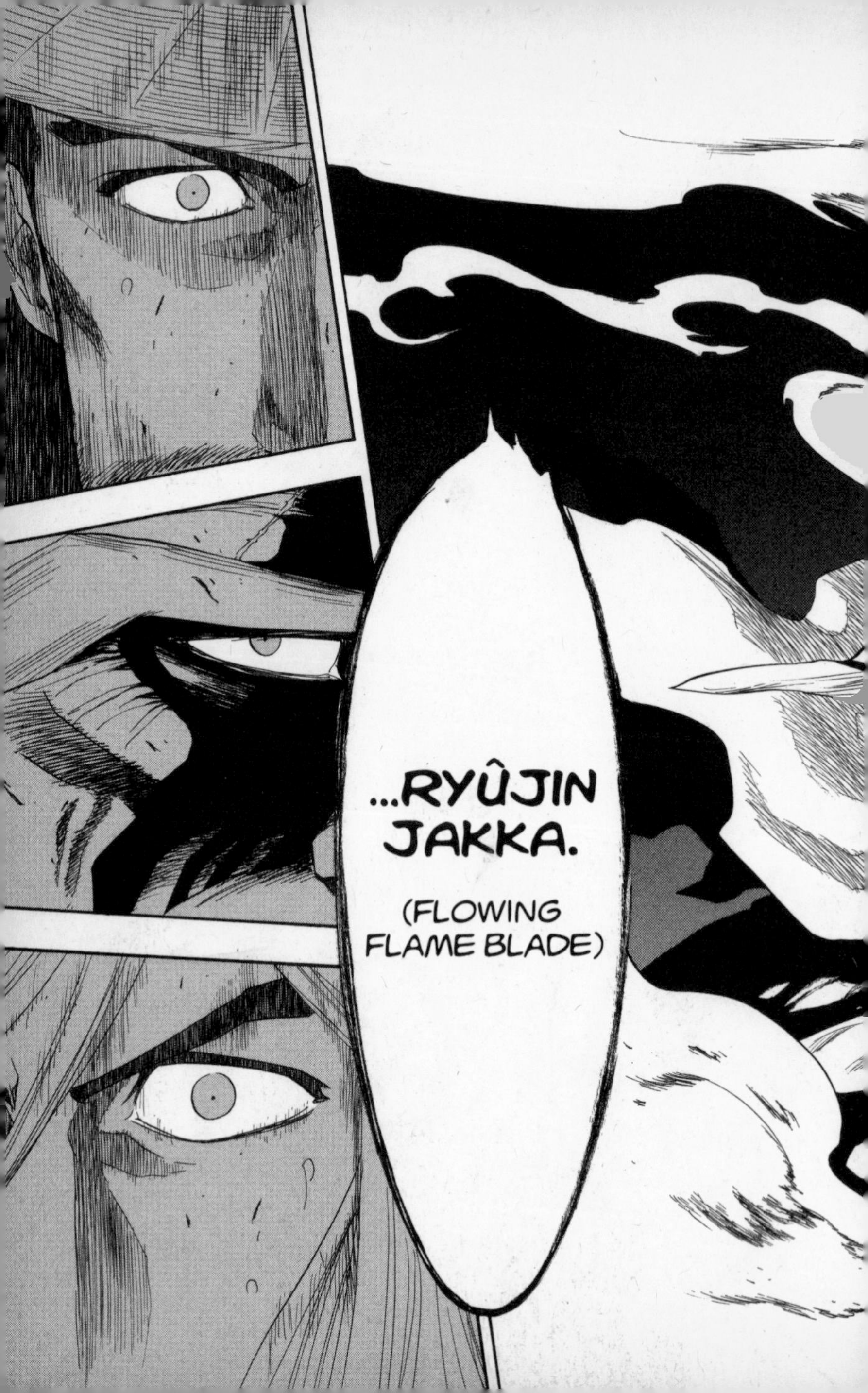
...RYÛJIN JAKKA.
(FLOWING FLAME BLADE)

JINTA! URURU! WHERE DID THEY GO?
JIN... WHERE ARE YOU?! JINTA!
EH?
WHAT?!
TH- THAT'S...
OH, NO!!

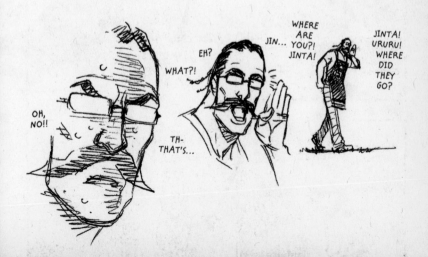

156. Welcome to Purgatory

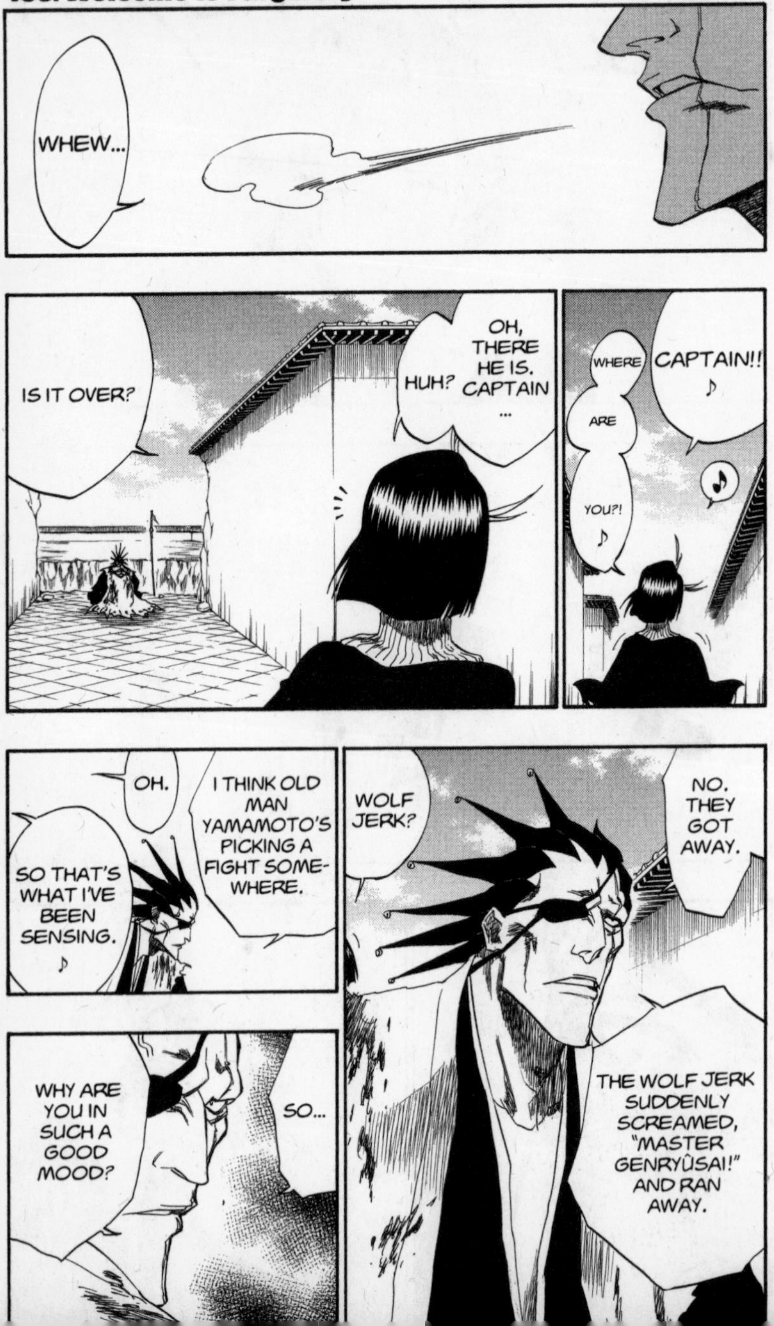
WHEW...
CAPTAIN!! ♪
WHERE ARE YOU?! ♪
♪
HUH?
OH, THERE HE IS. CAPTAIN...
IS IT OVER?
NO. THEY GOT AWAY.
WOLF JERK?
THE WOLF JERK SUDDENLY SCREAMED, "MASTER GENRYÛSAI!" AND RAN AWAY.
OH.
I THINK OLD MAN YAMAMOTO'S PICKING A FIGHT SOMEWHERE.
SO THAT'S WHAT I'VE BEEN SENSING. ♪
SO...
WHY ARE YOU IN SUCH A GOOD MOOD?

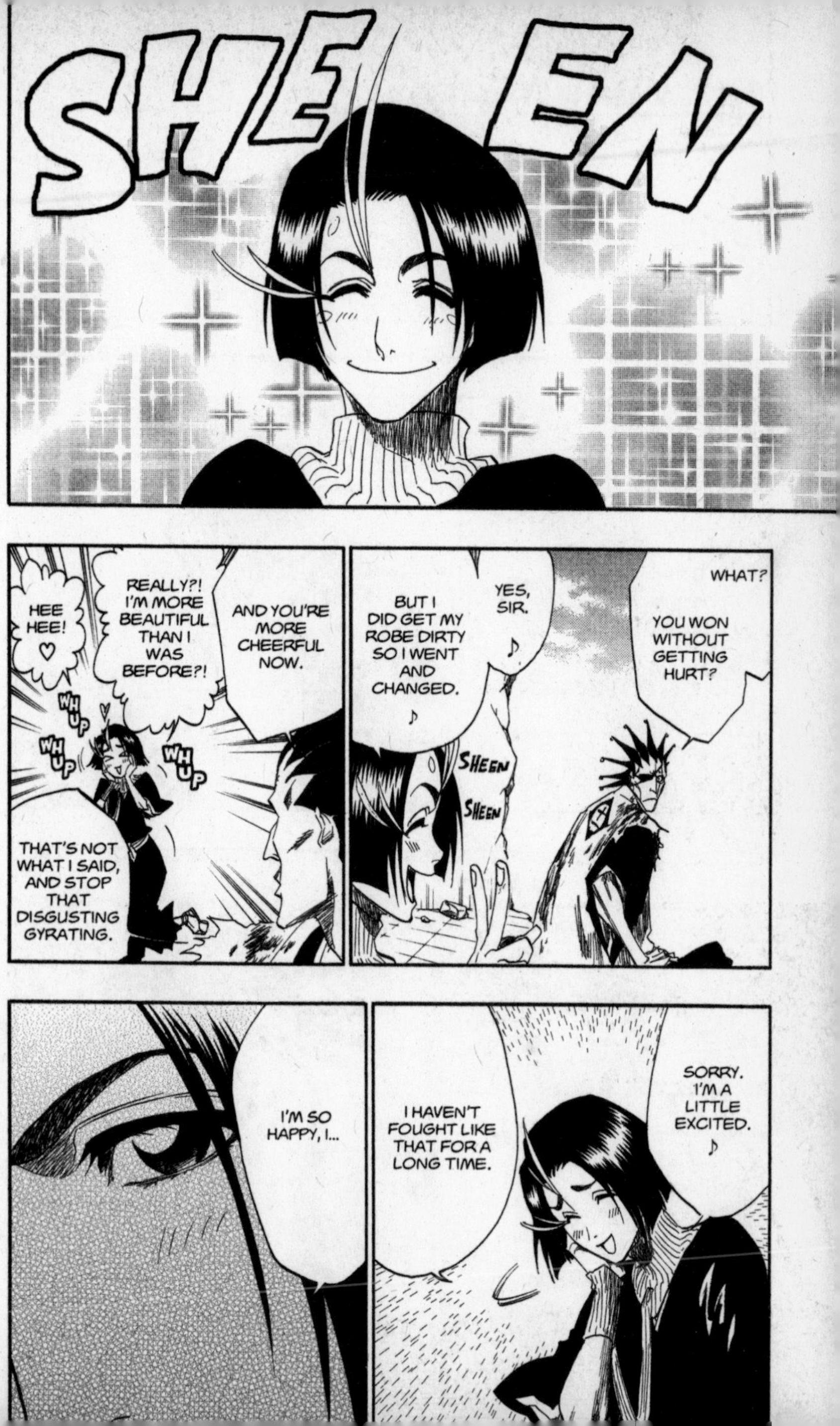
SHEEN
WHAT?
YOU WON WITHOUT GETTING HURT?
YES, SIR. ♪
BUT I DID GET MY ROBE DIRTY SO I WENT AND CHANGED. ♪
SHEEN
SHEEN
AND YOU'RE MORE CHEERFUL NOW.
REALLY?! I'M MORE BEAUTIFUL THAN I WAS BEFORE?!
HEE HEE! ♡
WHUP
WHUP
WHUP
THAT'S NOT WHAT I SAID, AND STOP THAT DISGUSTING GYRATING.
SORRY. I'M A LITTLE EXCITED. ♪
I HAVEN'T FOUGHT LIKE THAT FOR A LONG TIME.
I'M SO HAPPY, I...

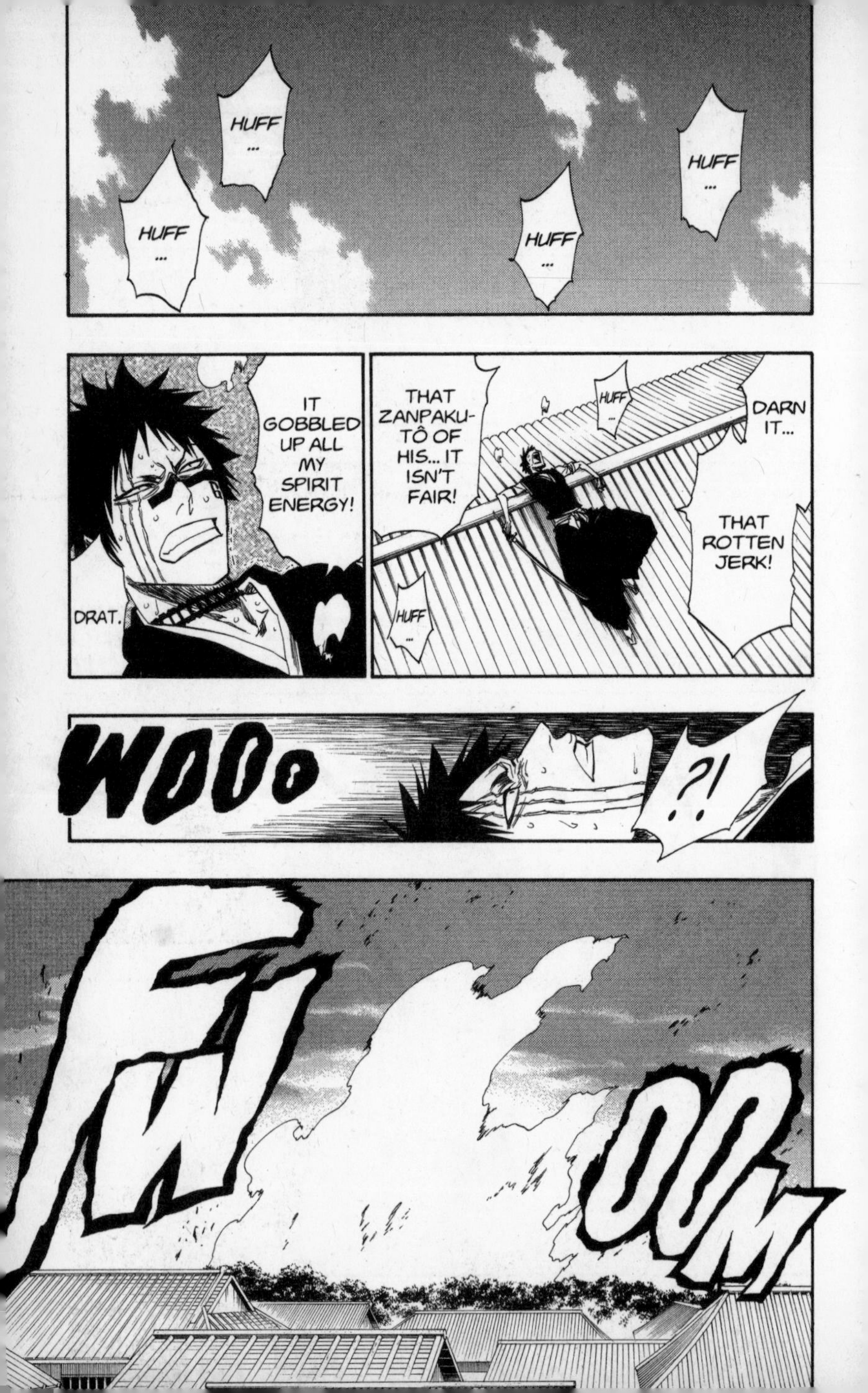
HUFF ...
HUFF ...
HUFF ...
HUFF ...
DARN IT...
THAT ROTTEN JERK!
HUFF ...
THAT ZANPAKU-TÔ OF HIS... IT ISN'T FAIR!
HUFF ...
IT GOBBLED UP ALL MY SPIRIT ENERGY!
DRAT.
?!
WOOO
WHOOM

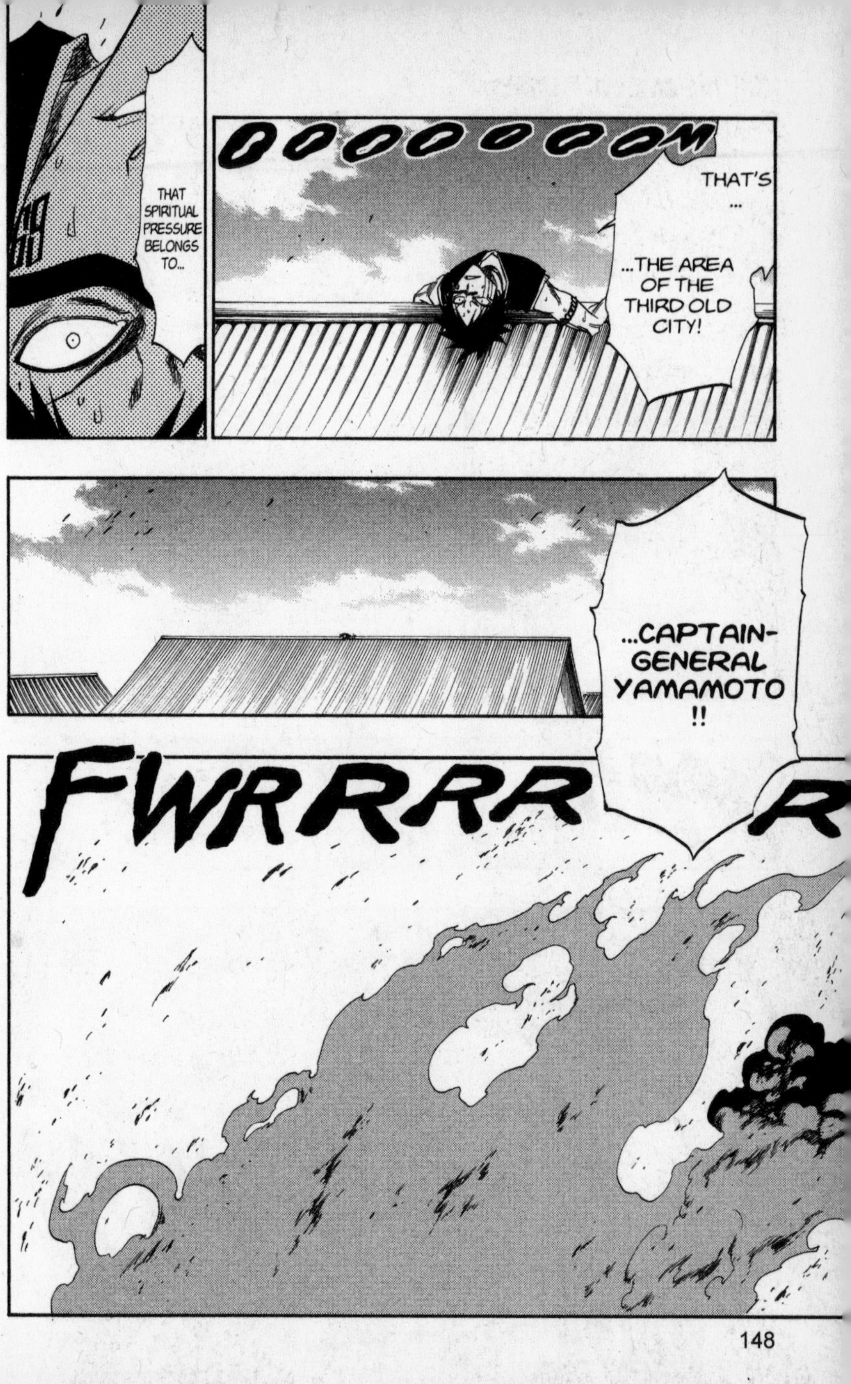
OOOOOOOM
THAT'S ...
...THE AREA OF THE THIRD OLD CITY!
THAT SPIRITUAL PRESSURE BELONGS TO...
...CAPTAIN-GENERAL YAMAMOTO!!
FWRRRRR

156. Welcome to Purgatory

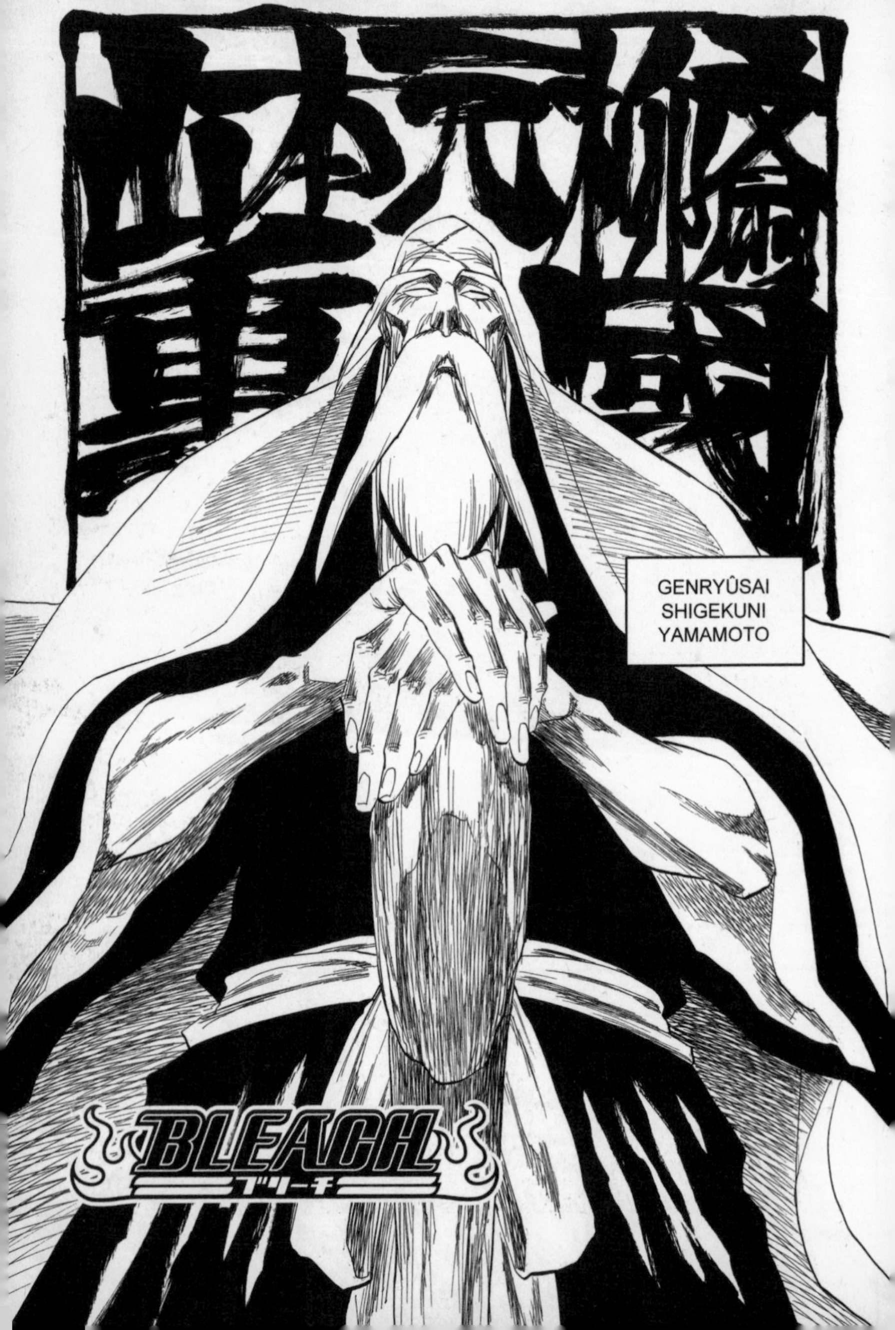
山本元柳斎重國
GENRYÛSAI SHIGEKUNI YAMAMOTO
BLEACH
ブリーチ

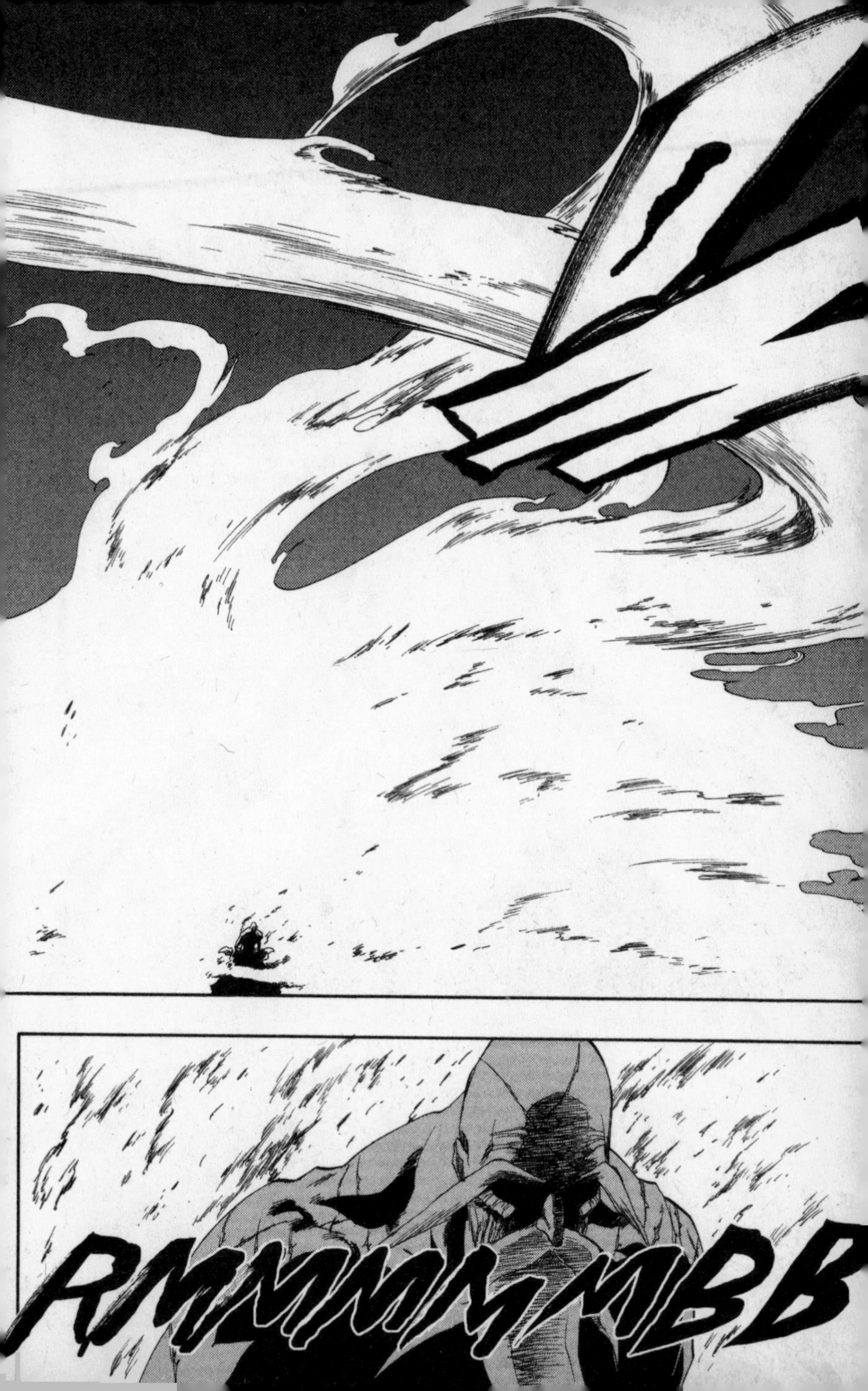
RMMMMMBB

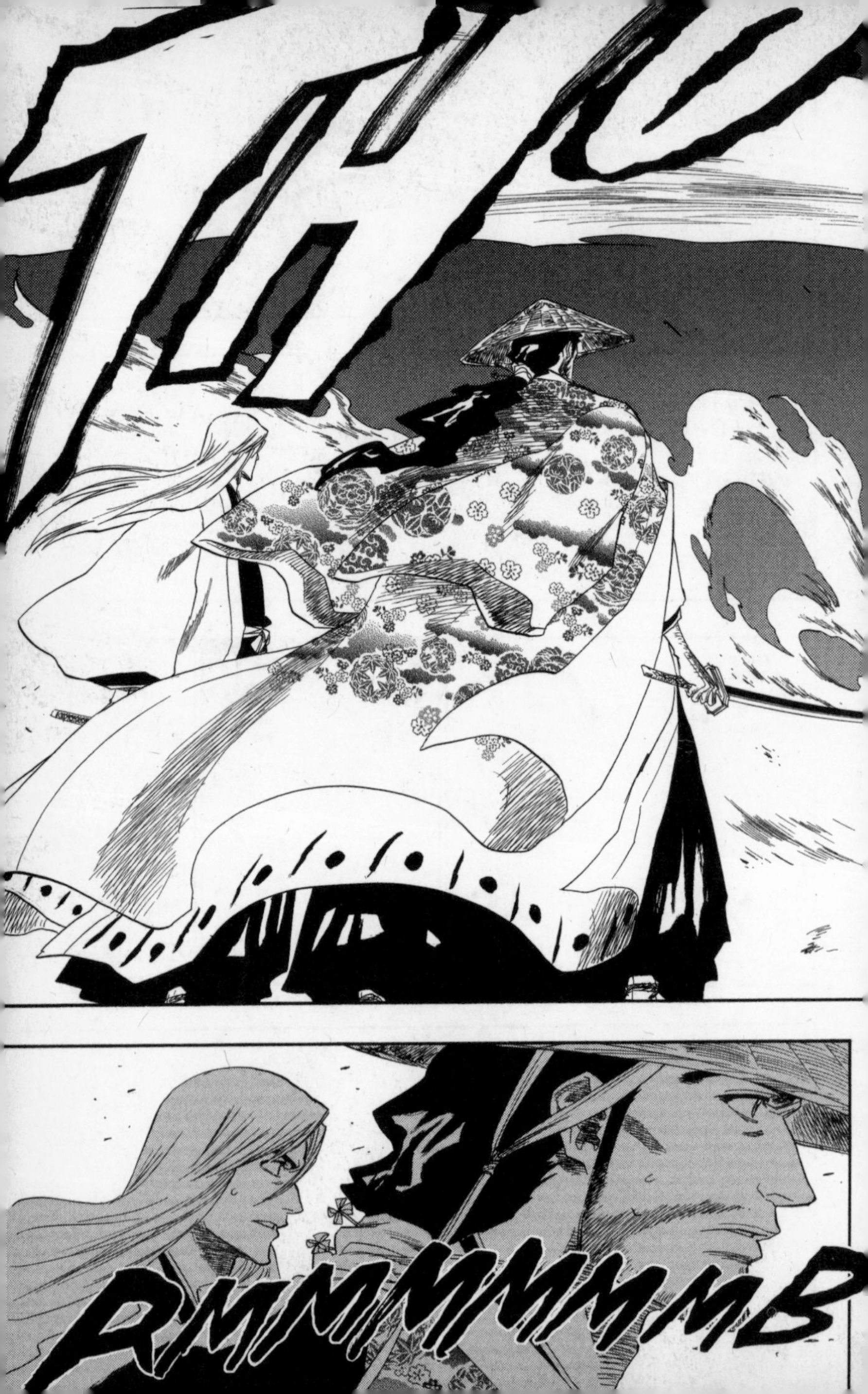
RMMMMMMMB

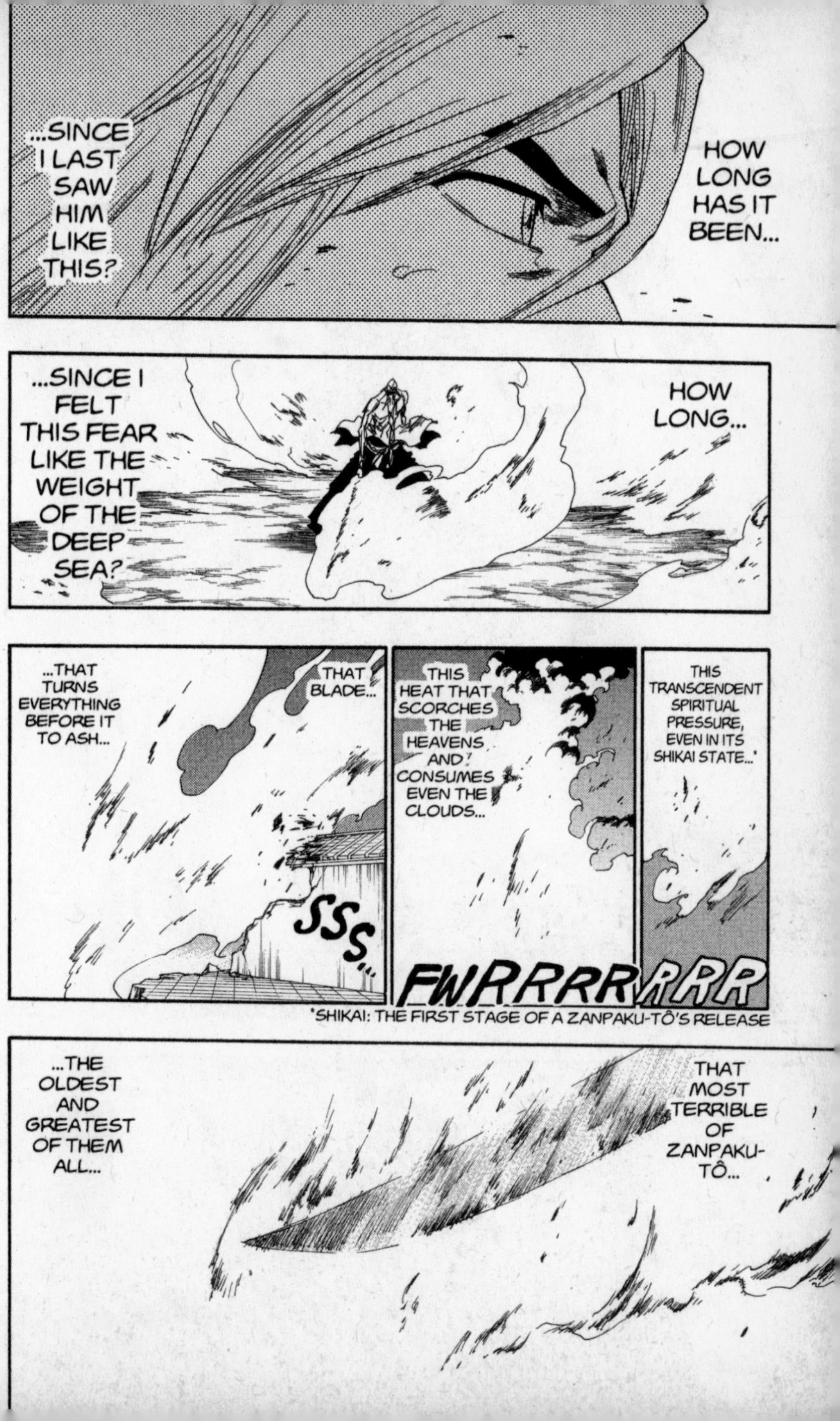
HOW LONG HAS IT BEEN...
...SINCE I LAST SAW HIM LIKE THIS?
HOW LONG...
...SINCE I FELT THIS FEAR LIKE THE WEIGHT OF THE DEEP SEA?
THIS TRANSCENDENT SPIRITUAL PRESSURE, EVEN IN ITS SHIKAI STATE...*
THIS HEAT THAT SCORCHES THE HEAVENS AND CONSUMES EVEN THE CLOUDS...
FWRRRRRRRR
THAT BLADE...
...THAT TURNS EVERYTHING BEFORE IT TO ASH...
SSS...
*SHIKAI: THE FIRST STAGE OF A ZANPAKU-TÔ'S RELEASE
THAT MOST TERRIBLE OF ZANPAKU-TÔ...
...THE OLDEST AND GREATEST OF THEM ALL...

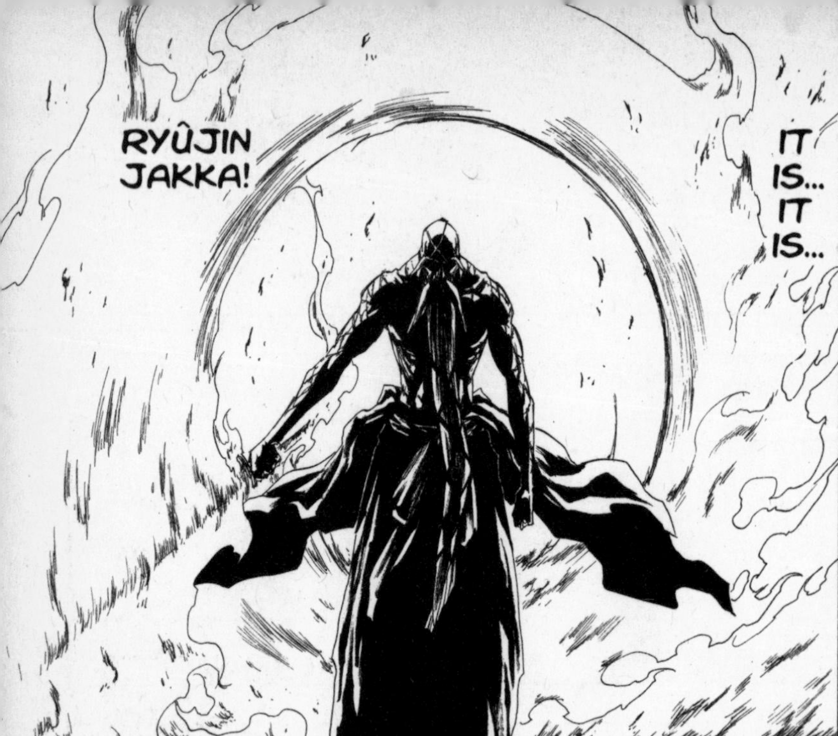
IT IS... IT IS...
RYÛJIN JAKKA!
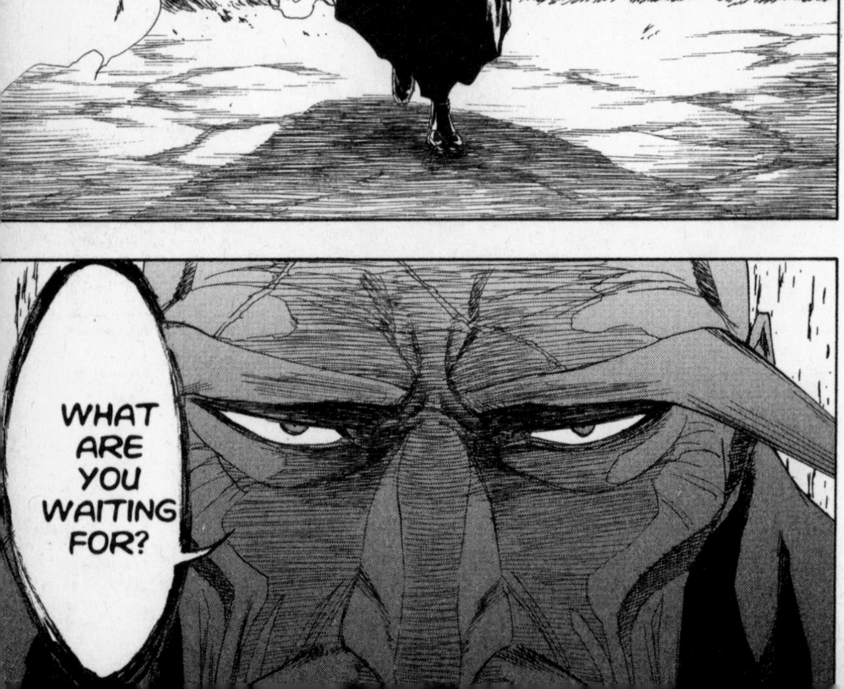
WHAT ARE YOU WAITING FOR?

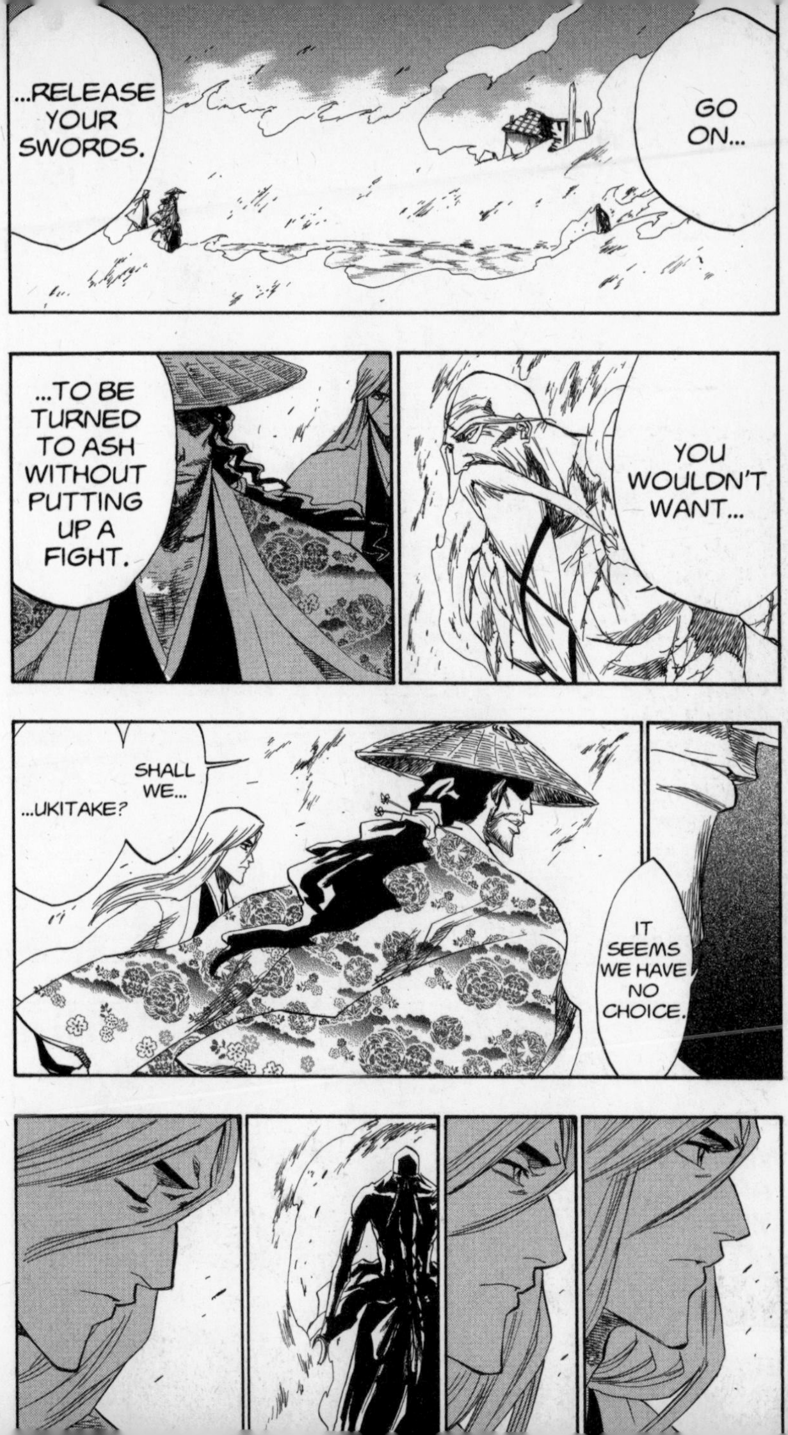
GO ON...
...RELEASE YOUR SWORDS.
YOU WOULDN'T WANT...
...TO BE TURNED TO ASH WITHOUT PUTTING UP A FIGHT.
SHALL WE...
...UKITAKE?
IT SEEMS WE HAVE NO CHOICE.

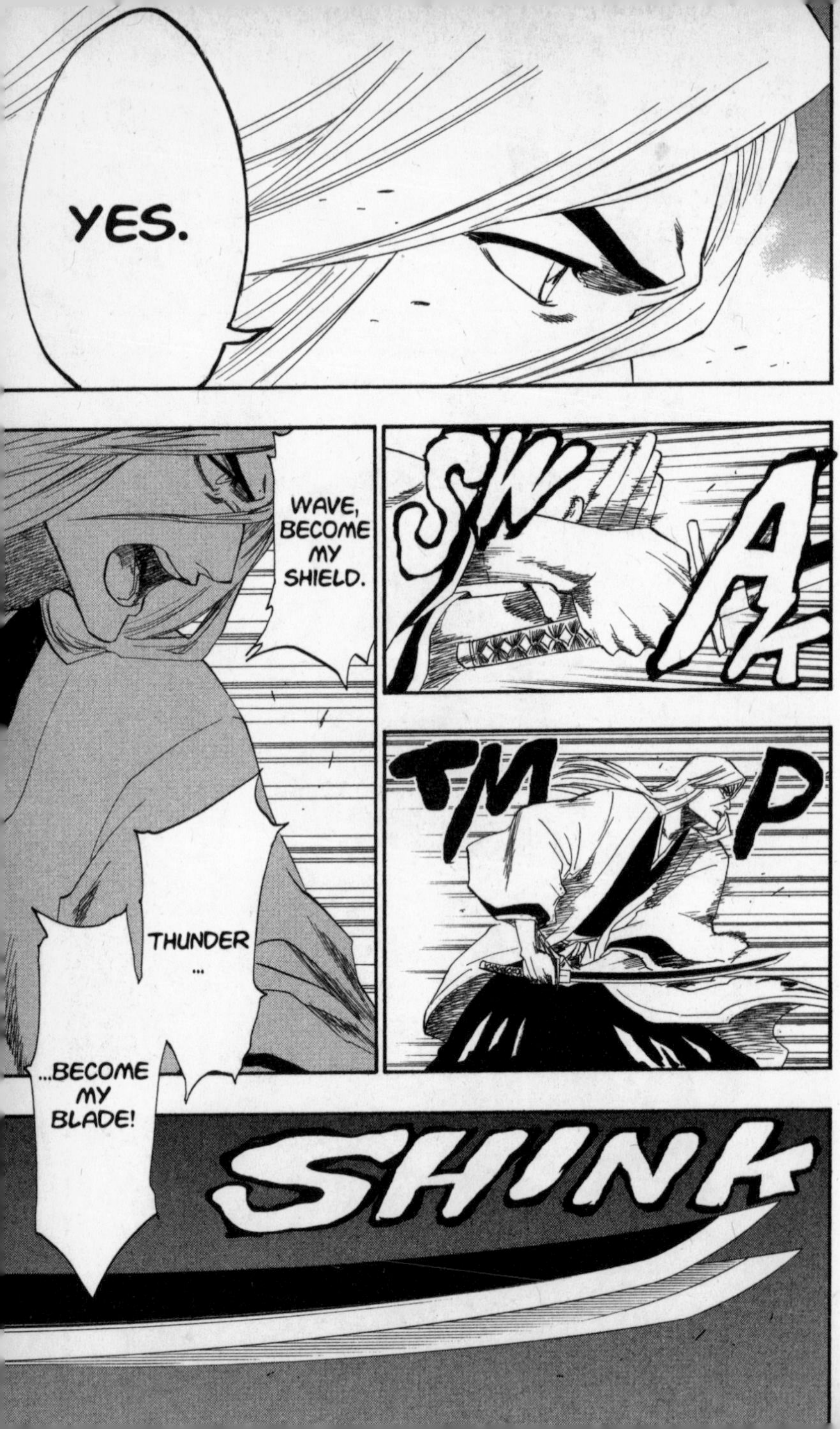
YES.
SWAK
TMP
WAVE, BECOME MY SHIELD.
THUNDER ...
...BECOME MY BLADE!
SHINK

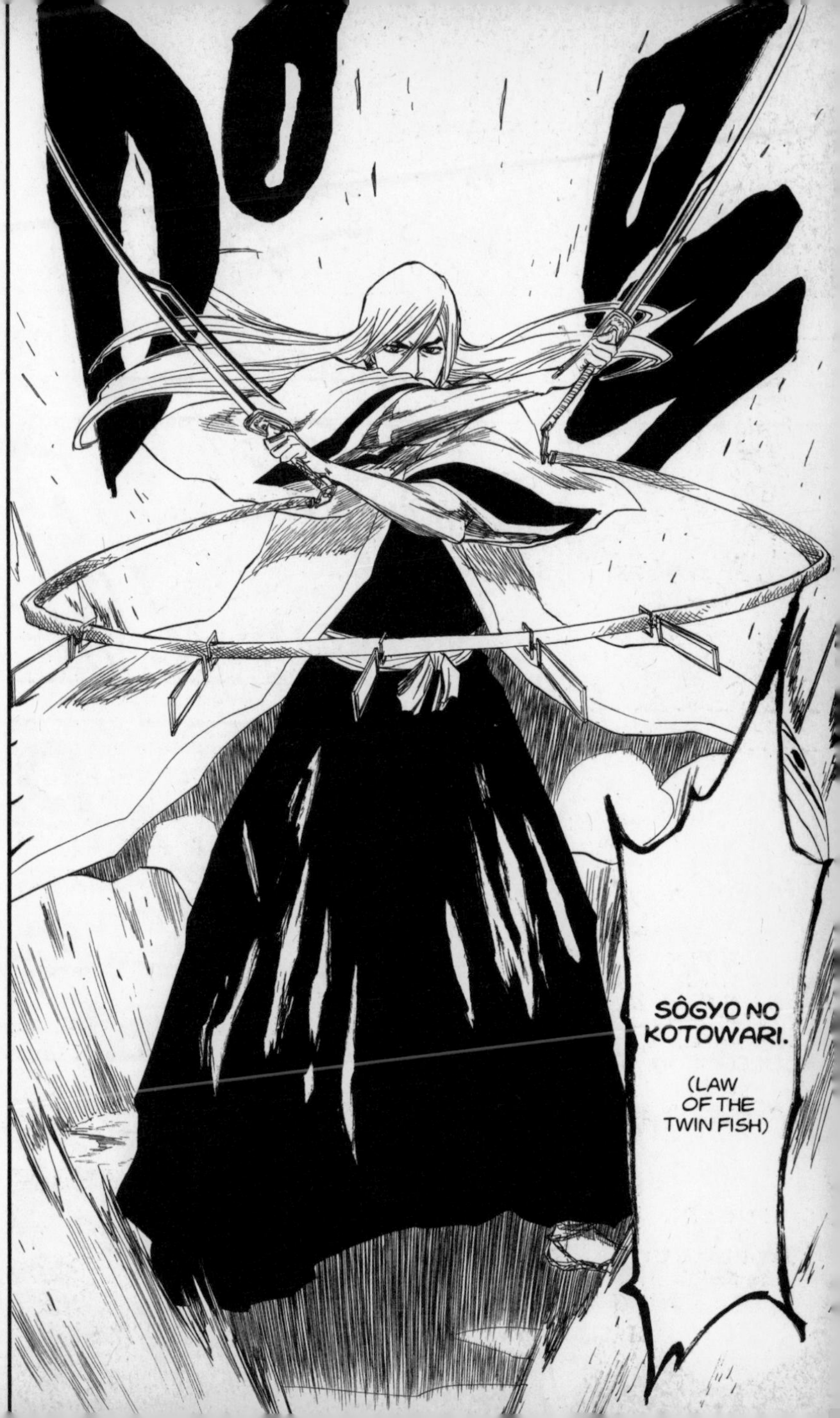
DOOH
SÔGYO NO KOTOWARI.
(LAW OF THE TWIN FISH)

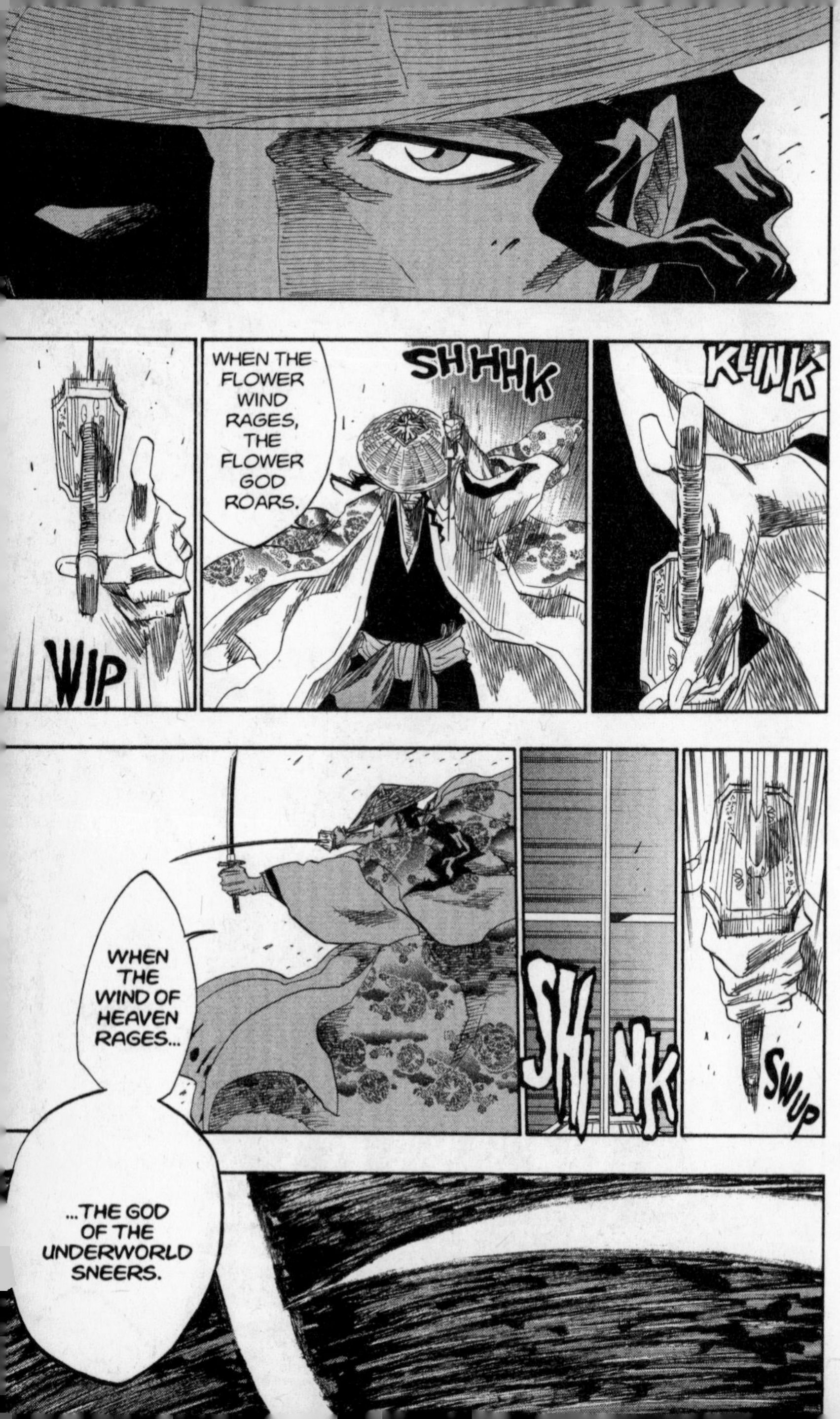
KLINK
SHHHK
WHEN THE FLOWER WIND RAGES, THE FLOWER GOD ROARS.
WIP
SWUP
SH NK
WHEN THE WIND OF HEAVEN RAGES...
...THE GOD OF THE UNDERWORLD SNEERS.

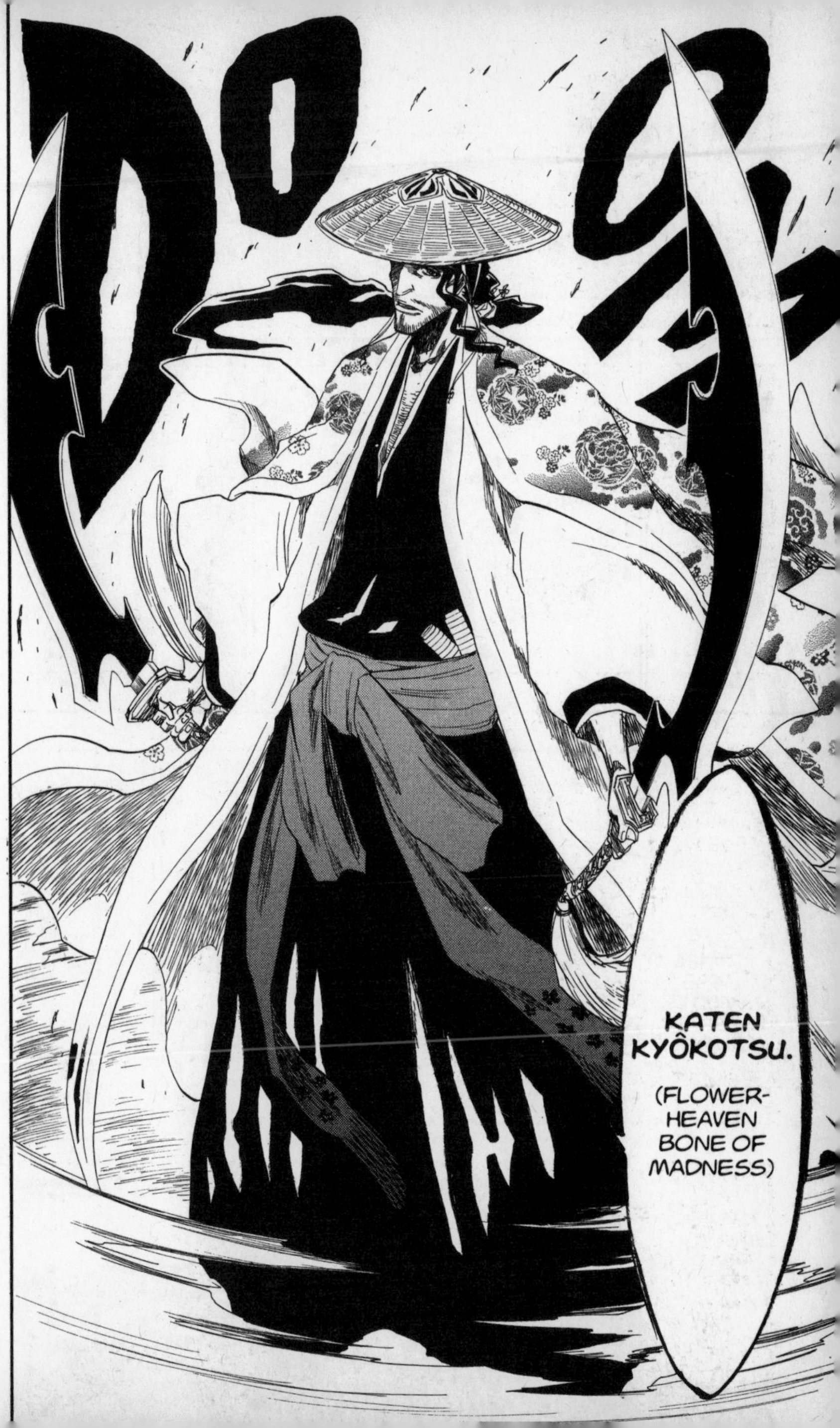
DOGA
KATEN KYÔKOTSU.
(FLOWER-HEAVEN BONE OF MADNESS)

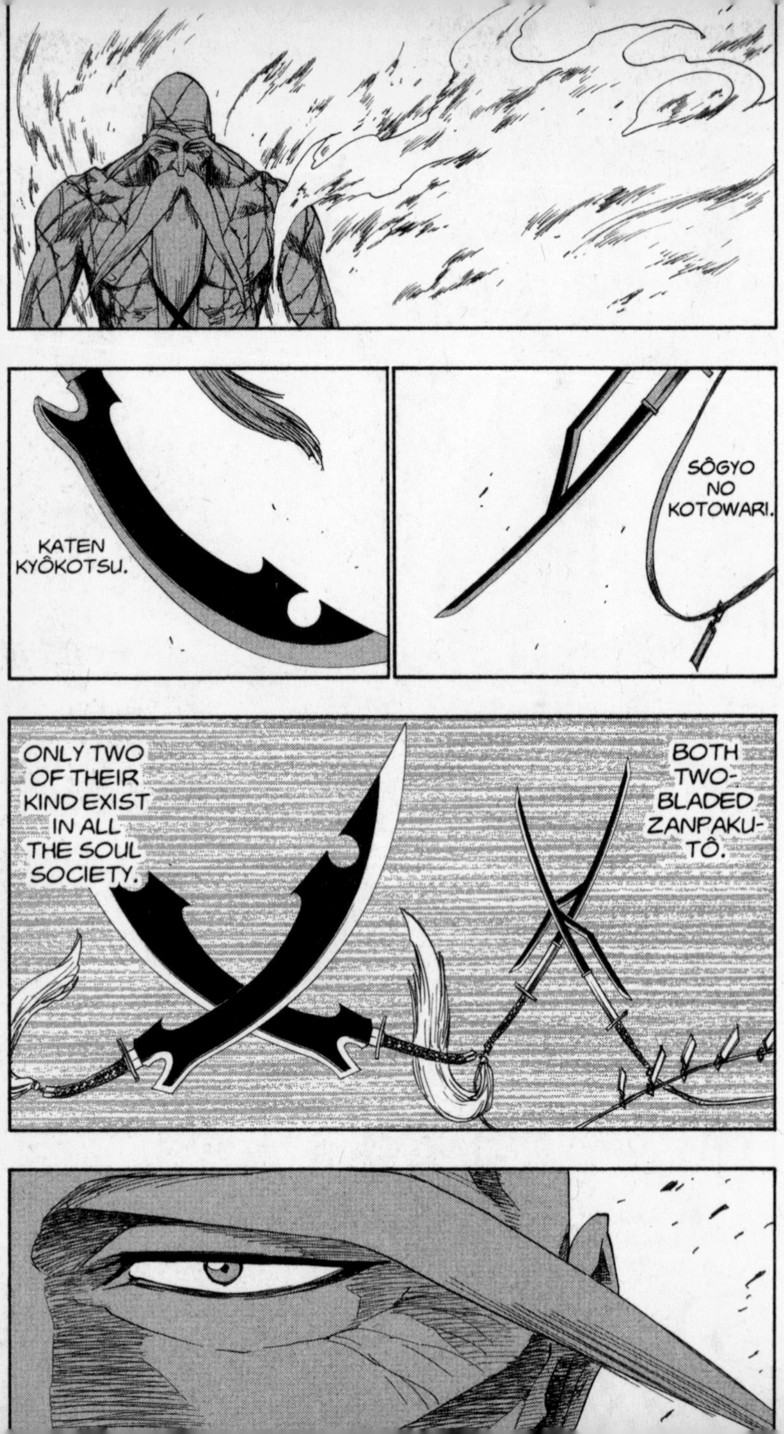
SÔGYO NO KOTOWARI.
KATEN KYÔKOTSU.
BOTH TWO-BLADED ZANPAKU-TÔ.
ONLY TWO OF THEIR KIND EXIST IN ALL THE SOUL SOCIETY.

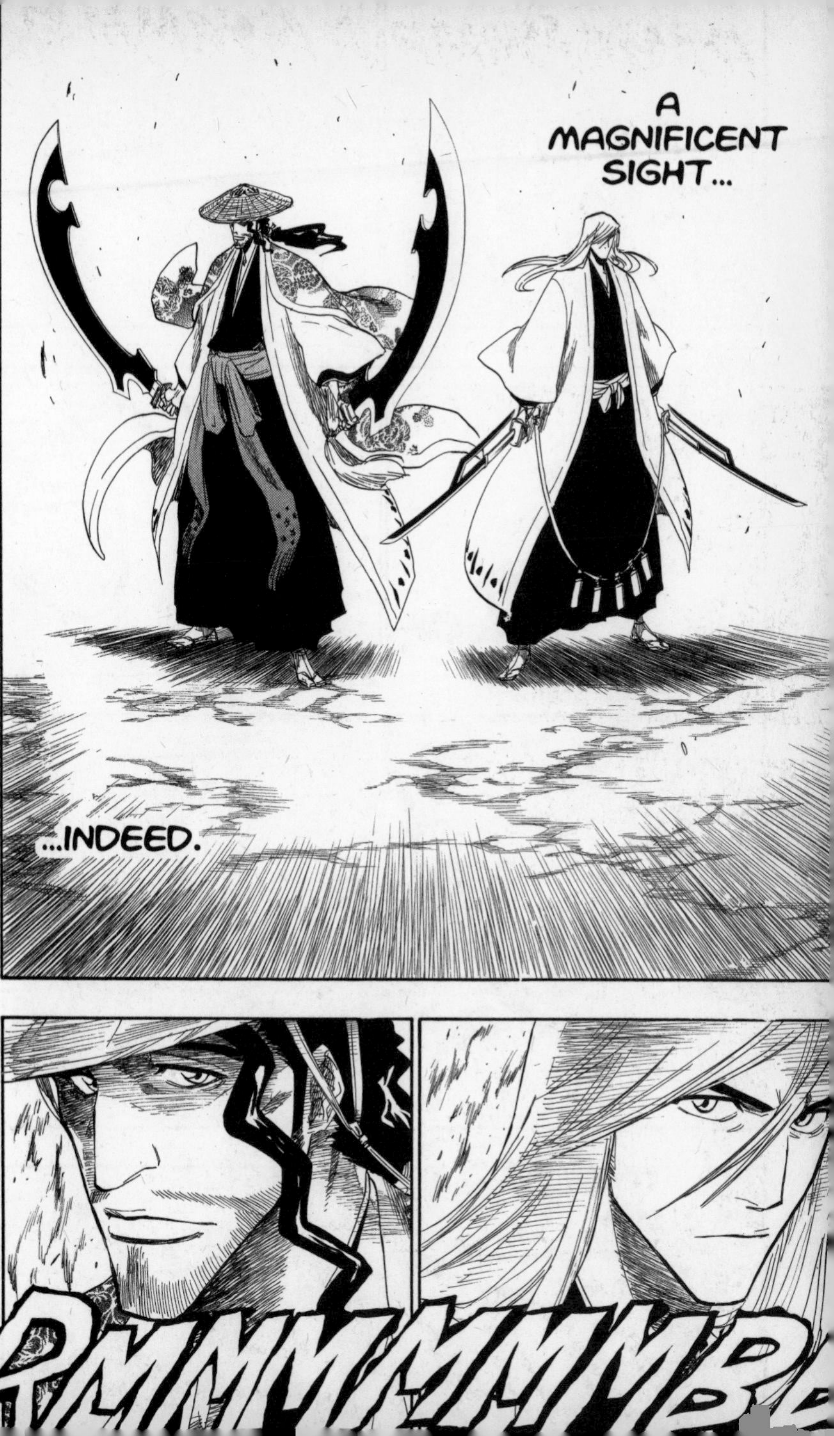

A MAGNIFICENT SIGHT...
...INDEED.
RMMMMMMB

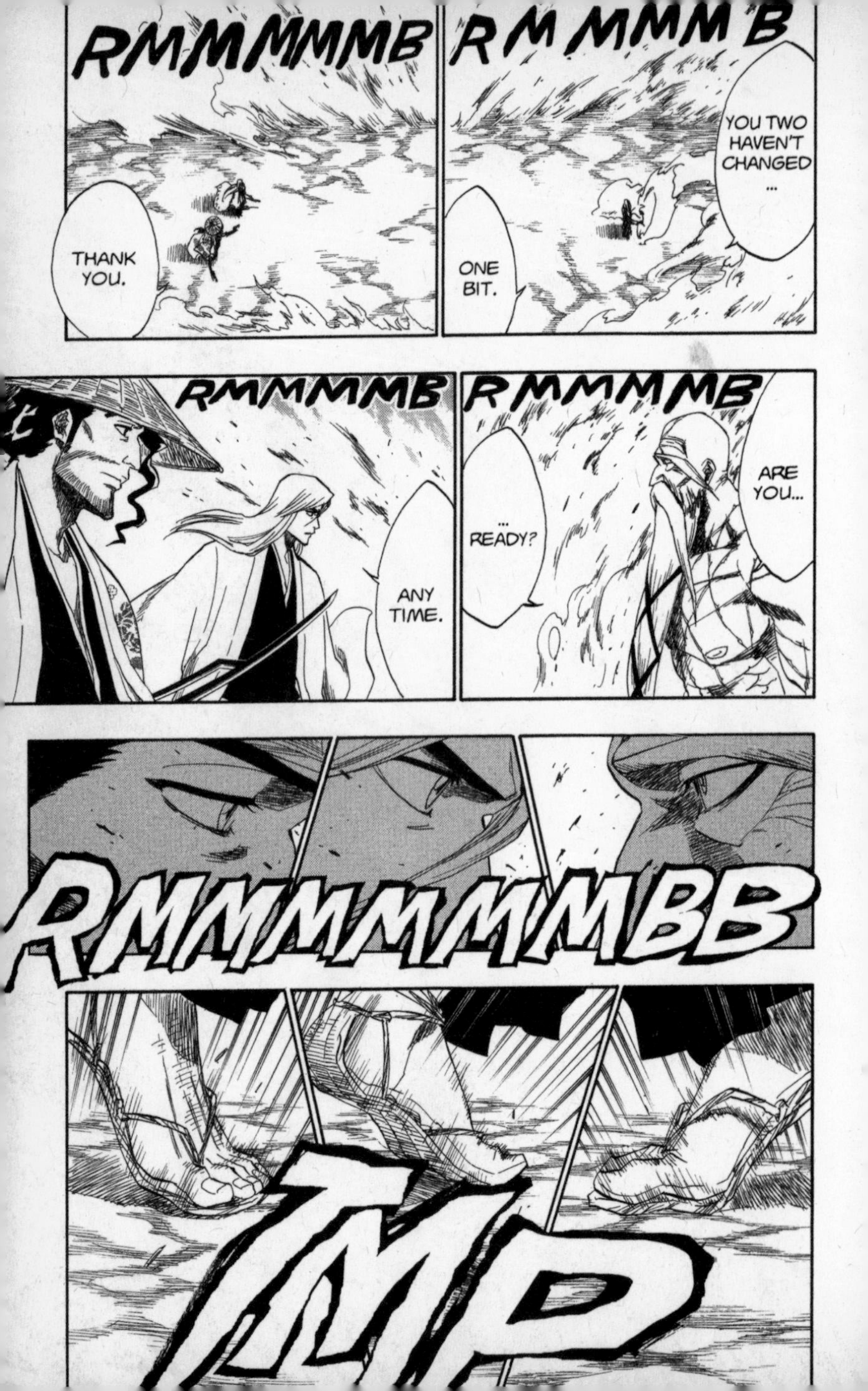
RMMMMB
YOU TWO HAVEN'T CHANGED ...
ONE BIT.
RMMMMMB
THANK YOU.
RMMMMMB
ARE YOU...
... READY?
RMMMMMB
ANY TIME.
RMMMMMMMBB
TMP

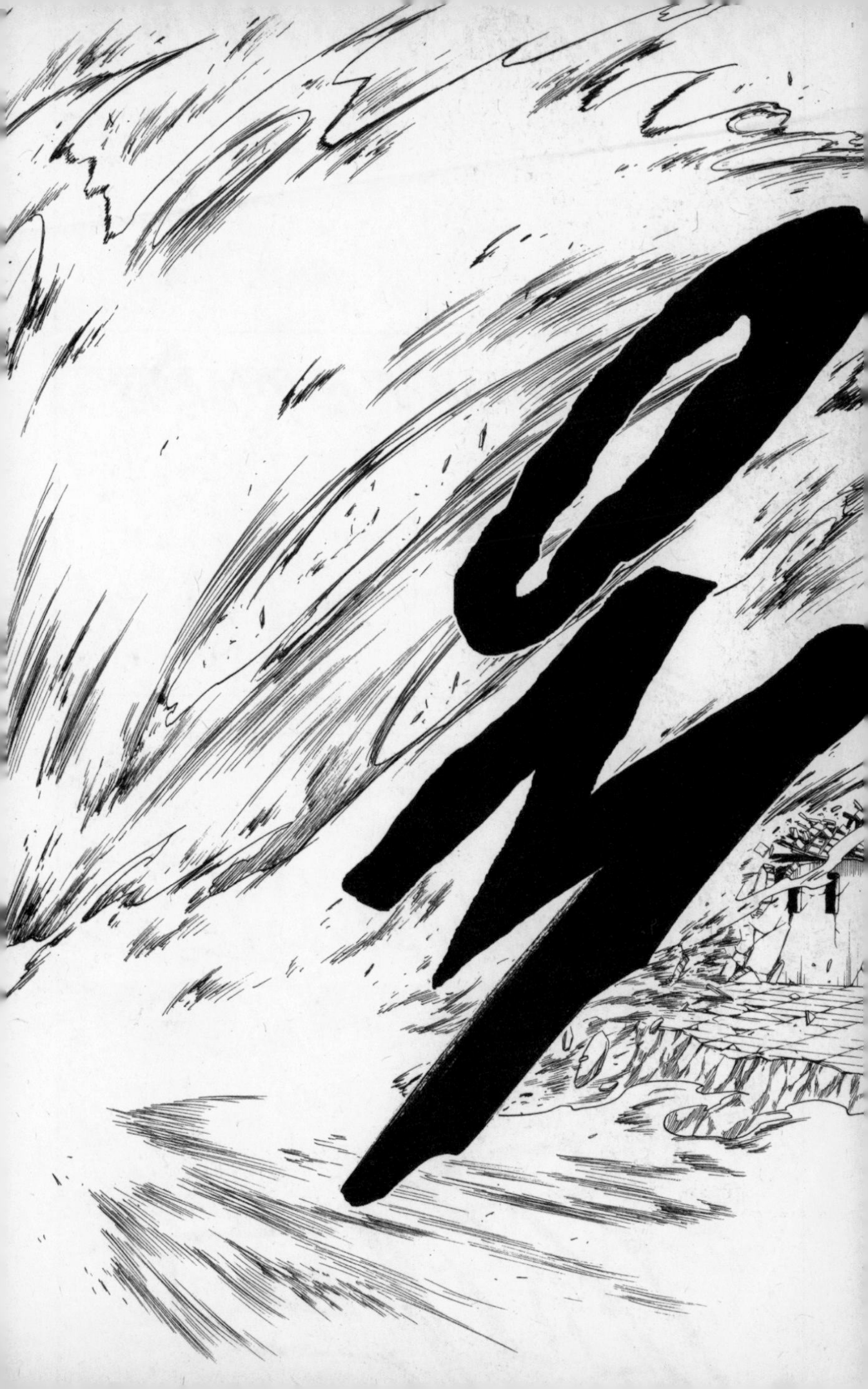

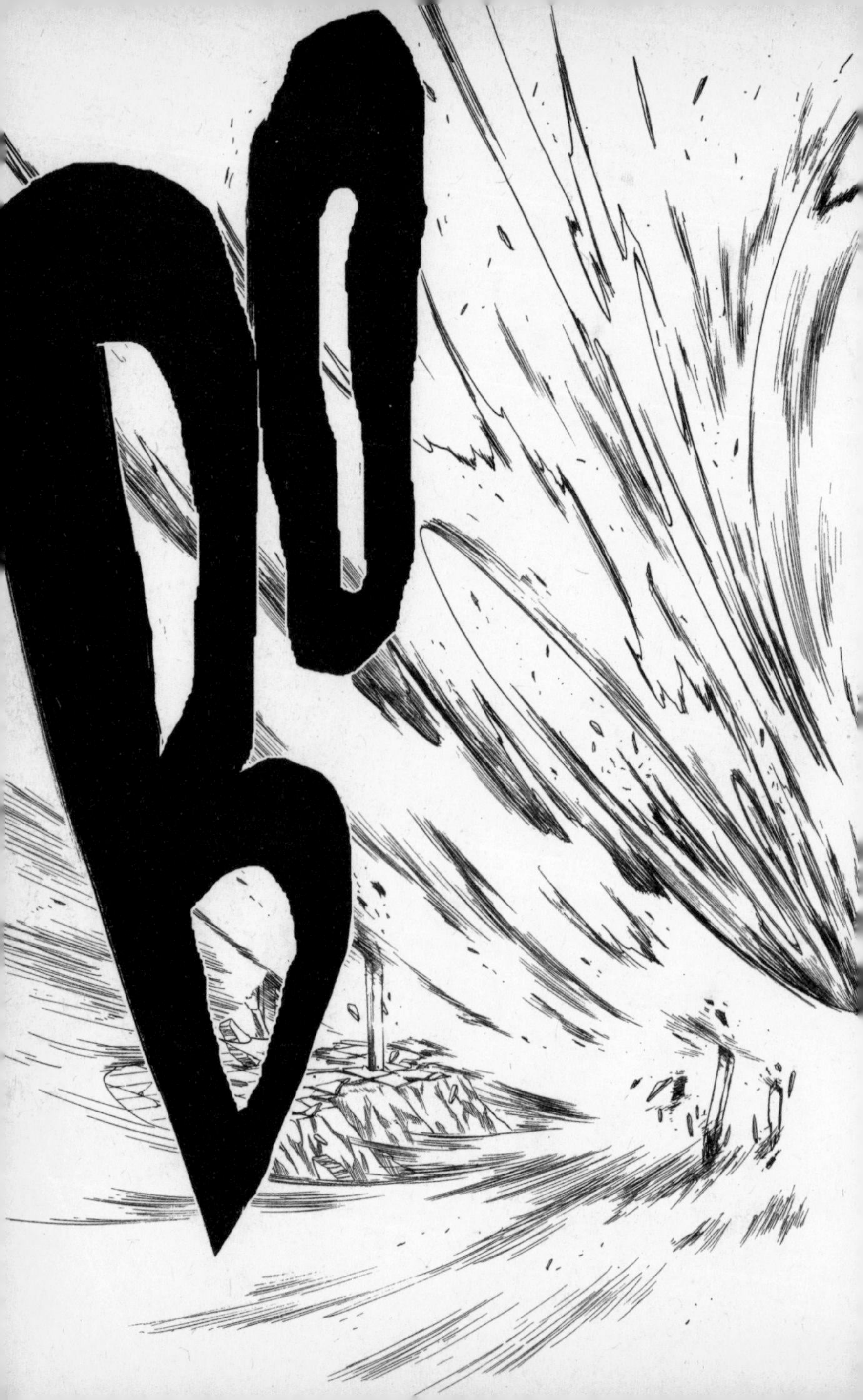

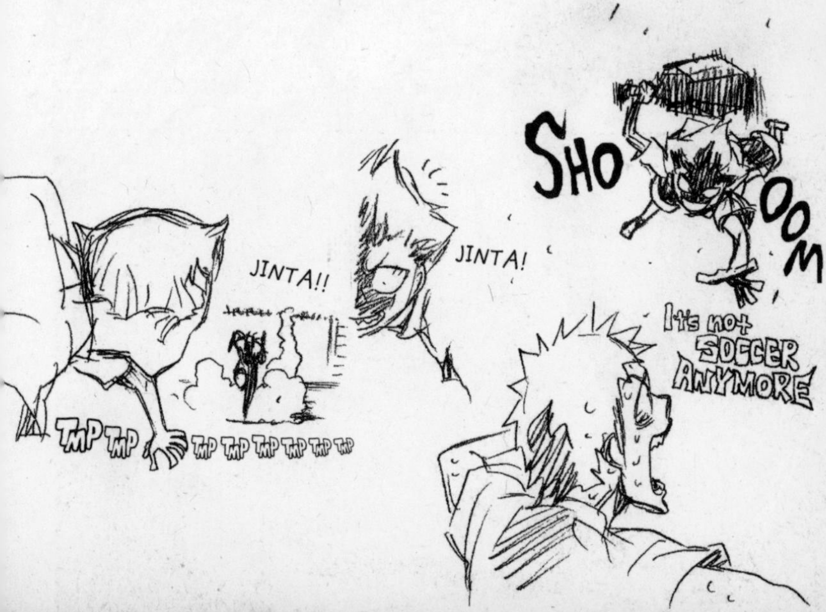
SHOOOM
It's not SOCCER ANYMORE
JINTA!
JINTA!!
TMP TMP TMP TMP TMP TMP TMP TMP

157. Cat and Hornet

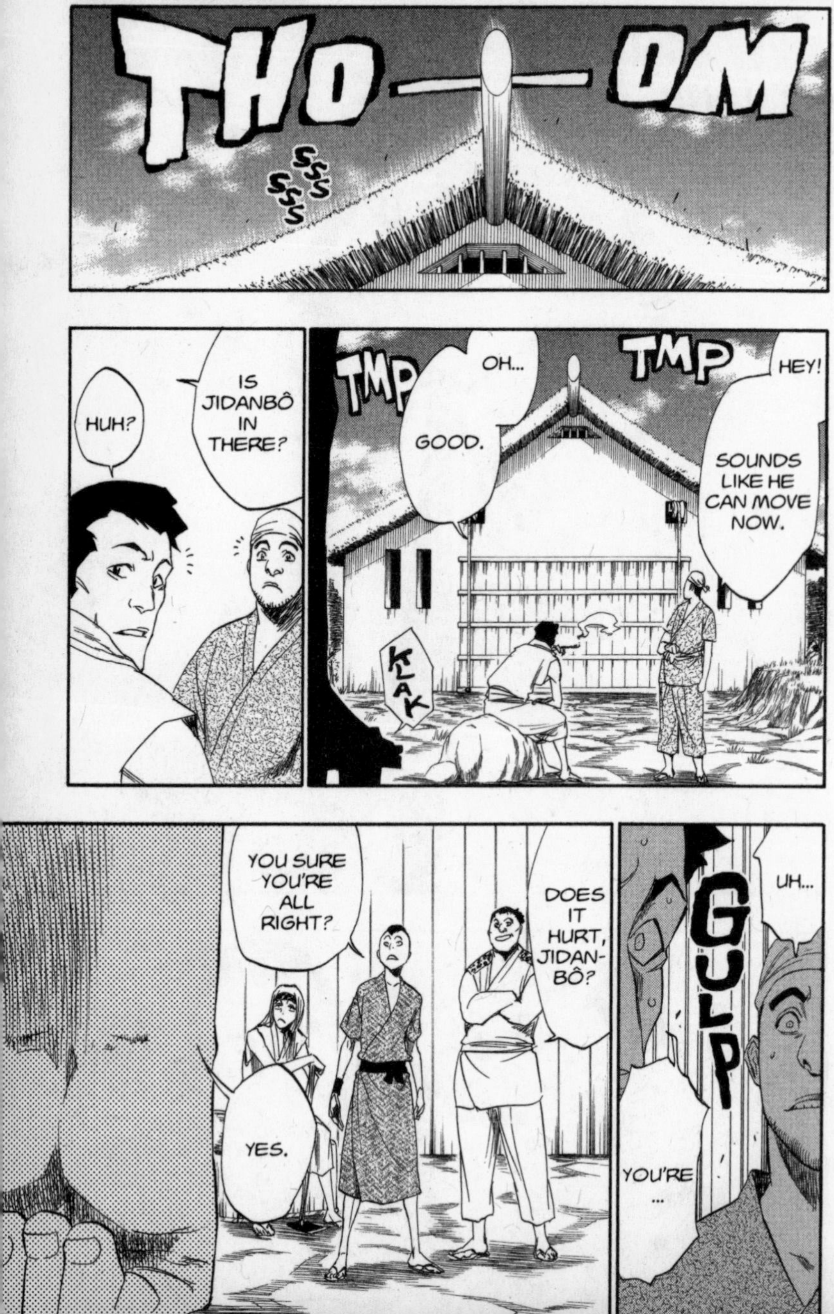
THO—OM
SSS SSS
TMP
HEY!
SOUNDS LIKE HE CAN MOVE NOW.
OH... GOOD.
TMP
KLAK
IS JIDANBÔ IN THERE?
HUH?
UH...
GULP
YOU'RE ...
DOES IT HURT, JIDANBÔ?
YOU SURE YOU'RE ALL RIGHT?
YES.

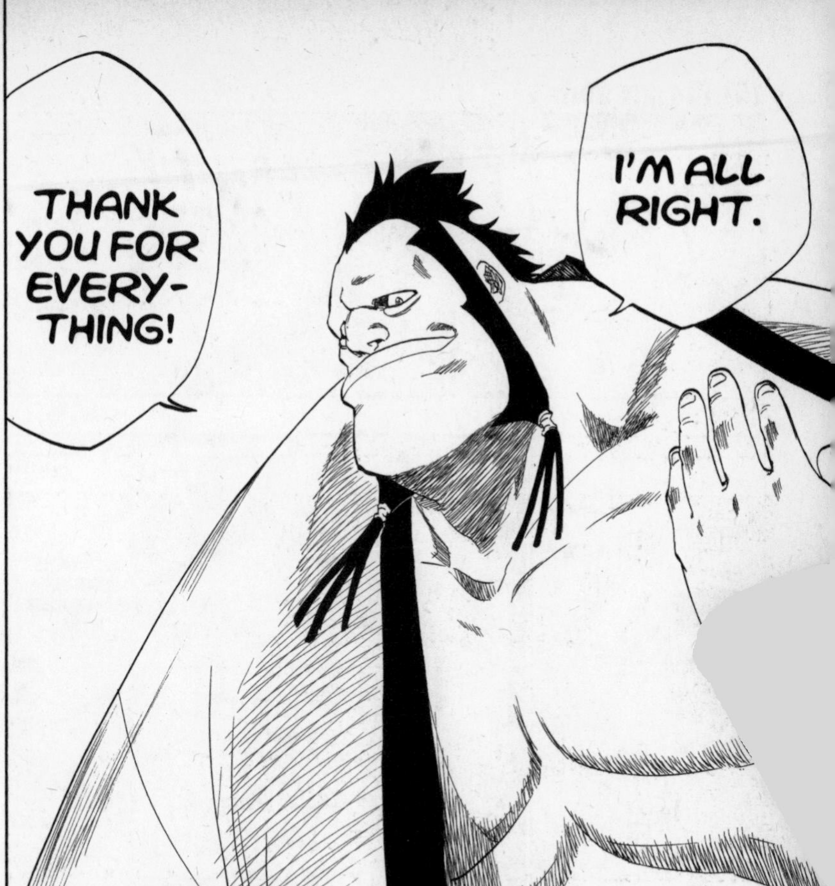
I'M ALL RIGHT.
THANK YOU FOR EVERY-THING!
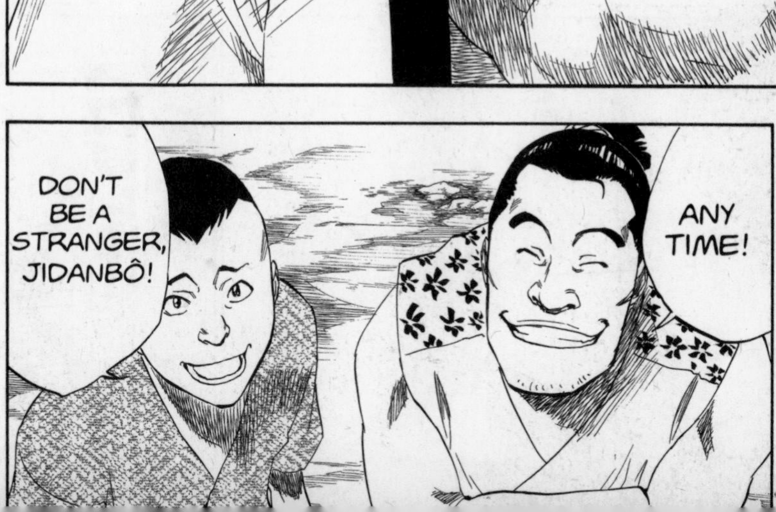
ANY TIME!
DON'T BE A STRANGER, JIDANBÔ!

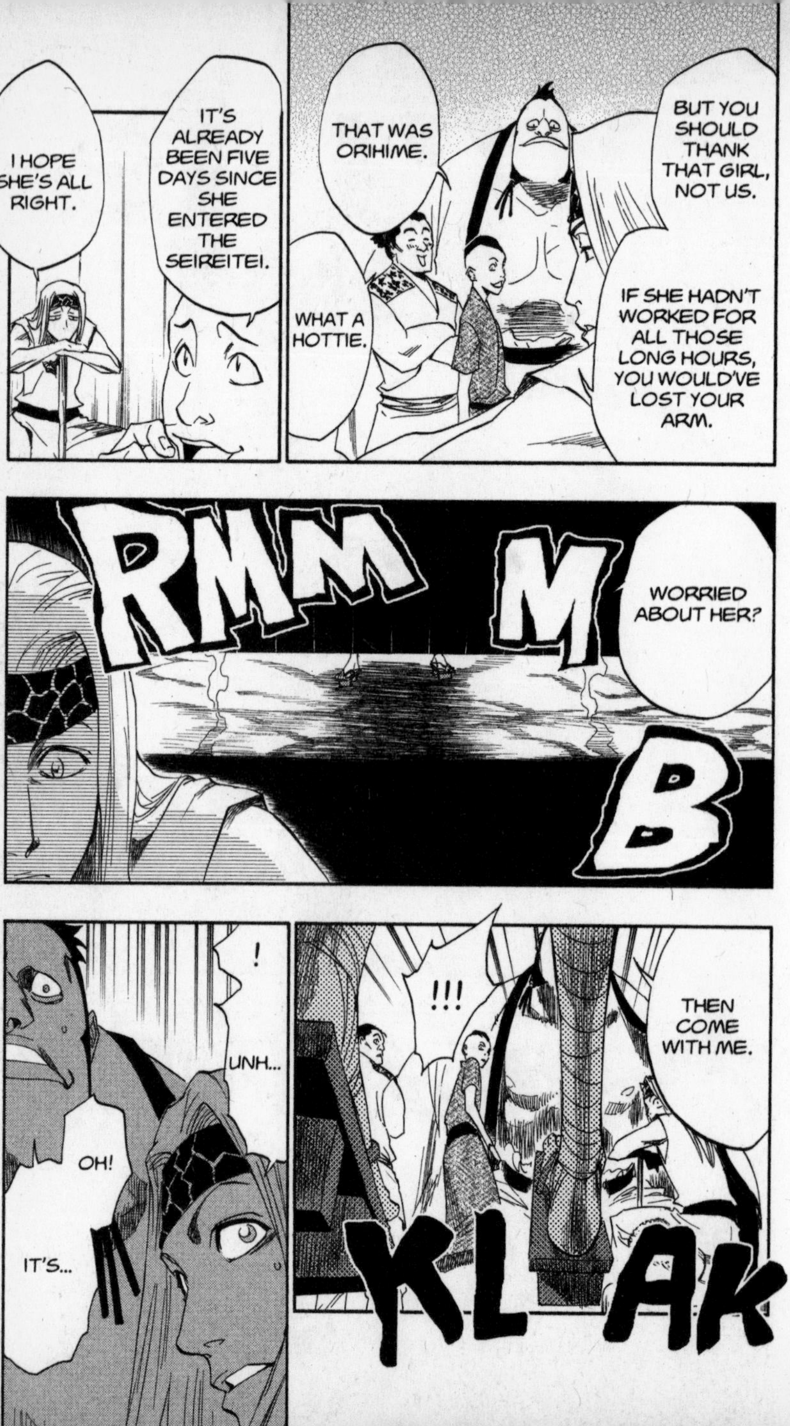
BUT YOU SHOULD THANK THAT GIRL, NOT US.
IF SHE HADN'T WORKED FOR ALL THOSE LONG HOURS, YOU WOULD'VE LOST YOUR ARM.
THAT WAS ORIHIME.
WHAT A HOTTIE.
IT'S ALREADY BEEN FIVE DAYS SINCE SHE ENTERED THE SEIREITEI.
I HOPE SHE'S ALL RIGHT.
WORRIED ABOUT HER?
RMM M B
THEN COME WITH ME.
!!!
KLAK
!
UNH...
OH!
IT'S...

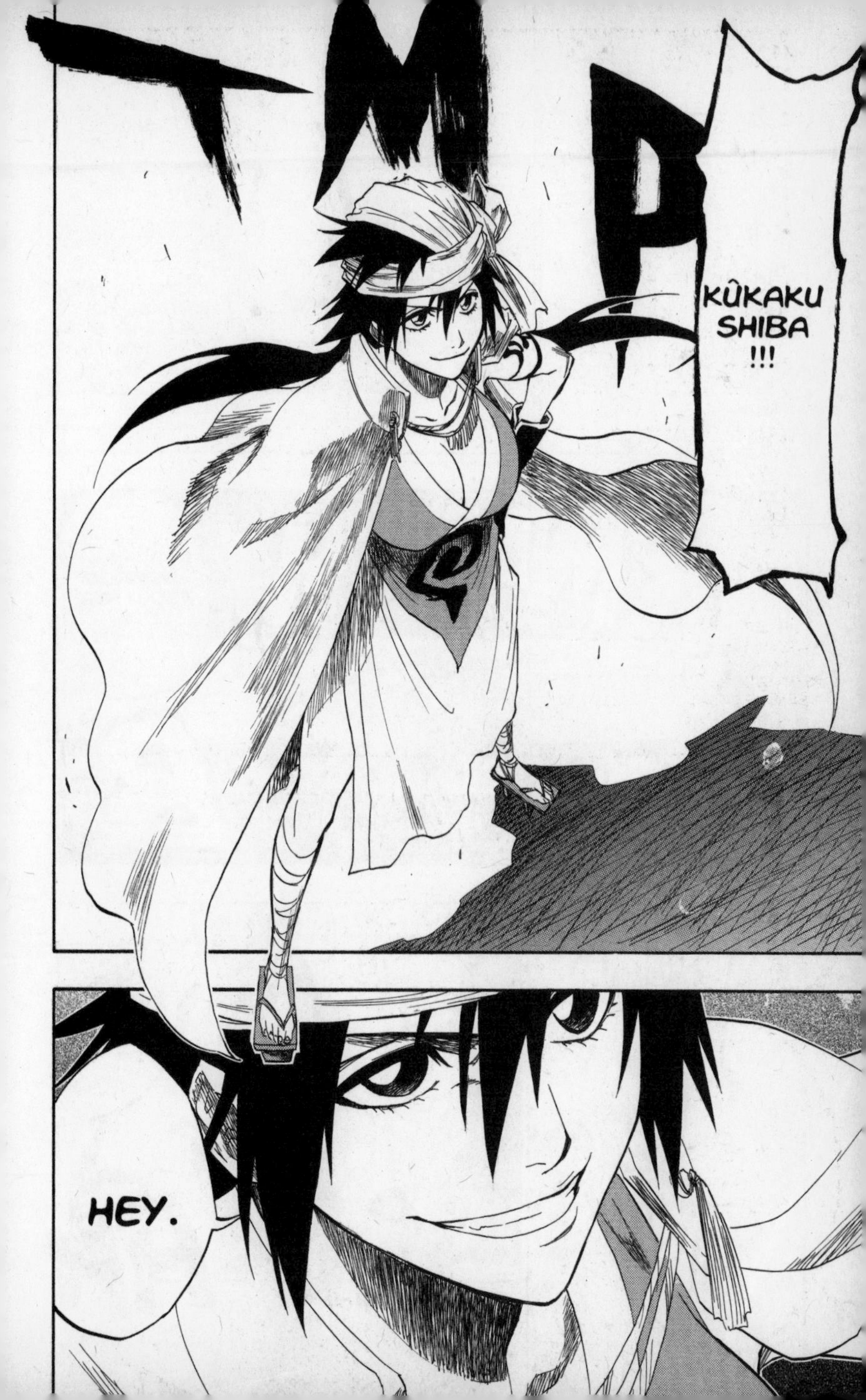
KÛKAKU SHIBA !!!
TMP
HEY.

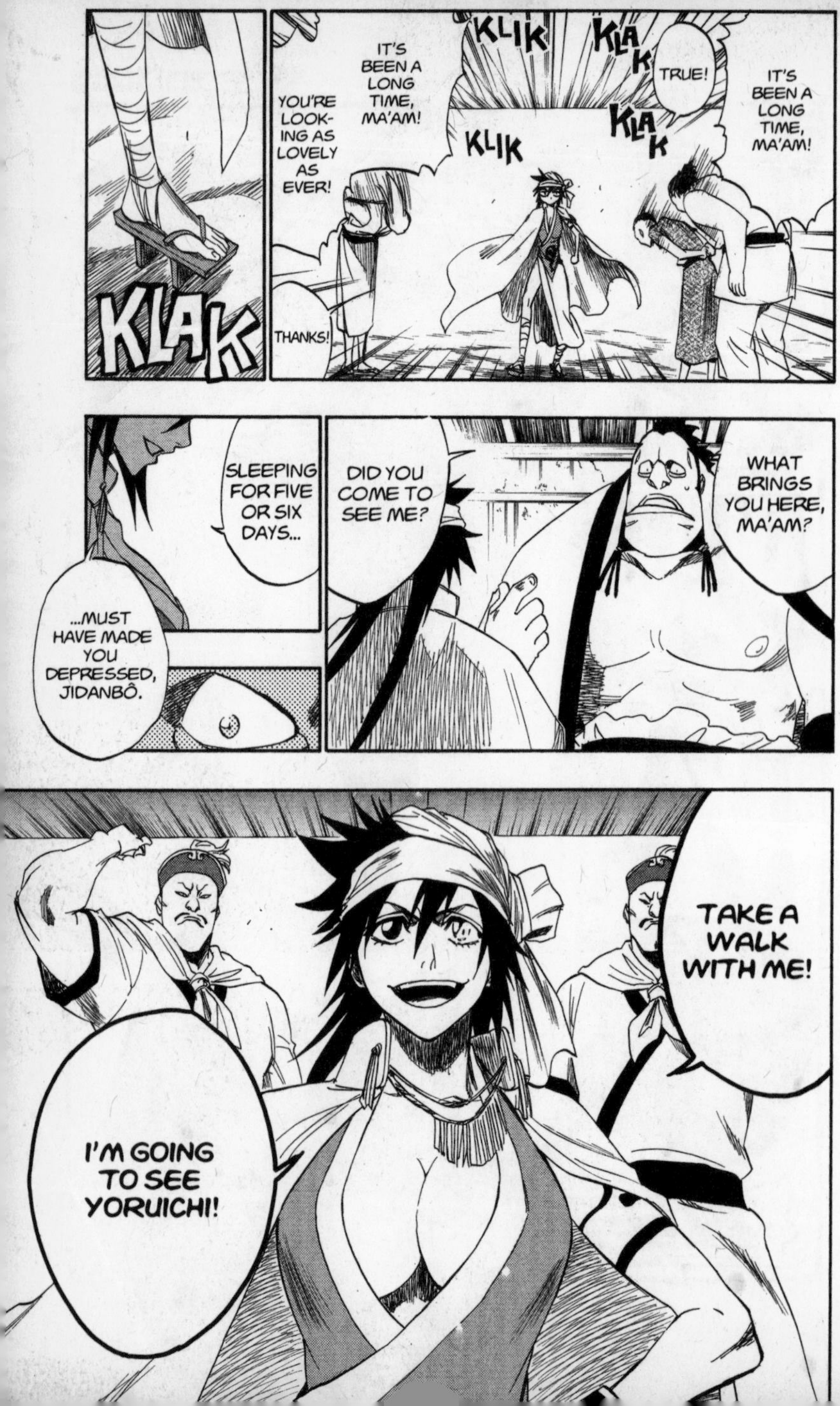
IT'S BEEN A LONG TIME, MA'AM!
TRUE!
KLAK
KLAK
KLIK
IT'S BEEN A LONG TIME, MA'AM!
YOU'RE LOOK-ING AS LOVELY AS EVER!
KLIK
THANKS!
KLAK
WHAT BRINGS YOU HERE, MA'AM?
DID YOU COME TO SEE ME?
SLEEPING FOR FIVE OR SIX DAYS...
...MUST HAVE MADE YOU DEPRESSED, JIDANBÔ.
TAKE A WALK WITH ME!
I'M GOING TO SEE YORUICHI!

157. Cat and Hornet

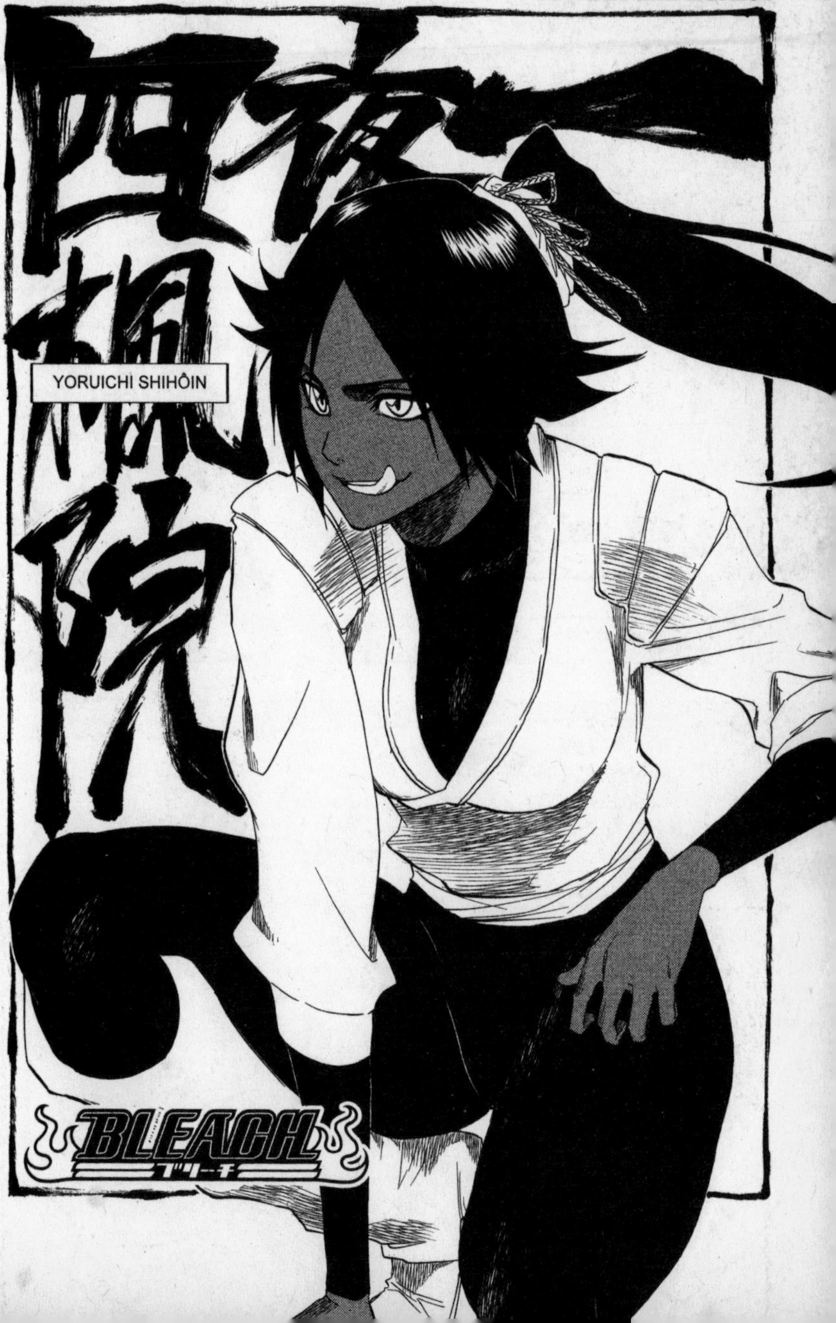
四楓院夜一
YORUICHI SHIHÔIN
BLEACH
ブリーチ

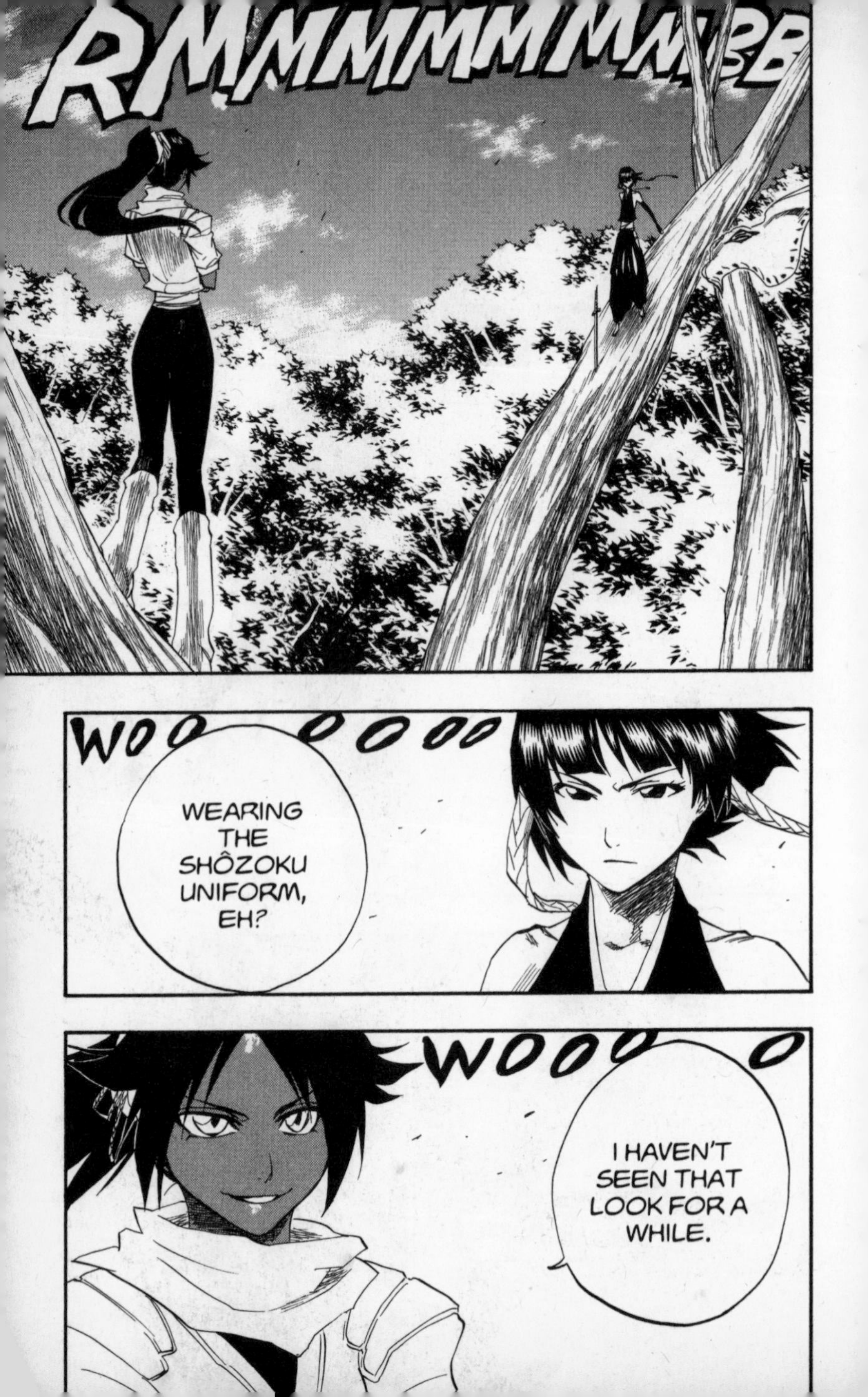
RMMMMMMMBB
WOO OOOO
WEARING THE SHÔZOKU UNIFORM, EH?
WOOO O
I HAVEN'T SEEN THAT LOOK FOR A WHILE.

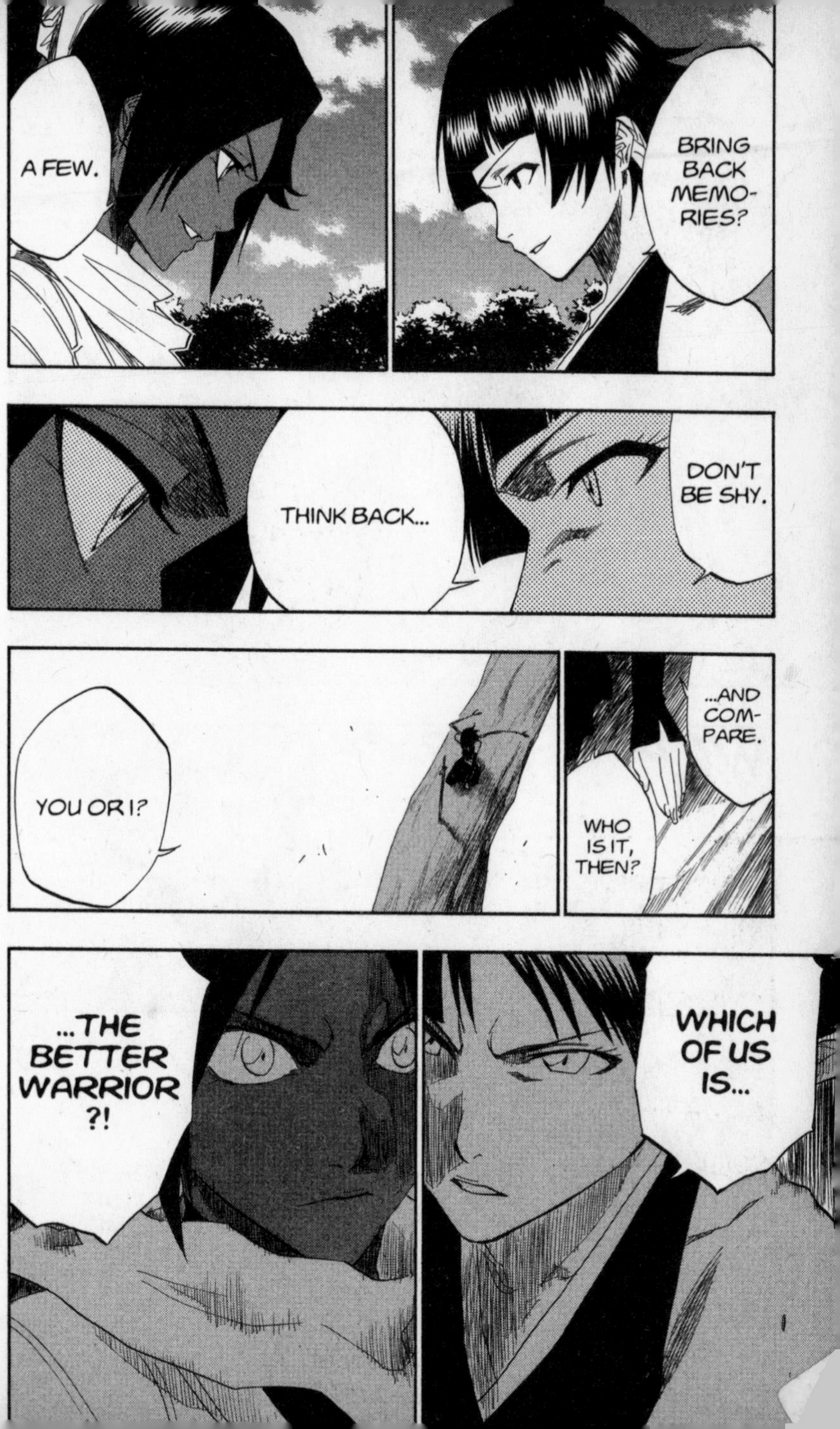
BRING BACK MEMORIES?
A FEW.
DON'T BE SHY.
THINK BACK...
...AND COMPARE.
WHO IS IT, THEN?
YOU OR I?
WHICH OF US IS...
...THE BETTER WARRIOR ?!

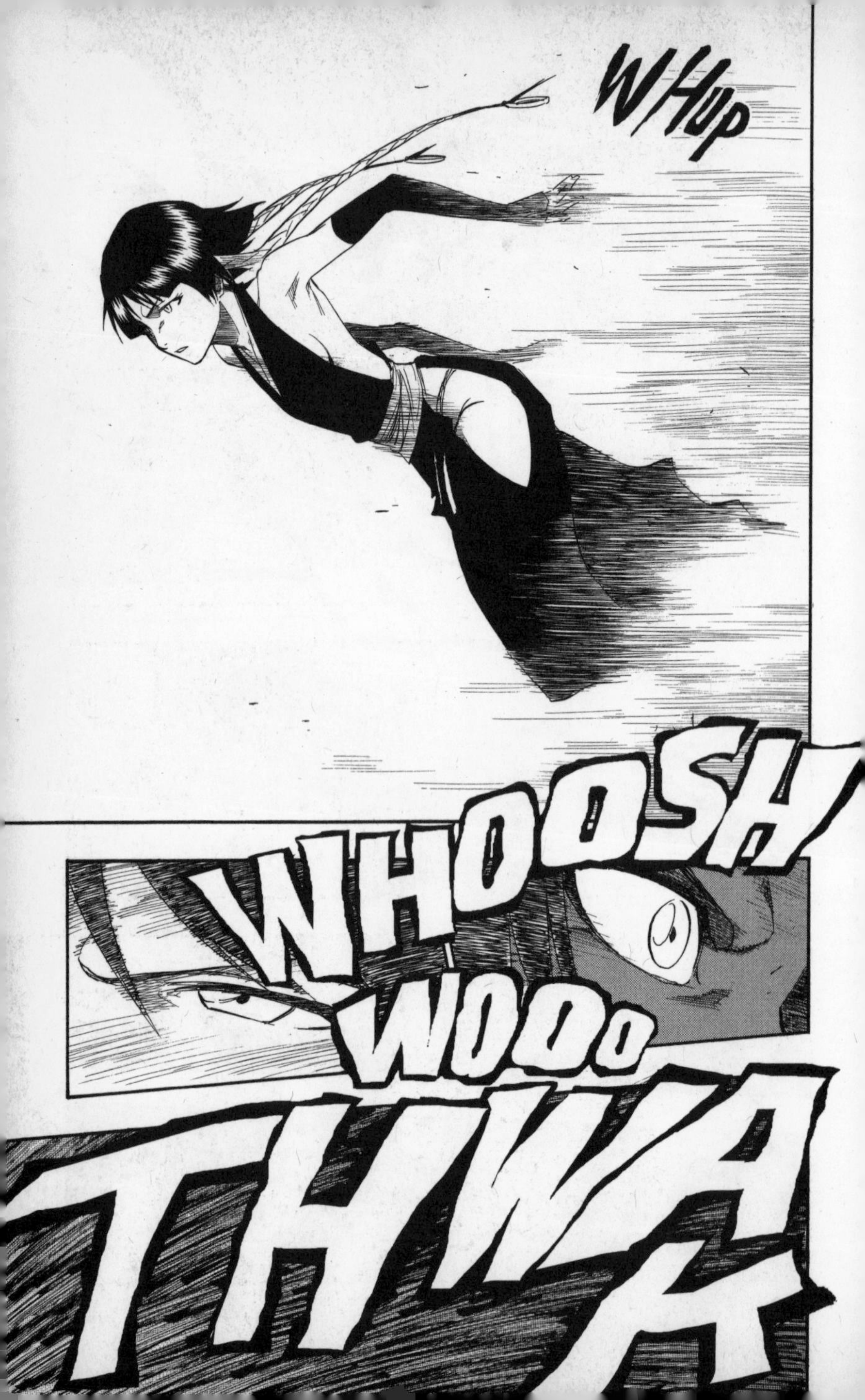
WHUP
WHOOSH
WOOo
THWA

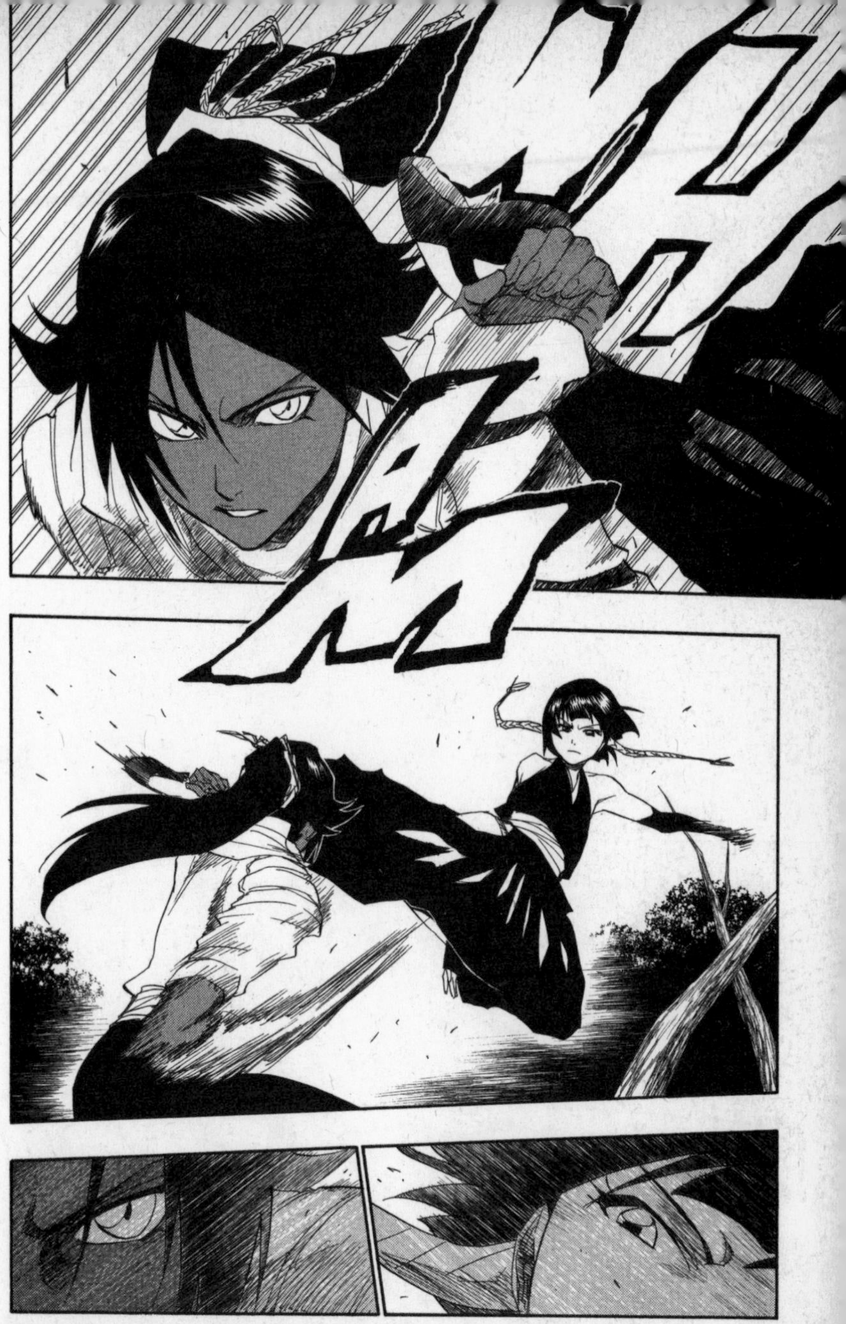

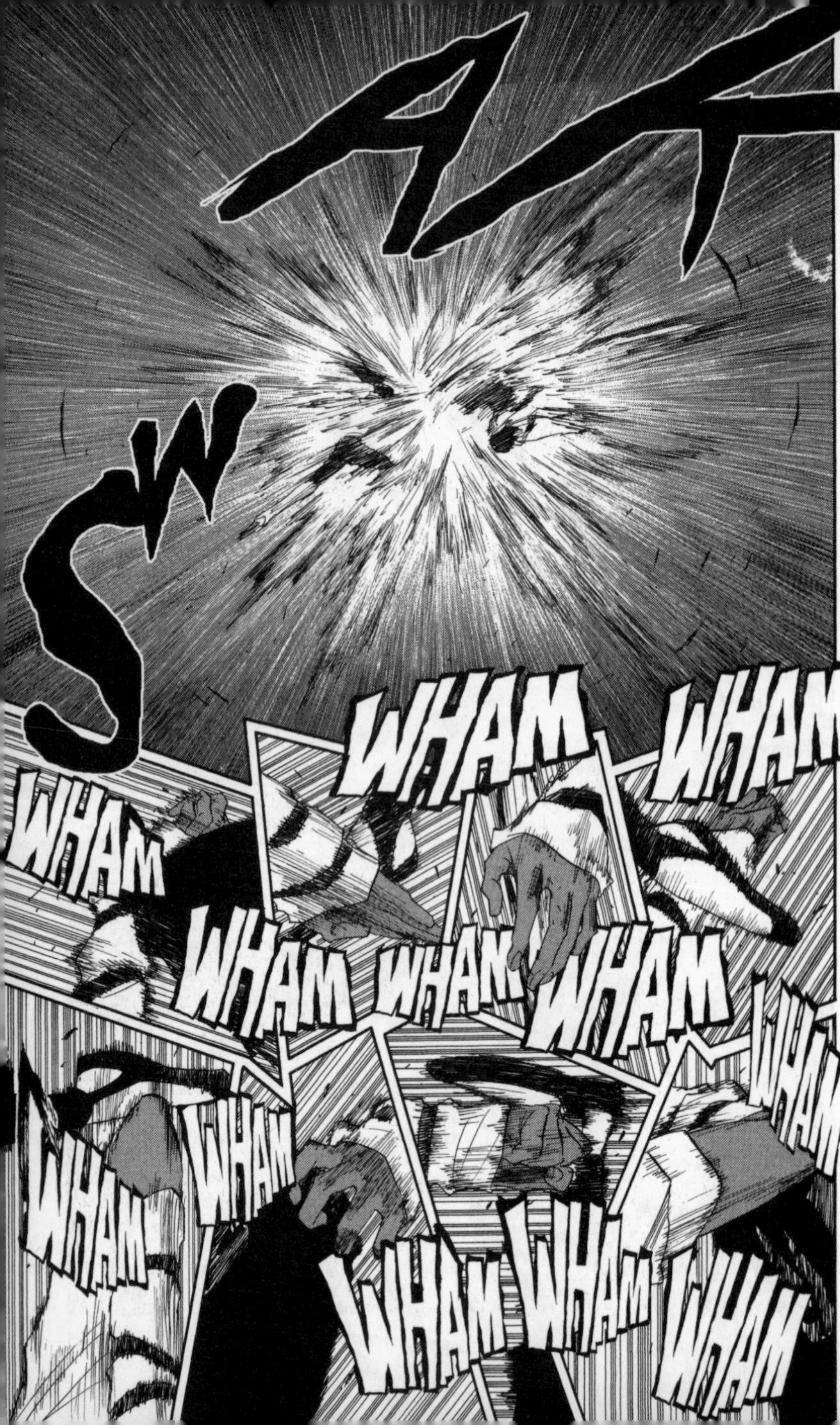
SWAT
WHAM
WHAM
WHAM
WHAM
WHAM
WHAM
WHAM
WHAM
WHAM
WHAM
WHAM
WHAM

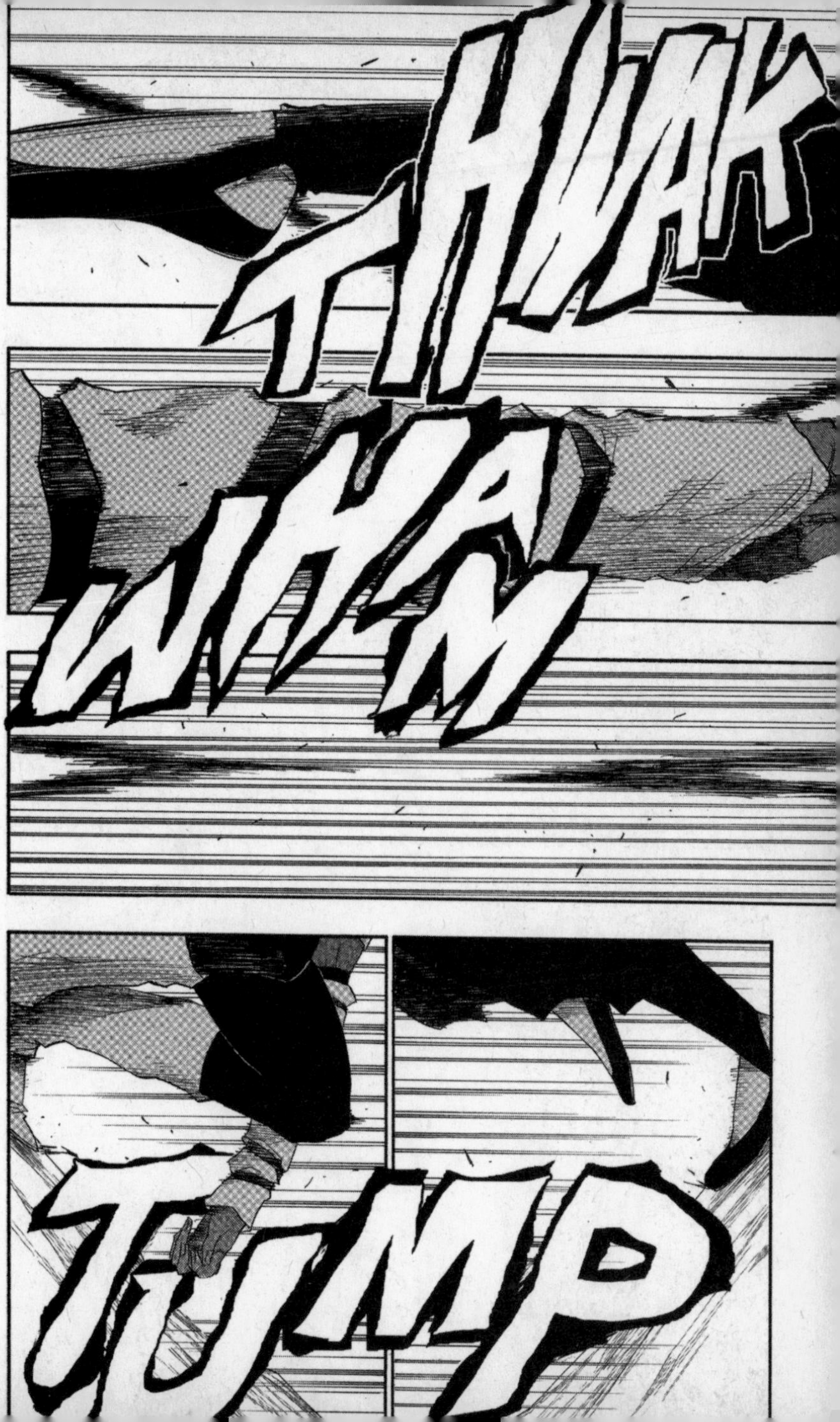
THWAK
WHAM
THMP

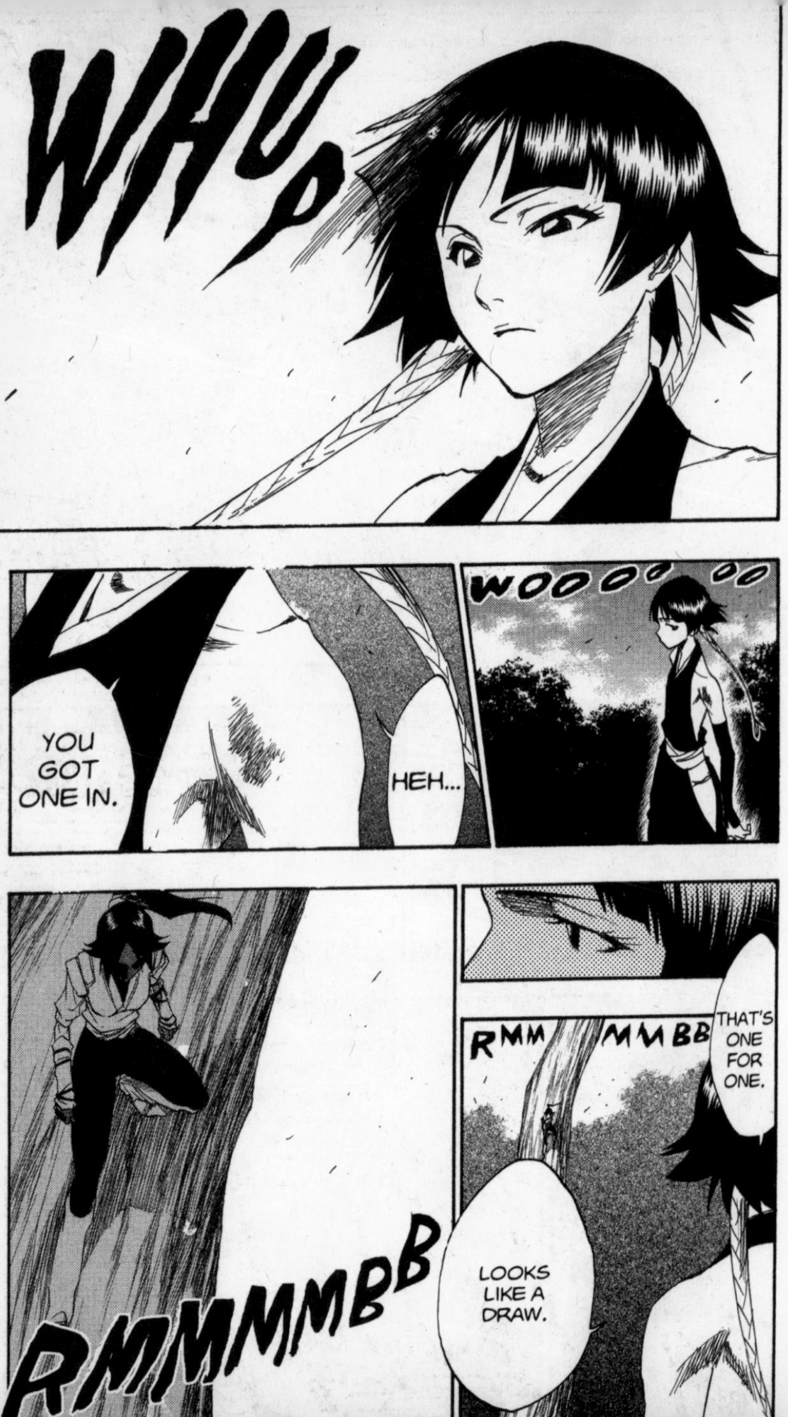
WHUD
WOOOO OO
HEH...
YOU GOT ONE IN.
RMM MMBB
THAT'S ONE FOR ONE.
LOOKS LIKE A DRAW.
RMMMMBB

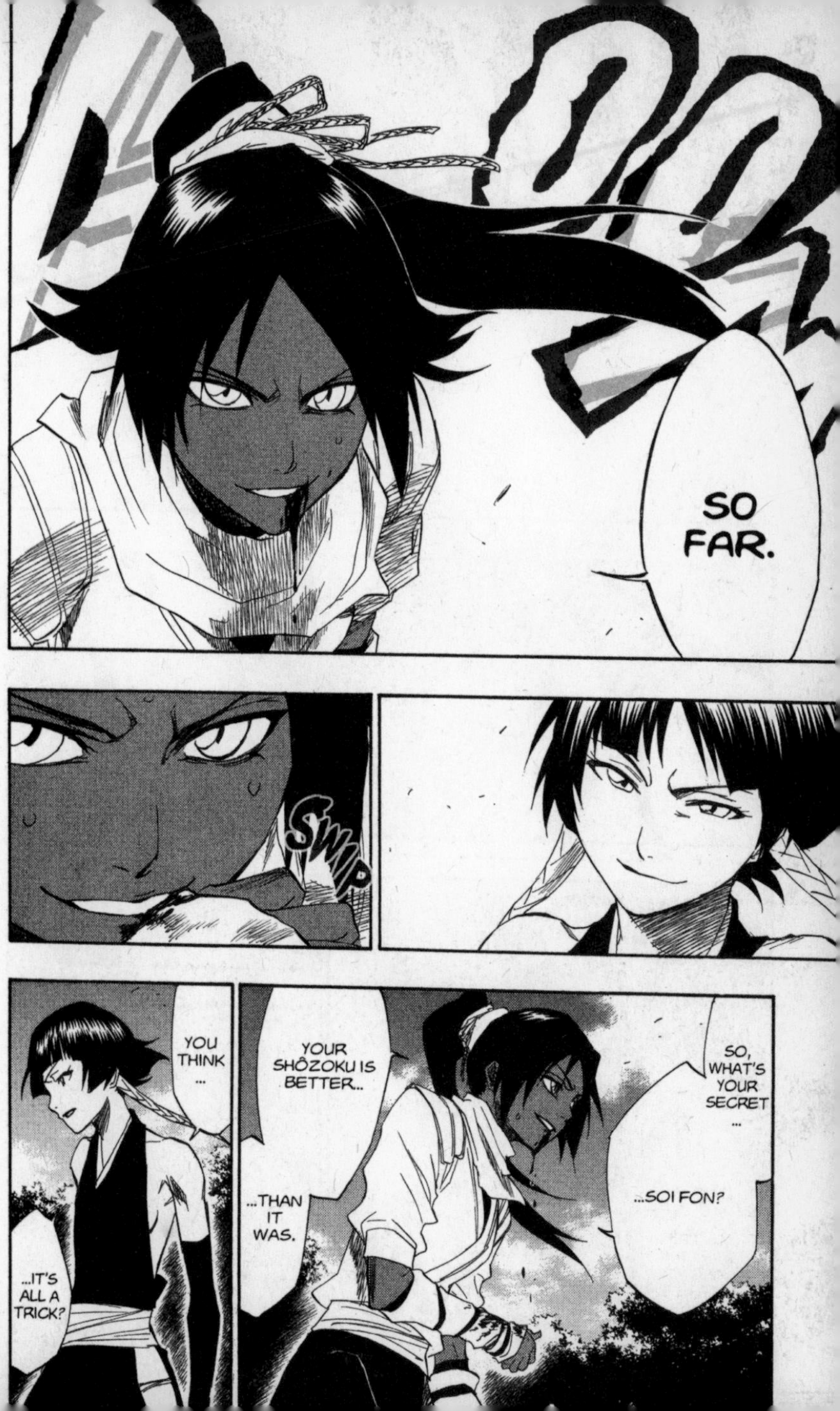
SO FAR.
SWIP
SO, WHAT'S YOUR SECRET ...
...SOI FON?
YOUR SHÔZOKU IS BETTER...
...THAN IT WAS.
YOU THINK ...
...IT'S ALL A TRICK?

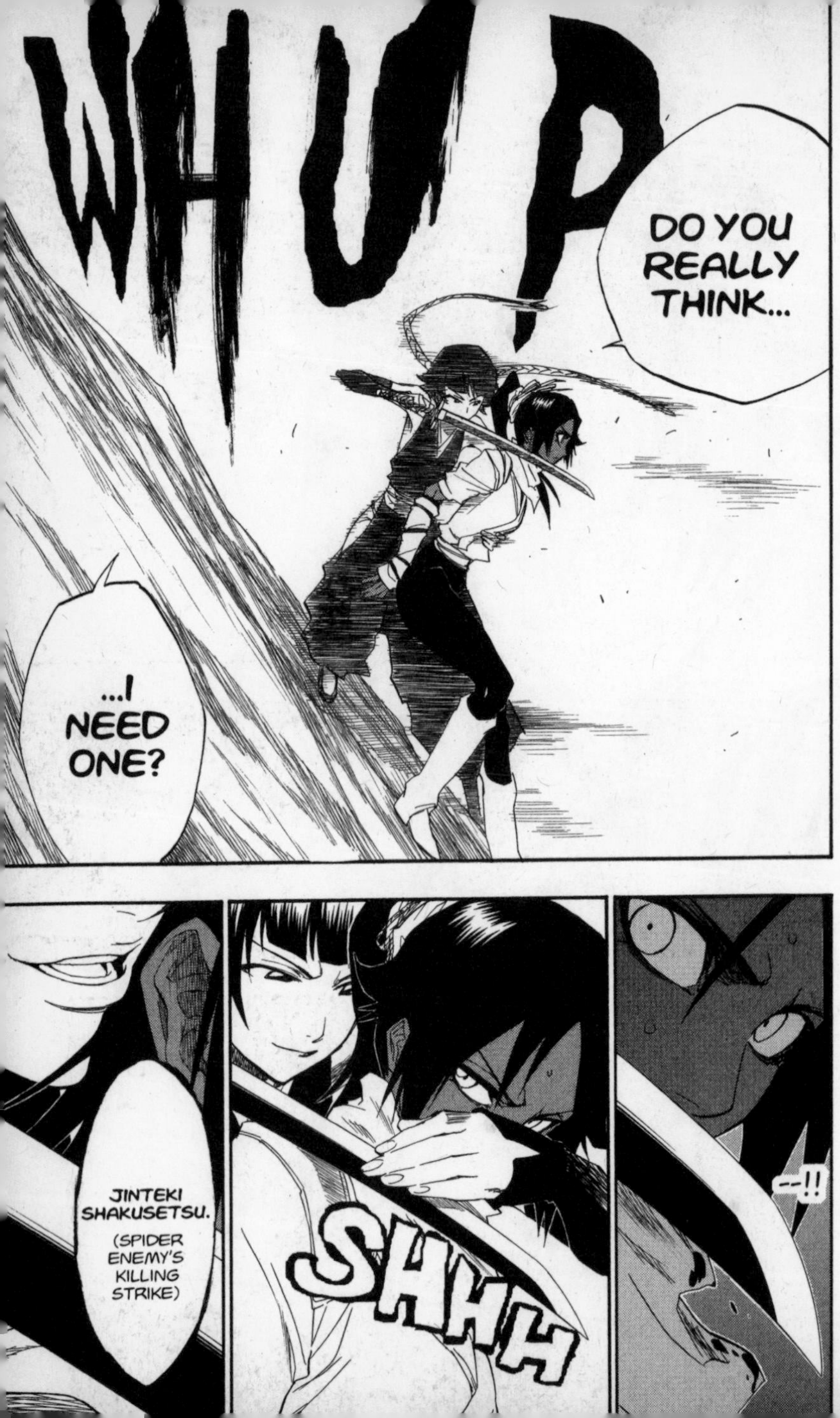
WHUP
DO YOU REALLY THINK...
...I NEED ONE?
--!!
SHHH
JINTEKI SHAKUSETSU.
(SPIDER ENEMY'S KILLING STRIKE)

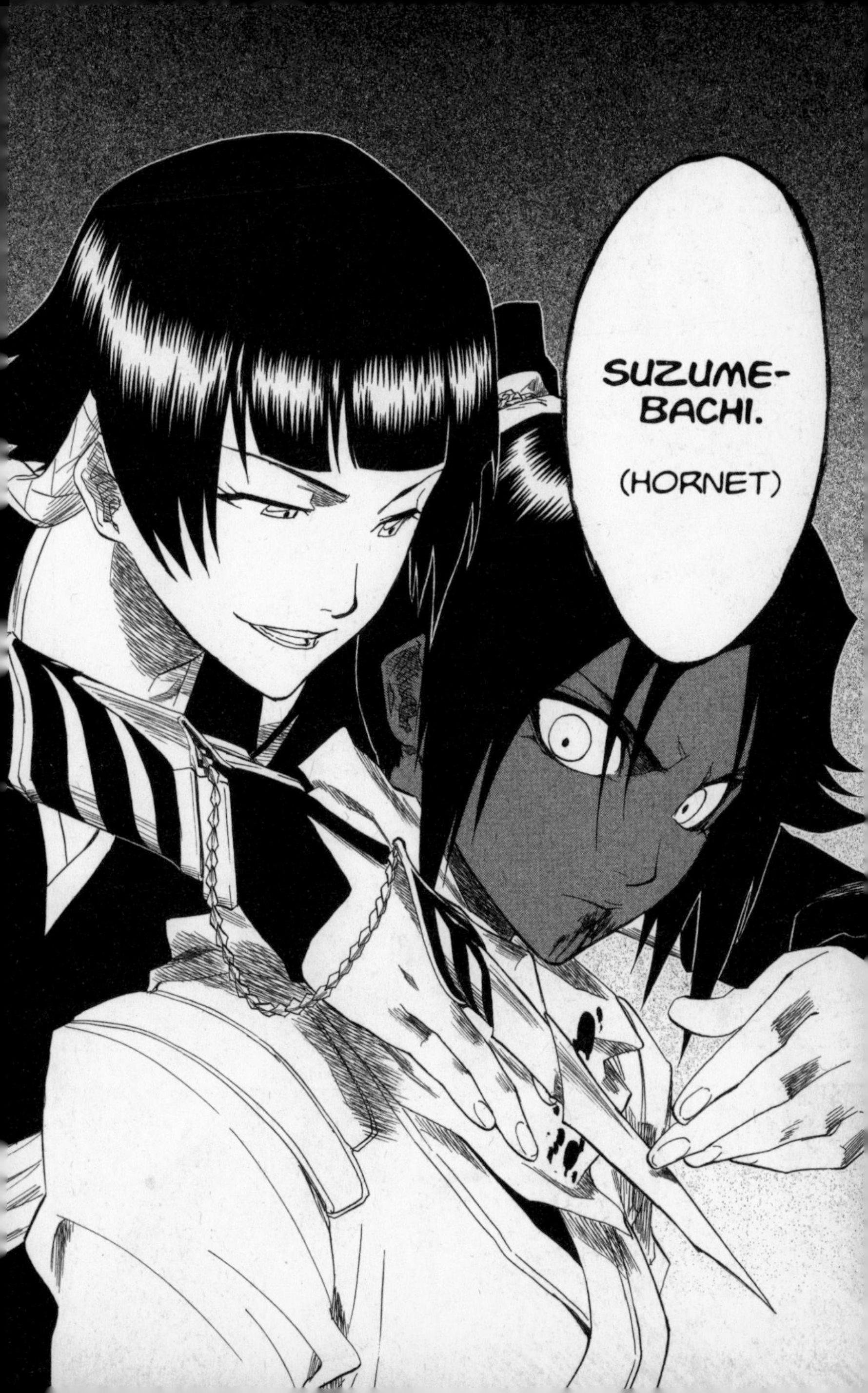
SUZUME-
BACHI.
(HORNET)

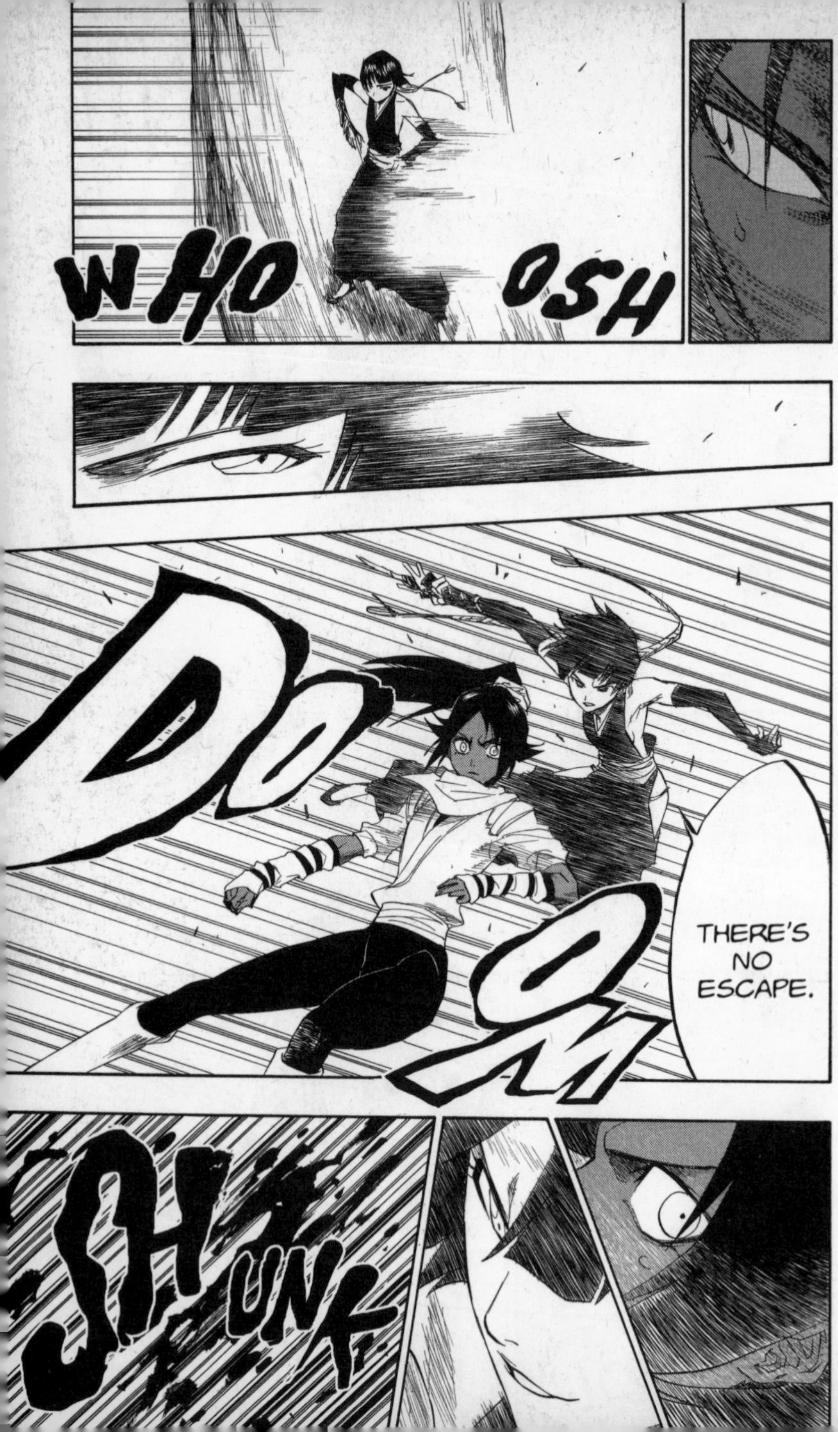
WHOOSH
DOOM
THERE'S NO ESCAPE.
SHUNK

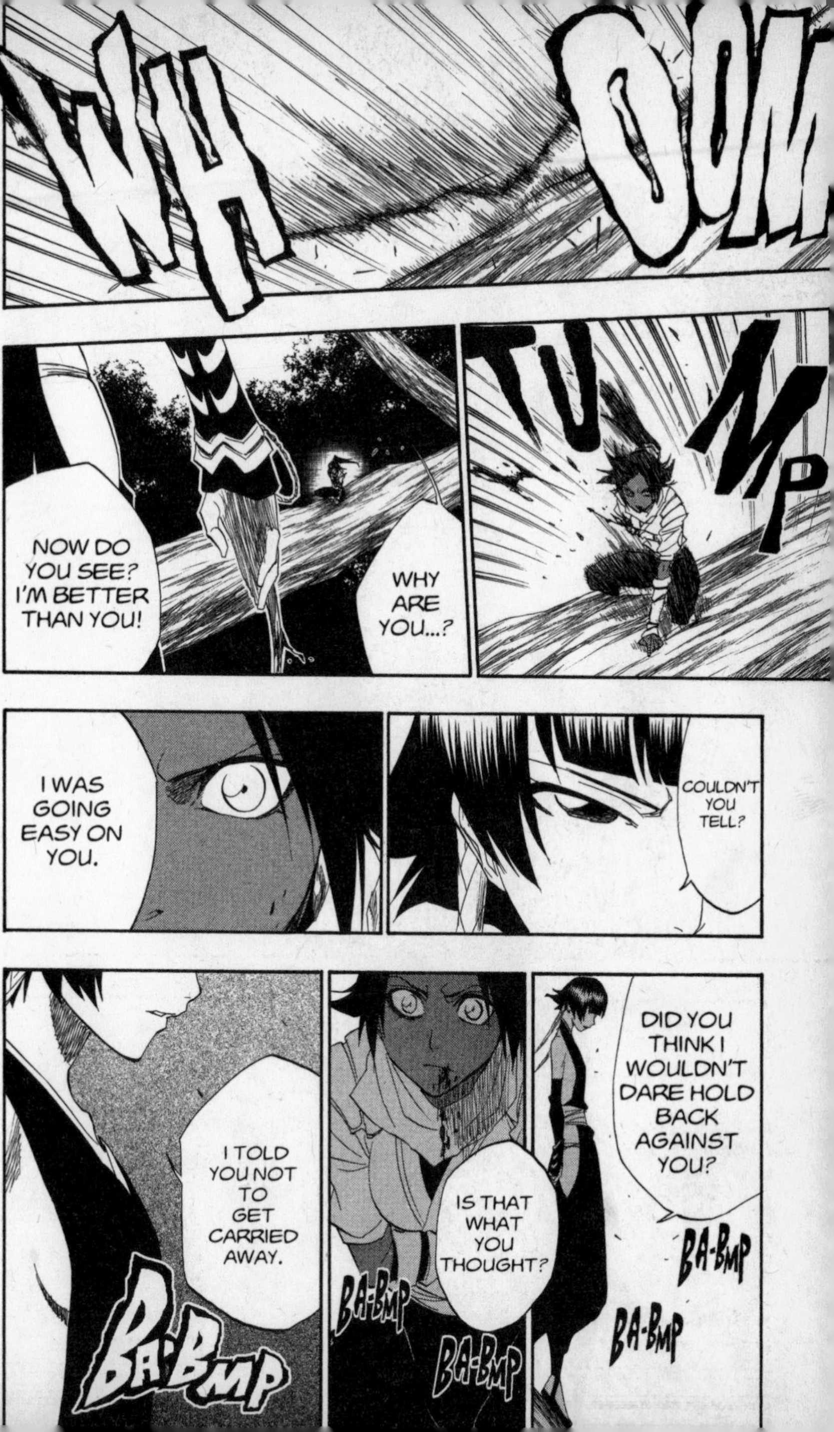
WHA OOM
TUMP
WHY ARE YOU...?
NOW DO YOU SEE? I'M BETTER THAN YOU!
COULDN'T YOU TELL?
I WAS GOING EASY ON YOU.
DID YOU THINK I WOULDN'T DARE HOLD BACK AGAINST YOU?
BA-BMP
BA-BMP
IS THAT WHAT YOU THOUGHT?
BA-BMP
BA-BMP
I TOLD YOU NOT TO GET CARRIED AWAY.
BA-BMP

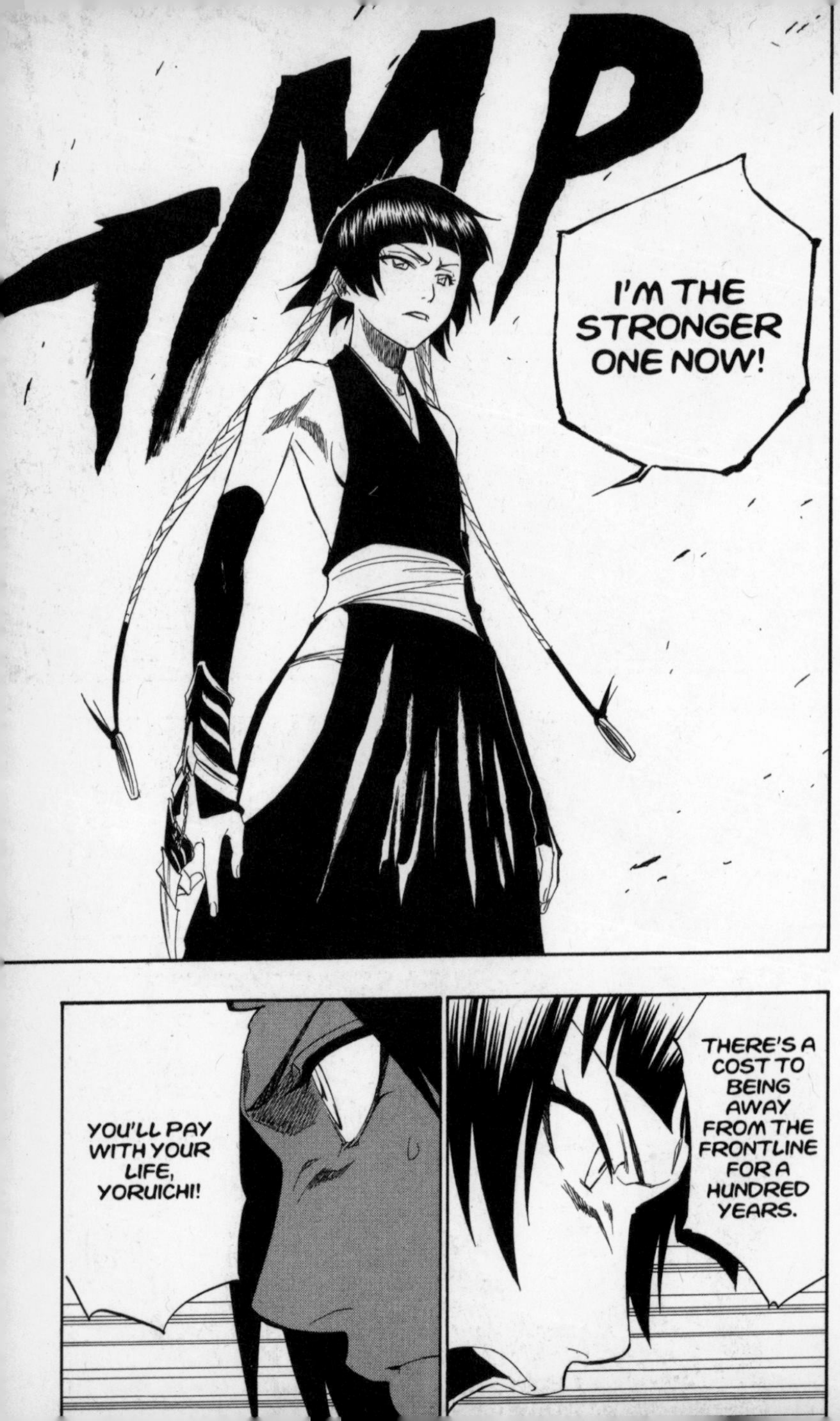
TMP
I'M THE STRONGER ONE NOW!
THERE'S A COST TO BEING AWAY FROM THE FRONTLINE FOR A HUNDRED YEARS.
YOU'LL PAY WITH YOUR LIFE, YORUICHI!

JINTA!!
DON'T USE YOUR INVINCIBLE IRON CLUB...
I FORBID IT!!
...ON A NORMAL PERSON!
I...
FOR-BID
IT!!

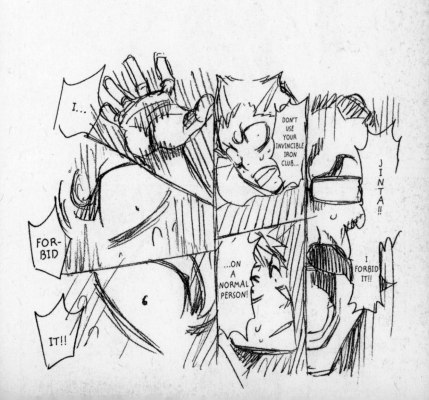

158. Sky Leopardess

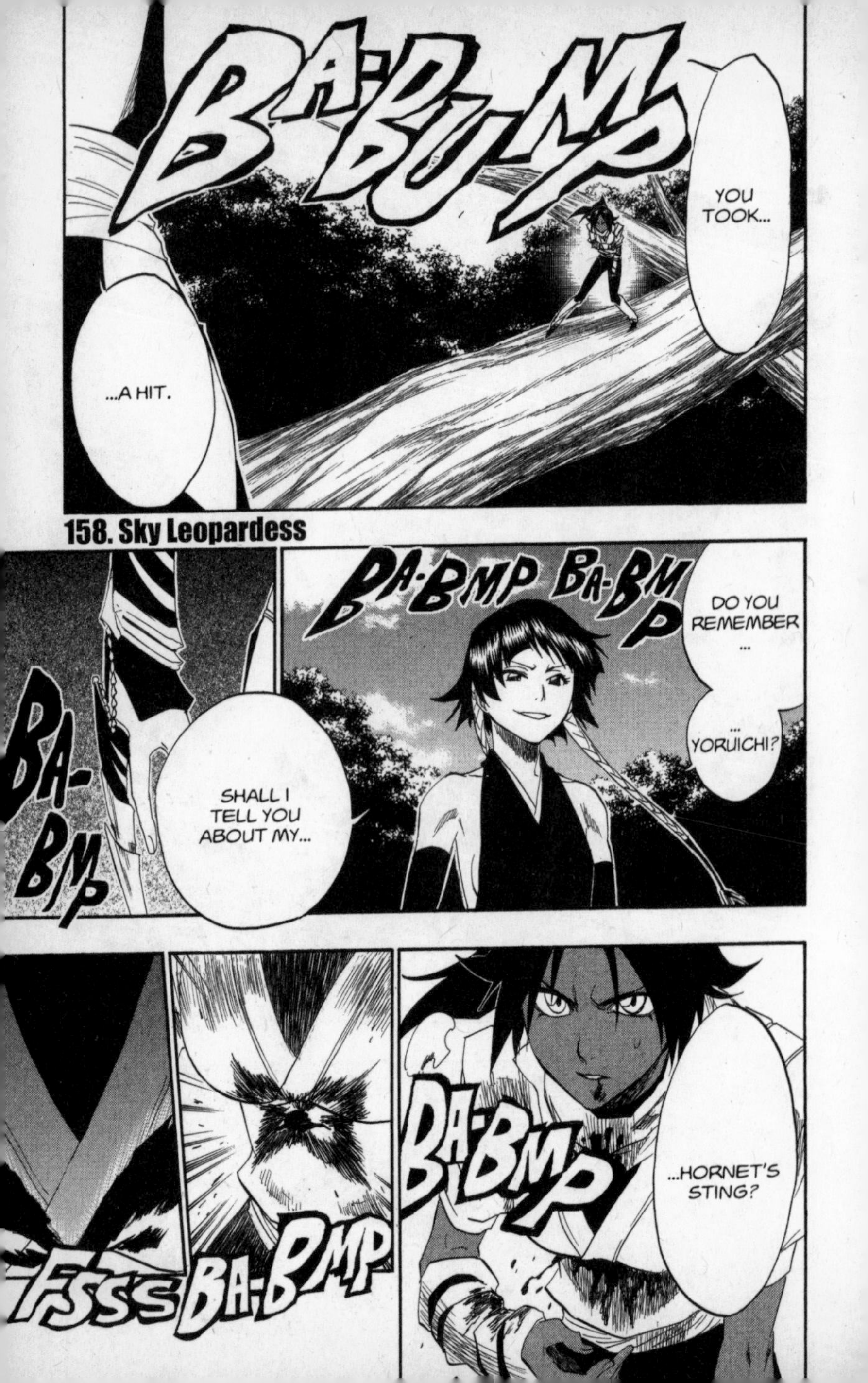
YOU TOOK...
BA-DUMP
...A HIT.
BA-BMP BA-BMP
DO YOU REMEMBER ...
... YORUICHI?
BA-BMP
SHALL I TELL YOU ABOUT MY...
...HORNET'S STING?
BA-BMP
BA-BMP
FSSS

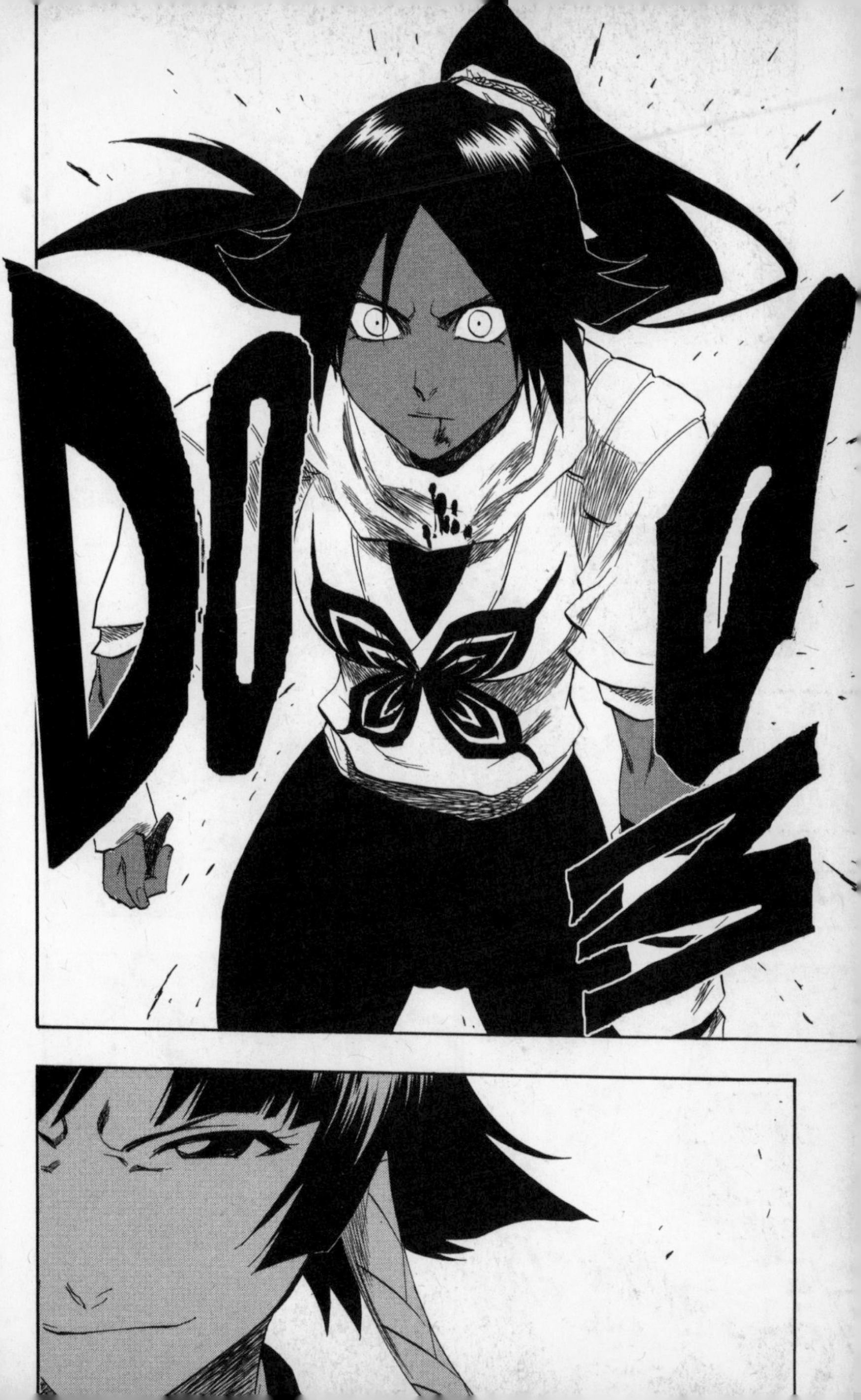
DOOM

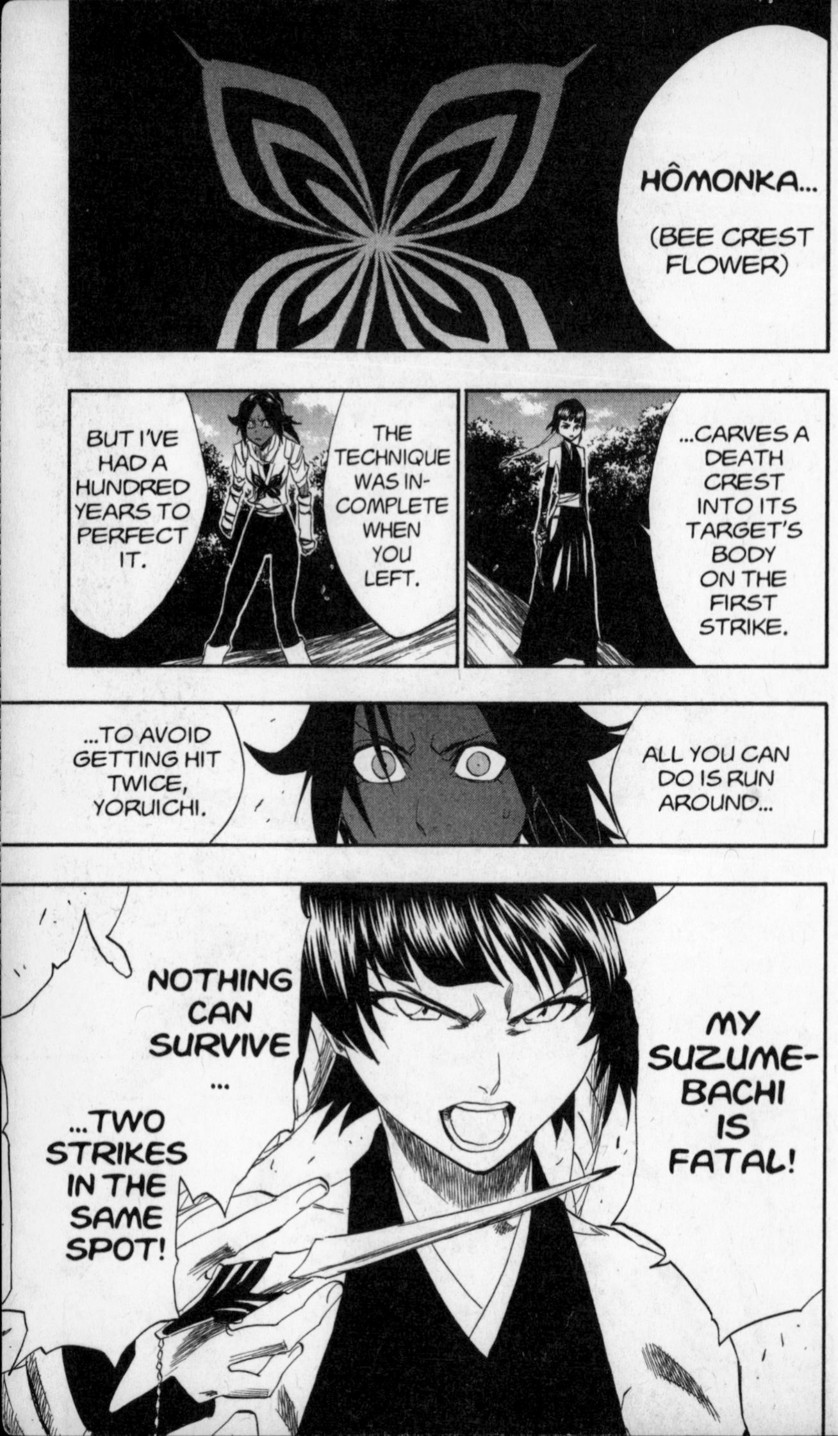
HÔMONKA...
(BEE CREST FLOWER)
...CARVES A DEATH CREST INTO ITS TARGET'S BODY ON THE FIRST STRIKE.
THE TECHNIQUE WAS IN-COMPLETE WHEN YOU LEFT.
BUT I'VE HAD A HUNDRED YEARS TO PERFECT IT.
ALL YOU CAN DO IS RUN AROUND...
...TO AVOID GETTING HIT TWICE, YORUICHI.
MY SUZUME-BACHI IS FATAL!
NOTHING CAN SURVIVE ...
...TWO STRIKES IN THE SAME SPOT!

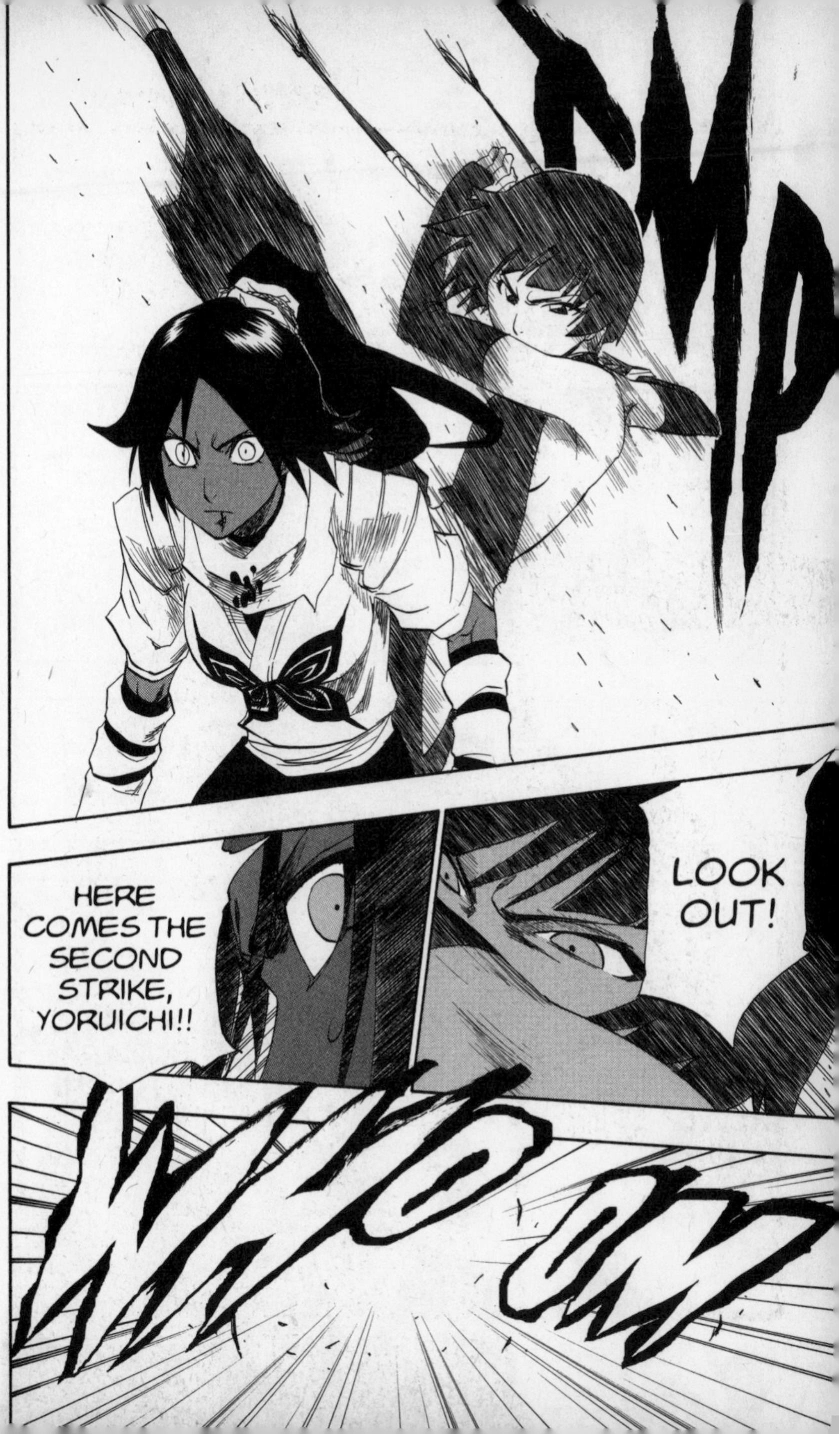
LOOK OUT!
HERE COMES THE SECOND STRIKE, YORUICHI!!
WHOOM

158: Sky Leopardess

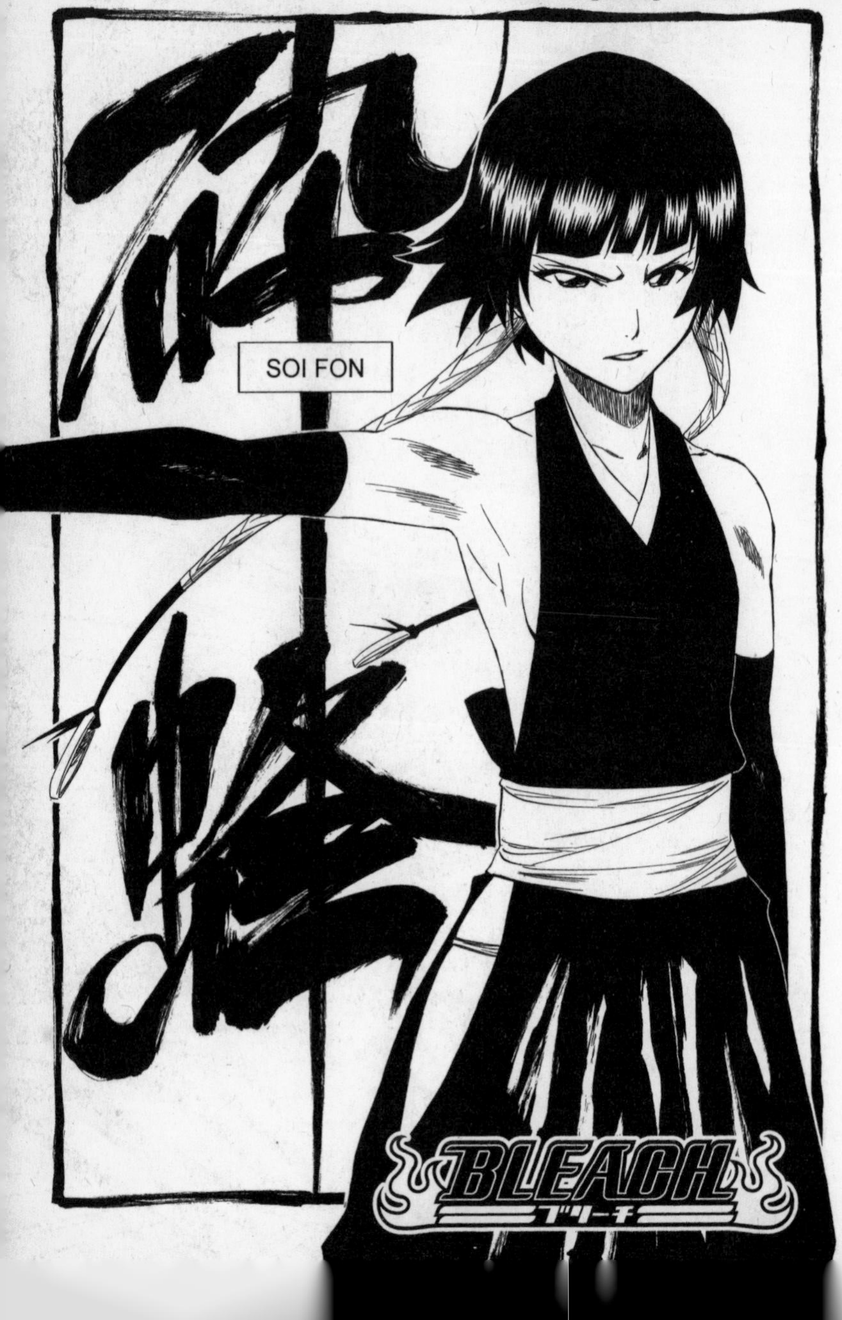
SOI FON
BLEACH
ブリーチ

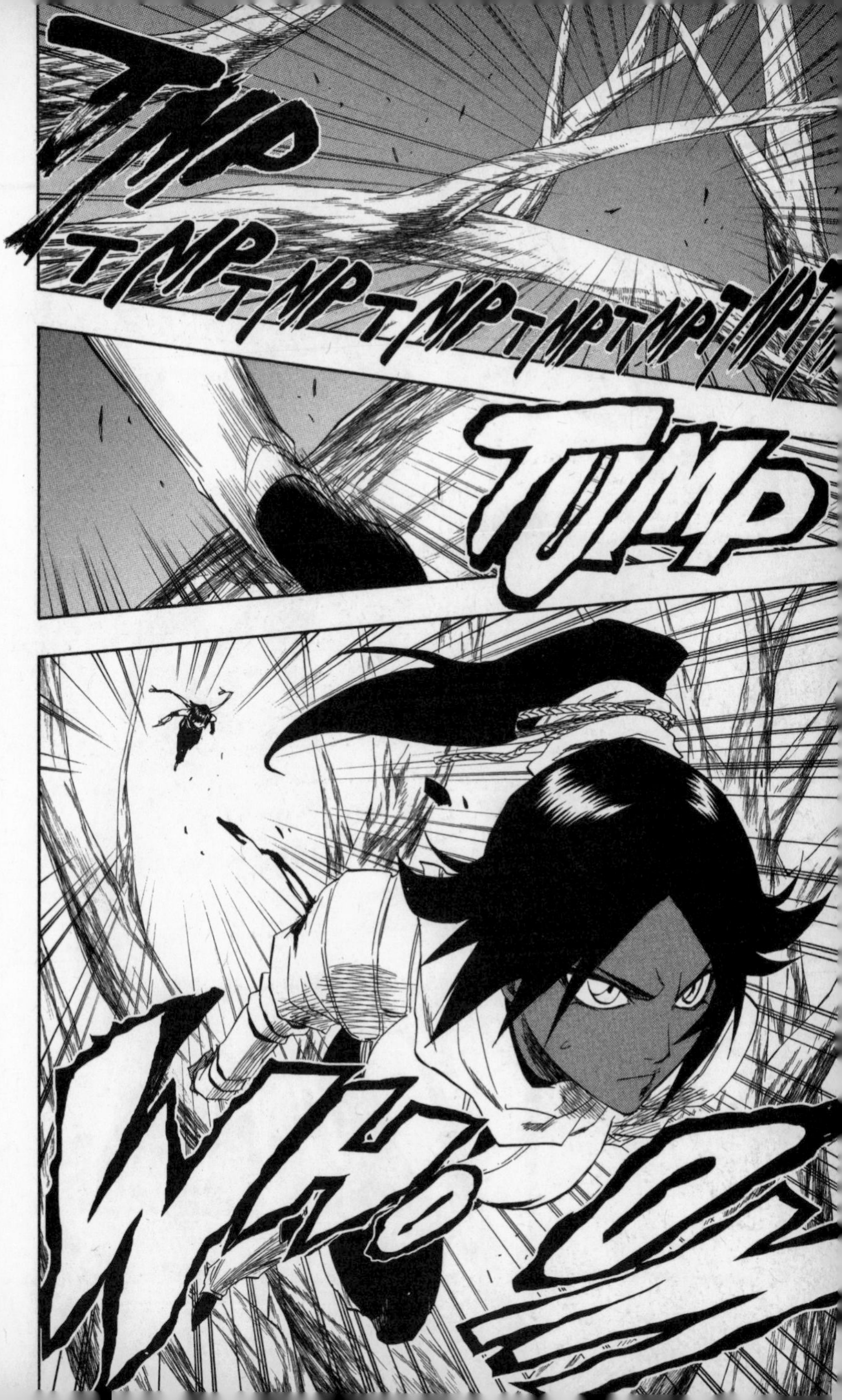
TMP
TMP TMP TMP TMP TMP TMP TMP
TUMP

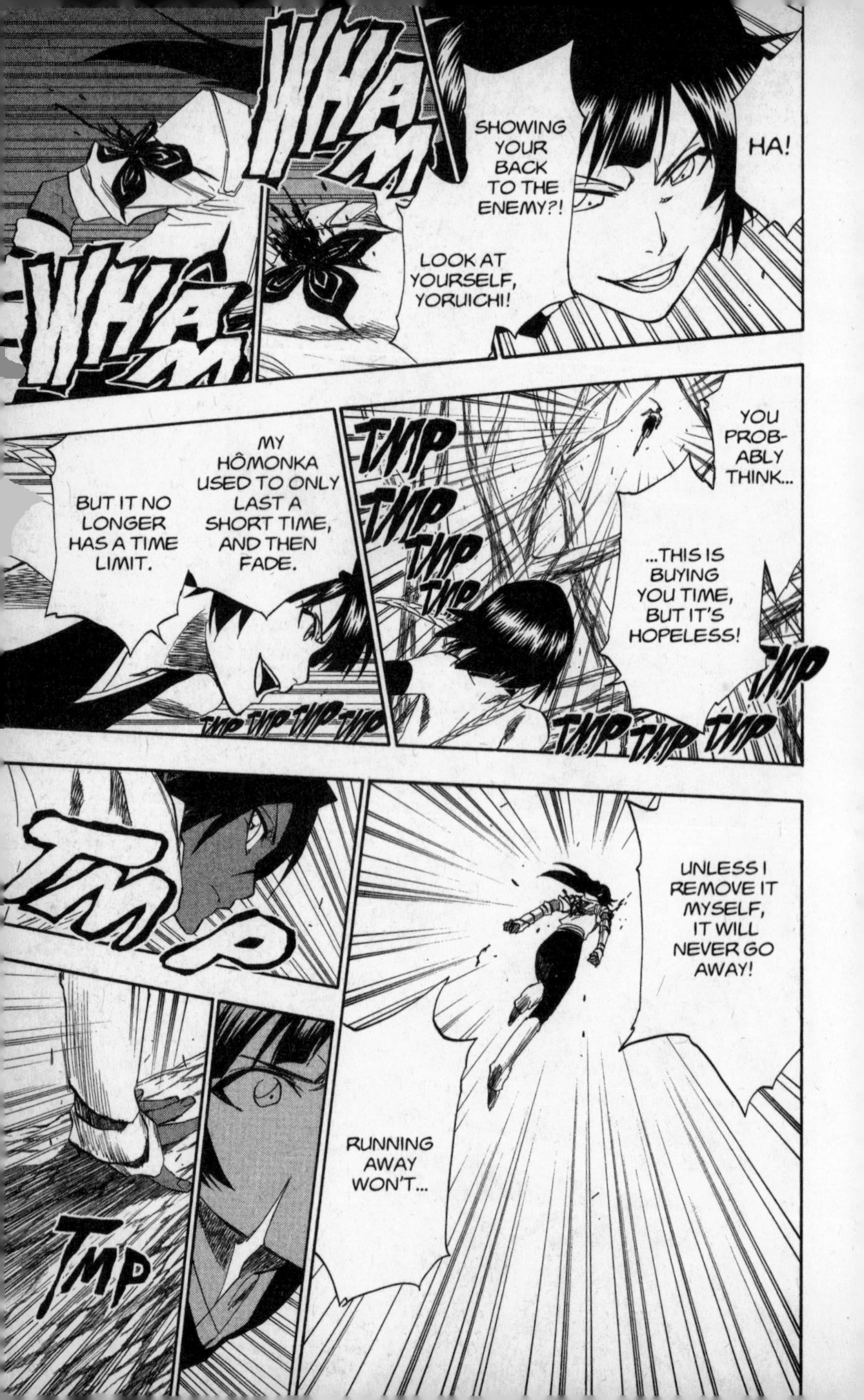
HA!
SHOWING YOUR BACK TO THE ENEMY?!
LOOK AT YOURSELF, YORUICHI!
WHAM
WHAM
YOU PROBABLY THINK...
...THIS IS BUYING YOU TIME, BUT IT'S HOPELESS!
TMP TMP TMP
TMP TMP TMP TMP
MY HÔMONKA USED TO ONLY LAST A SHORT TIME, AND THEN FADE.
BUT IT NO LONGER HAS A TIME LIMIT.
TMP TMP TMP TMP
UNLESS I REMOVE IT MYSELF, IT WILL NEVER GO AWAY!
RUNNING AWAY WON'T...
TMP
TMP

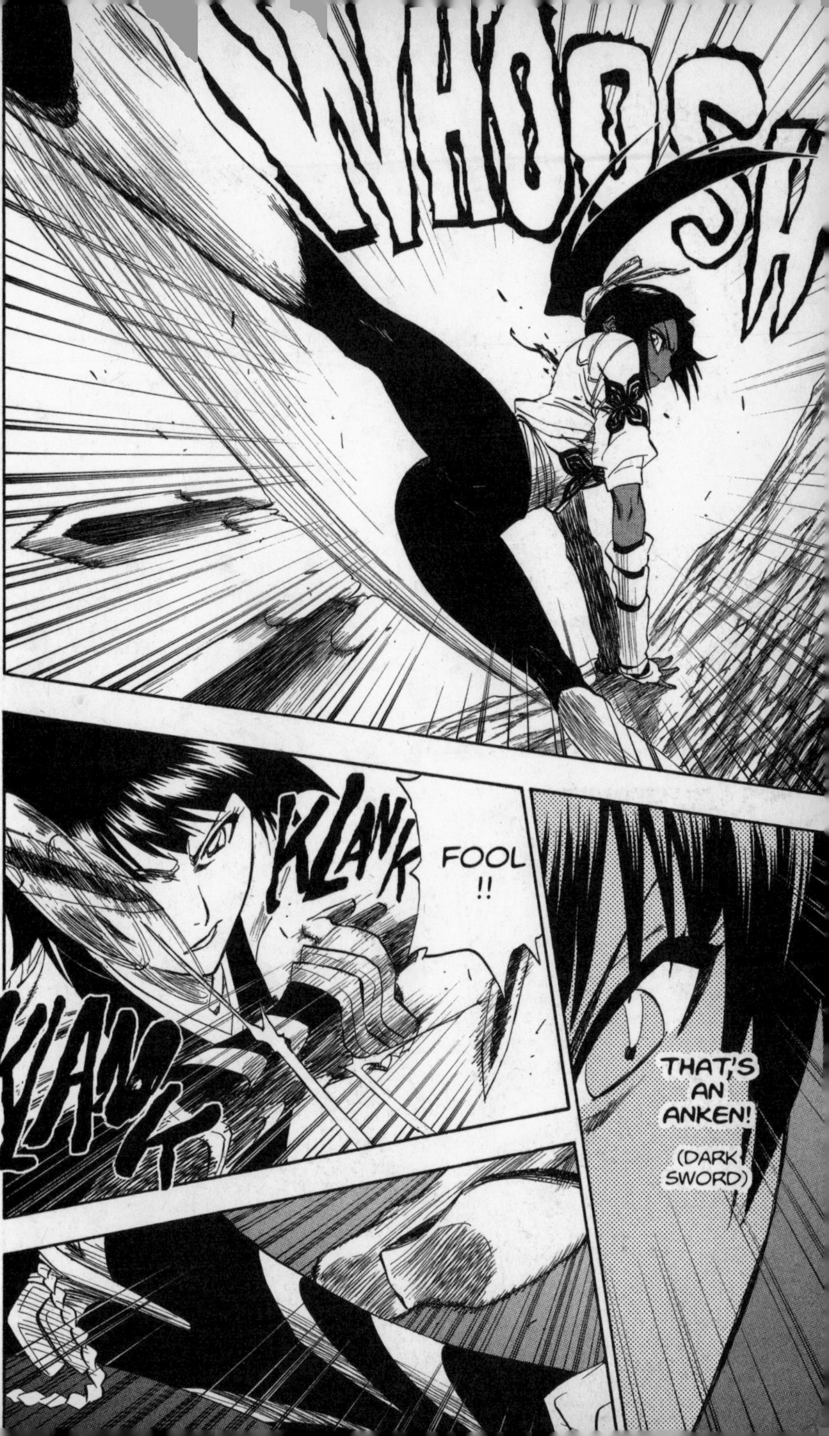
WHOOSH
THAT'S AN ANKEN!
(DARK SWORD)
FOOL !!
KLANK
KLANK

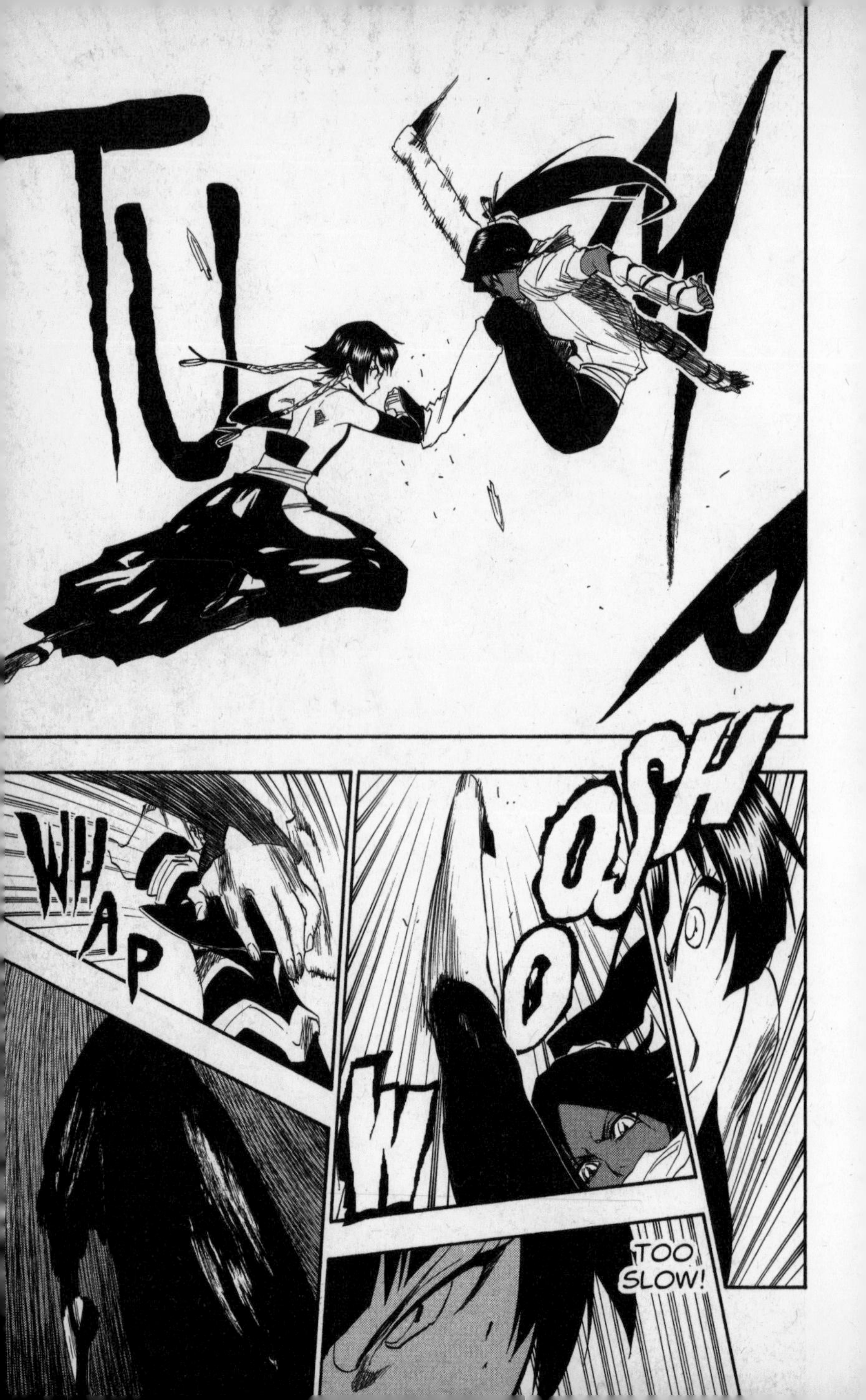
TUMP
WHOOSH
TOO SLOW!
WHAP

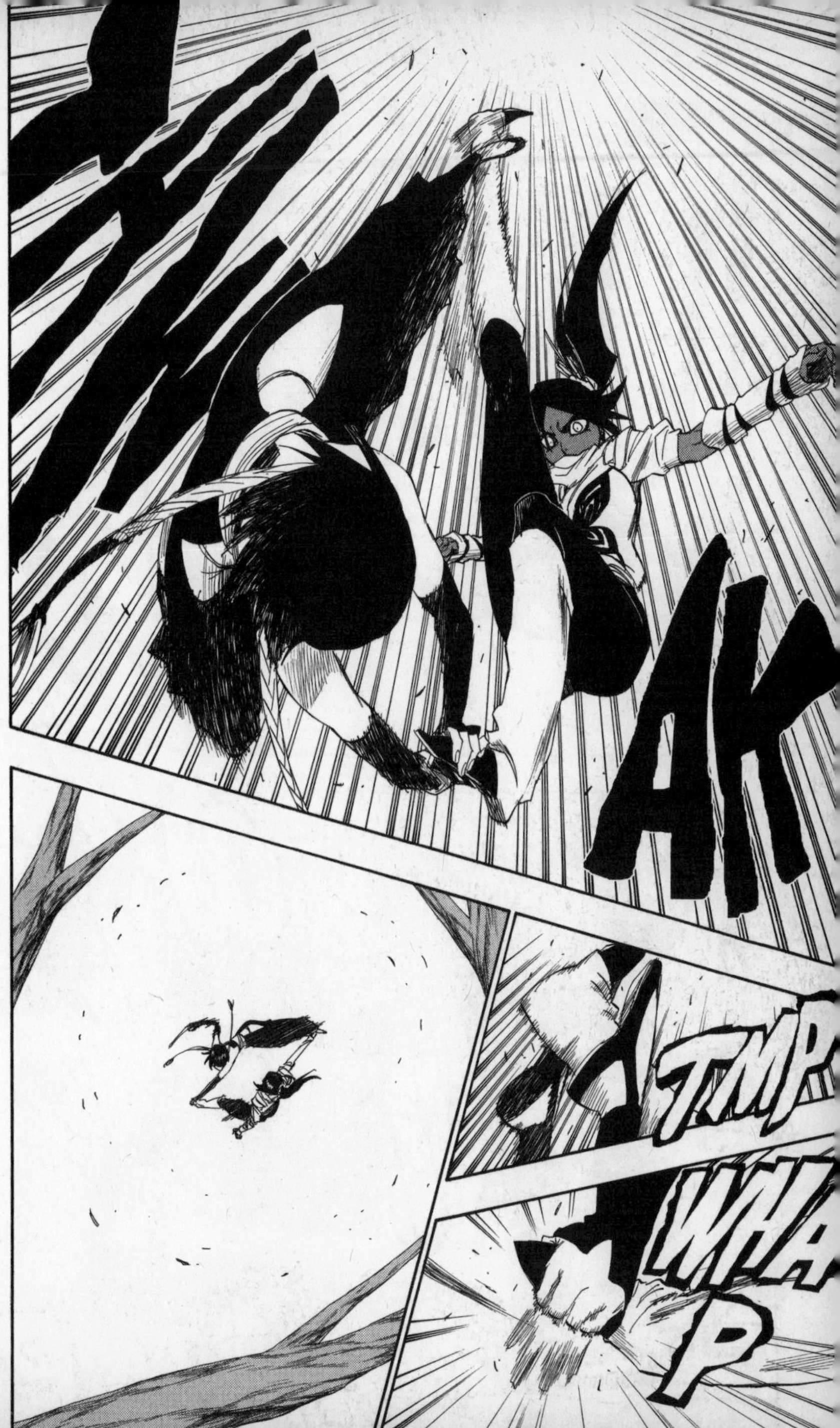
TMP
WHAP

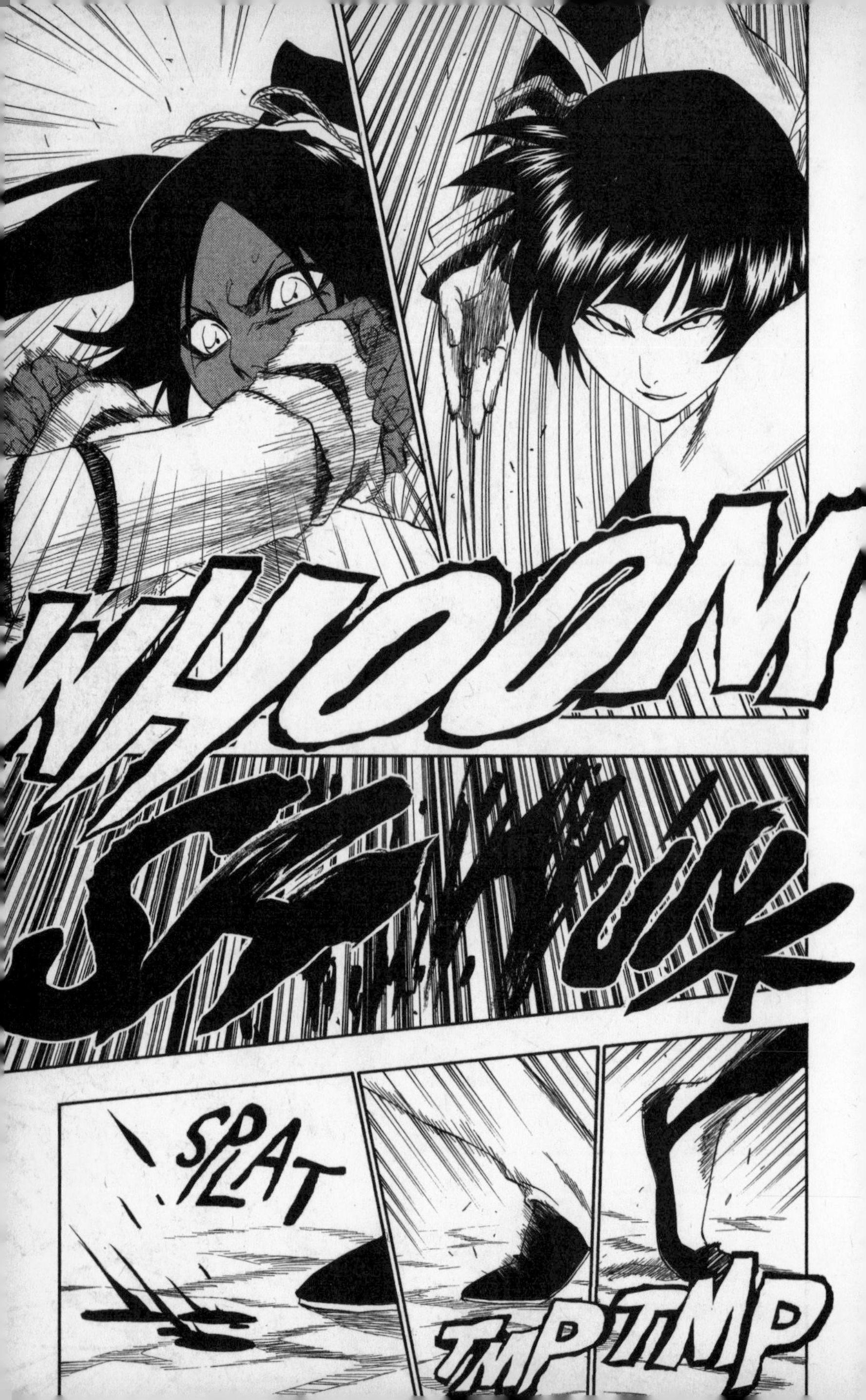
WHOOM
SHUNK
TMP TMP
SPLAT

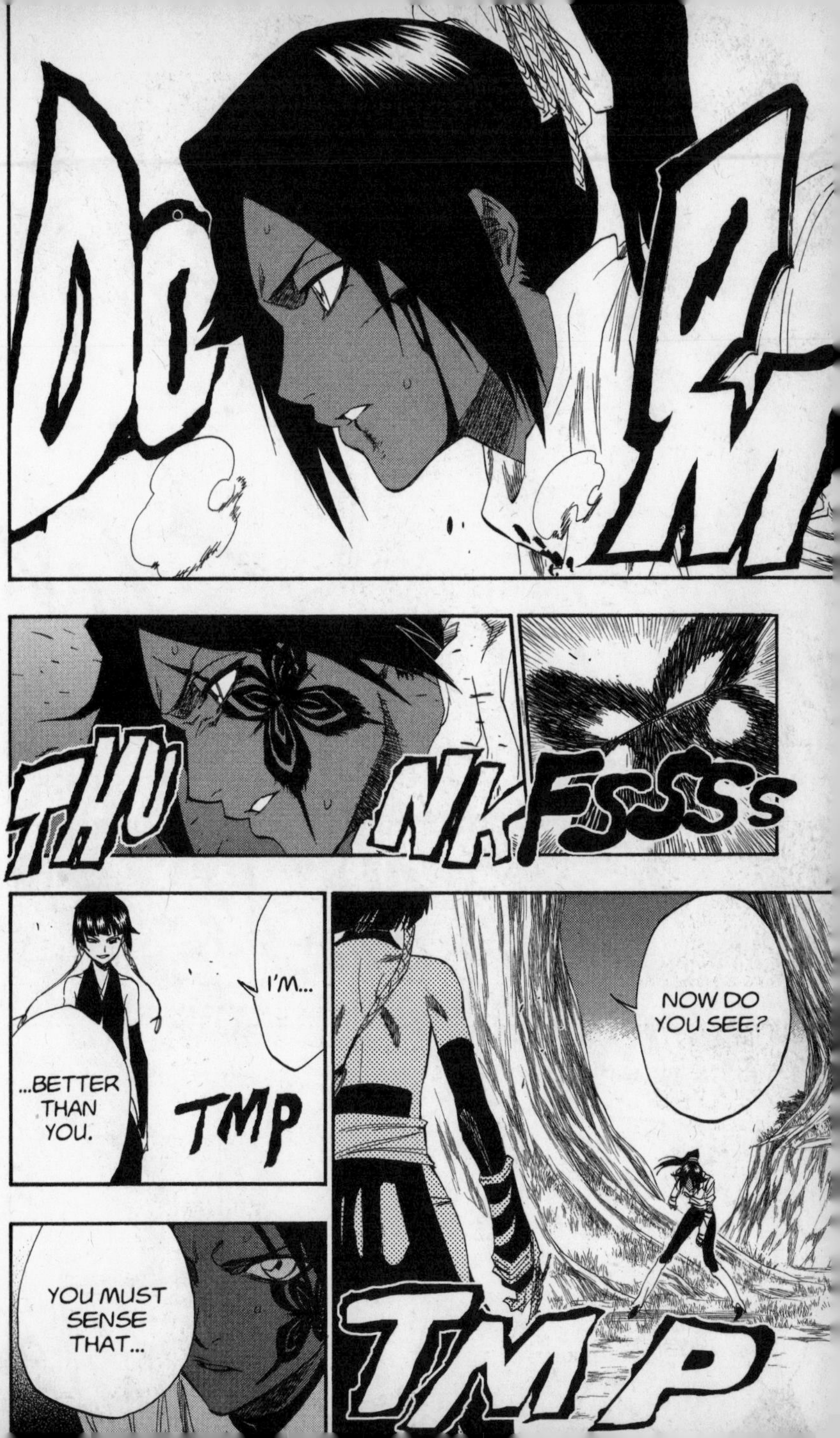
DOOM
FSSSs
THUNK
NOW DO YOU SEE?
TMP
I'M...
...BETTER THAN YOU.
TMP
YOU MUST SENSE THAT...

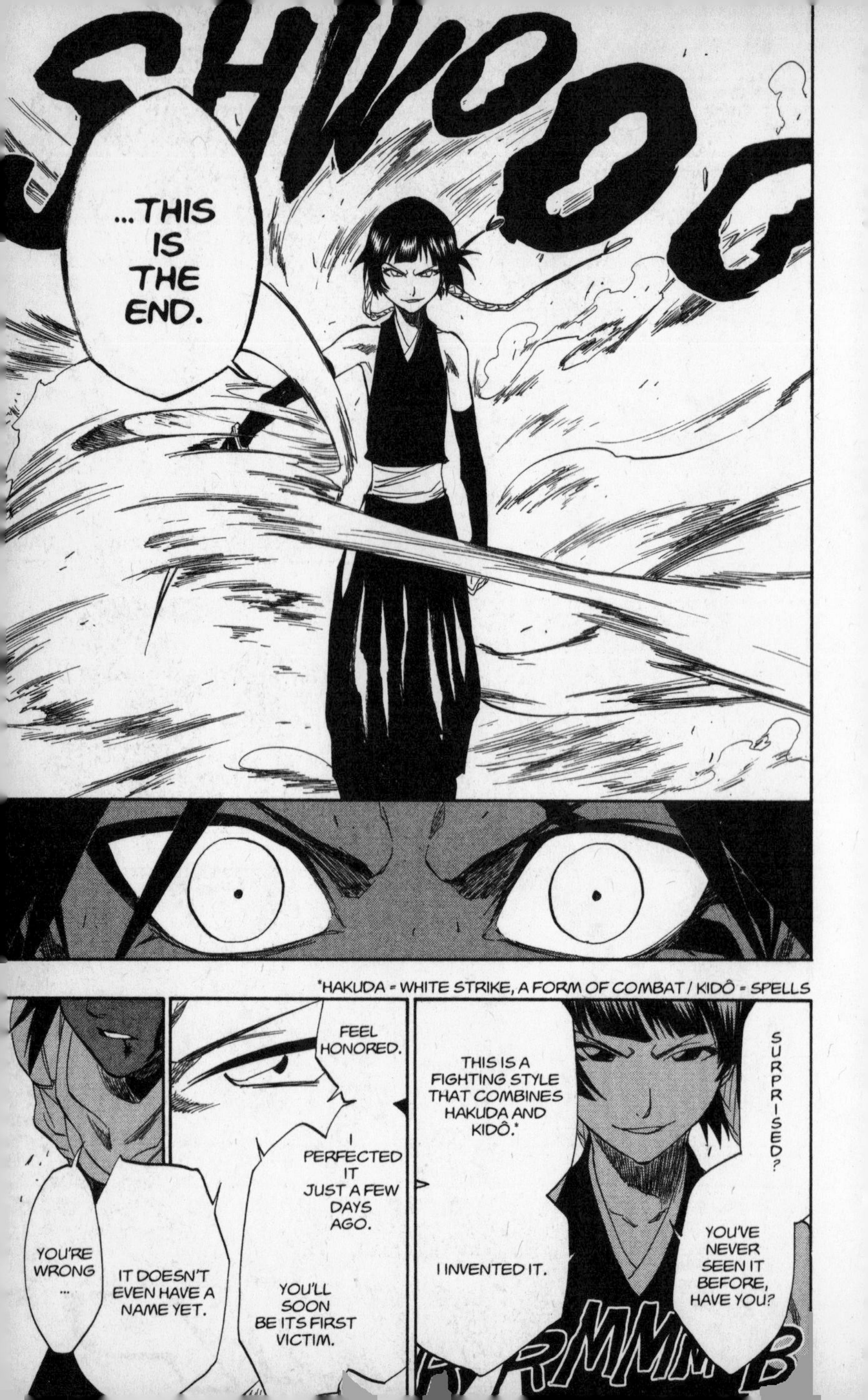
SHWOOG
...THIS IS THE END.
*HAKUDA = WHITE STRIKE, A FORM OF COMBAT / KIDÔ = SPELLS
SURPRISED?
YOU'VE NEVER SEEN IT BEFORE, HAVE YOU?
THIS IS A FIGHTING STYLE THAT COMBINES HAKUDA AND KIDÔ.*
I INVENTED IT.
RMMMMB
FEEL HONORED.
I PERFECTED IT JUST A FEW DAYS AGO.
IT DOESN'T EVEN HAVE A NAME YET.
YOU'LL SOON BE ITS FIRST VICTIM.
YOU'RE WRONG ...

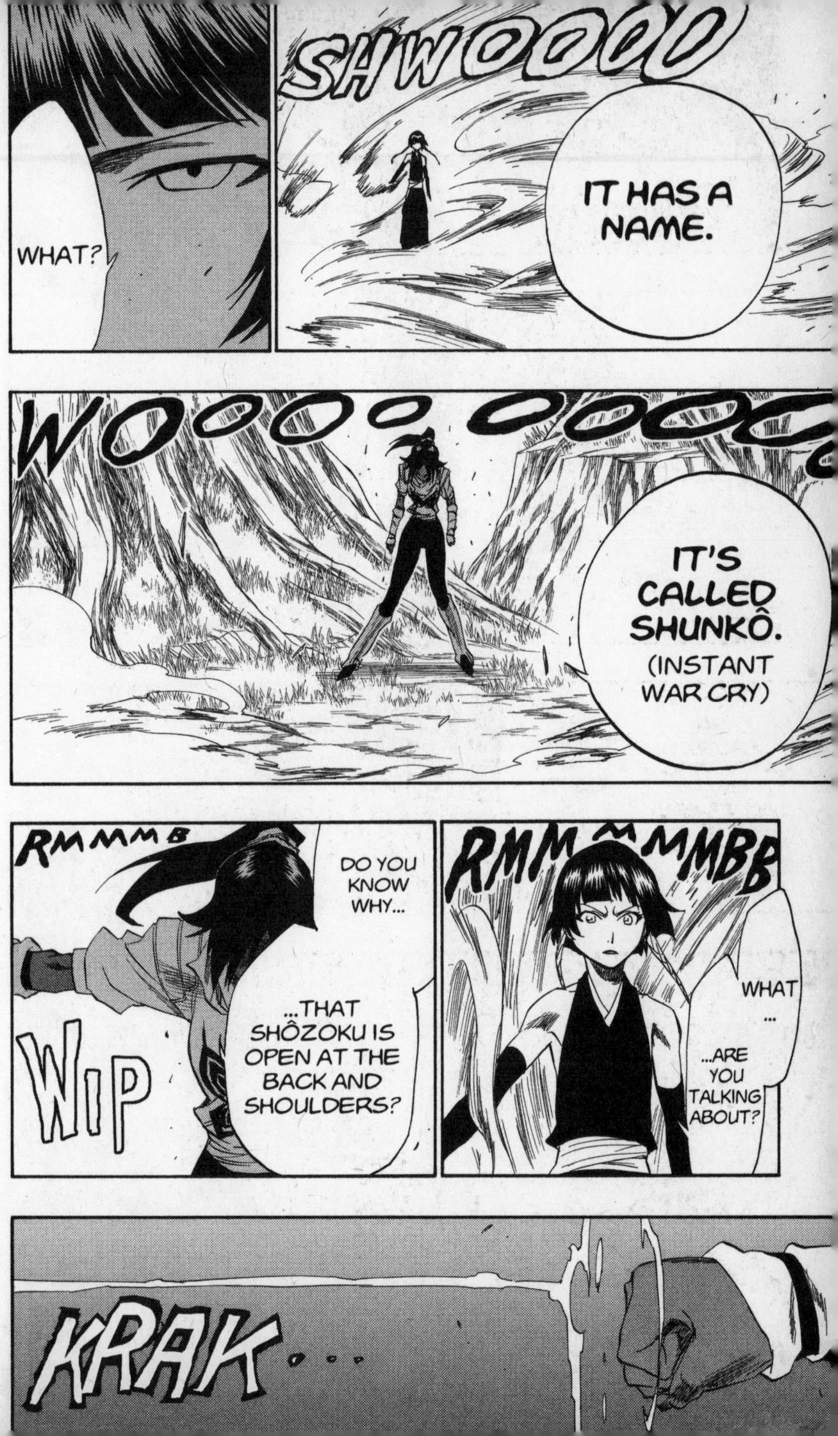
SHWOOOO
IT HAS A NAME.
WHAT?
WOOOO OOOOO
IT'S CALLED SHUNKÔ. (INSTANT WAR CRY)
RMMMMMBB
WHAT ...
...ARE YOU TALKING ABOUT?
RMMMB
DO YOU KNOW WHY...
...THAT SHÔZOKU IS OPEN AT THE BACK AND SHOULDERS?
WIP
KRAK...

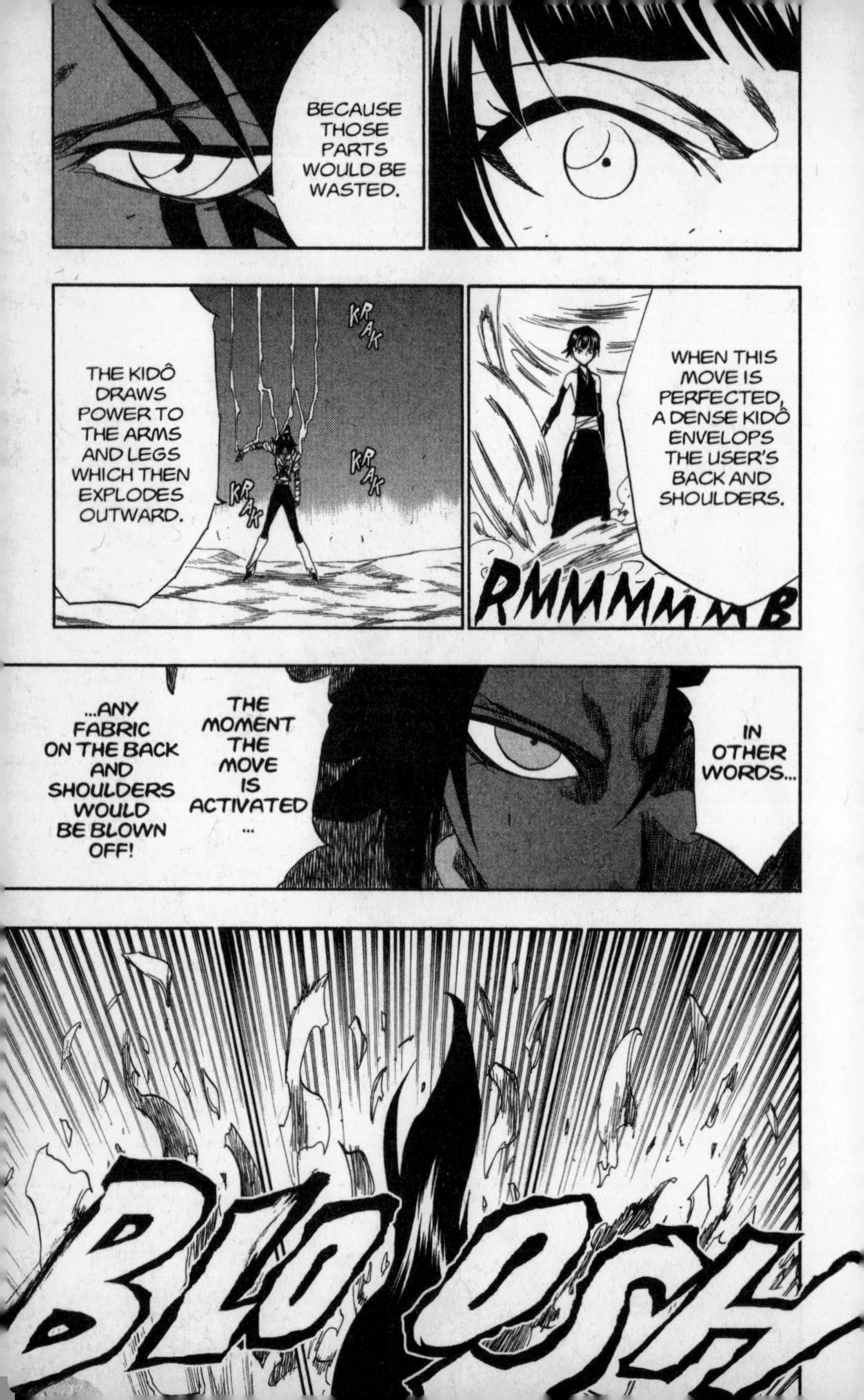
BECAUSE THOSE PARTS WOULD BE WASTED.
WHEN THIS MOVE IS PERFECTED, A DENSE KIDÔ ENVELOPS THE USER'S BACK AND SHOULDERS.
RMMMMMMB
THE KIDÔ DRAWS POWER TO THE ARMS AND LEGS WHICH THEN EXPLODES OUTWARD.
KRAK
KRAK
KRAK
IN OTHER WORDS...
THE MOMENT THE MOVE IS ACTIVATED...
...ANY FABRIC ON THE BACK AND SHOULDERS WOULD BE BLOWN OFF!
BLOOSH

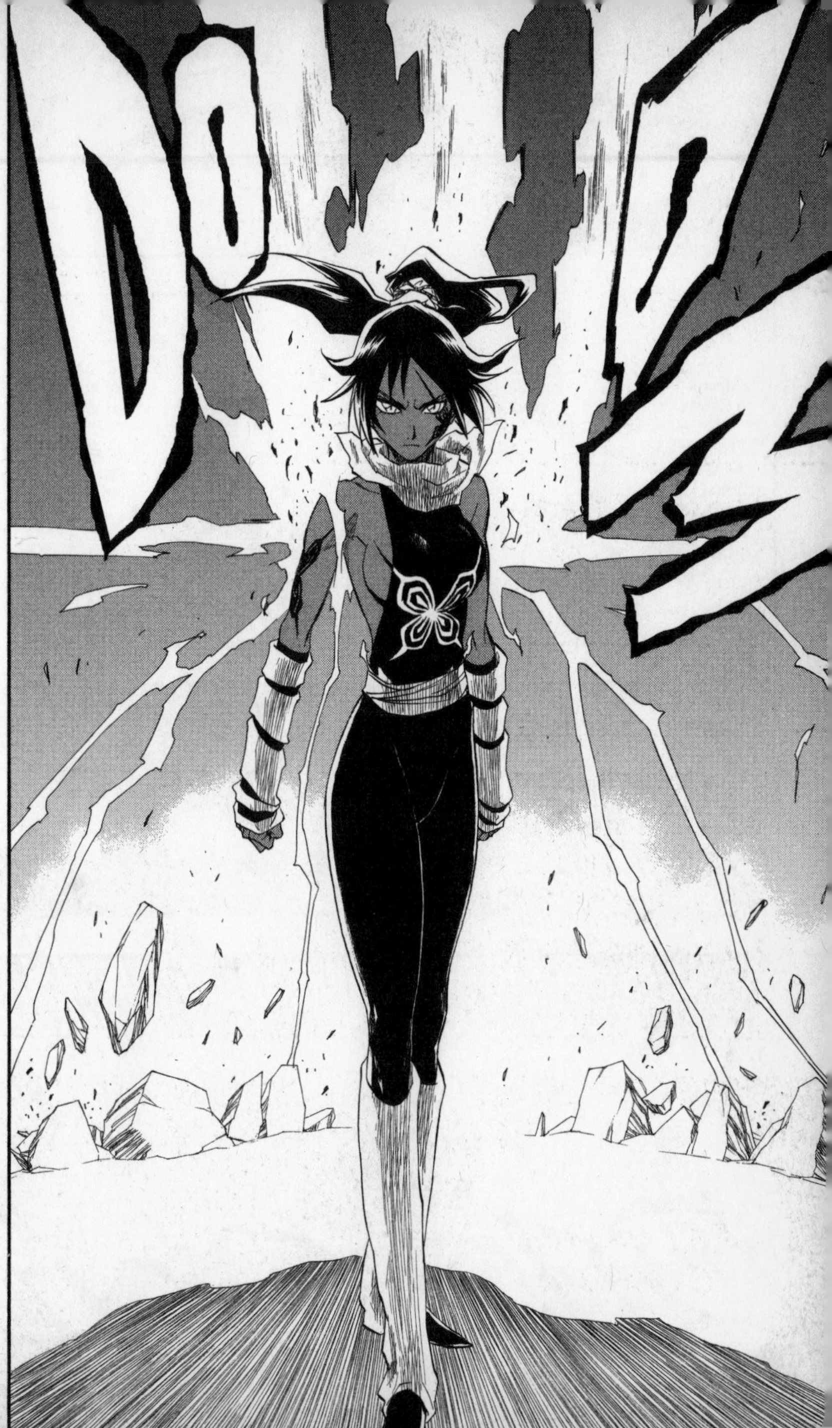
DOOM

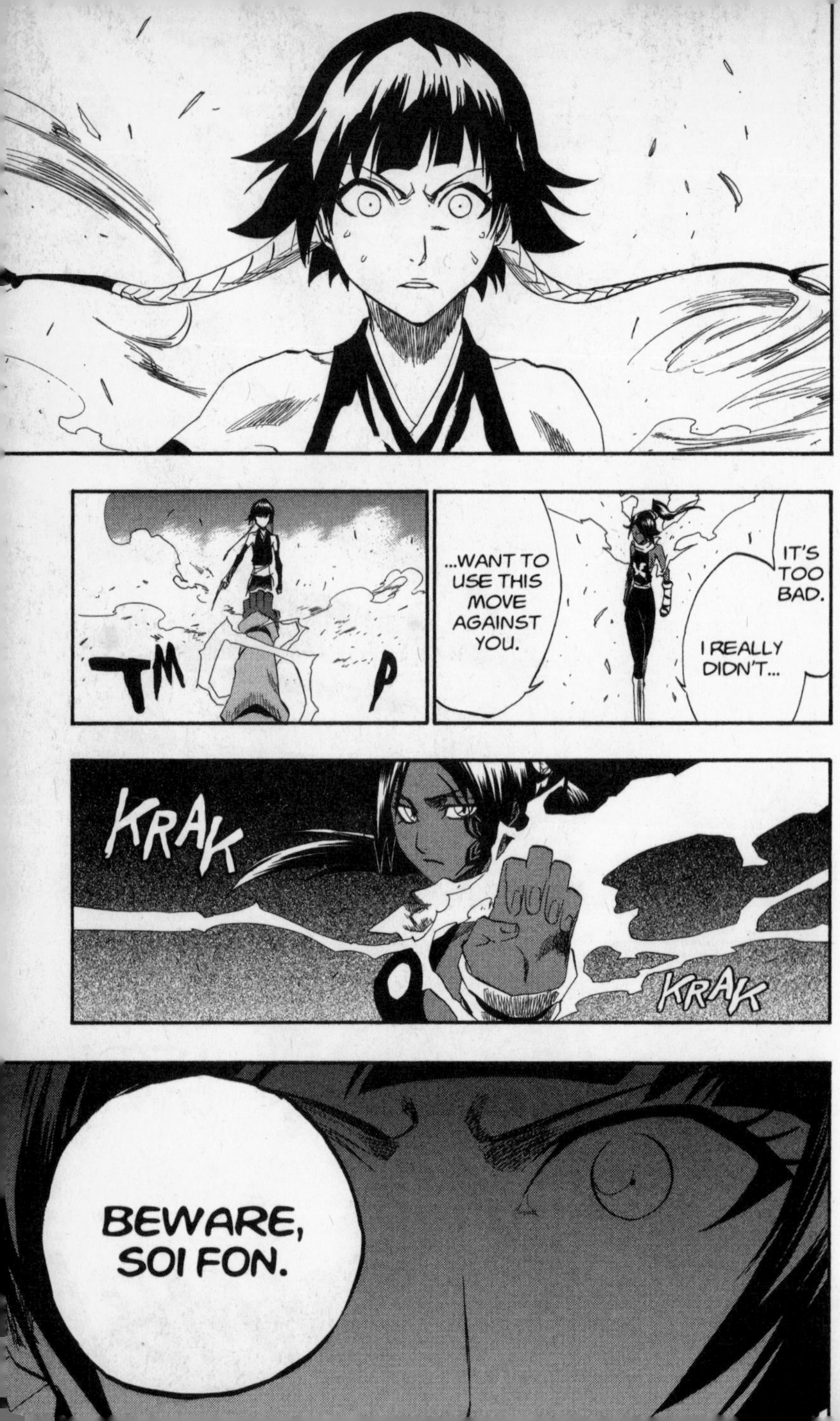
IT'S TOO BAD.
I REALLY DIDN'T...
...WANT TO USE THIS MOVE AGAINST YOU.
TMP
KRAK
KRAK
BEWARE, SOI FON.

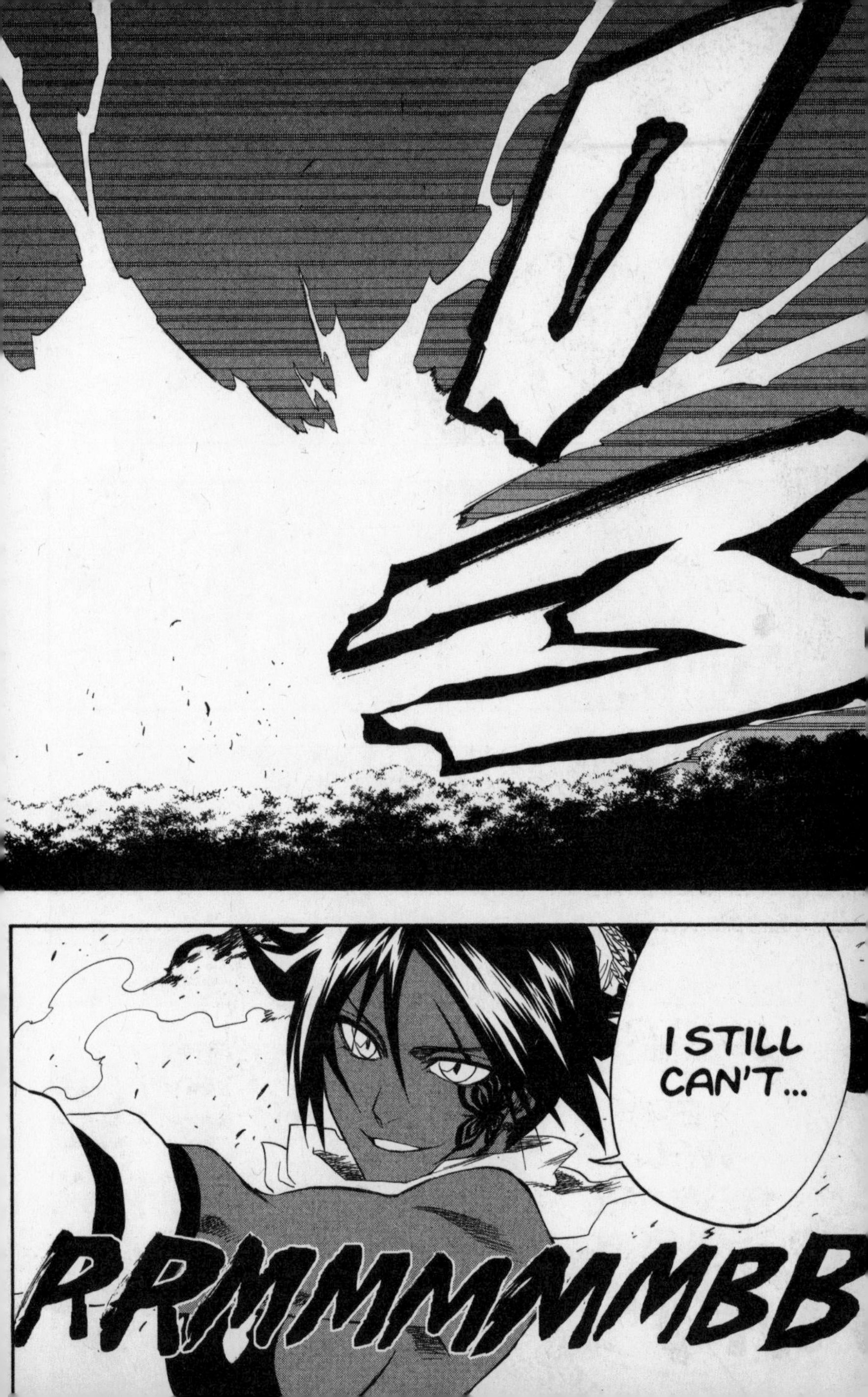
I STILL CAN'T...
RRMMMMMBB

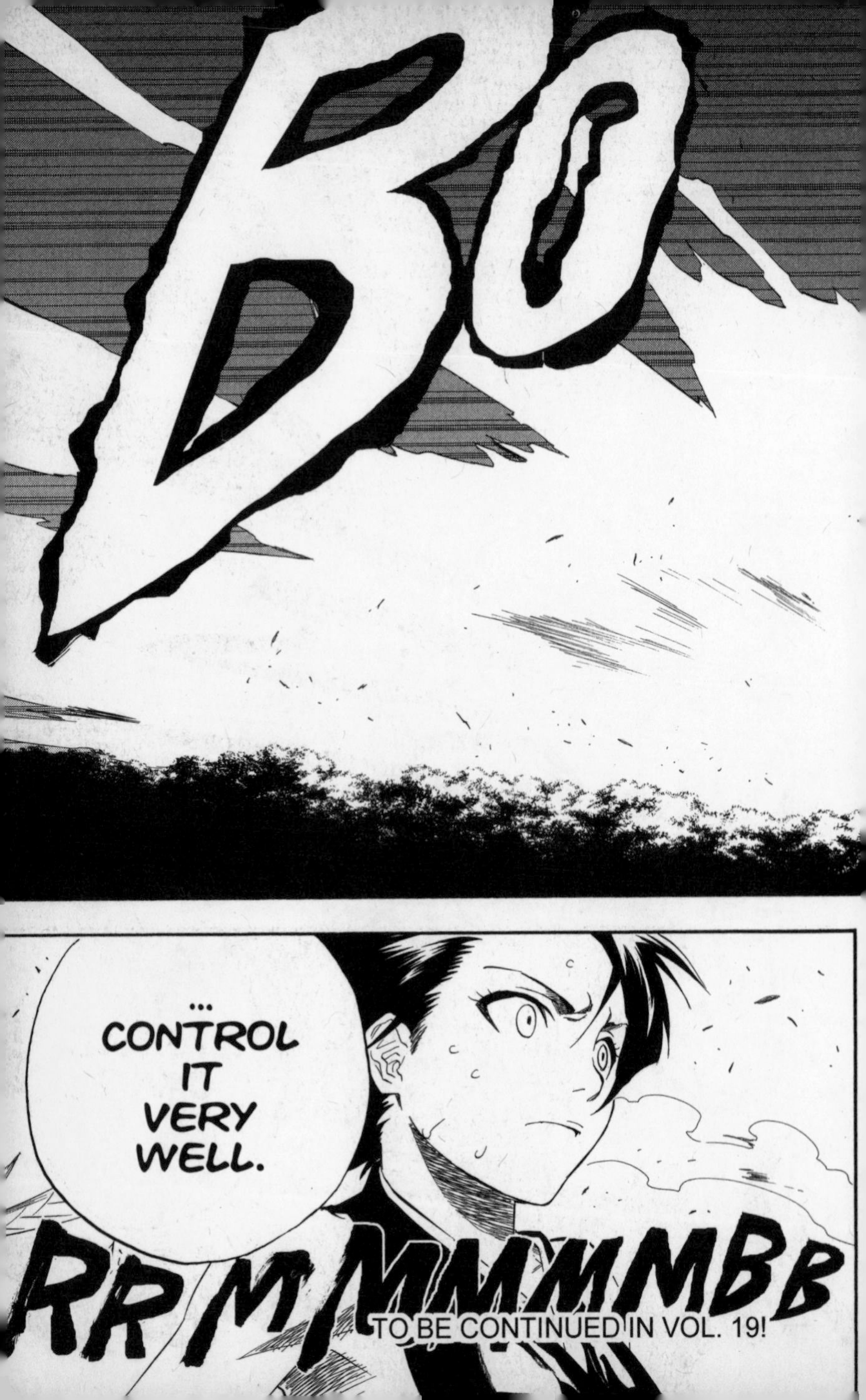
BO
... CONTROL IT VERY WELL.
RRMMMMMBB
TO BE CONTINUED IN VOL. 19!

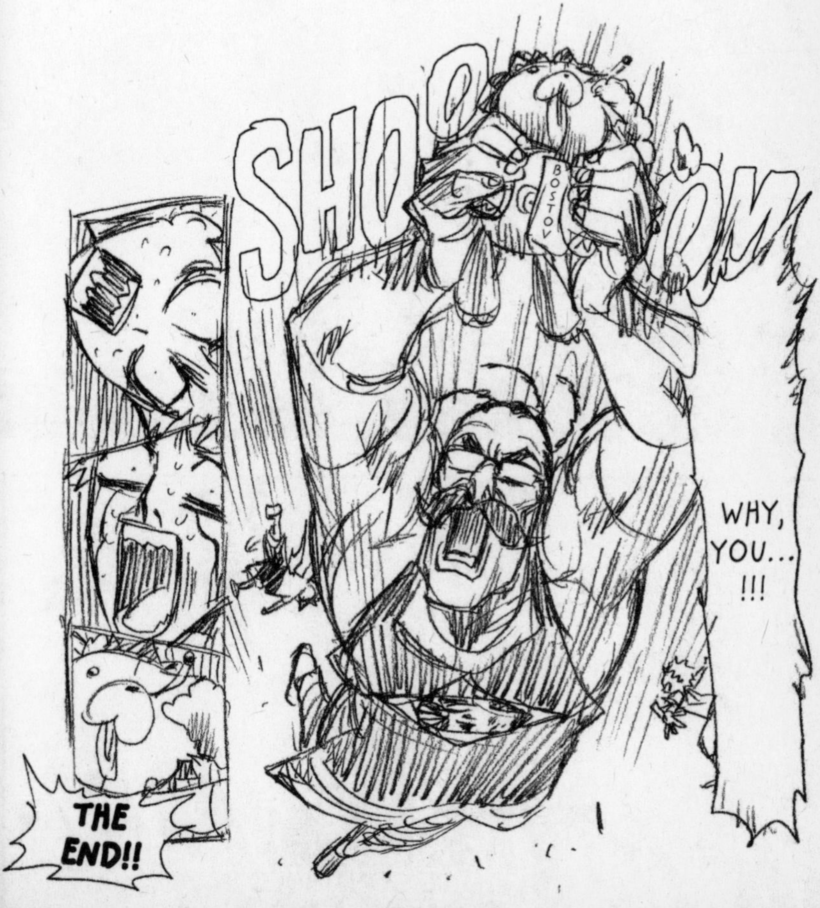
SHOOOOM
BOSTOV
WHY, YOU... !!!
THE END!!

★ ★ here is the data of **BLEACH!!**

13 COURT GUARD COMPANIES	浮竹十四郎	CAPTAIN JÛSHIRÔ UKITAKE 13TH COMPANY

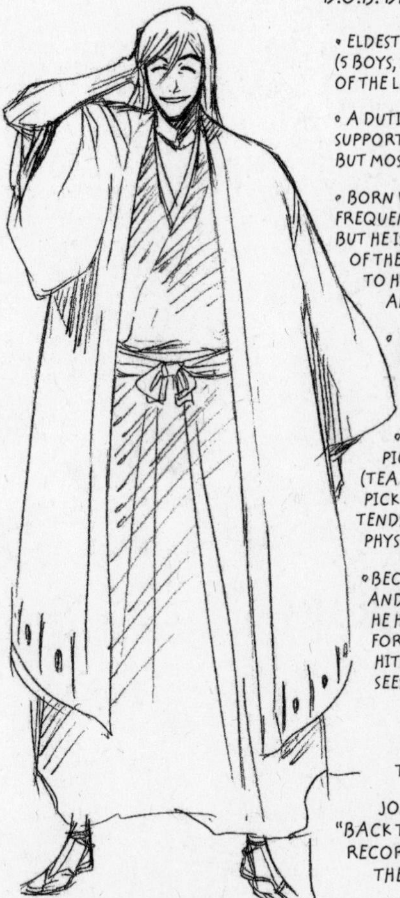

187 CM
72 KG
D.O.B. DECEMBER 21

- ELDEST OF EIGHT CHILDREN (5 BOYS, 2 GIRLS). HIS FAMILY IS OF THE LESSER NOBILITY.
- A DUTIFUL SON, HE NOT ONLY SUPPORTS HIS PARENTS AND SIBLINGS, BUT MOST OF HIS RELATIVES AS WELL.
- BORN WITH A LUNG AILMENT THAT FREQUENTLY INCAPACITATES HIM, BUT HE IS WELL LIKED BY THE MEMBERS OF THE OTHER COMPANIES DUE TO HIS AFFABLE PERSONALITY AND IMPRESSIVE SKILLS.
- HAS GRAY HAIR. HIS HAIR WENT GRAY OVER THE COURSE OF THREE DAYS DURING ONE OF HIS SICK SPELLS.
- HIS FAVORITE FOOD IS PICKLED *UME OCHAZUKE* (TEA POURED OVER RICE WITH PICKLED JAPANESE APRICOTS). TENDS TO EAT EVERYTHING, BUT IS PHYSICALLY FRAGILE.
- BECAUSE THE NAMES JÛSHIRÔ AND TÔSHIRÔ SOUND SIMILAR, HE HAS A ONE-SIDED AFFECTION FOR TÔSHIRÔ HITSUGAYA. OFFERS HITSUGAYA FOOD EVERY TIME HE SEES HIM.

THEME SONG

JONATHAN CAIN
"BACK TO THE INNOCENCE"
RECORDED ON "BACK TO THE INNOCENCE"

13 COURT GUARD COMPANIES	京楽春水	CAPTAIN SHUNSUI KYÔRAKU 8TH COMPANY

192 CM
87 KG
D.O.B. JULY 11

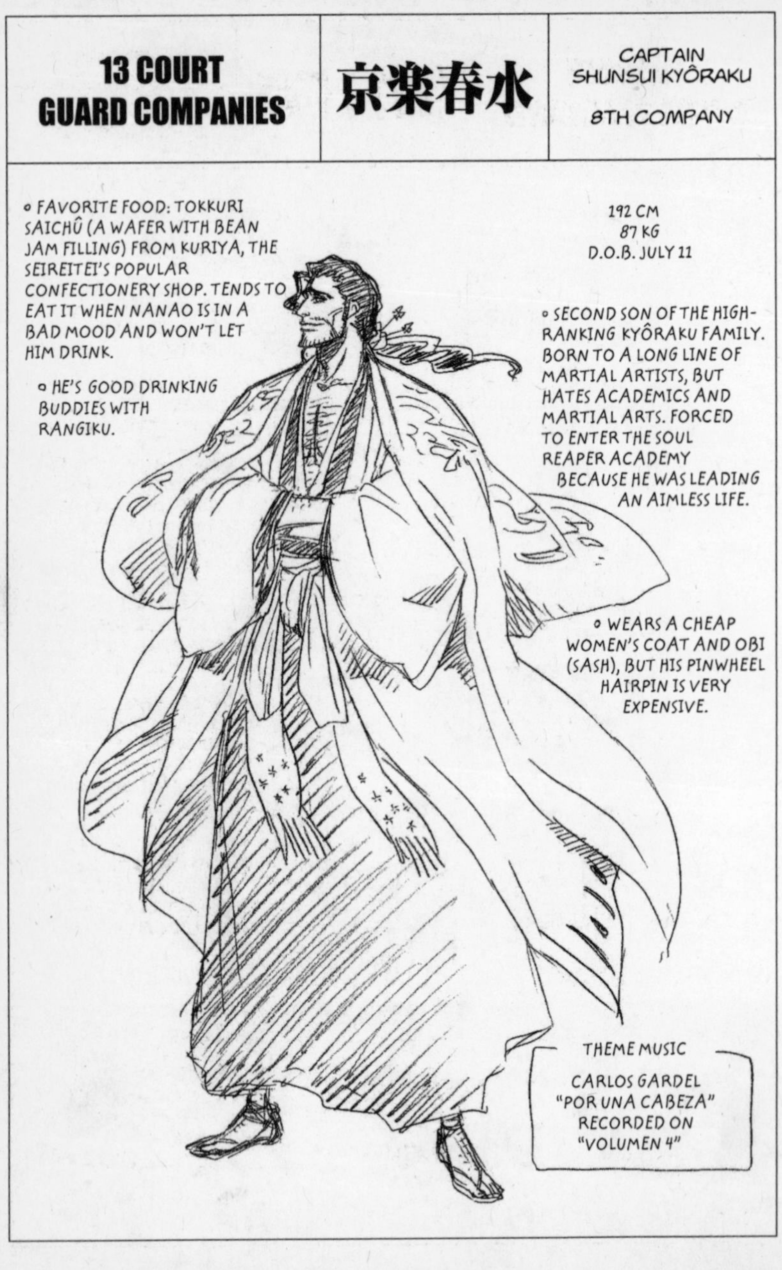

- FAVORITE FOOD: TOKKURI SAICHÛ (A WAFER WITH BEAN JAM FILLING) FROM KURIYA, THE SEIREITEI'S POPULAR CONFECTIONERY SHOP. TENDS TO EAT IT WHEN NANAO IS IN A BAD MOOD AND WON'T LET HIM DRINK.
- HE'S GOOD DRINKING BUDDIES WITH RANGIKU.
- SECOND SON OF THE HIGH-RANKING KYÔRAKU FAMILY. BORN TO A LONG LINE OF MARTIAL ARTISTS, BUT HATES ACADEMICS AND MARTIAL ARTS. FORCED TO ENTER THE SOUL REAPER ACADEMY BECAUSE HE WAS LEADING AN AIMLESS LIFE.
- WEARS A CHEAP WOMEN'S COAT AND OBI (SASH), BUT HIS PINWHEEL HAIRPIN IS VERY EXPENSIVE.

THEME MUSIC

CARLOS GARDEL
"POR UNA CABEZA"
RECORDED ON
"VOLUMEN 4"

Soi Fon reveals the real reason behind her treachery to
Yoruichi. Meanwhile, high above them, the battle that
will decide Rukia's fate comes to its bloody conclusion.

Available in June 2007

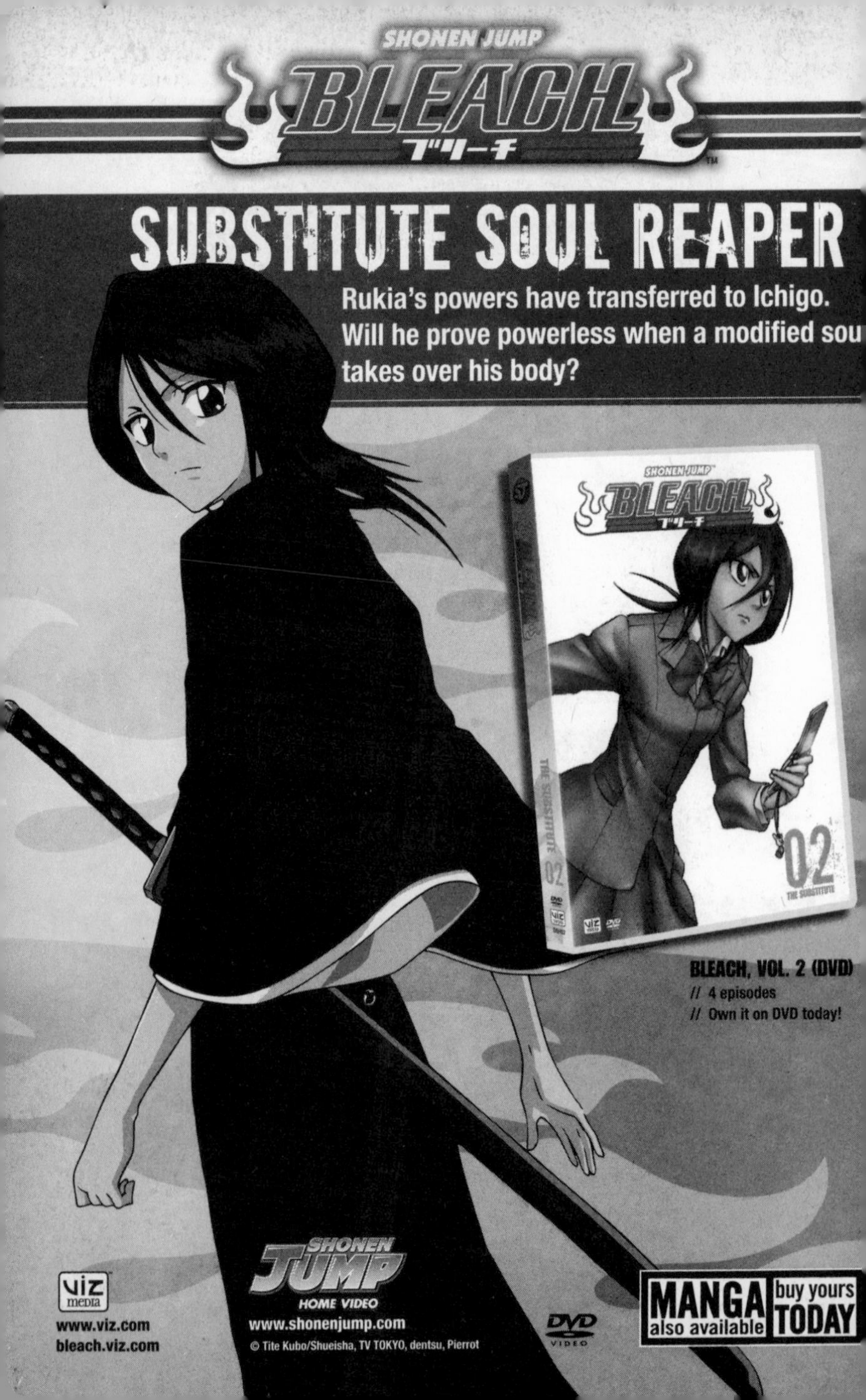
SHONEN JUMP
BLEACH
ブリーチ
SUBSTITUTE SOUL REAPER
Rukia's powers have transferred to Ichigo. Will he prove powerless when a modified sou
takes over his body?
SHONEN JUMP
BLEACH
ブリーチ
THE SUBSTITUTE 02
02
THE SUBSTITUTE
BLEACH, VOL. 2 (DVD)
// 4 episodes
// Own it on DVD today!
viz media
www.viz.com
bleach.viz.com
SHONEN JUMP
HOME VIDEO
www.shonenjump.com
© Tite Kubo/Shueisha, TV TOKYO, dentsu, Pierrot
DVD VIDEO
MANGA also available
buy yours TODAY

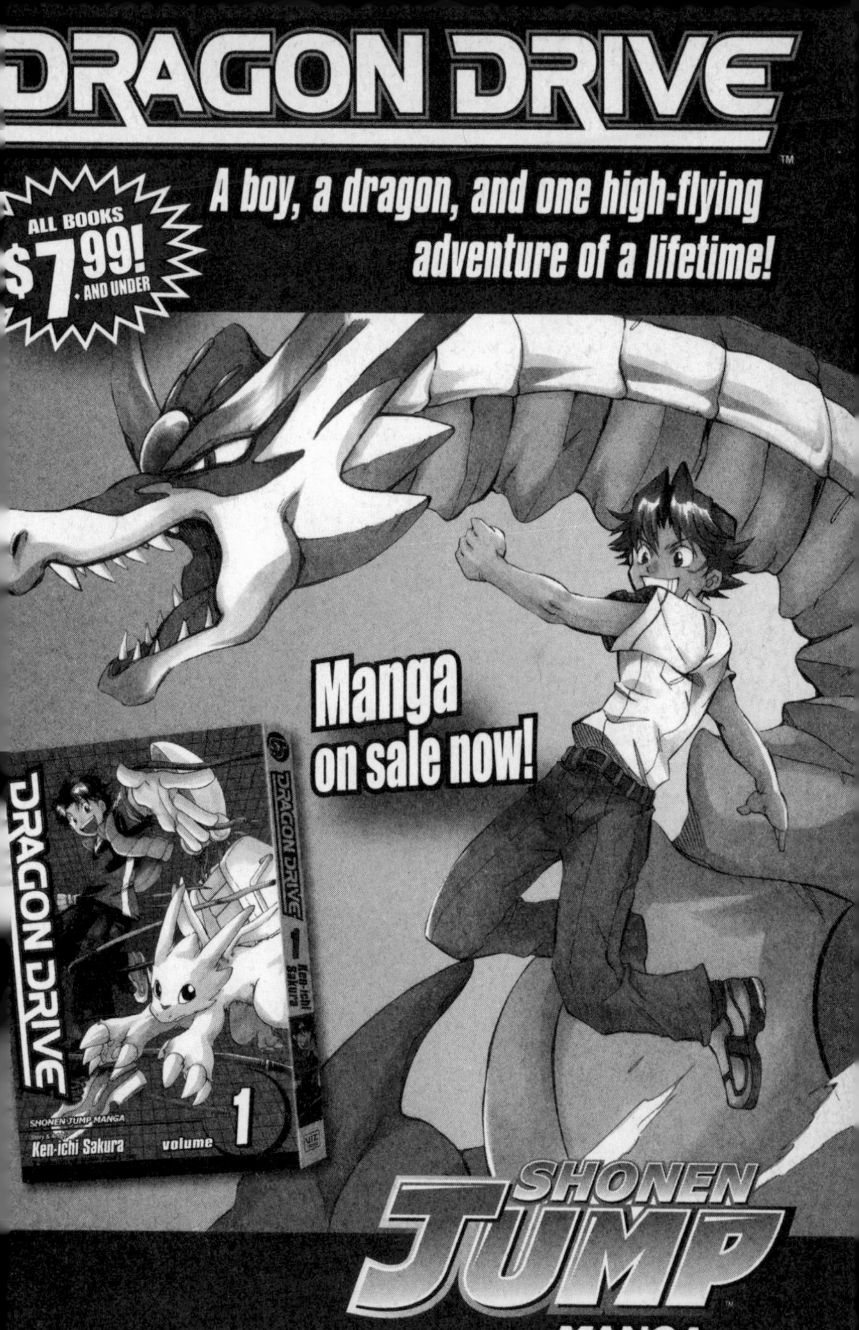
DRAGON DRIVE™
A boy, a dragon, and one high-flying adventure of a lifetime!
ALL BOOKS $7.99! AND UNDER
Manga on sale now!
DRAGON DRIVE
DRAGON DRIVE 1 Ken-ichi Sakura
SHONEN JUMP MANGA
Story & Art by Ken-ichi Sakura
volume 1
SHONEN JUMP MANGA
DRAGON DRIVE © 2001 by Ken-ichi Sakura/SHUEISHA Inc.

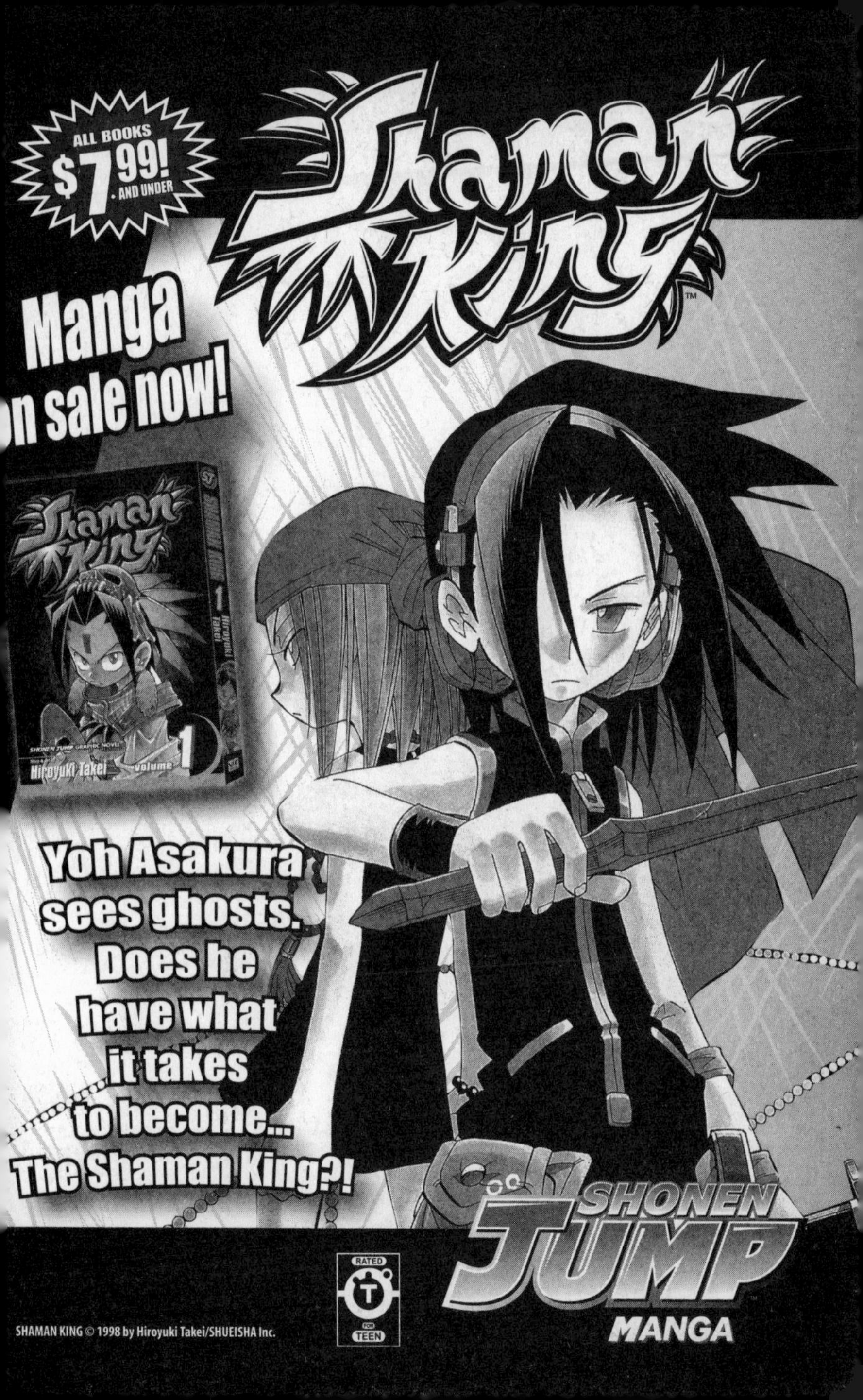

ALL BOOKS $7.99! AND UNDER
Shaman King™
Manga on sale now!
Shaman King
1
SHONEN JUMP GRAPHIC NOVEL
Hiroyuki Takei
volume 1
Yoh Asakura sees ghosts. Does he have what it takes to become... The Shaman King?!
SHONEN JUMP MANGA
RATED T FOR TEEN
SHAMAN KING © 1998 by Hiroyuki Takei/SHUEISHA Inc.

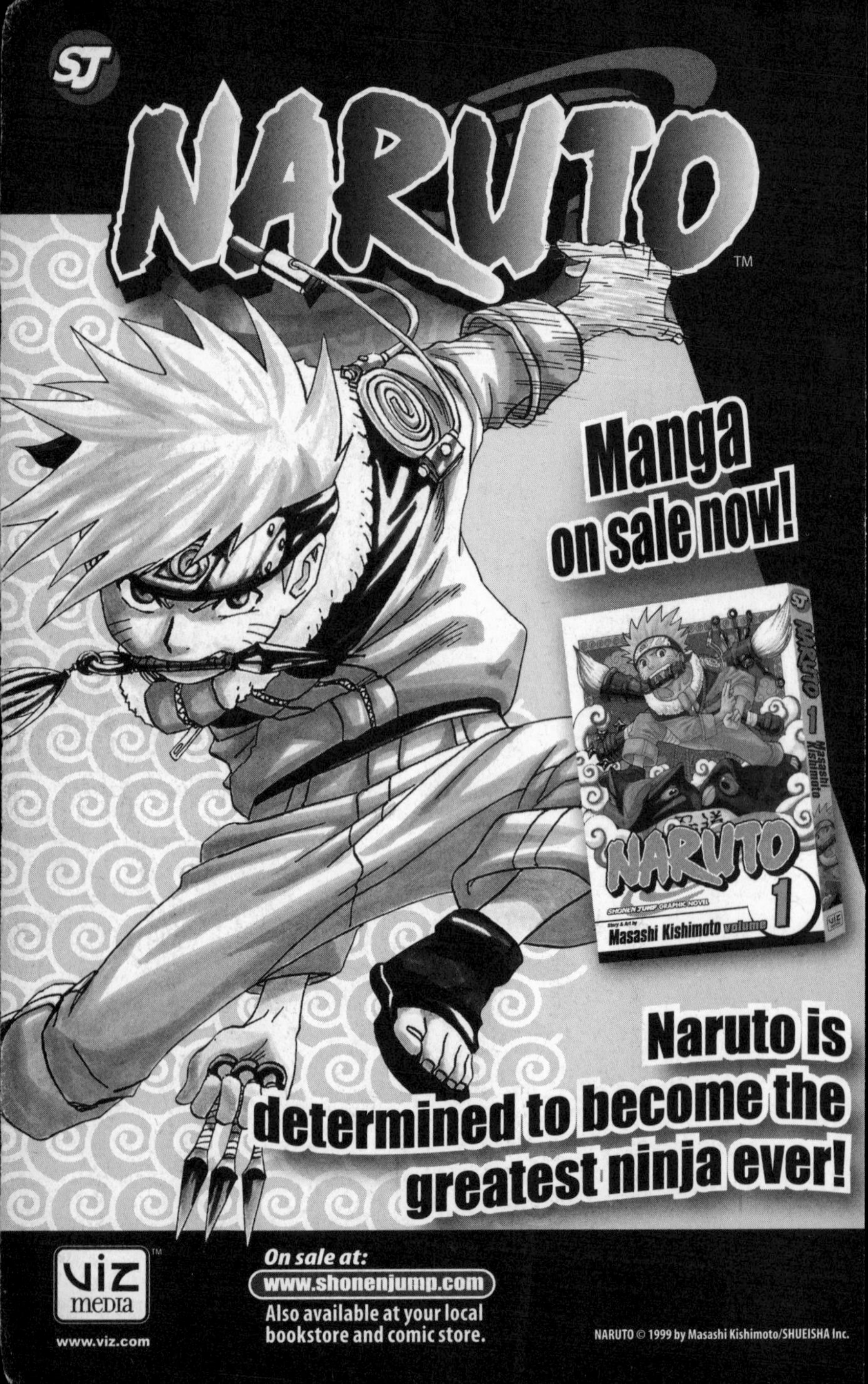
SJ
NARUTO™
Manga on sale now!
Naruto is determined to become the greatest ninja ever!
NARUTO 1
SHONEN JUMP GRAPHIC NOVEL
Story & Art by Masashi Kishimoto volume 1
VIZ media™
www.viz.com
On sale at:
www.shonenjump.com
Also available at your local bookstore and comic store.
NARUTO © 1999 by Masashi Kishimoto/SHUEISHA Inc.

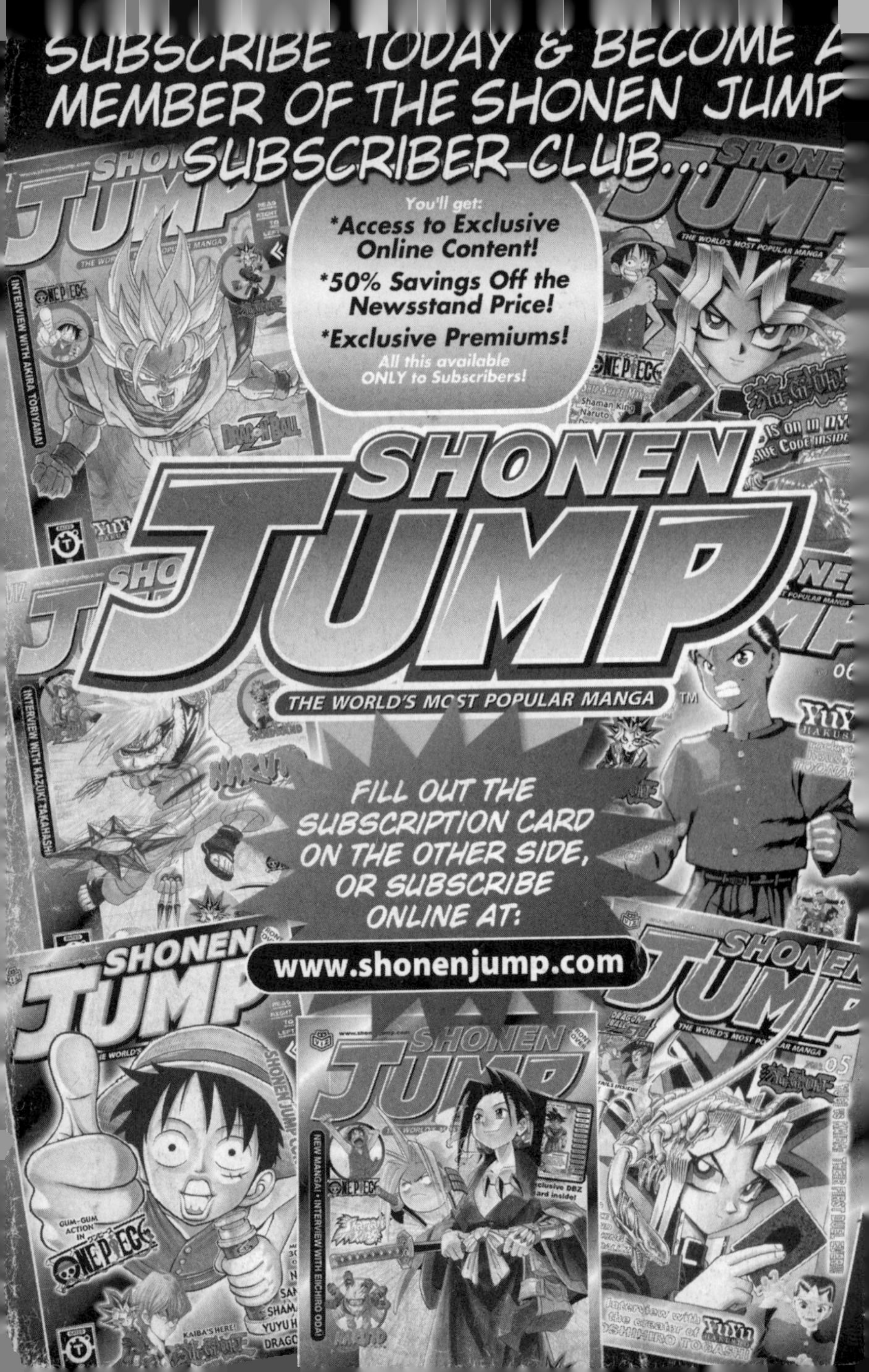
SUBSCRIBE TODAY & BECOME A MEMBER OF THE SHONEN JUMP SUBSCRIBER CLUB...
You'll get:
*Access to Exclusive Online Content!
*50% Savings Off the Newsstand Price!
*Exclusive Premiums!
All this available ONLY to Subscribers!
SHONEN JUMP
THE WORLD'S MOST POPULAR MANGA
FILL OUT THE SUBSCRIPTION CARD ON THE OTHER SIDE, OR SUBSCRIBE ONLINE AT:
www.shonenjump.com

SHONEN JUMP

THE WORLD'S MOST POPULAR MANGA

Save 50% off the ne...

SUBSCRIBE TODAY and SAVE 50% OFF the cover price PLUS enjoy all the benefits of the SHONEN JUMP SUBSCRIBER CLUB, exclusive online content & special gifts ONLY AVAILABLE to SUBSCRIBERS!

☑ **YES!** Please enter my 1 year subscription (12 issues) to *SHONEN JUMP* at the INCREDIBLY LOW SUBSCRIPTION RATE of $29.95 and sign me up for the SHONEN JUMP Subscriber Club!

Only **$29⁹⁵!**

NAME

ADDRESS

CITY

E-MAIL ADDRESS

☐ MY CHECK IS

CREDIT CARD:

ACCOUNT #

SIGNATURE

CLIP AN